MAC A. CAVES

ON THE ORIGIN OF GOD BY MEANS OF NATURAL SELECTION

ISBN: 978-0-967619-11-8
First Edition: 2019

ON THE ORIGIN OF GOD BY MEANS OF NATURAL SELECTION © 2015 by Mac A. Caves

Cover image by Hubble Project.

Cover and art by: Annie's Originals, Marianne Caves

Edited by: Annette Hatzman

Printed by: Kindle Direct Publishing, An Amazon.com Company
First Edition: 2019   ISBN-13: 978-0967619118

Published by: Chuparrosa Press:
       3460 MC3004
       Yellville, AR 72687
       www.thesecretofthegods.com

Library of Congress Control Number: 2019900750

Available from Amazon.com and other retail outlets
Available on Kindle and other devices

ON THE ORIGIN OF GOD BY MEANS OF NATURAL SELECTION is based in part on the concept from: **THE SECRET OF THE GODS**, by Mac A. Caves, First Printing, Copyright 1999, ISBN 0-9676191-0-6.

All references to historical events, cultures, civilizations, names, characters, and places are products of the author's research of aeons of documents and findings.

This endless task of finding truth from our ancient history is, with deep sorrow;

Dedicated to a Loyal Friend who lost his life due to the influence of a radical group, spreading religious ignorance and hate in America. God-Speed Ken; may you enjoy the mysteries of The Universe.

Kenneth Nelson Jr.
Departed this Earth Nov. 16, 2018

NGC 2174 - Constellation Orion
Galaxy: Milky Way - Orion Spur Arm
[same as Earth]: 243 LY - 1,360 LY away
Cover photo by Hubble project

Reader Comments

Congratulations Mac, thank you. I can't wait to read your next work of art.
Ken Nelson Jr. Bakersfield CA Nov-15-2018.

Darwin shook the world with his theory of evolution; Mac Caves in his book **ON THE ORIGIN OF GOD BY MEANS OF NATURAL SELECTION** shakes the world with his theory of Man colonizing the Earth and becoming Gods.
C R, San Marcos, California

Absolutely the most fascinating read about the origin of Modern Man, Civilizations and Religions. I particularly enjoyed the Maya connection to modern day Physics and Quantum Mechanics.
Math Teacher - Mountain Home, AR

Fantastic timeline of the evolution of God! LG - Needles CA

Brings to light so much history and the sordid past of our modern Churches. JF – Bakersfield CA

I said the same thing about Mac Caves' first book: This is the best timeline and logic that has ever been applied to history and the making of religions. In The Beginning Man did discover and colonize Earth. Janesville, WI

Christians should do their homework about their church beginnings instead of blind faith for what is taught.
JM – Dallas TX

I was never taught the possibility that Man discovered Earth. After reading this timeline of our history I am convinced Earth was colonized by Man and became the source for many ancient Gods. HT – Panama Beach City FL

ACKNOWLEDGEMENTS

First and foremost, to Marianne, my best friend, wife, life partner and resident archaeologist, for her brilliant work in piecing together the mysteries of *remnant civilizations* of the Americas and of the South-West United States. Her tireless assistance and encouragement to keep this work going forward has made it a reality.

A warm and special thank-you goes to our friends who provided readings of the manuscripts and enthusiastic comments.

To my "Big Brother Bob", for reviewing the manuscript and discussing this work for over twenty years.   A treasure of knowledge and guidance in understanding the ways of traveling tent preachers from the 1940's to today. His best advice for anyone close to these healing preachers, "keep your money and women out of sight".

And great appreciation for the fantastic editing by my favorite Editor Annette Hatzman, and for her time away from her family.

THIS BOOK IS EPIC HISTORICAL NON-FICTION

This work follows history in an effort to explain where we as "Man", Homo Sapiens Sapiens [Modern Man] originated and how our cultures, civilizations and religions developed.

Earth history
>   General Geologic history including the Last Ice Age
>   The last Comet Impact on Earth
>   Lost Civilizations and Species of the Pleistocene Extinction

Human history
>   Discovery of Earth by Man
>   Beginning of Man's Colonies on Earth
>   Rise of Civilizations
>   Creation of Religions

TABLE OF CONTENTS

BOOK I   THE BEGINNING

BOOK II   THE HOLY LAND CHRONICLES

BOOK III THE AMERICAS

BOOK IV FINAL SECRETS

INTRODUCTION TO THE AUTHOR

If you wish to know the mindset of the author of this work, go to the APPENDIX and read this section. I placed this in the appendix to avoid distracting from the focus of this historic work.

INTRODUCTION

The "Church" has perpetuated class distinction and ethnic prejudice since its beginnings. Early leaders of evangelism targeted the flotsam of society, outcasts, beggars and servants to gather easily persuaded people into the Cult. They were able to convince these followers they were not worthy to chart their own lives. This practice continues to acquire non-thinkers and those who have been educated to believe they belong to an identified victim group of Mankind's evils.

The Vatican spread victimhood along with racial and social prejudices by telling stories of God putting "Marks" on particular civilizations [black skin] and declaring Jews were descendants of Satan and that they had killed "Christ". If a child was disfigured at birth it was explained that this happened because God was punishing the parents for some sin. Women were to be punished all their lives for causing "Adam" to get laid, thereby spreading "The Sin Virus" through all of Mankind. For causing this grievous event, women would not be permitted to lead any church functions. Well, they could clean the crappers after the preaching. Of course, this Sin Virus can be altered with enough **faith** and donated **money**. These prejudices were continued in the Protestant religions as edicts from God.

I never believed [after childhood] in "UFO's", the presented fables of "aliens", magic, miracles, or anything which could not be logically explained. So much for my faith in any organized religion. I decided to research as much as possible everything I was taught about History, Life and God. It was amazing what I found, fueling further research.

Every religion you can name has been founded on the most ludicrous, inane suggestions of unexplainable miracles. The founders proposed visions, dreams, apparitions, direct conferences with God, on and on, and people fall for the stories. When children are taught any social view or religion, on a daily basis, throughout their formative years, it becomes real in their minds. Just put your hand on the radio or TV and send more money! You will be healed! Today Brother Pope can peer into a camera and extend "Blessings from God" to millions of people he cannot see, much less know about. And they receive the blessing [healing] through the television. Absolutely amazing!

In ancient times when few people were literate and most were open to the message that "God" and "Angels" appeared and conversed with special people, acceptance is understandable. When Emperors and Popes held an "Auto da Fe", cut your head off, or roasted a confession of heresy out of people with great ceremony, I understand following the religion. When your community and family banish you for heresy or non-belief, you will tend to go along.

What I cannot understand is when educated people accept a fable without any research. It is not that difficult with the "Information Highway" to find enough sources to form a valid opinion on any subject.

I am absolutely amazed at the information available due to our technology. This is because of how difficult research was several decades ago when I began researching history and religion. Today there is no reason for anyone with access to a library or the internet to be ignorant about any subject – NONE! One can decipher ancient languages, teach one's self how to read Mayan Codices, understand Quantum Mechanics and on and on. The information is there.

I recently found writings which have been known for over 2,000 years. Ancient chronicles of daily life I never knew about. Amazing! If I had another 70 years to study, I could not get to a majority of it. That is why I rely on professionals who devoted their entire lives to some miniscule part of our history and documented it. There are tens of thousands of dedicated people who have put together some piece of the vast puzzle of our existence.

There is nothing wrong with being ignorant about a particular subject; information will remedy the issue. However, education cannot fix stupid. Stupid is when an educated person refuses to believe proven fact but will rely on myth and fable. No Virginia, there is no Santa Claus, there are no green aliens picking up Humans, and no great all powerful, all knowing "OZ" which can speak and "make it so".

So, if you ever wonder why you act, believe or live the way you do, there is an answer waiting for you. Hopefully this work, based on available information, will cause you to wonder what is true, what is fable, and research the matter for yourself. If you must rely on "faith" for anything to be real, it is in the category of fable, sleight of hand or just plain BS. A belief in a Supreme Being does not equate to belief in an Organized Religion. Following the tenets of an organized religion is, as Granma used to say, "A whole 'nuther matter".

We, the inhabitants of Earth, "Man" if you will, have been ushered into two venues of thought relating to our "Origins". Both venues are equally destructive to independent thought.

The first venue, and oldest form of brainwashing, comes from the heavy burden of religious fundamentals taught from earliest childhood. The "Adam and Eve" creation fable is baseline thinking for organized religion. God made a doll from mud, performed CPR on it and IT WALKED! He then created another "being" to be "an helpmate" to the first "being", that is, He made an underling to serve the wishes of "First Man". This teaching has resulted in an almost inescapable mind-set of religious creationism and tunnel vision concerning history. It also created the illusion of an ever-watching destructive being that could zap infidels at will. Most damaging of all, this "history of God", for most of Mankind, replaced the natural bonding of Men and Women from partners in life to a system of dominance. In reality both have separate and important functions in pursuing a life partnership.

The second venue, the antithesis of the first, developed from two events. First, after working for over twenty years developing his manuscript "**On the Origin of Species, by means of Natural Selection**", Charles Darwin published it in 1859. Second, within a few years, [1864 CE] a monumental discovery occurred in the Neander Valley of Germany, which appeared to tie Darwin's Theory to the evolution of Man. Scientists proclaimed the discovery of Homo Sapiens Neanderthalensis, that is, Neanderthal Man. They also announced to the world, incorrectly, that Neanderthal was the final evolutionary link to Modern Man, Homo Sapiens Sapiens.

Recent DNA analysis has confirmed, beyond any reasonable doubt, that Modern Man is not a descendant of the evolutionary bipedal creatures identified as being precursors to Homo Sapiens Sapiens. These evolutionary precursors are identified as Homo Erectus, Homo Australopithecus and scores of other species which exhibited upright mobility, tool-making skills, and/or cognizant thought processes.

This evidence firmly puts Man in a unique species determination of "Sapiens". Man has not evolved from any other creature on Earth! All evidence points to the fact that Man has been on this Earth for several million years. Ancient Man was not isolated on the various continents; he traveled, sailed, traded and communicated between all of them.

The Sumerian Kings List indicates a continuous line of long-lived kings, ruling for over 254,000 years. Of course, *Academia* says this must be a myth.

Both venues of teaching, religious and scientific, proclaim Man is a product of Earth, either Divine or evolved. Little effort was expended to explore the possibility that, in the beginning, after the Earth was seeded by comets, most plants and animals evolved by means of **natural selection**, and also that, **In The Beginning Man Discovered Earth**.

With this indisputable information we can focus on the probable origins of Man and the evolution of our modern-era Gods.

If the "Garden of Eden" story, depicted in the "Year of Our Lord 1611" King James version of the Holy Writ, is true, then all of history, archaeology, ancient manuscripts, and geology are in error. The "Creation Story", which occurred 2,000 years after Jericho was occupied, is veiled allegory alluding to something entirely different than the creation of Man.

To understand our present we must search history, geology, anthropology and the rise of intelligent society. We began our journey aeons ago. Then, a catastrophic event, a comet impacting the Earth 12,900 years ago set our final path.

The revelations presented here are not new. Most have been widely published but have not been presented in a singular format and timeline. The historic and factual information contained in this work was derived from the notes and publications of thousands of professional historians, archaeologists, paleontologists, geologists, ancient language experts and cultural researchers. Some of these dedicated people, and thousands of assistants, lived and worked their entire professional lives on these archaeological sites.

Some components of this work have circulated in spoken and written history for aeons. Some of the most valuable information has come from recent archaeological sites and the deciphering of ancient text and hieroglyphs.

Religious dogma prevented all but a few individuals from surviving after attempting to compile, or reveal, the complete history of civilization and religion.

Albert Einstein [1879-1955] was aware that Man discovered Earth. The translations and discoveries found in the Mayan Codex in Germany provided the components of thought and advanced math which caused him to seek answers to the condensing of time in hyper-speed travel. In his thesis he explained how someone could travel thousands of light-years [A LY = about 5.88 Trillion miles] in a relatively short period of time. This of course is only a theory.

This book is not a discussion of whether God exists or not. Rather it is a revelation of what Man has created with the premise of God existing. This creation is labeled "Religion" and it is the most powerful and influential social control mechanism ever devised.

Organized Religion creates more control than any devised harsh treatment or punishment. Women, races, ethnicity, nationalism and any other defined group of people or popular followings have been subjugated to the whims and rules devised for religious worship. Organized religion holds greater power than any group of Corporations in terms of influence, monetary worth and gross annual income.

Others have thought for you since birth. This is what makes us who we are, it is our educational process. Knowledge comes in two forms; fact and myth. Organized Religion does not admit any inclusion of myth. It is up to each of us to research and determine fact from myth. Facts are real, tangible and provable. Myths are conjecture, assumptions, and conclusions no matter what they are based on. The most distorted areas of our education processes are history, science and religion.

According to ancient religious dogma, Gods were of virgin birth, including the Sumerians' and Egyptians' Gods. The founders of Christianity also used this myth and created the savior myth of Jesus [Yeshua]. In the Mayan civilization, their savior God Kukulkan was of virgin birth.

To understand our present-day concept of God we must journey into the distant history of mankind. To find the truth of our history one needs to realize the process of how each of us was made aware of religious and moral standards. As child we all were mentally programmed by parents, educators, religious leaders and those people we encountered during our early development. This is the normal process of life through generations of family growth and teaching.

Religious dogma, moral standards and history as taught by a common society and cultural nationalism are seldom challenged. That is, until we educate ourselves by researching each idiom of our indoctrination. The information is available, in libraries and online, established by tens of thousands of experts. We just need to find it and consider the validity of each area of research.

At some time in our pre-teen years we realized that reindeer cannot fly, rabbits do not lay decorated hard-boiled eggs and when a person is dead, they stay dead. We come to realize these fables are for no purpose other than to entertain us or to validate religious dogma for children. There is no real need for organized religion involvement in order to teach children right from wrong. We know what is right or wrong instinctively, it is just a question of social acceptance of our actions.

Most people do not know the history behind displaying a groomed and cosmetically prepared body for funerals. This practice was perfected by the Egyptians as a way to prepare the individual for resurrection and entry into eternal life in paradise. The concept of resurrection and an afterlife Paradise for believers and eternal damnation for heretics was conceived and taught by followers of ancient "Pagan" religions.

This concept was continued in various religions, evolving to the current Christian [and many other religions'] teachings, that a savior will return and cause all of the bodies of the faithful to reassemble, rise from the grave or ashes and enter paradise.

I published **The Secret of The Gods** in 1999 with research gathered as best I could for 20 years. The core values I held at the time have not changed. I was still blinded by a considerable amount of history and religious indoctrination as a young person.

Decades ago I was excited about "The Dead Sea Scrolls" discovery and deciphering. I thought, "Wow! Now we have evidence of what was the truth." I had begun writing these sections using "Dead Sea Scrolls" to debunk the myths in the "Holy Writ". I failed to realize these writings were no different in origin and purpose than the Holy Writ. Any argument of validity, without data from separate sources is meaningless. You cannot argue a negative into a positive.

I often say to rid your mind of mental blind spots [scotomas], to fully understand history. I failed to do that when I published **The Secret of The Gods** [**TSOTG**] in 1999. The Biblical narratives in **TSOTG** provide for a "cute" story, I was really proud of my dissertation. I abandoned all of the "Beginning", "The Holy Land Chronicles" and much more and started with recently deciphered writings. There is no difference in the two sources I originally used. The "writings of the Prophets" in the Dead Sea Scrolls is no different, except to provide entertaining reading, and to show how "Holy Writs' evolve.

If an archaeologist is trying to prove something in the Holy Writ, it will be proven. An academic trying to validate "scripture" using ancient religious scrolls will be successful.

I was fortunate to find up-to-date scientific reports and massive amounts of recent translations of ancient documents which provided new information and dating of events. This information was so revealing that I had to delete most of my previous work's conclusions and time frames. I relate this to you this so you will know not to rely solely on previously published material. Also, know the motives of the authors. My motive was, and is, to discover as much truth as possible and to counter Theologians' and *Academia's* fraud and various fame hunters.

Fide nemini [Trust no-one]; verify all claims from religions, governments and authors. With the vast knowledge available anyone can research and find the truth, if you actually want to know.

Recent claims by some "Researchers" are prime examples of the need for caution when reading published findings: One subject of the bogus claims was the testing of malformed 3,000-year-old skulls from Paracas Peru. The headline reads "**DNA test results confirmed: Paracas skulls are not human – Further testing planned**". Claims continued about DNA sequences of these non-human humanoids, identifications of "manipulated" sequences of mitochondrial DNA, on and on. The DNA scientist stated these beings had DNA "**mutations that were unknown to any man, primate or animal found on planet Earth**".

Now, "**The rest of the story**"; these "scientists" are making fortunes with appearances, selling books and making films based on their "findings". A fact checker researcher group reviewed the "scientists" backgrounds and found they have no qualifications in biology or genetics. The "geneticist" runs her own F rated lab [that means it is a hoax] and published a book on DNA from "Bigfoot". The only way to see the DNA report is to buy the book. Her other troubles included charges of fraud and tax evasion. Do you need more information to decide about this fraud? Probably not.

As Hitchens' razor states: "That which can be asserted without evidence, can be dismissed without evidence."

You will be subjected to "amazing" DNA discovery articles claiming new links to various Sapiens species of pre-modern man. Most are fanciful extrapolations by people wanting funding for their "research" and their "15 minutes of fame". So be skeptical and use logic and common sense to evaluate these claims.

Mystic Mountain
Courtesy of NASA Hubble Telescope Project

heic1007a Mystic Mountain - Carina Nebula - Hubble

The Fertile Crescent – Sumer - Colonized by Man 254,000 years ago when "First God" Alulim "Descended from Heaven" and became the "Foundation of Modern Religion".

PROLOGUE

Several million years ago Man first discovered Earth. The search for new worlds, adventure and expected riches brought expeditions to our solar system.   Successful research and mining colonies were established on Earth.   However, geologic data indicates many cataclysmic events occurred, some caused by comet and meteor impacts, and near impacts.

Each impact instantly resulted in mountains rising thousands of feet, canyons opening and volcanoes erupting.   This was followed by immediate and severe climatic changes causing worldwide floods of epic proportions. Accompanying these global disasters were four major Ice Ages in the last 750,000 years. There were at least 17 Glacial Periods in the past 2 million years. Geologic and fossil evidence verify these disasters changed the face of the Earth. If these events nearly wiped out plant and animal populations, they would certainly end any expedition based on the planet.

The Earth's Ice Ages occur on a cycle of about 100,000 years. The climate cools and the poles accumulate ice and sea levels lower, the climate warms and the sea levels rise. This is due to the variables of Earth's orbit and axis tilt, and the variation of the intensity of the Sun.

The explorations of the last several million years occurred in different eras, most likely between the Ice Ages. The adventurers originated from at least four different civilizations, possibly in different star systems. Each of these exploration groups left traces of their heritage, culture, civilizations and origins. Some traces were faint, others were colossal. All of these exploration groups left populations of workers behind to fend for themselves, surviving and becoming *Native Man*. These abandoned "native populations" carried with them customs, stories and folklore, the precursors of religion.

Man, a unique being of the Universe, did not mutate from primordial ooze with a series of subhuman ancestors, or be "created" by God making mud dolls and performing CPR on them. No one really knows the origins of Man, however if you believe that a Supreme Being is responsible, why would you mentally limit that Beings' ability to create Man anywhere in our Galaxy?

Religious Leaders and intellectual communities, holding to medieval mentalities, have explained away, or destroyed, all of the facts and clues which support the obvious, that Man exists beyond our Solar System. This type of mentality is termed *Western Thinking* and promotes the teaching of; until something is "discovered" by the Western World it never existed. In the Middle Ages this was akin to "The Earth is flat and is the center of the Universe."

The discovery of **The Dead Sea Scrolls** in 1947, and the **Nag Hamaddi** documents [Egypt] set the stage for a battle between the intellectual and religious circles, which continues to this day. These ancient writings are so controversial many of the documents will never be openly translated. Before the Scrolls could be hidden once again, some of the translations made it to the general public. Make no mistake about this information, if the world's religious leaders, cabals and organizations could put the genie back in the bottle, they would. The reason is that the "Scrolls" opened the door for examination of the "Holy Writs". This exposure led to determining that the "scriptures" have been continuously revised to fit the needs and goals of Organized Religion.

Recent discoveries of "Lost Gospels", in Greek and Coptic, indicate an extremely different view of Yeshua and his bride, Miriam of The Tower [translated as Mary Magdalene]. The Coptic script refers to her as "The wife of God".

I present a radically different view of religious history than that depicted in the King James Version of the Holy Writ. You will learn the truth about the Prophet Noah, that there was no "World Deluge" during his life and why this fable was perpetrated as a religious occurrence. Realistic and more accurate translations of the *Garden of Eden Incident* will show that "Adam" was a real person and that Eve was not his first wife. Also provided is evidence that Cain was not the son of Adam, and the answer to why he killed Abel.

For the past five thousand years, Man has sought answers to historical mysteries he simply did not understand. Several works on ancient civilizations, in print and film, have attempted to explain the history created by this unique group of celestial travelers. These efforts have only produced a series of unanswered questions and intellectual frustrations.

Answers to these mysteries are provided with unique clarity, without questionable events or fragmented answers. This unique approach provides you with an accumulation of information and knowledge presented in a new format, fascinating, and based on physical reality. Logic is applied to years of research, which includes history, ancient languages, religious writings, archaeology, geology, mythology and "Holy Writs". The world's most lauded intellectuals produced fantastic research material, yet their conclusions were clouded with the limitations of Western Thinking.

For my Masonic Brothers, this view of history reveals how the travelers established the Ancient Masonic Lodge, known today as Ancient Free and Accepted Masons. The journey to the East will prove to be an adventure into the lost secrets of your Craft.

The surviving group of explorers I follow developed advanced civilizations which extended from the Middle East to the Americas. From their centers of power on the Mediterranean Island of Thera to Teotihuacan in the Americas you will have a fascinating view of history in "The Old World" and in Central and South America. They brought advanced intelligence to the Americas over 20,000 years ago.

This period of history has never been presented with complete reality and clarity. Trade and communication existed between the Americas and the Mediterranean civilizations. The secret messages of the Nazca lines in Peru, and similar large-scale art in the Atacama Desert of Chile, will be explained. Influence from Teotihuacan developed the vanished mystery civilizations of the American Southwest.

Carefully developed religious, cultural, and scientific parables have provided past and present civilizations with mental scotomas. A scotoma is a mental blind spot which conceals truths and blocks your mind from identifying the keys to recognizing fact. To decipher these "keys," you must open your mind and go beyond the mental veils established throughout recorded history by the religious and intellectual community. As you do, your comprehension of historical anomalies will advance on a magnitude from sitting in a reed and mud hut on the Tigris River in 12,000 BCE, to riding in the Space Station orbiting the Earth.

Page one will raise the historical veil for a fascinating journey, beginning in our ancient past, continuous to present day. You will never again view recorded history as you have in the past.

Your journey through the mysteries of Time, of Man and Gods, has begun.

In the beginning, Man discovered Earth.

NGC 6888 – Courtesy of NASA – Hubble Telescope Photograph

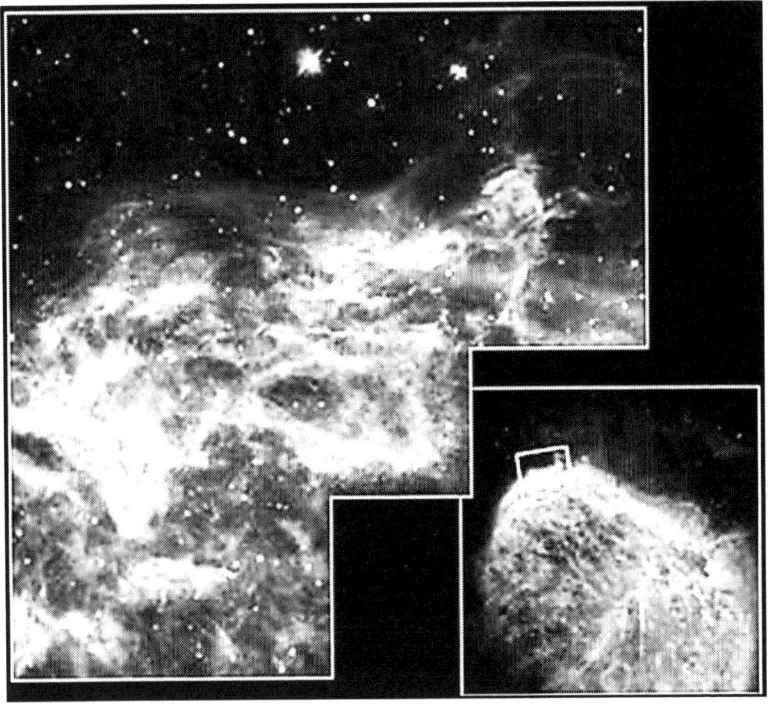

Book One

THE BEGINNING

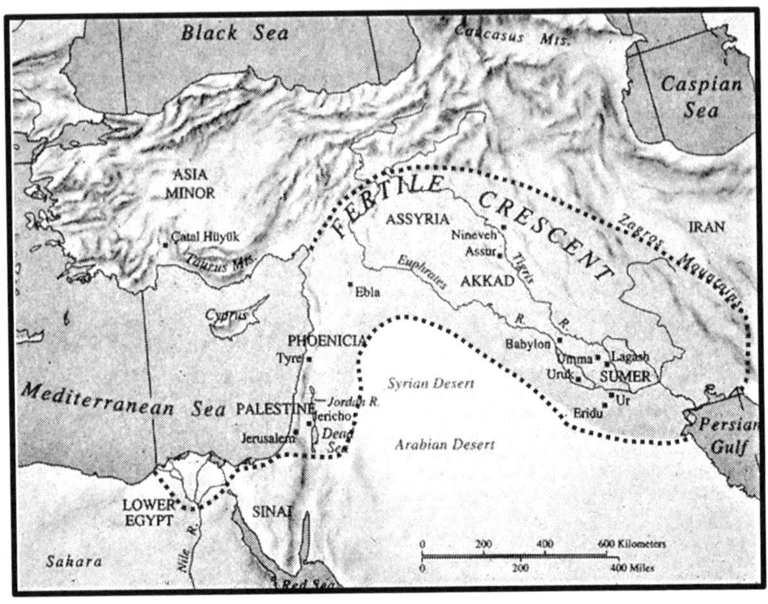

The Fertile Crescent, where Alulim descended To Earth and built the first Sumerian City of Eridug 254,000 years ago. His Sons and Daughters became Gods [Lords] to all in the Crescent.

Alulim came to lead and educate his people in this new frontier, Earth. He lived for the next 28,800 years.

After the Comet Impact and Pleistocene Extinction, with the accompanying Deluge 12,900 years ago, surviving Lords Bal and Yahweh revived the Civilizations of Sumer and began an epic journey for Mankind, Civilization and Gods. This set the foundations for Modern Religions.

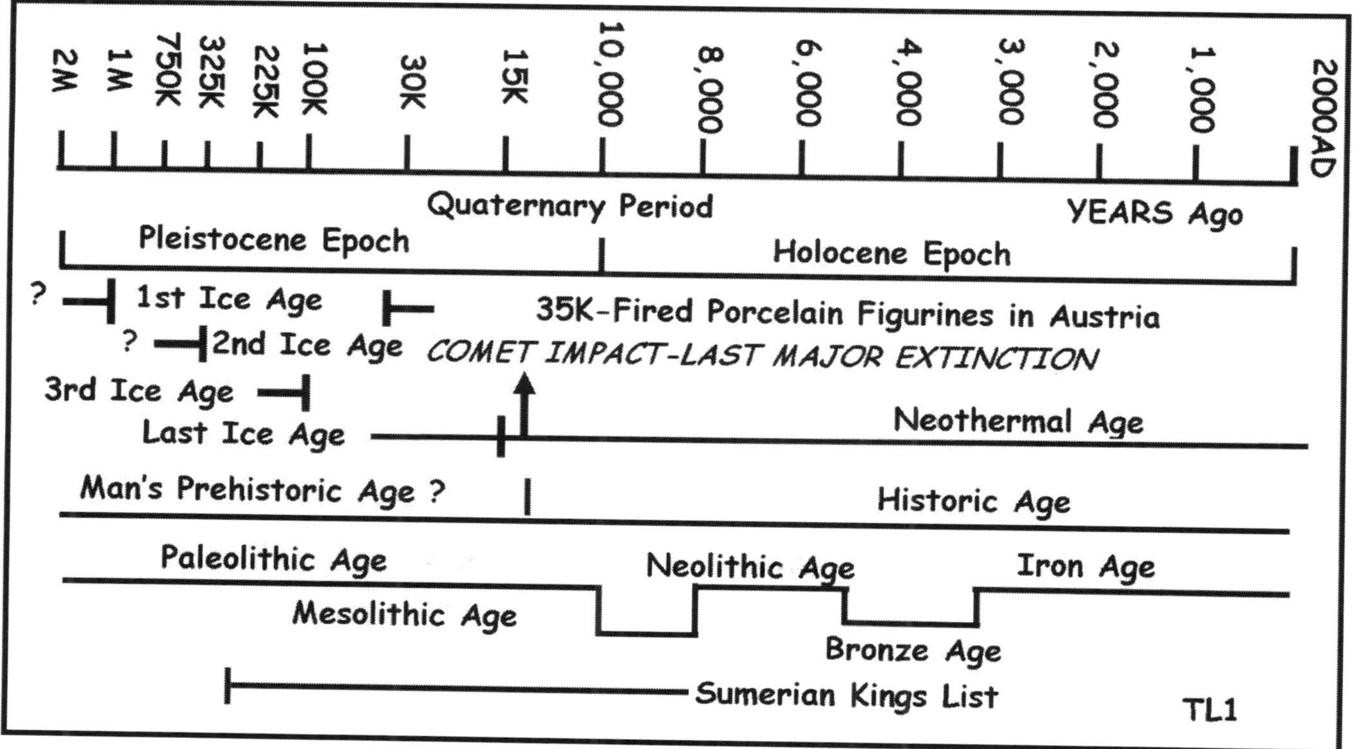

2000AD
1,000
2,000
3,000
4,000
6,000
8,000
10,000
15K
30K
100K
225K
325K
750K
1M
2M
YEARS Ago
Quaternary Period
Pleistocene Epoch
Holocene Epoch
? 1st Ice Age
35K-Fired Porcelain Figurines in Austria
? 2nd Ice Age
COMET IMPACT-LAST MAJOR EXTINCTION
3rd Ice Age
Last Ice Age
Neothermal Age
Man's Prehistoric Age ?
Historic Age
Paleolithic Age
Neolithic Age
Iron Age
Mesolithic Age
Bronze Age
Sumerian Kings List
TL1

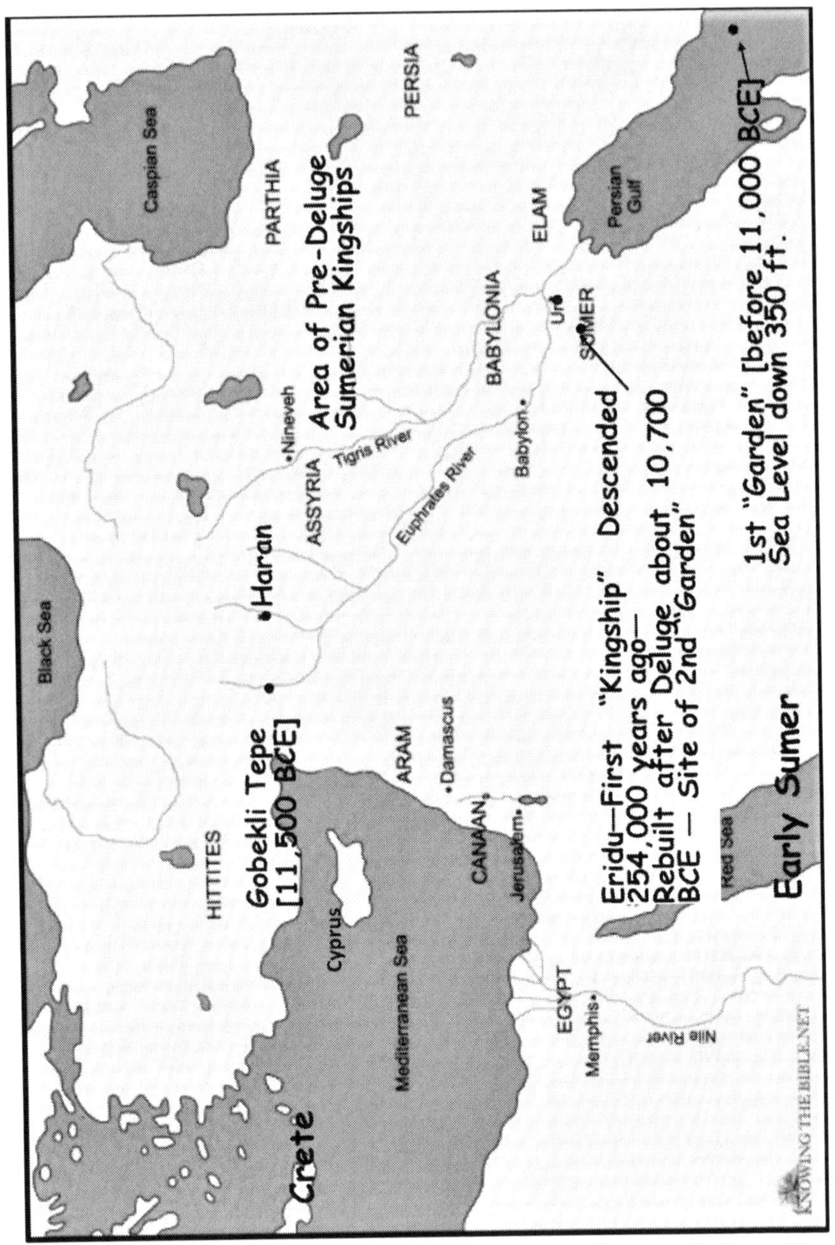

The Fertile Crescent – Sumer – Colonized by Man 254,000 years ago – Foundation of Modern Religion

Chapter
1

THE BEGINNING
Man Discovers Earth

The known Universe is immense, so beyond human comprehension it can only be explained as infinity. There is no beginning and no end. There is no point of reference that the human mind could fix upon to begin to comprehend the vastness of space. A small portion of space, as viewed through the Hubble telescope, contains a hundred billion visible galaxies with each galaxy containing three hundred billion stars and planets. Probabilities are there are many life-sustaining planets in our own galaxy, The Milky Way.

A prime example of other life sustaining planets in our Milky Way Galaxy is the Trappist- 1 solar system. **Trappist-1**, also designated as 2MASS J23062928-0502285, is a dwarf star that is slightly larger and much more massive than the planet Jupiter. It is about 40 light-years from our Sun in the constellation Aquarius. What is amazing is that 7 rocky, Earth-sized planets orbit this star.

Within this system of billions of planets, the probability of Earth being specifically located through the process of manned exploration is mathematically impossible. Several million years ago, most likely by using technology similar to ours and deep space probes, Man discovered Earth. The subsequent decision to explore this new world changed Earth forever.

Traveling through the vastness of deep space, an exploration team observed a bright planet covered with blue oceans and white clouds. This confirmed the photos and data of oxygen and water sent by the probe; there was evidence of life within this remote solar system. The travelers set their course to investigate this rare appearance of a life-sustaining world, suitable for colonization.

Exploration reflects the timeless human characteristic of a quest for knowledge, adventure, power and wealth. Man, the ultimate explorer, had extended his boundaries to include Earth. As with countless examples of Man making new discoveries, knowledge of Earth was disseminated throughout several civilizations.

Well before the last Ice Age travelers from a variety of Civilizations across the Universe launched exploration groups to Earth. The same group of explorers who colonized The Fertile Crescent 254,000 years ago established civilizations in the Mediterranean area and in The Americas. I am certain several other independent groups [of Man] established colonies in Central Asia, China and Africa.

Twenty thousand years ago the geomorphology of the Earth was vastly different than today. The Sahara was forest and savannah with numerous rivers and lakes. The forests of western North America had not yet developed and the present deserts of the Middle East were lush with grasslands and forest. Sea Levels were down about 430 feet from the present levels and the average temperature was about 40° F colder. North America's Death Valley was one of many glacial fed freshwater lakes. Massive Ice Age fresh water Lake Bonneville eventually became The Great Salt Lake of Utah. Many of its ancient shorelines are visible on the horizons.

The latest explorers' subsequent history of being stranded among Native Man by a comet impact, in the era of 12,900 years ago, created a series of historical anomalies, mysteries, religions and secrets. To date, these voids of history have not been adequately explained.

These stranded explorers conceived and nurtured many great civilizations and religions as sanctuaries to support their survival. Living as Gods, they were veiled in secrecy and protected by ancient religious rituals. However, the advances of civilization eventually overran their ability to control events. When this occurred, they relocated and began another more powerful sanctuary, waiting for rescue. This highly intelligent group of explorers is known as **The Lords of Sumer**.

These explorers colonized the Earth and fostered religion by portraying natural occurring events as spiritual. The Lords understood the Earth's equinoxes and solstices were important cycles of time and attributed these events to Gods' actions for their tribes to revere. These actions relate to today's most important religious ceremonies.

The civilizations created by **The Lords of Sumer** in the Fertile Crescent, after the comet impact, began with Sumer, Crete in the Mediterranean, Egypt, and the Indus River Valley Civilization [by a splinter group]. They had previously established advanced observatories and civilizations in the Americas.

In the Americas their influence is particularly evident in the Solar observatory ruins at Tiwanaku Bolivia. This site has been dated as functioning in 15,000 BCE, as an operating observatory. This means the construction was prior to that time. The Tiwanakuan Civilization was destroyed by portions of the comet impact of 10,900 BCE. The survivors of the Pleistocene Extinction gave rise to the Olmec, Maya, and *Mexican* of Teotihuacan [sometimes referred to as early Toltec] in Central America, and to the Pacific Coastal civilizations of South America, the Las Vegas Civilization and others.

The advanced civilization established at Tiwanaku constructed an elaborate Sun Temple Observatory and tracked variations in the Earth's orbit, axis tilt and star systems. Evidence of introduced intelligence in all the arts and sciences is discernable in each of the Lord's sanctuaries and developed civilizations.

There is compelling archeological evidence which supports the premise of many stranded groups of explorers. These men and women pursued their survival on Earth as Gods, developed their linage as tribes and assumed control of local populations. This is evident in most ancient cultures throughout the world. The mysteries of other groups of stranded explorers will not be addressed in this work, so as not to detract from the singular group we are about to explore.

The latest known exploration of the Earth altered the natural progression of Native Man. The populations of Native Man were remnant groups of previous exploration and mining activities over the past several million years. Native Man evolved socially from previous expedition workers, who for a variety of reasons, calamities and natural disasters, were left to fend for themselves. We must explore the earliest traces of Human existence.

To establish when the earlier explorations of Earth began, we need to look at the history of primitive Man. It is possible the explorations were in progress over several million years, from several different origins. This would explain the origin of different racial groups of people. The interaction of these groups would result in the wide diversity of distinct civilizations.

If you research the "**Academic Standard**" that Man evolved in and migrated out of Africa you will discover it is a myth. It is without foundation, without any proof that Eurasian civilizations expanded from black pigmented people in Africa. Black humans did migrate from Africa to the South East islands and to Australia and developed advanced civilizations in their regions. They later migrated and mingled with other races of people and enlarged the diversity of Human populations.

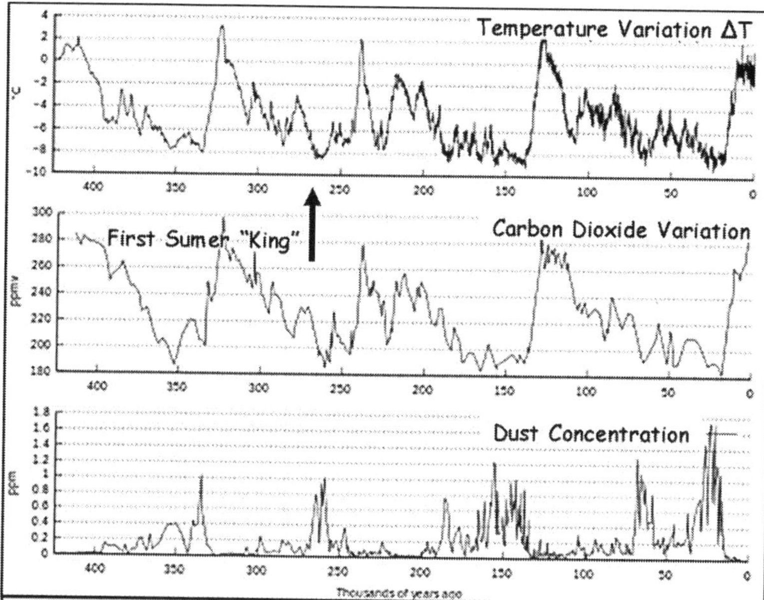

Top graph shows temperature changes. Lower part of graph indicate Ice Ages about every 100,000 years. 270,000 years ago began a warming trend when the Sumerian Kings List begins with the first "God" descending to lead Man. Other graphs show variations of CO_2 and dust concentration. CO_2 is produced by animals/other sources and absorbed by oceans and plants. During a Thermal Age increased Fauna releases more CO_2. Dust increases during arid Ice Ages.

EARTH GRAPHS FROM 400,000 YEARS AGO TO
PRESENT

Eon	Era	Period		Epoch	
					← Today
Phanerozoic	Cenozoic	Quaternary		Holocene	← 11.8 Ka
				Pleistocene	
		Neogene		Pliocene	
				Miocene	
		Paleogene		Oligocene	
				Eocene	
				Paleocene	← 66 Ma
	Mesozoic	Cretaceous		~	
		Jurassic		~	
		Triassic		~	← 252 Ma
	Paleozoic	Permian		~	
		Carboni-ferous	Pennsylvanian	~	
			Mississippian	~	
		Devonian		~	
		Silurian		~	
		Ordovician		~	
		Cambrian		~	← 541 Ma
Proterozoic	~	~		~	← 2.5 Ga
Archean	~	~		~	← 4.0 Ga
Hadean	~	~		~	← 4.54 Ga

Chapter

2

20,000 year old Sun Temple Tiwanaku Bolivia

GEOLOGIC AND ANTHROPOLOGIC HISTORIES

PRIMEVAL MAN

Chipped stone axes in Africa have been dated to approximately 2 million years. The footprints of Man, not Neanderthal, and absolutely not of Australopithecus or any other supposed evolutionary creature, were discovered in South Africa, preserved in stone dated well over 100,000 years. Fire pits from Asia to Southern Africa have been dated well beyond the footprints in stone and may exceed 200,000 years. A reconstructed skull of Homo Sapiens Sapiens has been positively dated to 130,000 years.

Ritual burials of ancient Man have been excavated in the area of present-day Israel and Jordan dating to over 100,000 years. The ritual burial involved decorating the body with red ochre pigment. Another ancient burial discovered in Australia, not of Neanderthal, showed identical red ochre ritual painting and dated to over 60,000 years.

The Sumerian Kings List was a remarkable find for history. It is so unbelievable to *Academia* that they dismiss it as "purely fictional myth" [redundant?]. Their basis for this is that there have been no ruins found which are classified before "The Great Flood" mentioned in the cuneiform tablets.

Academia also declares they cannot find any histories for these "Antediluvian [before the flood] Kings". My, My, what about that? It would be obvious to most people that when an epic flood occurs it destroys and buries most sites in its path. Well known to *Academia* are the cuneiform records found at Ashurbanipal's Library in Nineveh, written by Ashurbanipal, that state he read inscribed stones from "before the Deluge". Of course, *Academia* will declare this history as "fanciful prose".

The Holy Writ has some lineage histories before Noah, but that was 4,028 BCE, and doesn't mention any of these characters by name. The Holy Writ avoids mention of any kings or pharaohs until well after "Noah's Deluge", finally mentioning the King of Ur, King Ur-Nammu, and Egypt's Pharaoh when discussing Abram's travels. For the writers of the Writ to acknowledge any rulers of nations would discredit all of the narrative to Abram's time.

The Sumerian Kings List provides evidence of how the Earth was populated with Humans. As I said before, "In The Beginning Man Discovered Earth". This is just one of many exploration groups.

What really bothers *Academia* is that the first eight Antediluvian Sumerian Kings listed ruled for 241,000 years in different areas of The Fertile Crescent, beginning about 254,000 years ago. This period lasted through several Ice Ages, Thermal Ages and untold worldwide calamities. Further, none of these kings can be verified archaeologically, so *Academia* determined the tablets were made up for local political purposes to gain leadership positions. Do you think the clay tablet news boy stood on the street corner of Babylon yelling "breaking news we have ancestors"? I really don't think these ancient kings ran election campaigns.

Further consideration to believe these accounts of the first "Gods" is that Neanderthal is dated to over 200,000 years. It is very likely Neanderthal was labor for these "First Gods". Their remains have been found over most of Euro-Asia and North Africa. Of course, Neanderthal could have been survivors of a previous colonization by explorers.

From the translation of the Sumerian Kings List Tablets, for the first king listed:

"After the kingship descended from heaven, the kingship was in Eridug. In Eridug, Alulim became king; he ruled for 28,800 years."

The next list [post flood] was of the first dynasty kings of Kish [Sumer] begins with "*After the flood had swept over, and the kingship had descended from heaven, the kingship was in Kish*". The Gods ruled from Kish from 10,700 BCE to 4,700 BCE. The seat of power then moved to Uruk.

To understand what is presented by the Kings List, picture Ancient Sumer as the Empire, and the "Dynasties" are named after the city where the ruling God lived. Enormous ziggurat mud-brick temples were constructed at each of these cities.

If you research the deciphered document you will see precise year units [*sars* (units of 3,600 years), *ners* (units of 600 years), and *sosses* (units of 60 years)] for the reigns of the Antediluvian Gods. The Post Diluvian Gods [Kings] reigns are listed in years and I believe this is a mistake. The years listed are most likely the life spans of the "Kings".

The Kings List indicated 18,000 years just for the Kish Dynasty and this is an obvious error. To equate the years as a "reign" would date them beyond our Current Era. I believe *Academia* produced these obvious, erroneous findings to further cast doubt on any validity of the Sumerian Kings List.

"The Flood" or, "The Deluge" is dated to the Comet impact of 10,900 BCE. This Pleistocene Extinction Event would have destroyed most habitations in any flood plain, such as the gigantic flood plain of the combined Tigris and Euphrates Rivers. Eridug [Eridu] is said to be the first City of the Gods. It is also recorded as the first city to be re-built "after the Deluge". This would date the existing Eridu Site to about 10,700 BCE.

Today Eridu appears as many barren clay hills in a barren desert plain. The city was constructed in a marshy flood plain by digging the clay silt from the marsh bed and building clay mounds above water level. Research confirms this as fresh water shells are numerous in the ruins of the city. The builders then made sun-dried brick for constructing all buildings. The completed city had an extensive canal system and raised bed agriculture.

Raised bed farming was, and is, very successful with great yields of grains and other food crops. You will discover this method for farming, when locating a city in marshy areas, was a trademark for developing the Lord's civilizations. The Eridu site appears to be too far from the river channel to be irrigated, but looking at satellite maps, the ancient river channel went right through the city. This type of agriculture was necessary due to the still artic climate [glaciers and perma-frost] which existed around the Mediterranean to 45° N Latitude until the forests began to return after 8,000 BCE.

The Assyrian and Babylonian Gods' names were often exchanged and reversed. A few things to remember to keep the Gods somewhat organized. First was the Father of all "Earth Gods" who descended from the sky, **Alulim**, with female consort Gods in *Heaven* and *Earth*. This name was changed several times to Ellil, El [Lord], Anu, An and so on. He was the leader of the Pantheon of Seven Gods who ruled Earth.

"Heaven" is a term which was coined from the Sumerian words for "The Stars" and "Paradise" to enhance the stories for Christianity. Paradise was a Sumerian word for a peaceful place of beauty and wealth where the Gods dwelt. The Sumerians knew exactly what "The stars" referred to; The Universe.

From these Seven Gods came sons and daughters with humans, who became the kings, queens and princes of various civilizations. The names change but the structure remains, particularly with the original "Seven Holy Beings".

The cornerstone for these ancient religions is an established trinity of Gods: The father god, the virgin mother god baring the offspring Son, most often representing a Teacher and Savior of Man. The Savior deity was constantly referred to as the "Sun God" in ancient religions. This trinity of gods has remained in religions to this day.

The last ice age, and previous ones, obliterated any traces of civilization under the ice sheet coverage. 30,000 to 40,000 years ago, at the beginning of the last Ice Age, the Woolly Mammoth and other large fauna [animals] were hunted by both Homo Sapiens Neanderthalensis [Neanderthal] and Homo Sapiens Sapiens. The game animals were killed for food and shelter in Europe, Eurasia, Mongolia, and in North and South America. During this same time period [32,000 BCE], exceedingly fine, fired porcelain figures were produced in present-day Austria. Exquisitely carved ivory figurines and animals were produced at several sites through-out the world. Fantastic cave-art paintings were being done near Lascaux, France by Cro-Magnon.

During the next 20,000 years these skills diminished in the local populations.

Homo Sapiens Neanderthalensis was named and identified after fossils were discovered in the Neander Valley in Germany in 1856. Neanderthal lived in the Feldhofer cave of this valley for a considerable time, leaving evidence of a remarkable people. Contrary to popular belief, Neanderthal had a brain larger than modern Humans, stood upright, was about 5 feet tall and weighed approximately 180 pounds. They were heavy boned, muscular, strong, stout and intelligent. They also were very adept at surviving in extreme cold climates.

Neanderthal may have been the result of genetic engineering to produce a breed of tireless workers. Of course, they could have been simply a remaining civilization exploited by the original Sumerian Gods as a labor source. An earlier expedition of explorers could have simply left these workers to fend for themselves when the expedition was over. Their origins can be traced to about 200,000 years ago, and, according to popular *Academia* they survived to about 20,000 BCE, finally becoming extinct. I do not claim to have unique knowledge about them, just sensible conclusions. Just as later civilizations would be devastated by introduced disease, this could be a reason for their demise. The Spanish eliminated at least 130 million people, in South America, in a few years with smallpox and a few other diseases.

The same result occurred in Central and North America when the Conquistadors contacted indigenous civilizations. The northern contact with Europeans eliminated close to 100 Million people with the various disease epidemics.

Neanderthal's range was from Central Asia to Europe and North Africa, and they were constantly pushed south and west by the advancing Ice Age and by advancing Homo Sapiens Sapiens.

I must interject the most recent debate on evolution. The 2010 discovery of *Denisovans* [bone fragments found in Denisovan Cave] in Russia set off a new flurry of evolution debates. What was "found" were bone fragments from two cranial caps and a metacarpal; a finger bone. Other cranial bone fragments were found 4,000 kilometers away in China. Although the cranial fragments resemble Neanderthal, the researchers are convinced they discovered a new species of Homo Sapiens due to DNA results. I think it is a bit early to devise an entire civilization on a few bone fragments. I only mention this because so many people get taken in by "new findings". So far, "Sapiens" have not been linked to early Hominids by DNA.

Having noted the extinction of Neanderthal about 20,000 BCE, as is widely held in the academic culture, the following is extremely provocative. A manuscript produced in 922 CE [Current Era] by Ahmad Ibn Fadlan, an ambassador for the Caliph of Baghdad, recounted his travels to the Artic North with Vikings. It is an interesting account of his travels, and of doing battle with a hairy race of people in the Artic regions. The point I am coming to is, his description of these people is of "Neanderthal".   This was over 900 years before Neanderthal was discovered or named. Academics vehemently deny that Ahmad's description is of Neanderthal. We certainly would not want facts to cloud the established norm.

There are written accounts of contacts with similar groups of "hairy, ill-tempered and bad smelling night hunting groups of humans" during the late 1700s CE and early 1800s CE in the Pacific Northwest Coastal and inland Territories of North America.

The Neanderthals were in conflict with Cro-Magnon Man. The term "Cro-Magnon" has resulted in a perception of a sub-species of Man, the cave dwellers, due to early cartoons and Hollywood depictions. Most of us envision hunch-backed, hairy, long armed pre-humans who were evolving. 19th and 20th Century *Academia* gave this civilization a name based on the name of a rock shelter in southwestern France.

They were just like you, Human, that is Homo Sapiens Sapiens. *Academia* is now proclaiming Cro-Magnon was a sub-species human, now extinct. I have recently found this statement and do not believe it. It is just another fad of *Academia*. When I see scientific proof, as in full DNA comparisons, I might change my mind.

In the 1800s it would have been heresy to proclaim Man existed before the time of Adam's "creation", or about 4,200 BCE. It also would end any academic's chance of retaining employment or tenure. Realizing this, the academics used terminology which confused the commoners and hid the truth in plain view. Early film makers perpetuated the vision of Cro-Magnon as pre-human beings. Cro-Magnon was Homo Sapiens Sapiens, Modern Man. They made and fitted their clothing, produced fine art, had family and tribal cultures, and to the detriment of Neanderthal; they conquered their territory.

In the Upper Paleolithic Age [40,000 years ago to 12,000 years ago] Cro-Magnon civilizations [Aurignacian, Solutrean and Magdalenian] moved into southern Europe from the near-east Fertile Crescent [Levant].   These civilizations combined with the Perigordian civilizations which were already established.   None of these civilizations were of black descent.

These early humans were in the category of Paleolithic [Old Stone Age] groups, classified as hunters and gatherers.   Some anthropologists rely on the following definitions for the developmental level of "Early Man."   Anything prior to 8,000 BCE is classified as Paleolithic [Stone Age], 8000 to 6000 BCE is Mesolithic [Middle Stone Age], and 6000 to 3000 BCE is Neolithic [New Stone Age].

In their continual search for spirituality and self-identification Stone Age humans painted or scraped drawings and pictures at special locations.   Usually the paintings were on the walls of caves and petroglyphs were produced on rock faces and depicted everyday life and cultural mythology.   The art clearly represented events or mythology of that time.

There has been considerable speculation regarding the meaning of the strange figures depicted in their art, however there is little evidence these Pre-Paleolithic humans received outside influence on their daily lifestyles. What they did have were stories of old, mythology derived from those original "Sumerian Kings" and abandoned workers. The stories were retold, generation-to-generation, and held sacred by the clan's Shaman.   This mythology established the oldest form of "religion".

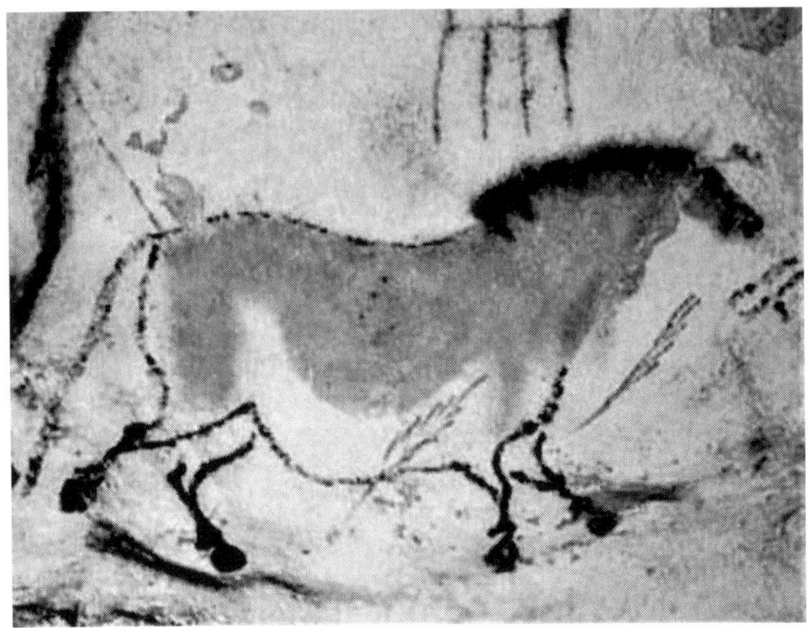

17,000 BCE Lascaux Cave Painting by Cro-Magnon
Southern France

21,000 BCE Altamira Cave Painting by Solutrean
Culture in Southern Spain

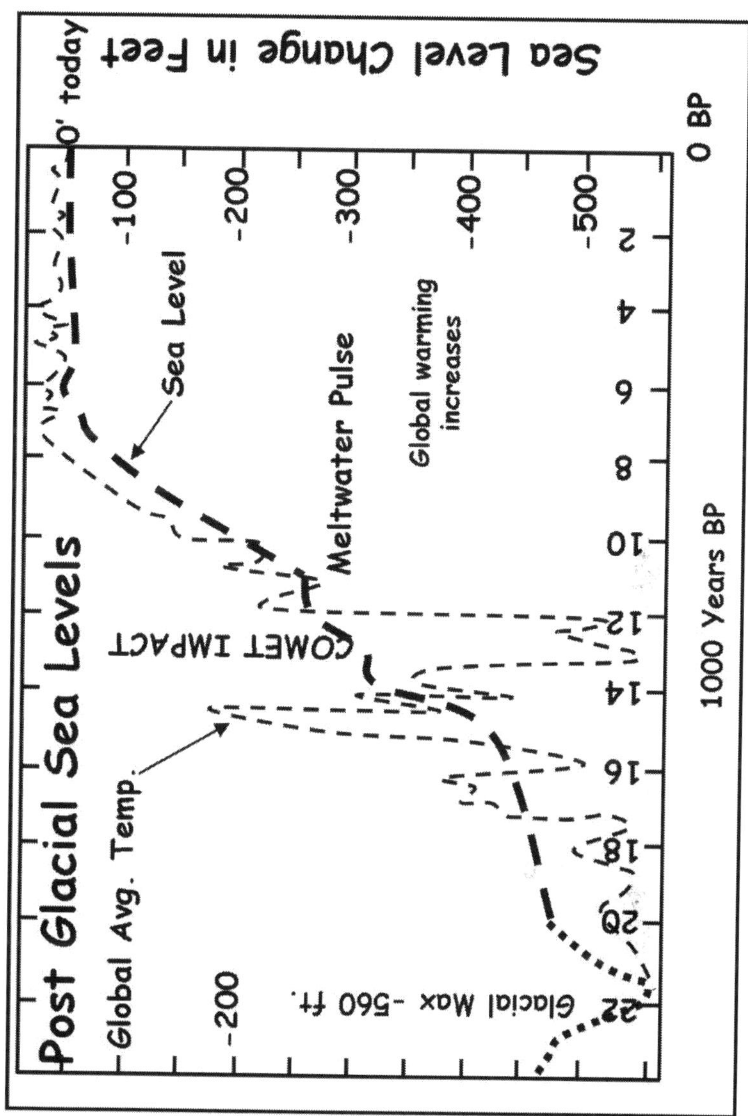

Pleistocene Sea levels - 15,000 years ago

At the glacial maximum the sea level was at -560 feet of today's sea levels exposing seamount land bridges worldwide. The sea level had risen to -260 feet at the time of the Comet Impact of 12,900 years ago.

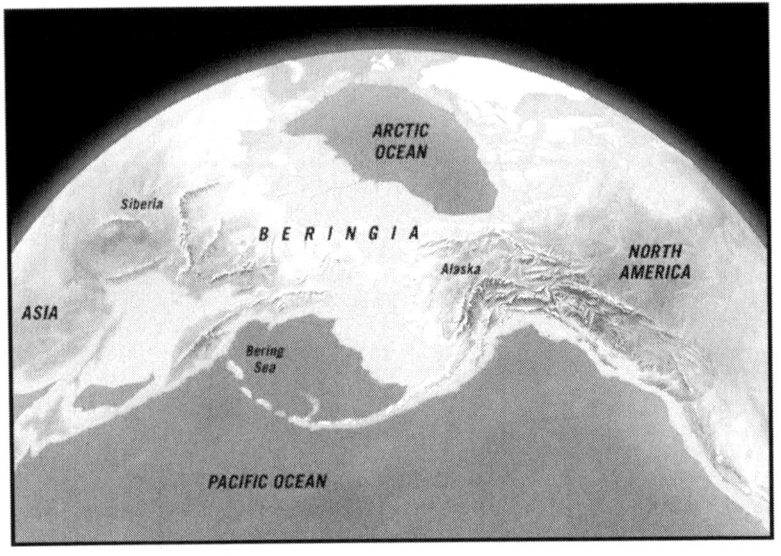

Pleistocene Sea Levels 15,000 years ago

Chapter

3

Wooly Mammoths

THE LAST GREAT EXTINCTION

COMET IMPACT

Approximately 12,900 years ago, a comet struck the Earth at several locations. Major impact sites were in the North American and Polar ice sheets, South America, Eurasia, Pacific Ocean and the Atlantic Ocean. The comet strike resulted in the last world-wide extinction of large herbivores and civilizations. This is referred to as the Quaternary Period, or Pleistocene Epoch Extinction worldwide.

Dr. Richard Firestone and Dr. William Topping of Lawrence Berkley National Laboratory, and Geologist Allen West, along with over 20 scientists published their findings in 2005. Of course, *Academia* has been trying to show the findings are not supported. Sound familiar?

"Our research indicates that a 10 kilometer [6.2 miles] wide comet, which may have been composed from the remnants of a Supernova explosion, could have hit North America 13,000 years ago".   [Dr. Richard Firestone, et al]

The 12,900 years ago Comet impact discovery by Dr. Firestone and team was a history clarifying scientific report; his summary report and reply to skeptics in Academia who claim no impact occurred, is detailed in the Appendix of this writing.

Since the release of Dr. Firestone's group's findings other researchers have followed with their own investigations and have corroborated his findings.   They have found the "Event Boundary Layer" of high concentrations of typical elements from space in forms of spheroids and other nano-shapes interspersed with carbon fallout. One of the premier research groups is NARCIS of the Netherlands, whose finds included an impact site from this Comet near Belgium.

Comets typically will break-up due to gravity as they near a planet and will strike in many locations at 30,000 to 40,000 miles per hour. The North American **Laurentide Ice sheet** impact was the greatest, with near equal and smaller impacts around the globe. The most immediate inflow of fresh water into the Pacific Ocean came from the **Cordilleran Ice Sheet** which covered the western half of North America.

The first destructive force from an impact is the thermal shock wave. It moves out at super-sonic speed, leveling everything for close to a thousand miles in every direction, killing most animal life. Next the heat generated sets everything ablaze and the rebound of ejected material filled the atmosphere with ice and debris, resulting in a global winter and then the rains began. Instant super-cold freezing temperatures returned rapidly after the impact.

Sea Levels rose from -560 feet in 20,000 BCE to -360 feet in 13,000 BCE and to -250 feet when the comet impacted the Earth. Sea Levels rose from -52 feet in 6,000 BCE to -30 feet of today's levels by 5,500 BCE and increased +10 feet over todays' level in 4,000 BCE. Sea levels continued to rise with a gradual increase to present day. Global average temperatures were about 40° F colder at the glacial maximum and sea levels were -170 meters [-560 feet] exposing vast areas as dry land.

During and after the comet impact, debris and thousands of meteors rained on the Earth. Over 500 large craters have been documented near the Carolinas' coastline [USA]. I would urge readers to research these findings.   To fully cover this event would require years of writing.

The comet impact created massive Tsunamis, centuries of floods, vegetation dying, massive meltwater draining into the oceans and widespread volcanism. This was followed by 1,400 years of global winter, ending about 9,500 BCE. This global winter is referred to as the Younger-Dryas period. This event left the stories of "The Great Flood" in all ancient civilizations.

The Younger-Dryas period is believed to have been caused by the collapse and melting of the North American and Asian Ice sheets [up to 2 miles thick]. The massive fresh water influx changed ocean currents resulting in extensive weather changes and raised sea levels hundreds of feet. This new weather pattern eventually changed the Sahara from lush savanna, lakes and forest to one of Earth's largest deserts.

The global winter created large deserts, glaciers returning and loss of forests and grasslands. At the end of this period the Earth steadily warmed and sea levels continued to rise.

In geologic terms this was The Quaternary Period, and the end of the Pleistocene Epoch. Over 200 species of large animals, all over the Earth, became extinct at this time and the event is known as the "Pleistocene Extinction". Percentages of megafauna in the extinction ranged from 14% in Africa to +85% in Eurasia, North America, Australia and South Pacific Islands.

In North and South America most all of the large animal species became extinct. These extinct species included; the horse, camel, mastodon, mammoth, cave bear, giant sloth, saber toothed tiger and many others.

Evidence of the Pleistocene Extinction was found in 1940 as mining equipment was clearing tundra north of Fairbanks Alaska and discovered frozen animal remains. These rotting carcasses were strewn in jumbled piles for hundreds of miles. The remains included mastodons, lions [possibly Tigers], horses, wolves, bears and many more species mixed with tundra, peat and trees. The New Mexico Professor issuing the report stated;

> **"The evidence immediately suggests an enormous tidal wave which raged over the land, tumbling animals and vegetation within its mass, which was in turn quick-frozen".**

At present, Fairbanks Alaska is 400 miles north of the Gulf of Alaska, 450 miles south of Prudhoe Bay and about 400 miles east of the Bering Sea. The town is at an elevation of 450 feet and is just south of the Yukon River. The Tsunami [tidal wave] traveled from the Canadian Basin [North Pole] through the dry Bering Sea area, over 400 miles up the Yukon River valley and deposited its rubble at an elevation of over

700 feet above the Pleistocene sea levels. I have not computed the height and speed of the Tsunami, but it must have been massive and fast.

At the date of impact, sea levels were down about 250 feet [60+ meters] which put the Bering Sea and the Chukchi Sea in dry land. The islands north of Canada, extending to Greenland, were all connected by dry land [except for glaciers]. The only ocean water was in the Canada Basin and in the Eurasian Basin on either side of the North Pole. For a Tsunami to have caused the destruction in Alaska and Siberia, the impact would have had to be at or near the North Pole.

Identical Tsunami destruction was found in Siberia. The estimate of large animal remains buried along Siberian rivers is several million. One specimen of Mastodon, excavated in 1902, was so quick frozen and preserved that researchers found buttercup flowers in its mouth, and undigested food in its stomach. The large Siberian ivory tusks are still mined for today.

Upper Pleistocene civilizations on all continents were lost in this great comet strike. In North America, an impact on the 2-mile-thick ice killed most of the Human population. The Clovis Civilization vanished. In Europe near the areas of southern Spain and France the Aurignacian and Solutrean civilizations were decimated. Central and South American civilizations suffered similar extinction fates, although there were more pockets of survivors.

The Comet Impact ended the Clovis Civilization, which vanished with evidence of their sites found from the East Coast to the West Coast. The civilization was named from a spear point first identified near Clovis New Mexico.

Clovis flint tool making skills were distinct and extraordinary, using pressure flaking rather than a striking technique. This flint tool making skill was mirrored in the Aurignacian and Solutrean civilizations located in Europe near the areas of Spain and France. Also, very interesting is that both civilizations in Europe and the Americas used a spear throwing device called an Atlatl. The survivors on both continents continued to use the atlatl and bow-and-arrow as weapon systems.

There are hundreds of "megalithic sites" located around the globe, which present continued mysteries of the civilizations which constructed the massive stone block sites. Advanced civilizations in

Africa ceased to thrive, leaving stone observatories abandoned. The African Dogon civilization charted the sister stars, Sirius A and Sirius B in the Pleiades cluster [Tarus Constellation], which were not known to modern astronomers until powerful telescopes were constructed. These stars are so close together they cannot be differentiated without the use of a telescope. These civilizations thrived from Cape Town to the Mediterranean Coast, Egypt and into the Sinai. One of the great civilizations established by Africans would come to be know as the Phoenicians of Gibraltar.

In Europe and Asia most Upper Pleistocene Cultures ceased to exist after the comet strike, including Neanderthal. Although the Earth was in an Ice Age there is considerable evidence of several temperate zones, through the glaciers, in the Americas and in Asia. Ocean levels rose about 100 feet from 15,000 BCE to 13,000 BCE, indicating a warming and more temperate climate. Large game and Human groups would naturally gravitate to these areas. From the British Isles to Iran and Upper Mongolia to Siberia there were hundreds of principle cultural sites which were destroyed. Again, there were pockets of survivors. These extinction survivors were extremely important for the rise of civilization in the Levant, an area which indicated continued habitation.

Although the climate was warming, glaciers and permafrost extended to southern France, with treeless steppes south to 45° N latitude in Europe. Glaciers were widespread from the Atlas Mountains in North Africa eastward across Europe north of the Mediterranean. Reforestation began after 8,000 BCE.

Artic seas with pack ice extended almost as far south as the permafrost. The oceans were a few degrees warmer than land and also contained some warm currents. A very large warm current ran north close to Japan, into the North Pacific Ocean.

To summarize these Earth and climatic change events for an overall view of Earth's history coming out of the last Ice age, the following is presented:

During The Pleistocene Epoch, 20,000 years ago [18,000 BCE] is the date of our last Ice Age maximum advance, with the sea levels down about – 170 meters.

12,500 BCE to 11,000 BCE the Antarctic warmed and sea levels began to rise, the North Atlantic and North Africa areas warmed and rains began to establish Sahara savannas. There were oscillations of extreme cold lasting 1,000 years or more.

12,900 years ago [10,900 BCE] The Pleistocene Comet impacted Earth, resulting in the extinction event and massive changes to the climate. This was followed by 1,400 years of intense cold worldwide, known as The Younger-Dryas Period.

The Pleistocene Epoch ends and The Holocene Epoch [Post-Glacial Period] begins about 10,000 BCE.

9,500 BCE to 7,500 BCE: The climate warms, sea levels rise, Europe and North American forests reestablish and the Sahara is full of Savannah and lakes until about 4,000 BCE when sea levels were about 3 meters higher than todays' levels.

4,000 BCE: Climate dries and weather patterns shift resulting in the current Sahara and other major deserts of the Earth.

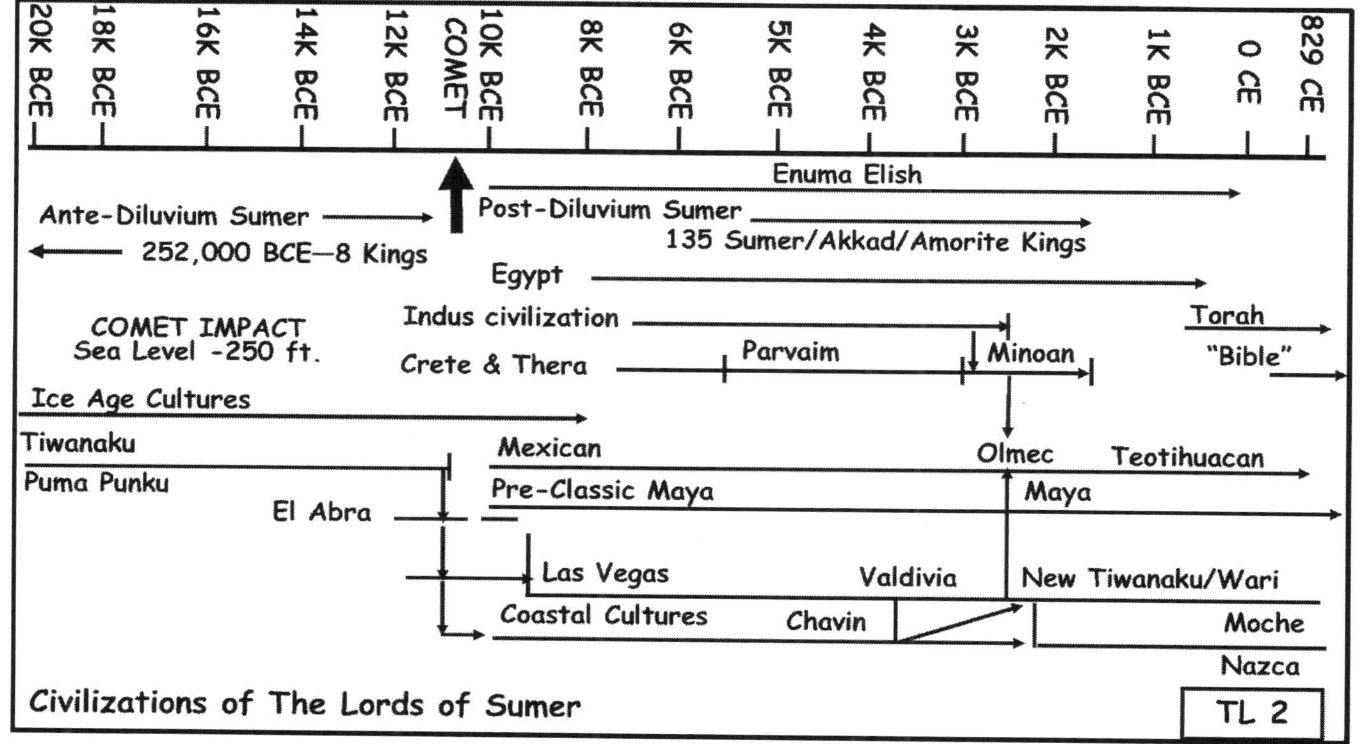

20K BCE
18K BCE
16K BCE
14K BCE
12K BCE
10K BCE
COMET
8K BCE
6K BCE
5K BCE
4K BCE
3K BCE
2K BCE
1K BCE
0 CE
829 CE
Enuma Elish
Ante-Diluvium Sumer
Post-Diluvium Sumer
252,000 BCE—8 Kings
135 Sumer/Akkad/Amorite Kings
Egypt
COMET IMPACT
Sea Level -250 ft.
Indus civilization
Torah
Crete & Thera
Parvaim
Minoan
"Bible"
Ice Age Cultures
Tiwanaku
Mexican
Olmec
Teotihuacan
Puma Punku
Pre-Classic Maya
Maya
El Abra
Las Vegas
Valdivia
New Tiwanaku/Wari
Coastal Cultures
Chavin
Moche
Nazca
Civilizations of The Lords of Sumer
TL 2

Anu – Father of the Gods in his winged Sky Disk

Chapter 4

Ninurta god shooting down another winged disk

THE LORDS OF SUMER

In the Middle East, humans thrived in the Fertile Crescent. This is an area located between the Mediterranean Sea and the Persian Gulf and is in the form of a crescent. The crescent begins on the shores of the Mediterranean Sea near the Gaza Strip and continues northward through Israel, Lebanon, and Syria. The northern area of the crescent extends beyond the Euphrates and Tigris Rivers into Turkey. The eastern area is flanked by Iran, where the crescent turns south through Iraq to Kuwait and the Persian Gulf.

This group of explorers expanded their operations to colonize Earth near the end of the last Ice Age, about 20,000 BCE. This would correlate with establishing some advanced civilizations and observatories such as Tiwanaku in South America and the Gobekli Tepe complex in present day Turkey.

The Sumerian Lords were successful in locating and mining valuable materials with labor provided by local and conscripted members of various civilizations. They only shared technology with select groups of Native Man. The Lords had developed a ruling council to oversee the activities of the various exploration groups and to maintain order. This council is referred to as "The Seven Gods" and several other descriptions throughout the different cultures and civilizations including the Minoan, Egyptian and Tiwanaku in South America.

I believe the explorers observed the comet approaching Earth and all who could, departed our Solar System in great haste. This departure and subsequent impact stranded many groups of explorers on an undeveloped world, Earth.

The men and women who discovered Earth were traveling to explore new worlds. If they were escaping from a natural calamity within their own solar system, they would have stayed and tried to survive the comet impact. Their sudden departure was in response to imminent danger. The main body of the exploration group returned to their homeland, wherever that may be. Their departure was necessary for survival, with the priority to return and rescue the surviving parties. The subsequent history and survival of these stranded people will clearly show they expected to be rescued.

The comet impact of 12,900 BCE destroyed their ability to carry on business as usual. The comet destroyed settlements, workers and equipment. Council leaders Yahweh and Bal had established their respective tribes prior to the comet impact. The tribes of the other council members sometimes supported the effort of the council leaders, Bal and Yahweh.

Yahweh's tribe was located in the Southern Fertile Crescent, centered in the southern Euphrates River Valley [present day Persian Gulf]. In 11,000 BCE the Persian Gulf did not exist, as the ocean levels were down about 260 feet.

Bal established the territory for his tribe in the Northern Fertile Crescent, centered between the Tigris and Euphrates rivers [present day Turkey] and it continued east into Persia.

I believe these tribes were the source for the first biblical creation story, where Yahweh's tribe [of Semitic culture] lived in the lower Euphrates River Valley. "Adam" was his firstborn son, of a selected wife, and was provided a wife of suitable bearing. It is possible this is the fabled "Lilith" from the tribe of Bal [of present-day Nordic culture, later known as Canaanites], who entered the union which was orchestrated as a unity marriage. This would have been before the comet impact.

In Lord Bal's established area of influence in present day Turkey, an incredible find has been revealed. A great archeological discovery was recently announced about a site named Gobekli Tepe, located near the Turkey/Syria border.

Gobekli Tepe has been dated to over 13,000 BCE. It is a remarkable temple complex with circular, interconnected kiva rooms surprisingly similar to the American Southwest civilizations' kivas. The animals and snakes carved on the temple supports are extremely similar to Mayan carvings. Gobekli Tepe was purposefully backfilled, covered and abandoned by 9,500 BCE. This was most likely a reaction to climate change due to the comet impact, as evident by the massive statues which were destroyed.

You must view the program produced for Gobekli Tepe, if only for the absolutely amazing statements from *Academia*. This amazing complex was attributed to Paleolithic ***"Primitive Hunter-Gathers"*** who roamed the area. The presentation was accompanied with film of diminutive African hunters in little clothing, holding bows and arrows, dancing around a campfire.

The producers could not use "Perseverance of Neolithic Artisans" because the site was too old, so they reverted to "Primitive Hunter-Gathers". Look at the site photo and convince anyone that the huge T-shaped stone supports were thought of, made in a stone quarry and placed in this site by hunters who did not have permanent campsites.

The huge stone bust carvings of the leaders of the civilization that occupied Gobekli Tepe should convince anyone that this was an advanced civilization.

As a note about the depiction of "Hunter Gathers" constructing Gobekli Tepe; it is really a stretch to show the construction of the site and the magnificent bust carvings and claim these hunters did the work. There were great ancient civilizations which once flourished in Africa, but they are not part of this group in the Levant. Also, the African cultures were well beyond the "Hunter" level of development. *Academia* has demeaned those civilizations for centuries, depicting most in a constant state of Paleolithic development.

After the Comet impact the stranded explorers were faced with global disaster, no clear leadership and a lack of subsistence. As with any great power vacuum the struggle for leadership began. The result was a great cosmic war centered on Earth. This war is documented in the histories of most ancient civilizations, including the Biblical history of the Hebrew Tribes. If you read the banned books of The Holy Writs, you will see this ancient history in some detail. This same battle is described in great detail in Sumerian epics and other ancient writings.

Stone and terra cotta heads of Sun God Mitra at Gobekli Tepe

Gobekli Tepe Column carved with hand baskets for Gods

Much Later Assyrian God with "hand basket" [a Royal Seal]
[See Olmec God with "hand basket" in The Americas]

According to *Western Holy Writs*, at the end of the battle for supremacy of the Earth, Lord Yahweh's group was victorious and in charge. Lord Bal's group [Bel or Satan] was defeated and doomed to a tortured, shackled life deep below the Earth's surface in a fiery hell. History does not support this theory.

During the rise of the Sumerian civilization, the first use of the title *Lord* [translated from "Bal" and "El"] appears in their recorded history. The title was used to describe anyone who ruled the land. The founders of Sumer were the Lords of the land. They were **The Lords of Sumer**.

The Sumerian account of the war is recorded in the "**Enuma Elish**", which contains **"The Epic of Gilgamesh"**. This Epic and the **"Athra-Hasis Epic"** are tales very similar to the Old Testament [OT] account of creation and Noah's Flood, except it is recorded with the half-God Gilgamesh. These accounts attribute creation to Lord Bal and that he was the victor in the cosmic war. The recording of this Sumerian myth was dated to the 4th millennium BCE, possibly about 3,500 BCE, well before the Holy Writ attributed to the Prophet Moses. A very important point of ancient history about Lord Bal; he had many names in various civilizations and one of these names, Anu, translated as The Invincible Sun God, another name translated as The Feathered Serpent and The Flying Serpent.

Lord Yahweh was also known by several different names, Lord of the Mountain, El Shaddi, one of the Elohim [Pantheon of the seven Gods] and a few others. In the Hebrew Religion the phrase "Ruach ha' Kodesh" is the name for Yahweh's spirit and is curiously in feminine form. The Vatican changed this to masculine form in their Greek translation.

The end of the war left two main factions of explorers in the Fertile Crescent. One was led by Lord Yahweh and the other led by Lord Bal. These factions continued their conflicts for domination of The Levant through their respective Tribes, or families, of their own linage.

An ancient myth of catastrophic destruction, around the time of the fabled cosmic war, was translated from a Tibetan document and titled the "Lhasa Record", by Colonel J Churchward in 1931.

> **"When the Star of Bal fell on the place where now is only the sky and the sea, the seven cities with their golden gates and transparent temples, quivered and shook like the**

**leaves in a storm; and, behold, a flood of fire and smoke
arose from the palaces."**

Archaeological evidence in ancient sites, on all continents, indicates many groups participated in the great cosmic war. Strange and mysterious stories have surfaced throughout history, indicating many of the groups did not survive. The exploration party of the Fertile Crescent not only survived, they established a new ruling council and one of the first known advanced civilizations. Considering the success of these two groups, it is apparent they consisted of a large number of personnel. Legends and written accounts suggest the number to be from several hundred to a thousand people, along with the vehicles and weapons necessary to insure long-term survival.

Following the comet impact and 1,400 years of global winter [9,500 BCE] the surviving inhabitants of this area established stable tribal units on small farms. Domestic animals were primarily herds of cattle, sheep, and goats. Their tools and weapons were made of stone, flint, and chert. They lived in huts of mud, rock, willows and reeds, built near the many streams and rivers. Primitive settlements such as Jericho were established. The people began a slow process of creating and improving crude pottery, which provided for the storage of food.

By 8,500 BCE the Lords regained full control of the Crescent. Large temples and ziggurats appeared in the Fertile Crescent between the Tigris and Euphrates Rivers, known to archaeologists as Central Mesopotamia. The explanation by archaeologists for the sudden flowering of civilization is that it was "a remarkable event." Historians refer to the event as "an unusual perplexing phenomenon." The center of power was the temple of Tel-Kish, south east of Babylon. The reigning Gods changed cities often and built many ziggurat temples.

Considerable attempts have been made to adequately define how civilization, arts, sciences, mathematics and architecture, suddenly emerged in the region. Some historians simply state the cultural event is unexplainable, as the available information did not provide a clear answer to any questions.

In place of answers or simple speculation, there are very noncommittal statements, such as:

**"It is very difficult to clearly state who they were, or
where their culture originated. Such questions cannot be
answered with a premise of factual certainty."**

These statements were simply products of professionals operating within the blinding limits of *Academia*. What they may have suspected could not be clearly stated without connecting historical information, and evidence, to prove their conclusions.

It was crystal clear to the historians and archaeologists that an advanced civilization moved into an area previously populated by Stone Age people. The problem the academics had is that no known advanced civilization existed at that time. The most advanced of civilizations in this area, outside of the Lord's influence, were in the Paleolithic phase.

The emergence of a civilization devoted to pure science and engineering genius could not have occurred without the aid of **introduced intelligence**. The predominate assertion, that primitive Man, who was at that time trying to improve his clay pots, had also formulated governmental structure and used structural engineering and astronomy to plan and build cities, is ridiculous.

The Council of Lords established a base of palaces known as mythical **Parvaim** [Paradise] on the Mediterranean island of Thera. Lord Bal established his tribal base in southern Turkey and northern Iran. Lord Yahweh established his tribal base in southern Iraq. Archaeology, and history, indicates these groups began the classic Sumerian civilization in the Fertile Crescent in the era of 9,000 BCE.

Sumer was located on the southeastern end of the crescent, within the country of Iraq and the present Persian Gulf. It became known thousands of years later as "The Cradle of Civilization." The region is a vast area, located between two great rivers. The Tigris forms a natural boundary to the east, and the Euphrates guards the western boundary. Annual rains produced floods, providing a positive impact by bringing new silt and fertilizing the entire area. The abundant source of water provided for irrigation of the surrounding lands. This region was ideal to meet the needs of the exploration party. Another fertile area would later be developed and evolve into Egypt.

The only serious security problem the group later faced was from renegade followers of Lord Bal in the North and in an area located east of the Tigris River. The entire eastern region is flanked by the Zagros Mountains, which extend northward into present day Turkey. Barbaric tribes would later populate this mountainous region.

Within the boundaries of the two rivers the Lords cleared eighteen known building sites. *Academia* claims these sites are the first evidenced cities built on Earth. The combined cities, known as the Sumerian Civilization, are the remnants of Earth's first, known, advanced civilization. *Academia will not admit that the ruins of Tiwanaku Bolivia are 20,000 years old, insisting the Inca built this site 2,000 years ago.*

The cities of Sumer were carefully located to ensure domination of the entire area. The northern Euphrates cities had suitable ground for agricultural development. The northern-most city was Mari; to the south were Sippar and Kishi. In the center of the region were the cities of Abu-Salabikh and Nippur. In the South, towards the Persian Gulf, were the cities of Shuruppak, Eresh, Uruk, and Ur. 7.5 miles southwest of Ur was the city of Eridu. On the eastern boundary of the region were the cities of Adab, Umma, Kidingir, Pa-tibira, Larsa, Girsu, Lagash, and Nina for a total of eighteen cities.

Eridu is the oldest city of Sumer and is the site of the Temple and Palace of God Enki [Marduk]. Eridu is mentioned in the Sumerian Kings List as the first city of the First God Alulim descending from the Sky 254,000 years ago. It is also one of five cities built before "*The Deluge*". Several researchers believe Eridu to be the site of the mythical Tower of Ba'Bel.

One or more "Lords" governed each of these cities. The exact population of the Sumer region has not been determined. Estimates place the population between eighteen and twenty thousand residents for each city. The entire region supported a population of 360,000 to 400,000 people.

In the early development phase of Sumer, the construction of massive structures reinforced the Lords' status as Gods. Two types of buildings were completed as the first structures of Sumer. The first was a massive multilevel temple that housed the Priests and was the center of religious ceremonies.

The first temples were built on cleared areas ranging from twenty-five acres to one hundred seventy acres allowing for future expansion of the complex. To Paleolithic Man, the temples projected the awesome power of the Gods who lived there and were worshipped with great reverence and fear.

The second structure to be completed was a massive fired brick flat-topped pyramidal tower with outside stairways and a shrine at the top, known as a ziggurat. Ziggurats were built on the cleared temple areas and along the boundaries of Sumer as observation towers. From the top of the structures all intruders were quickly discovered.

Archaeologists have concluded the first temples and ziggurats were constructed in the era of 8,500 BCE. Considering the time of construction, historians attempted to explain the events leading to their construction. They described the structures as being located in simple farming communities and villages, and further stated the emergence of such structures was unexplainable.

Different historians use various terminologies to arrive at the same conclusion of the event being unexplainable; however, the use of descriptive terms also causes problems. In describing this historical time, most historians refer to the civilization as an urban society. The following is an example of the weak attempts to sidestep the sudden development of these monuments:

> **"One may conclude the early growth of Sumerian urban society is very complex. Such complexness may well be beyond any perception to explain the event."**

The statements and physical evidence produced by these archaeologists needs to be examined using logic and common sense. These "simple farming communities" were mud huts with reed roofs, located on or near the banks of rivers. The "urban society" consisted of family units living in the Stone Age. They used stone hoes to till their gardens. The hoe was a rock sharpened on one side and tied to a wooden pole. The people used sharpened sticks to punch holes in the ground for planting seeds in small plots. They cooked their food over open pit fires. Their clothing was made from plant material and animal hides, and their tools were made from sharpened rocks and sticks. This best of cultural states existed all over the world.

These "Simple farming communities and urban society" is the level of cultural development that existed *after* the temples were built. Historians insist the construction of the ziggurats and temples is attributed to the abilities of the Neolithic culture. To further cloud the issue of possible introduced intelligence, the elitist intellectual community introduced the phrase "These accomplishments were the result of the **Perseverance of Neolithic Artisans**". You will encounter this terminology quite often when researching ancient civilizations. It means - **We don't really know how this happened, or when it happened.**

The ziggurat was similar to a pyramid. The base was 150 feet by 200 feet with a height of 80 feet. The structure had a wide, stepped staircase leading to the upper-most platform. Each wall was built with layered brick on a perfect horizontal plane, not a huge heap of stones or brick, and the entire structure was solid. Archaeologists and engineers have described the structure as follows:

"The Sumerian engineering skills can be described as sophisticated as those of twentieth century engineers."

The walls of the Ziggurats were bowed horizontally and vertically. The purpose of this sophisticated engineering was to create the visual perception, from a distance, of straight lines. Each ziggurat was built exactly alike and there were numerous platforms found in the region. The ancient descriptive name for these structures translates somewhat as "Stairways to the Gods."

For those historians who continue to support the argument that these Stone Age people built structures of mathematical precision, consider this: The level of cultural development, before the Lords of Sumer arrived was; there was no concept of mathematics or measurements. There were no metal axes, shovels, metal hammers, masonry trowels, construction levels, string lines, compasses, squares, plumb bobs, or plumb lines. There were no construction tools of any kind that are required to build buildings. There was no evidence of kiln-fired brick in these Stone Age cultures prior to the Lord's intervention.

To further describe the level of cultural development, or non-development, there was no written or pictorial language except for the stelae and cuneiform of the Temple Priests. There were no houses, no towns, no cities, because there were no bricks. And last, for those same historians, there was no motivation to build anything other than simple huts to meet their immediate needs. The local inhabitants simply lived their lives based on the things they had, the same as we do today. If the people of that time had the plans, the tools and the motivation, they could not read. This should be sufficient to explain why it is absurd to believe these primitive people could have built the advanced structures, without *introduced intelligence*.

The Lords, using primitive Man for labor and Lodge members for supervision, and their own engineering skills and tools, built the massive Sumerian structures. One of the tools would have to be a transit, which an exploration survey team would have. The transit is a sophisticated instrument used in construction projects to determine exact horizontal and vertical measurements. You cannot build an inclined, eighty-foot high building with accurately measured angles, without some type of transit. The completion of the Ziggurats and temples provided the Lords of Sumer with security and safe havens to continue their survival. I will discuss "Lodge Members" in depth as we continue this journey into our beginnings.

Primitive Man had never seen sophisticated construction, much less an eighty feet tall structure. He could not compare it with anything in his entire world. The ziggurats and temples provided the visual effect of dominance and instilled fear in anyone who wandered into the area. These dominating structures projected the absolute power of the living Gods. In combination with the visual effect of the structures, the Lords killed all intruders of their domain. This established a taboo region clearly inhibiting encroachment by outsiders.

A temple at Gobekli Tepe, constructed for Lord Bal The Sun God, in the northern area of the crescent was dated to 12,000 BCE. It had been abandoned and hidden by backfilling the entire site, possibly after the comet impact.

The Lords established villages near their compounds and began to develop larger agricultural areas. To improve production, engineering skills were used to build dams, drain swamps, and control flooding. Later, after the climate continued changing, a system of canals delivered water to the desert fringes. The newly created farms produced food for a growing population and provided surpluses for export.

As 6,000 BCE ended, the villages around the temples became towns with city-like characteristics. The infrastructure of civilization was well in place. The abundance of food, created by vast fields of agriculture, provided a firm economic base.

Sea Levels had risen about 200 feet from 9,000 BCE to 5,500 BCE. This increase flooded the lower Euphrates River Valley and created the existing Persian Gulf. The Persian Gulf lies southeast of the city of Ur. In later years, the Lords used Ur as a conduit for trade goods transported to and from the Gulf.

The Island of Bahrain is a small island just off the coast of present-day Iraq, in an inlet known as the Gulf of Bahrain. The island is 27 miles long, north to south, and 10 miles wide, east to west, and has numerous fresh water springs. Archaeologists found a large number of ancient Sumerian burial mounds on the northern upland slopes. Also discovered was an unusual fired brick docking facility, which provided the island's only shipping port at that time.

The shipyard dock had a massive brick wall preventing access to the rest of the island. The wall served to deter the curiosity of traders wanting to see what had been stored on the island. Bahrain was an island seaport and storage area for the mainland civilization and served as a resort area for many of the Lords. Many historians believe the Island of Bahrain to be the legendary lost Sumerian paradise of Dilmun.

The next cultural expansion was promoted by the introduction of the potter's wheel and mass-produced pottery, a valuable trade item. The combination of agricultural products and mass-produced pottery sustained the civilization for centuries.

By 10,000 BCE bread, beer, the musical harp, and the weaver's loom were introduced to native Man. Other items, such as baked clay molds were used to produce and stockpile vast amounts of brick for the thriving community. The plow and a new form of ax facilitated the labor of the growing population in Sumer. The first axes containing socket holes to insert handles were from this period.

All of these items have been attributed to native Man, who had yet to understand how to make a wheel. The introduction of these tools was limited to the people of Sumer. Most everyone else on the planet was still chasing animals with sharp sticks and stone tipped poles.

Although the region was well suited for agriculture, stone and timber products were located great distances from Sumer. This problem was overcome by extending trade routes into the outer regions.

The temples were the focus of religion and power during each level of cultural development. The temples housed the Gods, central government and the affairs of state and trade. They were also training centers for specialized crafts such as weaving, pottery, and the use of tools, and the most important, metallurgy.

Marduk - firstborn of God Enki

METALLURGY and THE WHEEL

By 5,500 BCE, an advanced load bearing transportation system was necessary to serve the needs of a growing population. To facilitate further growth, wagons and carts were necessary to bring raw metal, stone and timber from sites in the Zagros and Taurus mountains. The abundance of produce from extensive agricultural areas also required load-bearing wagons. This new form of transportation served to facilitate corporate business between the Sumerian cities. This historic milestone, of the introduction of the wheel, was attributed to native Man.

On the surface the subject of man's first use of the wheel appears to be rather boring. Historians and anthropologists usually discuss the invention of the wheel in very general terms. What is usually not explained is the requirement to include an element necessary for the creation of the wheel itself. That element is hardened metals.

The requirement for hardened metals presents a problem because according to *Academia*, the metals did not exist. This is quite similar to the explanation that native Man created wheat. The wheel was another significant event which historians explained in very general terms because it required the introduction of advanced intelligence that native Man did not possess. Historians did not express this concept because they feared peer ridicule and would have been out looking for a new line of work.

Archaeologists found evidence that iron was smelted in Syria and Iraq centuries before 5,500 BCE. Smelting means; producing iron and steel items. These were not just "back yard" enterprises producing a few items.

The solution to explaining the problem of advanced intelligence was solved again by the use of the pseudo intellectual term, *Neolithic Artisans*. To understand the complex issues of making a wheel we need to understand the history of metallurgy. The following is a typical explanation of the development of metallurgy, provided by our academic community [paraphrased]:

> **By 4500 BCE, Neolithic Artisans discovered how to locate and mine deposits of oxide ores. Native Man soon discovered the technique to extract copper from oxide ores by heating them with charcoal. The surge in the use of**

metals continued unabated. About 3000 BCE, Neolithic Artisans discovered how to improve copper metal by the addition of tin. A new alloy was produced that resulted in the creation of <u>man's first hardened metal</u>. The new alloy, bronze, was harder than copper, and provided a sharper cutting edge. The Bronze Age continued well into 1200 BCE when Neolithic Artisans produced iron in the form of weapons and tools. Iron production quickly replaced items made of bronze.

This explanation appears to have all the answers regarding the evolution of man's development of metals. That is, unless you apply logic to the statement. And remember the use of the term, "*Neolithic Artisans.*"

The conventional wisdom of the intellectual community is that Neolithic Artisans discovered by the addition of tin, copper was improved and the alloy produced bronze. They continue to present the discovery and use of bronze as a typical example of the remarkable persistence of the people of that historical time. The work "typical" leads to the misconception that the event was occurring all over the world. Applying logic and reality to this question, of the discovery of tin, results in a simple answer. Neolithic Man did not possess the intellect or motivation to locate, mine, mill and process tin ore without the aid of introduced intelligence.

For Stone Age Man to mine and produce specific metals, he needed the skill of geologic exploration. This skill, this science, is dependent on knowledge of basic geology to find the specific ore being sought.

Some ore bearing strata emerge on the surface as an outcrop or primary deposit. However, outcrops are extremely rare. Most ore deposits are beneath the surface. If a prospector is fortunate enough to locate a placer deposit [surface deposit of sand, gravel and ore], it does increase the possibility of locating the primary ore deposit.

After locating the ore deposit, it must be mined and processed. This is difficult if you do not have metal tools to reduce the large ore-bearing rocks to small pieces. The last step in the process is refining. The metal must be separated from the ore by a smelting process, which requires extreme heat and sometimes, chemical reactions. After smelting, the combined metal product must be refined again to obtain a pure metal. Also, you need a furnace complete with bellows to smelt the ores.

The first people to record the art of metallurgy were the Sumerians. They were masters of metallurgy and recorded this activity in 5,500 BCE. How could a "natural evolution" of the discovery and use of metals occur without introduced intelligence? The Americas civilizations also developed advanced metallurgy techniques of alloys, plating and casting. Their most durable alloy was copper-nickel bronze. The Sumerians used copper-tin alloy which was less durable.

In 1963 the Encyclopedia Britannica clearly stated that the previous theories concerning the chronology of the discovery and use of metals were incorrect. There were no specific time frames for each discovery and use of different metals. The perception that iron was not in use during the "Bronze Age" is a distortion of history. The labeling of specific times in Man's history as *Stone Age, New Stone Age, Bronze Age* and *Iron Age* has caused irreparable damage to anyone searching for true history. These terms only apply to a specific civilization, in a specific location, at a specific time.

Some historians, archaeologists, and anthropologists continue to be so myopic in thought; they do not know how the terms "Bronze Age" and "Iron Age" came to be used. Nor do they know how the dates associated with these terms were established, or, why these terms continue to be used. Many of these intellectuals could not tell you that these terms, which are used to label and classify so much history, originated from the Greek writer, Hesiod.

Hesiod was an 8th Century BCE Greek poet, historian, and philosopher who divided all of history into five periods. His classification began with the oldest history, mythology, that of the "Gods' rule on Earth," and was labeled *The Golden Age.* Hesiod's divisions of history continued, using metals on a declining scale of value, to illustrate his belief that Man's moral stature had also declined. His divisions had nothing to do with the order of discovery of metals. Hesiod's classic periods were, *The Golden Age, The Silver Age, The Copper Age, The Bronze Age,* and the last, his own time, was *The Iron Age.* Iron was not commonly used until 1,200 BCE and was placed last in the sequence of metals in his dissertations. Therefore, 1,200 BCE is commonly called the beginning of the Iron Age.

The correct view is that gold, silver, copper, tin, and iron and other metals were all mined, processed and used at the same time in the Sumerian civilization. Most ore bearing mines produced several metals which included iron. Long before 5,500 BCE some very intelligent "Neolithic Artisans" were directly influenced and guided by the engineers and scientists of the stranded expedition. Unfortunately, for academic presentations, we have historians who do not read Britannica, or study Biblical history. Seven [or more] generations from Adam, in the lineage of Cain, a master metalworker named Tubal-Cain was born.

Genesis Chapter 4 Vs. 22
And Zil'lah, she also bare Tubal-Cain, an instructor of every artificer in brass and iron:

[From the NIV Bible: **"Tubal-Cain, who forged all kinds of tools out of bronze and iron."** The ancient phrases of this passage also translate "**Tools for agriculture and construction, but there were also weapons**"].

So, why not translate the entire ancient passage, as it should read in modern day language? Try this as gleaned from ancient manuscripts, stelae and inscriptions:

"Seven generations from Adam, in the year 6,000 BCE, in the lineage of Cain, the first-born son of Lamech was named Tubal-Cain. He was a Master metal-smith, teaching craftsmen in all the arts of metalworking. He produced everything from gold jewelry to steel swords. He made iron and brass hammers for driving nails and working stone. Tubal-Cain also made farming tools and steel plows."

For the balance of this book, do not forget this important revelation of the use of **IRON** prior to 6,000 BCE. This is The Holy Writ stating that by 6,000 BCE iron was used for construction tools and weaponry. I believe the reason for the lack of steel and iron artifacts from this period is that everything made of iron was easily recycled or rusted. Iron was too valuable to be wasted.

Iron is widely mentioned in the Armana Tablets, circa 1,400 BCE. These Akkadian-Canaanite Cuneiform tablets recorded correspondence between the Egyptian Pharaohs and the kingdoms in the eastern Mediterranean and Sumer. Iron ore was readily available as surface concretions, in various forms, in desert areas where erosion processes left the nodules of iron oxides in plain view. These oxides would have been the easiest ores to gather and process.

The other direct references to iron weapons in ancient text are found in Sumerian epics such as the **ENUMA ELISH**, story of Marduk [Bal], the God of all cosmic order, and of **GILGAMESH**, a Babylonian hero half-God. Both are translated from 2nd and 3rd Millennium Akkadian cuneiform. The Epic of Gilgamesh was found in the Palace of Ashur'Banipal in Nineveh, inscribed on 12 tablets. Unfortunately, the origin of these epics can only be dated by association and speculation, as with the Holy Writ. As the "Holy Writ" of Sumer, it was copied many times to maintain religious history.

The **ENUMA ELISH** tells the story of the cosmic war between Lord Yahweh and his group and Lord Marduk [Bal] and his followers. However, it relates the creation story from the perspective that Lord Bal was the victor and Creator God of the Universe.

I have digressed from the timeline; however, the last bit of information is crucial to understanding how we all have been led down the path of "Truth and understanding concerning Man and history."

Researchers of the origin of the wheel clearly state it first appeared in Sumer. They also *imply* that hardened metal tools were required for cutting and shaping the wood. The wheel was constructed using three carefully cut planks. The planks were clamped together with a series of copper clasps, and a metal hub was attached to the center plank. A stationary axle extended to each wheel hub and the wheels were attached to the axle by linchpins. The Sumerians later constructed the wheel hub with lubricated roller bearings to ease friction on the axle. Do we have Neolithic Artisans designing roller bearings?

The researchers did not identify specific metals used in the construction of the wheel but did provide very good descriptions. Each wheel was fitted with metal hoops. The hoops or rims were kept in place by metal braces on the inside and outside surfaces of the wood. From this information we can conclude the Sumerians had produced hardened metal saws, tools, wheel hoops and braces.

Although the author refrained from describing the tools as iron or steel, there never has been, or ever will be, a copper saw capable of cutting and shaping heavy wooden planks. And last, you must have a hardened metal file to produce the teeth of the saw. This information was well known to historians and archaeologists, yet none will concede that native Man was introduced to metallurgy by intelligent people from across the universe. Instead of recognizing introduced intelligence, the intellectuals continue to grind out the same scotoma producing misinformation.

Tin ore, cassiterite, which contains tin oxide [SnO_2] is not considered to be an extremely rare ore, although many continental regions do not contain ore deposits. Cassiterite is a colorless crystal when pure but appears as black or brown crystals when iron oxides are present. Ore deposits are usually found in alluvium deposits or streambeds. There are "hard rock" ore formations which occur in volcanic intrusions and thermal vent settings. Most Cassiterite is associated with granite formations and the ore is usually about 1% tin.

There are two allotropic forms of tin, alpha [α] and beta [β]. White tin, known as β-tin [metallic], is stable above 13.2° C [60° F] and is a soft and malleable metal. Grey tin, known as α-tin [non-metallic] is powdery and used in specialized electronics and advanced technology. β-tin reverts to α-tin below 13.2° C, unless it is alloyed with another metal. Tin is very similar to lead in appearance and softness. It melts at 232° C [450° F] and for super fine particles it melts at 177.3° C [351°].

Tin ore is located much the same as gold and is often found while prospecting for gold. After concentrating the tin ore, it was necessary to heat the ore in a crucible with charcoal added to remove the oxide and powdered limestone added to remove other impurities. This step required the mixture to be heated to 1,400° C [2,550° F] which caused a slag of tin, other metals and impurities to form. If iron was present in the ore, it required temperatures of 2,800°F [1,538°C] to melt the iron, so the Tin would be processed first.

After several more smelting steps, adding more carbon and applying air through a bellows system to maintain high temperatures, the resulting slag of tin, iron and other metals are ready for the final procedure.

The slag was finally furnace heated to about 500° degrees F and the molten tin ran out of the slag. The Tin was collected in a kettle or ceramic bowl, then kept heated and stirred with green wood poles producing aeration, steam and introducing more carbon to the process. This removed the remaining impurities which surfaced as slag. The Tin was about 99% pure when the process was finished. The remaining slag was then processed to remove other metals.

The primary sources of present-day tin production come from South America, Indonesia, Thailand, England, Germany and Portugal. The area of Mesopotamia where the Sumerian civilization emerged has no known commercial tin deposits. There are small, isolated tin deposits in the Zagros Mountains of Iran, east of Iraq, and in the Taurus Mountains of Turkey to the north.

Archaeologists from the Smithsonian Institution have recently discovered an ancient mine in the Taurus Mountains of Turkey which produced tin and iron. The information provided by stone tools and pottery shards indicated people might have lived in the mine around 4,000 BCE. There was no indication or information given to determine when the original mine was started. This is no doubt one of many small, isolated tin and iron deposits in the region.

The Lords needed to sustain a growing market in bronze, and sources for tin were located in England, Portugal and Thailand. Tin ingots could easily be shipped from these locations by ship and caravans. Sumer exported the bronze technology to Thailand in 5,000 BCE, as indicated by archaeological finds in the region of Ban Chaing. Tin was mined in the British Isles prior to 6,000 BCE in colonies developed and administered by Sumerian Priests. Evidence of their astrological observatories has been widely publicized.

Although I condensed the smelting process, it is ludicrous to attribute the discovery of this metallurgy solely to *Neolithic Artisans*. Although primitive smelting processes were used, the Lords used and guided primitive Man through the process of constructing furnaces with bellows to achieve the necessary heat. Their instructions to use available materials provided the necessary chemical reactions to reduce the ore to pure metal.

While researching the uses of Tin, I realized there was more to the story than simply producing bronze for trade goods. Tin in several of its' states is used to build sophisticated communication devices and is used in many other electronic applications. It is also used in the production of nuclear power systems [and weapons]. I think the Lords had use for this and many of the other rare-earth elements which are produced in the overall smelting process.

Some historians have identified the Sumerian civilization as possessing hardened metals prior to the widespread use of the wheel in 4,500 BCE. Others assumed or inferred that all Neolithic civilizations followed an evolutionary process initiated by the Sumerian civilization. Finally, the primary issue is: Was the discovery and use of metals an evolutionary process, or was it the result of introduced intelligence to native Man?

The information presented here is not intended to prove anything. It is provided in the context that you have the ability to use your own logic in deciding if the information is factual, or plausible.

The Sumerians possessed hardened metals thousands of years before anyone else on the planet acquired the skills to copy the process. Neolithic people throughout the planet did discover how to locate and use soft metals such as gold, silver and copper. Raw copper, as a naturally occurring metal, was used for tools and trinkets prior to 10,900 BCE. There was never a "*natural*" evolution of the process of mining and smelting copper, nor in the production of Bronze, by adding Tin at a ratio of 10% to copper.

The secret to the Sumerians' possession of hardened metals was iron. Iron ore is common and is found all over the globe. To produce bronze, you first had to have iron kettles and ladles to be able to smelt or process tin ore. Someone had deduced this fact a long time ago. You had to have iron first, not last. This is the reason that in 1963, Britannica published the information regarding metallurgy, which stated the former belief. The practice of stating that the history of metals can be divided into clear-cut periods is oversimplified. Copper, bronze, and iron were made and used simultaneously.

An extremely unusual steel dagger was recovered from the Pharaoh Tutankhamen's burial. The dagger was 3,000 years old, steel and had not rusted. This steel [iron] was mentioned in the Armana Tablets as iron from the Gods and well predated this tomb. Some tablet references stated this iron was "the bones of the Gods". An analysis of the steel revealed it was an iron-nickel-cobalt alloy, presumably smelted from a meteorite. A matching meteorite with this metal analysis has not been located.

The reason given by *Academia* for the meteor conclusion follows:

> **"No one on Earth could produce such high-quality steel in those times".**

The ancient Americans' metallurgists alloyed nickel-copper to produce a very durable bronze. They also produced polished steel bowls which did not oxidize and vanish over the centuries of exposure to the tropical climate. The ancient *Neolithic Artisans of the* Americas' steel alloy was, and this is really a mystery to *Academia*, an iron-nickel-cobalt alloy.

What originally caused confusion regarding the sequence of metals is very simple, practicing **Academicism**. Defined as: **The uninspired working within some traditional mode**. That is, our learned academics would never challenge **Western Thinking**. This mind-set is: If the modern western civilizations did not invent or find an item or process, it could have never been accomplished.

The Lords did possess vehicles at the end of the Great War of the Heavens.   They simply flew to the nearest deposits of tin and established trading communities with the local warlords. Their travel to these sites established their position as Gods. After they initiated the mining process with local labor, the ore was smelted at the same location. The value of the metal ingots to the local warlords would have been limited to the trade items provided by the Lords. The association of the local warlords to the living Gods was priceless, providing them with the highest status possible. As trade routes were established the Lords transported the ingots to Sumer by ship and caravan, where bronze became the most valuable trade item of that period.

By 5,500 BCE the Lords completed the foundations necessary for a successful civilization. Long-range trade and sailing routes extended east to Thailand, west to Britain and south to Africa, with numerous ports along the way. Other trade routes extended northward across Syria and into Asia Minor and on to Western Europe. The trade routes were a feat accomplished by the use of intelligence instead of hostile aggression, well maybe a little local aggression. With the foundations of Earth's first civilization completed, the Lords of Sumer began the next phase of their plans for rescue.   The Lords focused their energies on the development of several new empires. During this development period the Lords maintained contact with their sites in the Americas.

7 Planets [comparison] which orbit Trappist – 1, a red dwarf star 40 light years from Earth. Several of these planets could sustain life. [Courtesy of NASA]

Ancient Egyptian Mural showing Stone cutters using
well-formed metal chisels

Cuneiform symbol for God An [Anu]

MASONIC SYMBOLS OF THE CRAFT
NOTE THE SUN AND MOON GODDESS SYMBOLS WITH
OBSERVANCE OF THE SEVEN REINING GODS USING
STARS

THE ANCIENT LODGE OF FREEMASONS

By 8,500 BCE when villages grew into towns, a new class of builders and craftsmen emerged. The Lords selected and trained the craftsmen in the use of special tools and building techniques, math, sciences and astronomy. This class of craftsmen would later build the magnificent cities of Sumer. The Lords created a fraternal order to train these craftsmen and to instill social skills, discipline and the all-important need to worship one Supreme God. The members would be known through aeons as Free Masons.

This Fraternity of craftsmen insured the containment of knowledge from the general public. These highly skilled craftsmen were the first members of the Ancient Order of the Masonic Lodge. They are known today as Ancient Free and Accepted Masons [AF&AM]. Education was mandatory for the early craftsmen. They were trained in the arts and sciences of writing, grammar, geometry, logic, music, astronomy, math, metallurgy, building skills, architecture and the use of tools.

They were also taught the skills necessary to live and communicate in a civilized society. This type of instruction does not appear to be significant in today's world. You must remember the peers of these craftsmen were living in tents made of animal skins or crude huts and were illiterate. The knowledge and education the apprentice Masons received placed them thousands of years ahead of their peers.

As the early Masons were trained, each detail of the training became secrets of the Lodge. All tools received social and religious significance. Advanced mathematics including algebra, geometry, and trigonometry were the sole secrets of Grand Masters of the Lodge. Each level of training required an oath of secrecy. This oath carried a severe punishment, sometimes death, for revealing any secret to Masons of lesser levels of knowledge, or to persons outside the Lodge. The oaths were administered with great ceremony before the members of the Lodge to ensure compliance.

The punishment for revealing Lodge secrets prevented the spread of knowledge among the general population. The most important aspect of the first Lodge's social training was the new concept of a Universal God, described in Masonic teaching as the **Great Architect of the**

Universe. One of the Lords would impersonate the "Universal God" while the rest were His emissaries [or angels]. This concept released early Masons from their life-long religious superstitions. The Lodge provided them with the answers to the forces of nature and reinforced their status of self-worth. The early Masons were no longer subservient to the many Gods worshipped by the general population. The Lodge would evolve to Priesthoods, overseeing countless empires for thousands of years. Throughout the Lodge development Masons were fiercely nationalistic bounded with a universal belief in caring for their family and those who could not care for themselves.

The Ancient Lodge was in place prior to any development of Judaism or Christianity. This is important to understand as the Lodge members followed the religion of the empire they were living in. The ancient Gods worshipped were; The Sun God, The Virgin Moon Goddess and their offspring Son. These symbols are present in today's Lodges. The symbol carried by the Senior Deacon is The Sun God, and that of the Junior Deacon is The Moon Goddess. Of course, these are symbolic only and are subservient to The Great Architect of the Universe.

The beginning of the Masonic calendar is in 4,000 BCE, *Anno Lucis* or Year of Light. The Hebrew calendar begins in 3,777 BCE, which I suspect is the same point in history. I also believe this is when the history of Yahweh's favorite tribe begins to be recorded by the Prophet Enoch in Parvaim.

There can be no doubt the Lords created the Lodge to serve their own needs. They needed a secure, reliable method to promote the cultural phases within their crafted society. Also needed was the physical expertise of specially trained craftsmen to build their cities and provide security for the Lords. It is clear the Lords considered knowledge as power, and knew the sharing of power could result in a loss of control over primitive Man. Any future level of cultural development depended on the Lords' specific needs.

CEREAL GRAINS

When reading historical and educational material, we assume it is factual and has been carefully researched. Published information provides the individual pieces of the puzzle to man's history, and the pieces of this puzzle must be fitted to gain a factual picture of our ancient past. In many instances, information has been carefully researched but published in a theme to satisfy the popular concepts of the time. This resulted in a distorted view of our distant past.

The great majority of older references will seldom mention a date older than 4,500 BCE to 5,000 BCE. This is a result of centuries of intellectual and religious brow-beating about the "Age of Man." To propose any dating of man's activities or history that did not correspond to Biblical chronology was considered heresy. Naturally all technological breakthroughs must have occurred after this time.

An example of distorted research is the reports which attempted to prove that *Neolithic Artisans* domesticated wild grains to produce cereal grains. The following cereal grain research is interesting.

Man's earliest successful civilization was dependent on agricultural production. The primary product was cereal, which are different forms of grains. A researcher stated that **"Around the year 5000 BCE, Neolithic Artisans domesticated wild grains and produced wheat"**. You need to re-read the last achievement attributed to New Stone Age Man. It says, <u>around 5,000 BCE</u>, remember what I said about historians and the "Age of Man"? The truth is; "cereal grain" is documented to be cultivated in 11,000 BCE at Gobekli Tepe and for making beer in the Paleolithic classification, Old Stone Age. Not to be confused with the beer brand **"OLD STONE AGE"**. Next, the achievement continues, **"Neolithic Artisans domesticated wild grains"**. If you believe they did, you may as well believe **"And God spoke and it was so."** These Stone Age people suddenly became Geneticists and Botanists.

Statements regarding domestication of wild grains were similar to those attributing the building of complex structures to *Neolithic Artisans*. Information from an encyclopedia stated: Cereal grain production was believed to have emerged sometime in the Neolithic period [6,000 BCE to 3,000 BCE], and there was insufficient evidence to indicate a more specific time. Further, all successful civilizations were founded on agricultural production of cereals and Wheat is believed to be one of the first crops grown by ancient Man.

Another source stated the origin of cereals is still a mystery to biologists of today. Why would something so simple still be a mystery? The reference should have clearly stated; "Present day biologists cannot duplicate a feat attributed to Primitive Man over 13,000 years ago."

Geneticists from America and Japan spent twelve years trying to develop wheat from wild grasses found in and around the Sumerian area. The geneticists were unsuccessful and gave up their attempt. A geneticist is a scientist in the field of biology who specializes in plant genetics and hybrids for crop improvements, including using gene manipulation. So, we have teams of scientists, working under ideal laboratory conditions for years, trying to duplicate a 13,000-year-old feat attributed to Primitive Man. They failed.

This leads to the possibility that wheat may have originated as a process of nature. This is the answer most intellectuals prefer, over the obvious, but that does not work either. The geneticists confirmed there are no wild cereal grains. Wheat would have to originate from three or more wild grasses to satisfy the "process of nature theory." The attempt to create a wheat plant resulted in a search that extended across Asia Minor to Afghanistan. Because wheat does exist, and did provide an important part of the foundation that civilization evolved from, the feat is still attributed to native Man. I don't believe it. At present, our geneticists cannot do it. With the information we have, it is absurd to believe Primitive Man accomplished this biological feat.

The statement that the origin of cereal grains continues to be a mystery to biologists should be rewritten. It should read; *"Wheat could not have originated without the help of introduced intelligence far beyond that of twentieth century biologists."* There is the overwhelming possibility that our last group of explorers introduced the seed for the original cereal grains. Wheat and barley emerged in simple farming areas before 11,000 BCE Pleistocene Comet Impact.

It is most likely that the exploration teams had local farmers grow this crop, and others, for staple food. Evidence of beer production and roasting meat in Sumer has been documented prior to 11,000 BCE. Sounds like Texans settled there.

Sumerian Cuneiform inscription in monumental archaic style

WRITING AND RECORD KEEPING

By 6,000 BCE the Lords were building the first of the magnificent cities of the Sumerian region. The temples originally provided secure living quarters but were later converted to house the central administrative authority. The Lords now lived in large estates located near the temples.   These estates were known as "Edens", walled gardens or beautiful plains.

Temples governed by the Priesthood were the repositories of all ancient knowledge. Beyond Temple life less than 1% of the population was literate and this remained the case for thousands of years. The first known Sumerian writing system was pictographic proto-writing. This system evolved into the use of Cuneiform [wedge shaped] symbols. Some historians state the Sumerians developed Cuneiform writing by 5,000 BCE. I suspect the earliest recovered pictographic writing form was in place by 11,000 BCE.   According to records recovered from **Nineveh** a form of cuneiform was used before **"The Deluge"**.

The oldest Cuneiform tablets recovered by archaeologists contained about two thousand different signs. As the writing became more efficient, the number of signs was reduced to about six hundred. This writing developed into the Proto-Semitic script, which is deemed the "mother of all alphabets."

LANGUAGE DEVELOPMENT

When communicating with ancient Man the Sky Gods [Lords] used their own language, ancient Sumerian. This dominant language replaced but did not terminate the local tribal languages known as Hamito-Semitic. The original Sumerian language was used exclusively by the ancient Lodge.   Modern linguists have determined the original Sumerian language is not related to any other language, living or dead, and it is an *extinct language.*

During this period of earliest communication, it would have been natural for the Lords to begin communication in their own language. This is the secret to the lost language of Babylon, the language of the visitors from across the universe.   They spoke what we would recognize as ancient Sumerian, which was lost to invaders when the Lords abandoned the area and the Lodges adopted the common languages.

Information from Webster's Dictionary and Thesaurus [Paraphrased and extended]

The most ancient of languages in the Fertile Crescent was derived from the language family, Hamito-Semitic. Its branches are; Semitic, Egyptian, Berber, Cushitic, and Chadic.

The Semitic branch is divided into eastern and western sub-branches. The eastern sub-branch consists of the extinct Akkadian language [cuneiform writing], which produced two variants, Assyrian [northern], and Babylonian [southern]. The western sub-branch consists of the Northwest Semitic and Southwest Semitic. From the Northwest Semitic are derived Aramaic and Canaanite.

Canaanite produced Hebrew, Phoenician, Moabite and many others, all of which became extinct at some time. Aramaic was the primary common language of the Hebrews and is still in use, though not widespread. Hebrew was the written and religious language used by the elite, the priests. Hebrew script was developed from the pictographic Phoenician script, a derivative of the Minoan language. Ancient Hebrew became extinct prior to the Christian era and was revived in the 19th Century as Modern Hebrew. Sargon The Great used the Akkadian [Semitic] language in Sumer, which, as civilizations progressed, produced variations, and survived as cuneiform inscriptions.

The Minoan languages were preserved as "Linear A" and "Linear B". Linear A is undeciphered and was a depiction of the original language of The Lords of Sumer. Linear B was developed as a common form of communication in the Mediterranean Civilizations.

Traditional Jewish exegesis [a critical review of text] such as Midrash [Genesis Rabbah 38] says that Adam spoke Hebrew because the names he gives Eve – "Isha" [Book of Genesis 2:23] and "Chava" [Genesis 3:20] – only make sense in Hebrew. Of course, this rational is based on writings produced about 700 BCE.

The following is out of this timeline sequence, but is needed for understanding two very important issues. The first is the timing for "The development of written language" and the second issue is the establishment of written language prior to "The Deluge". Ashurbanipal is the basis for clarifying these two issues.

Ashurbanipal ["the god Ashur is creator of an heir"] [668-627 BCE, the last great king of Assyria. In the Hebrew Tanakh he is called As-e-nappar. He created a huge library at Nineveh, which he promoted as his greatest achievement for mankind.

He ruled the Assyrian Empire which included Babylonia, Persia, Syria, and Egypt. Ashurbanipal was a patron of the arts and established his library of more than 30,000 clay tablets at his Nineveh Palace. The Library contained the ancient Holy Writ, preserved in part in the Enuma Elish, and original stories of the Great Flood.

Ashurbanipal could read and write cuneiform in many variations, signing his own works. A translation of one of his writings follows:

> **"I, Ashurbanipal, within the palace, understood the wisdom of Nabu. All of the arts of writing of every kind, I taught myself to be the master of all. I read the cunning tablets of Sumer and the dark Akkadian language which is difficult to rightly use; *I took my pleasure in reading stones inscribed before the flood.* The best of the scribal art, such works as none of the kings who went before me had ever learnt, *remedies from the top of the head to the toenails, non-canonical selections, clever teachings, whatever pertains to the medical mastery of* [the gods] Ninurta and Gala.**

Ashurbanipal dispatched orders to all kingdoms he ruled or was friendly with to gather all written works for his library.

Ashurbanipal establishes that written communications existed "before the flood". I have always believed that any great civilization required written communications in order to exist. If you can accept the premise of very ancient civilizations with advanced intelligence, then written communications are in existence at that time. Western Thinking does not allow for this to be true because writing was developed by "*Neolithic Artisans*". Another fact established by this King is the medical knowledge, from before The Deluge, available to cure many ailments "from head to toe-nail".

Only Priests were taught to read and write this newest form of communication. From the art of keeping financial records, ancient Man learned he could express himself with the construction of sentences. The earliest expressions were in the form of poems [songs]. Later these expressions grew to personal stories and epic tales of local rulers, ancient Gods and mythology. These early writings are an excellent example of the human trait of adapting intelligence for one's own personal use.

The Sumerian scribes provide us with a view of the Lords from thousands of years ago. They describe their city Gods as possessing all human traits, falling in love, being the fathers of children, and quarreling among themselves. They also describe the Lords as being immortal and all-powerful absolute rulers. Native Man was described as nothing more than their servants. If a servant angered or disrespected a Lord, the punishment was immediate death.

The temple administration ran according to strict business standards and methods. All receipts and expenditures were recorded on clay tablets. In the temple compounds Lodge apprentices were taught building skills, reading, writing, and basic math.

Based on Ancient Legends, the Lords of these Estates had their own "families," their lineage passed on through the "best of the best" women available. Ancient writings indicate the Lords took all the "wives" they wanted from locals and from Brother Lords' "families." The firstborn sons of the Lords managed the large estates and became legends as "The Sons of Man", and half-Gods as in the legend of Gilgamesh. These "half-Gods" also became the High Priests of the Lodge.

The Lords began devising a grand plan for their rescue soon after the comet strike. They used the Sumerian civilization as the beginning of the plan. As the population of the cities grew, the Lords relieved themselves of administrative duties, using priests for these tasks. The priests conducted and recorded the cities' business and Lodge records.

The Lords of Sumer's long-range planning and building equates to extended life spans far beyond normally anticipated. These life spans of thousands of years are recorded in Biblical and Egyptian history, and the Sumerian Kings List. If living for thousands of years is a myth, then are these records of old, the Holy Writs of several religions, and ancient civilizations in the same category?

Based on biblical history everyone in charge was male. Women of the Bibles were relegated to domestic roles and advising their spouses. By contrast, Women of the Lord's groups became powerful Goddesses in the Sun God religions.   One powerful woman is recorded as the Emperor of a Sumerian Civilization.

The eighteen known cities the Lords created operated as one corporate force mirroring the operational structure of the Ancient Lodge. The city of Nippur functioned as the administrative center of authority and maintained the region's trade records.

The Sumerian cities provided Nippur with a constant flow of intelligence from their respective areas and allowed for balanced management of the entire civilization. This strategy was unique for its time. If one or more cities fell to an invading force, the corporate structure of the region would continue. Unlike all civilizations to follow in this area, the Sumerian Lords built their civilization inwards without attempting territorial expansion.   This policy clearly distinguished them from their barbarian counterparts, who used brute force to expand their empires. Instead of aggression, the Lords used trade to obtain the items and power they desired.

The early history of Sumer records intermittent battles between "Sky Gods", using their flying machines of destruction to establish supremacy of various regions. Many of these conflicts occurred Pre-Deluge, most likely between the offspring of the supreme delegation of gods.

In the early formation of the civilization, the Lords used any and all means to preserve their crafted society. They insisted on total subservience and discipline, devoid of independent though or behavior. Their methods of dealing with native Man reinforced their status as Gods. Lords Yahweh and Bal were firmly established as almighty Gods.

During the years of preparation for the building of the cities, mountain tribesmen from the Zagros Mountains began raiding along the Sumerian borders. The tribesmen were allowed to raid the outer settlement areas as long as they did not pose a threat to the temple and township areas.

The Lords used a sophisticated strategy to counter the raids. Instead of building border fortifications or engaging in extended warfare, trade was established with the raiders. This policy extended control over the tribesmen by providing them with wheat, barley, and oats.

Successful trading was blended with gratuitous bribes for the tribal chieftains. Few tribal chiefs would allow harm to come to those who provided the wealth. The Sumerians completed trading alliances outside their regions to obtain the materials necessary to build their cities. Each alliance served to ensure Sumerian regional security against all but small raiding parties. The growth of the region continued uninterrupted.

To acquire the necessary building materials and metals for the cities, long-range trade routes were established extending to Syria, Turkey, and Iran. Later routes extended across Iran into Afghanistan and Pakistan. Overland and sea routes extended to the British Isles in the West, Thailand in the East, and to Mongolia in the North. Sumerian traders established communities along these routes, with Emissaries of the Lords overseeing the local operations. The trade routes were a monumental achievement providing the Sumerian civilization with vast amounts of wealth.

Pottery and bronze were the principle items for trade, along with grain and other merchandise from the Sumerian community. Trade and bribery ensured the Sumerians' continued survival among these barbarian warriors. Also, their caravans were able to cross territorial boundaries in relative safety.

In many of these outlying "trade colonies" the local Emissary, or Lord, established solar and lunar observatories to monitor time and enforce religious dogma. Remnants of these structures can be found today on most every continent. These local Lords developed families and were regarded as living Gods, leading to the development of several ancient religions. Religion was evolving by natural selection. In cuneiform writings it is noted that one God was reincarnated at least six times. This suggests the God's children or a relative replaced the God when he died.

The trade routes enabled the Lords to search for metal bearing ores over vast reaches. They needed ore that could be mined, refined and converted into ingots at the same location. The barbarian kings profited and gained considerable status and respect from these mining activities and trade agreements.

By 5,500 BCE, the temples in Sumer had become estates surrounded by cities of magnificent architecture. To assist the functioning of a well-organized productive community, the Lords introduced a new form of time management. The Sumerian civilization was the first to use the sixty-minute hour, the twenty-four-hour day, and the annual calendar. Codes of Law and a public justice system were established to govern the growing population.

During this time of accomplishment and tranquility, a powerful priesthood emerged in the cities. Their duties were to serve the local city Gods and assume control of city administration at each temple. This priesthood was the first visible authority of the Ancient Lodge.

A new policy allowed traders, merchants, and tribesmen uncontrolled access to the cities, and desert tribesmen settled in the region. As the strict discipline of the Lords was relinquished, the citizens exhibited a surge of independence in their life styles. Cuneiform writing reflects this independence in the poems and stories of the people. The stories provide insight to newly acquired freedoms such as fathers taking care of family problems, or of the citizens recording stories relating to the Lords themselves. This freedom of expression was unheard of in previous times.

With the priests controlling the cities' administration, the Lords were able to avoid public scrutiny. This provided greater freedom of movement and allowed the Lords to leave the area unobserved. City residents would assume their living Gods were still within their walled estates.

In Sumer, the Lords released their administrative duties to the Lodge Priests and city kings. Historically, native Man had begun to self-govern. This absence of absolute authority was the beginning of the decline of the Sumerian civilization. The city kings began to wage war among themselves.

THE DECLINE OF SUMER

While building their empire, the Lords had sown the seeds for its destruction. Caravans traveling the trade routes carried tales of cities of wonder, filled with food, jewels and precious metals. Wandering desert tribes and bands of traders were attracted in far greater numbers than it was possible to capture and kill. The tribes moved to the fringes of Sumer, settled in the region and many were assimilated into the local population.

Lord Yahweh could not control the constant and successive invasions into his domain of southern Sumer, from Lord Bal's followers. He abandoned his "Eden" and moved his tribe to Canaan. Lord Bal was soon worshipped as The Sun God and in Babylon as The Feathered Serpent. The Moon Goddess was also very popular in the households. This local selection of Gods is known in evolutionary terms as "Natural Selection". The pantheon of Gods was referred to as "Elohim" in the local language. Some Gods were elevated in status while others were cast aside. This is Social Evolution at its finest.

The Sumerian cities formed a loose alliance to fend off invading barbarians. History shows the city kings did not have the discipline or intellect to effectively resolve their territorial problems. With the lack of leadership and discipline, the entire civilization began a final decline around 2,600 BCE.

As the Lords left Sumer a progressive infiltration of Assyrians, Akkadian-speaking people from the North, began. The Assyrian calendar begins in 4,765 BCE. By 2,575 BCE the entire Sumerian region was settled by a race of warriors known as the Akkad. In 2,334 BCE, "The Akkad", Sargon the Great, came to power during a rebellion of the Akkad population in the city of Kish. Shortly after the rebellion, Sargon formed an army and overthrew the king of Urak. Sargon continued to overthrow each city and after a series of brief wars he ruled the entire region. The Lodge in this region was now free to chart its own course and create its history without the Lords' direct influence.

Warrior Kings expanded their empires, subduing neighbors and accumulating wealth. They learned they could not become rich and powerful with the total destruction of the regions they subdued.

Other than killing defending armies, they usually left the remaining civilization in place. As the warrior king entered the cities, subservience and paying homage to the new ruler was the order of the day. After disposing of the local king and his close advisors, everyone of administrative value was brought before the victor. If these administrators valued their lives, they swore allegiance to the new ruler and business continued as usual. The invaders were usually assimilated by the local population and the cultures merged.

Sargon appears to have been quite pleased with the social structure of his new conquests. He adopted many of the Sumerian customs and passed new laws to ensure the social conscience of the community continued uninterrupted.

The influence of the Ancient Lodge is evident in the strict social laws Sargon established. One specific set of laws ensured social justice by protecting the weak and the poor in society. In the formation of the new laws, Sargon specifically used the phrase, ***"Providing for the care of Widows and Orphans."*** These reforms of ancient times have endured and are timeless in the Masonic bylaws of the Blue Lodge. Sargon the Great [Sargon I, Sargon the Akkad] ruled for almost sixty years. 800 years later King Hammurabi would issue the 200+ Codes of Hammurabi from Nippur. He gave honor to Gods Bel and Marduk while repeating the social foundation of protecting widows and orphans. It would appear that worshipping Lord Bal was not all "evil-doing".

During this time of regional warfare in Sumer, there were monumental building accomplishments in Egypt. The two largest pyramids were completed by 2,520 BCE.

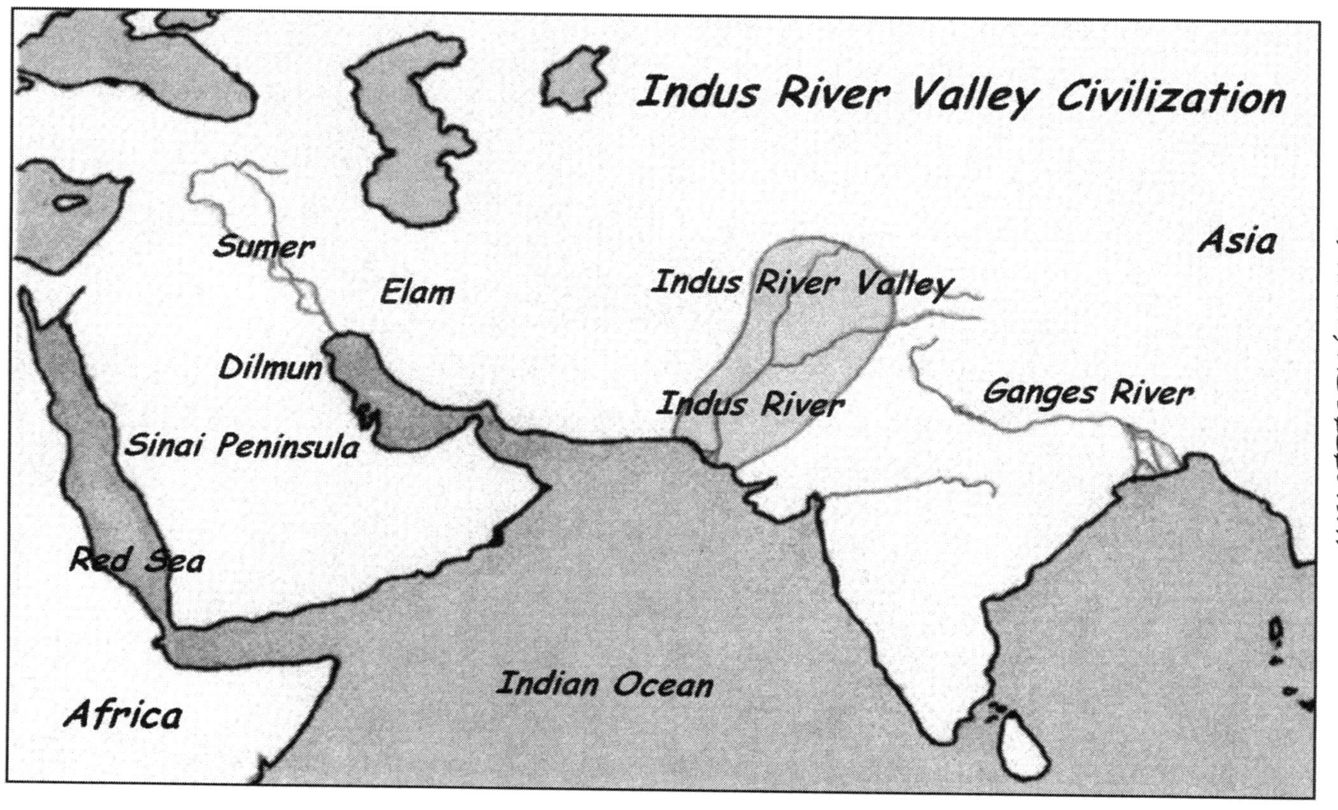
Indus River Valley Civilization
Asia
Sumer
Elam
Indus River Valley
Dilmun
Indus River
Ganges River
Sinai Peninsula
Red Sea
Africa
Indian Ocean

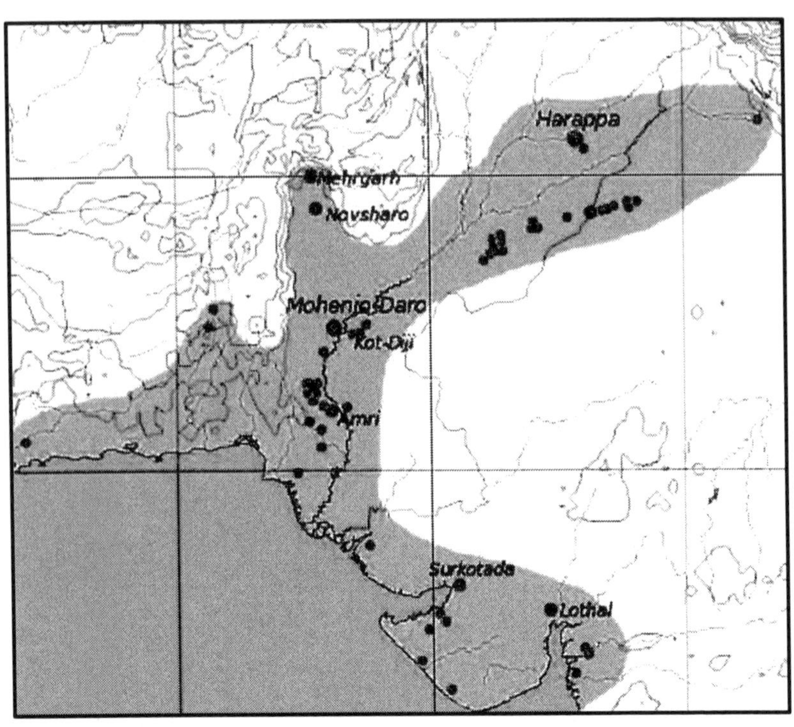

The Cities of The Indus River Valley Civilization
The area was referred to as "The Black Dirt Nation"
with two safe harbors for large sailing vessels.

Chapter
5

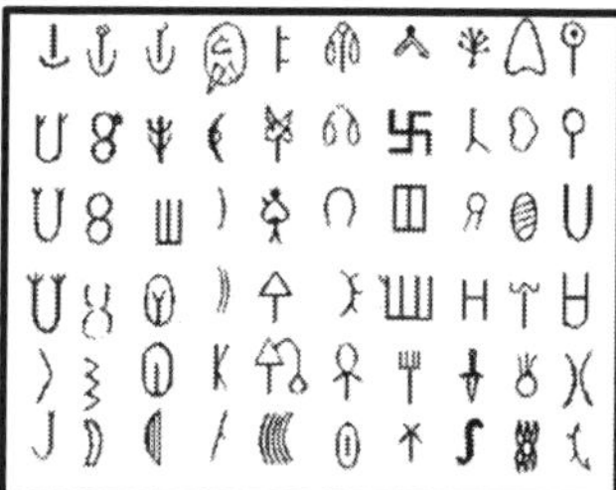

Undeciphered Indus Script

THE INDUS RIVER VALLEY CIVILIZATION
[7,000 BCE - 1,800 BCE]

A Life without the Lords Oversight

By 3,850 BCE, a group of Lords from Elam, accompanied by highly trained craftsmen and their families, had created another great civilization. They used a well-established long-range sea trade route to relocate this group, sailing from the Island of Bahrain, ancient "Dilmun". About 7,000 BCE an advance group from Sumer had located The Indus River Valley using sea-going trade routes to the area.

Large sea-going galleys, powered with up to three decks of oars and sails provided transport of personnel and trade goods to the Indus ports. The same types of galleys were used in the Mediterranean and Atlantic to travel to the Americas. This group of Lords began the new civilization known as the Indus River Valley Civilization.

The language group assigned to the Indus civilization is "Dravidian". This was also the language of Elam, part of the Fertile Crescent, which bordered Sumer on the East and continued south along the Persian Gulf. The Sumerians labeled the Indus people Meluhhaites, or those who lived in Meluhha.

The Indus River Valley is in present day eastern Pakistan. To the West of the Indus Valley is Iran, to the north and northwest is Afghanistan, and on the eastern border is India. The Indus River Valley continues south to the coast of the Arabian Sea. The Lords of the Indus group built an urban civilization whose foundation depended on agriculture and trade. The Lords blended with the civilization they created without drawing undue attention to themselves, maintaining the new policy of total secrecy.

The Indus civilization was unique and without equal for their advanced engineering techniques and city planning skills. Engineering and architectural skills were the trademark of the Lords of Sumer, far beyond other civilizations, but did not compare to the Indus civilization. The lack of "God" leaders, grandeur and opulence compared to Sumer, indicates this specific group of Lords did not concur with the dominance methods of the leaders of the Sumer Lords.

In contrast with Sumer, no monumental structures for leaders were built; no evidence of palaces with kings and armies, or great religious temples with ruling priests has been discovered. All inhabitants enjoyed equal status. I believe this was the first true Representative Democracy established by the Lodge.

The lack of opulent life styles and grand palaces leads to the conclusion that the builders were a group of Masonic Craftsmen without the Royalty of The Lords. This conclusion is further supported by the history of the region. The Indus civilization was conspicuously absent of royal ruling lineage, massive displays of wealth, or royal ceremonies. Instead of a royal lineage, a council of ruling priests [advisors] governed the civilization.

The predominate religion of the Indus was the Sun and Moon Goddess and the all present Great Bull. The religion was somewhat low-key and was near equal to that in Crete. Evidence of women priests equal in status to men, detailed labyrinth layouts, and bull leaping dominated the ceremonies.

The ruling council was formed by the Masters of the Lodges. This is demonstrated by findings that all citizens were treated equally. The Indus civilization was the first known Masonic community without royalty.

Historians have noted the Indus civilization produced truly remarkable and sophisticated cities. The cities of Mohenjodaro, Harappa, and Kalibangan seem to have suddenly emerged. One historian noted the sudden emergence of civilization in the Indus Valley duplicated what had occurred in Sumer, which later became a part of Mesopotamia. These cities actually surpassed Sumerian development in sophistication and planning.

An archaeologist who excavated some figurines stated **"Some mistake must surely have been made; that these figures had found their way into levels some 3000 years older than those to which they properly belonged".**

Before 3,850 BCE the area was developed for farming and beef production with modest towns. Two major cities suddenly emerged on the Indus River, four hundred miles apart. Historians concede the cities were not the result of successive building phases.

Each city was built using a standard grid system, with a massive sewer system built before construction of the streets and buildings, and the sewer manholes matched the layout of the streets. You cannot be sure of this detail in modern construction.

The Indus cities were carefully planned with straight brick paved streets intersecting at right angles. The sewers were large enough for workers to conduct cleaning and repair work. The sewer system was specifically engineered to provide manholes at intersections of the streets. Each city had two and three storied houses with balconies, enclosed courtyards and water wells. The houses had inside bathrooms with flush toilets and showers connected to the city sewer system with clay pipes.

Observations of the plumbing and toilets that used water, in the Indus Valley cities of Harappa and Mohenjo-daro, cited they had a flush toilet in almost every house, attached to a sophisticated sewage system." Also, that the Indus systems of sewerage and drainage that were developed and used in cities throughout the Indus region were far more advanced than any currently in use in rural areas of the Middle East and more efficient than those in many areas of Pakistan and India today."

The cities were surrounded by massive walls which protected the community from frequent floods in the Indus valley. The walls also provided security and a great vantage point for the guards.

One of the major cities had an enormous swimming pool, which was deemed to be a "religious bath". Could it be just a swimming pool? They had dentists, doctors, engineers, sports and "soccer moms", why not a place to swim? Of course, *Academia* always appoints the use of water in ancient times as a religious experience.

The housing neighborhoods were divided specifically for trade brokers, artists and craftsmen. Raw materials were imported from distant sources to produce trade goods, jewelry, ceramic and metal figurines. These artists produced molds for seals, which identified trade goods, individuals and local areas.

Many of these "seals" were stamps showing the symbols for the Indus language. The Indus "writing system" is another language system of the Lords which is yet to be deciphered. There are near 1,900 identified separate script symbols. I suspect the key to deciphering all of the various scripts of the Lords; Sumer, Indus, Minoan, Teotihuacan and others, is to view these symbols as a "Key". Keys are no more than symbols which are associated with a sound, phrase, word or number. This is one way in which Egyptian hieroglyphs were used for complete words. This system of communication was used by the Lodge and required years to master. Key script, or symbols, are meaningless to anyone not specifically trained to recognize them.

The mass-produced individual uniform script and symbols stamps were unique to the Indus, as no other civilization accomplished this printing practice until the Gutenberg Press in 1440 CE. Also unique were paired positive and negative stamps for producing jewelry items. One seal represented the Ritual Mazes used worldwide in the Sun God labyrinth ceremonies.

Indus Script and The Great Bull associated with worshipping the Sun God

Indus paired seal stamps which could be used to stamp thin metal for signets and jewelry

The overall cultural area of the Indus region was about eleven hundred miles from east to west, and eight hundred miles north to south. In the south, like Sumer, the area extended to the Indian coast, where the port city of Lothol was built.

The Port of Lothol was an engineering marvel, built with kiln-fired brick, and completed with a brick dockyard measuring 730 feet by 120 feet. All brick produced in the Indus area were uniform in size. Access to the dockyard was by a hand-dug channel that leads outward to the open sea. The channel is considered a unique engineering marvel for this time in history and has never been duplicated. Archeologists consider the engineered channel and the building of the dockyard an amazing feat, crediting native Man with an intellectual level far beyond that of other civilizations throughout the world. Archaeologists and historians refuse to consider that this amazing feat was the product of introduced intelligence. *Academia's* attitude continues to be "*How could these Neolithic Artisans do this?*"

The Indus civilization's ability for accurately measuring length and weight was not developed over centuries, they arrived with these skills. All weights and measures were uniform and precise. An Indus measurement scale was marked with divisions as small as 1.7 mm. The scale weights were uniform throughout the civilization. The base weight unit was an ounce [28 grams of modern weight] and scale weights were produced from 0.05 unit, doubling up to 2 units and proceeding from 5 units to 500 units. They also could determine the mass of objects, which was very useful in the gold trade for determining purity. The Indus merchants also used touchstones to determine the purity of gold.

Researchers believe the Indus were "Influenced by the Near Eastern Neolithic" because of "Domesticated wheat varieties, early phases of farming, pottery, other archaeological artifacts, domesticated plants and cattle herds." The agriculture and beef production are dated to before 5,000 BCE. Really? influenced by Sumer! What a guess. How about; "The best engineers, craftsmen and business leaders arrived from Eastern Sumer [Elam] to create the most advanced civilization known at the time."

I would not be surprised that the planners for the Indus sent advance parties to the region to determine if a full-scale civilization was feasible, probably about 7,000 BCE

An interesting historical tie to the Sumer region was deciphered from Cuneiform tablets and Stelae in Southern Iraq. The Akkadian King

Naram-Sin, 3rd King after Sargon the Great, mentions great and wondrous trade goods arriving from the "black-dirt" land of [the Indus].

Naram-Sin became full of himself and declared that he was King of the Gods and the Universe. From his palace in Akkad he had his name inscribed throughout the kingdom as equal to the Council of Gods.

This was an open challenge to the position of God Enlil who was head of the Council of Lords at that time. God Enlil prohibited all Gods from supporting Naram-Sin or traveling to his Kingdom. This would end all trade to and from his kingdom.

In response to this trade embargo Naram-Sin attacked Enlil's Temple in Ekur [Eridu] and caused severe damage to the structure and the resident priests. The Lords acted swiftly and without mercy. They sent an army of mercenaries to Akkad who destroyed the city, leaving all of the people and animals rotting in the streets.

In 2001, archaeologists discovered the Indus Valley Civilization utilized advanced dentistry. Evidence of cavity repairs with fillings and full tooth crowns was found in burial sites. This is the oldest known evidence for drilling and repairing teeth in people. The dental work is dated to 7,000 BCE, indicating the advance craftsmen brought the knowledge and dental tools with them.

According to *Academia*, "*their discoveries point to a tradition of proto-dentistry in the early farming cultures of that region*". I cannot believe they missed an opportunity to use "*The Perseverance of Neolithic Artisans*".

All cities show evidence of population growth planning. Each city's population was maintained at about forty thousand people, supporting a large farming community that produced cotton, wheat, barley, and rice.

Cotton was farmed for the first time in the history of this area and was used to weave cloth for local use, trade and export. Indus trade extended to Sumer, Egypt and the Mediterranean, especially Crete. Other trade routes connected Southeast Asia and Eastern Africa. The extensive textile trade was due to the Indus civilization producing the first wooden, hand driven cotton gin. This enabled one person to do the work of many, removing the cotton seed from the cotton fibers. This local "discovery" is known as the Churcka cotton gin.

To keep the advance of civilizations around the world in perspective, the production of cotton goods in the Americas at this same time is comparable. Also, the knowledge of noble metals and alloys in the Americas was on, or above, the same level as the Indus people.

The city used night watchmen housed in small guard posts throughout the city. The administration buildings were large multistoried structures, housing the priests in comfort, and provided office space for the city administration. The administration buildings and the family houses contained plumbing which provided hot and cold running water.

Climate change and drought began taking a toll on the Indus River Valley around 1900 BCE. This drought also affected a large portion of the Fertile Crescent. Once again, the Lords found a force they could not control. The Indus civilization and its wealth began relocating to Egypt's Nile Delta and to Crete. There they enhanced the Minoan trade networks and supported the migration of Hyksos settlers into the Delta for the construction of Egyptian monuments. The Hyksos were also fleeing drought and famine in Canaan.

The Indus Civilization came to an end due to extreme drought about 1,800 BCE. They could no longer provide crops to feed the population and the cities were totally abandoned by 1,700 BCE. Aryan invaders encountered this region in 1,500 BCE and took over the remains of this once great civilization, known for many "firsts" in the ancient world.

The wealth of the region would continue to attract invaders who would battle the previous conquerors of the land. Without strict discipline, intelligence, and meticulous administration, the civilization began a rapid decline. In future years, residents of the land wandered through the ruins of once great cities and wondered who in their distant past could have created such marvelous works of architecture.

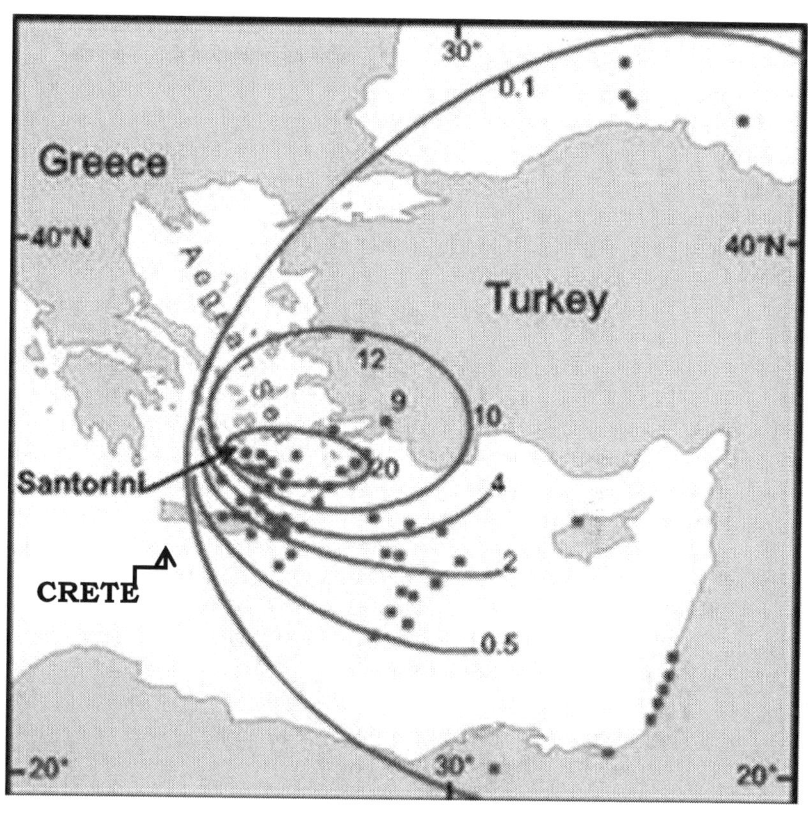

The Island of Thera [Santorini] exploded in a volcanic eruption in 1628 BCE

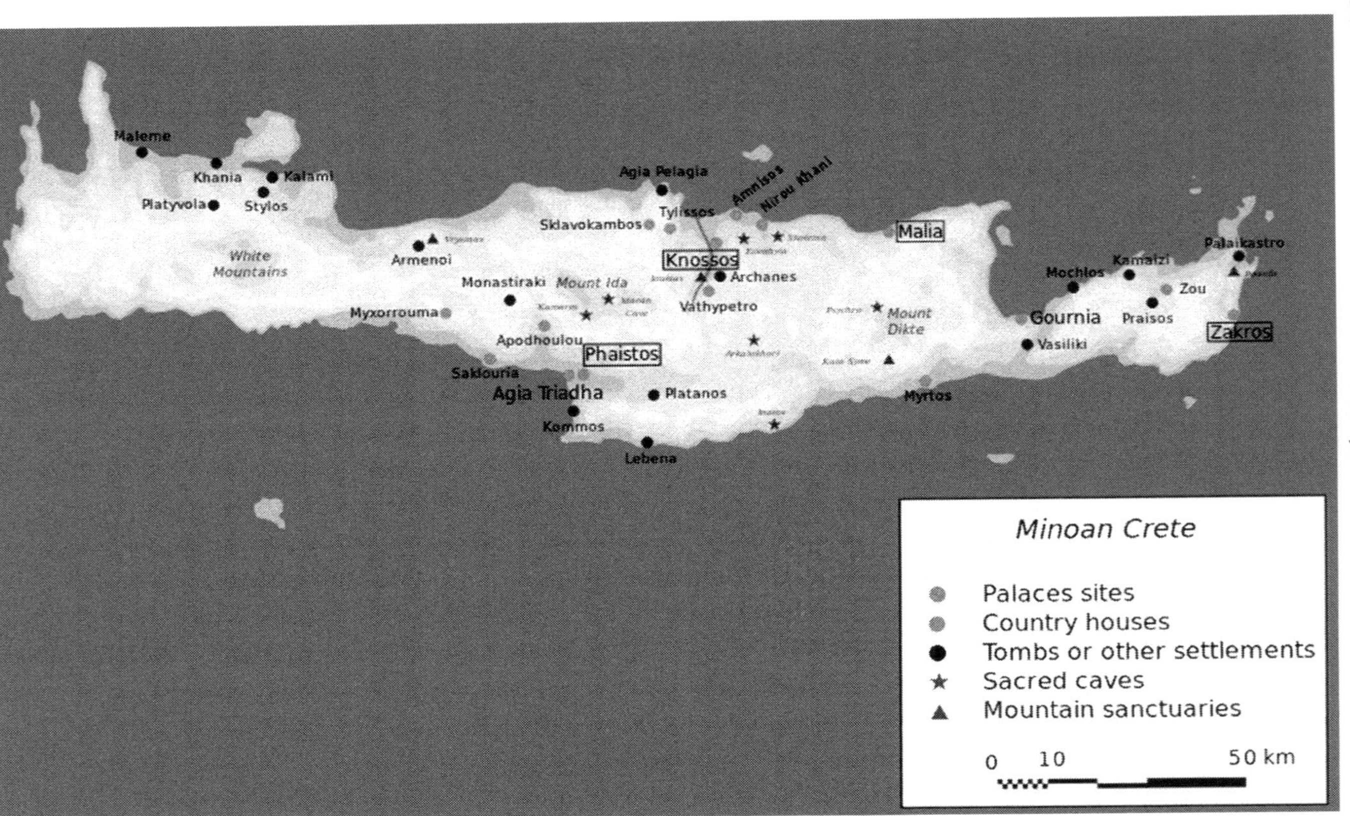
Maleme
Khania
Kalami
Platyvola
Stylos
White Mountains
Agia Pelagia
Amnisos
Nirou Khani
Tylissos
Sklavokambos
Malia
Palaikastro
Armenoi
Knossos
Kamaizi
Mochlos
Zou
Monastiraki
Mount Ida
Archanes
Gournia
Praisos
Myxorrouma
Vathypetro
Mount Dikte
Zakros
Apodhoulou
Vasiliki
Phaistos
Saktouria
Agia Triadha
Platanos
Myrtos
Kommos
Lebena
Minoan Crete
Palaces sites
Country houses
Tombs or other settlements
Sacred caves
Mountain sanctuaries
0   10   50 km

TL 4 MINOAN

2000 CE

YEARS BCE

0 BCE

Years BCE	Event
1,100	Lords abandon "Nail" occupation
1,550	Minoan Civilization fails
1,600	Lord Bal's group completes move to The Americas
1,628	Thera explodes, North Crete, N. Egypt and Med area destroyed By Tsunamis and volcanic ash
1,650	Thera and Minoans at height of power and success-Phoenicians rule seas and trade
1,900	Indus Lords move to Crete and Egypt Mycenae colonized
2,000	Grand Palaces expanded on Crete
2,600	Lords leave Sumer— to Crete
3,200	Minoan Civilization established—building palaces and cities and industries
6,500	Lords establish "Parvaim" on island Of Thera [Santorini]
7,000	Egypt has organized farming
8,000	DNA analysis show Paleo colonists on Crete arrived from the "Levant"
11,000	Wheat-beer in Fertile Crescent Sun Temple deliberately buried At Gobekli Tepe in Turkey
10,900	Comet impact of Earth causes Pleistocene Extinction
18,000	Tiwanakuan Civilization and Sun Temple in South America

AB 01	AB 21	AB 31	AB 54	AB 76	AB 123
AB 02	AB 21^f	AB 34	AB 55	AB 77	AB 131a
AB 03	AB 21^m	AB 37	AB 56	AB 78	AB 131b
AB 04	AB 22	AB 38	AB 57	AB 79	A 131c
AB 05	AB 22^f	AB 39	AB 58	AB 80	AB 164
AB 06	AB 22^m	AB 40	AB 59	AB 81	AB 171
AB 07	AB 23	AB 41	AB 60	AB 82	AB 180
AB 08	AB 23^m	AB 44	AB 61	AB 85	AB 188
AB 09	AB 24	AB 45	AB 65	AB 86	AB 191
AB 10	AB 26	AB 46	AB 66	AB 87	A 301
AB 11	AB 27	AB 47	AB 67	A 100/102	A 302
AB 13	AB 28	AB 49	AB 69	AB 118	A 303
AB 16	A 28b	AB 50	AB 70	AB 120	A 304
AB 17	AB 29	AB 51	AB 73	A 120b	A 305
AB 20	AB 30	AB 53	AB 74	AB 122	A 306

Standardized Table of Minoan Linear A Script
[Undeciphered]

Chapter
6

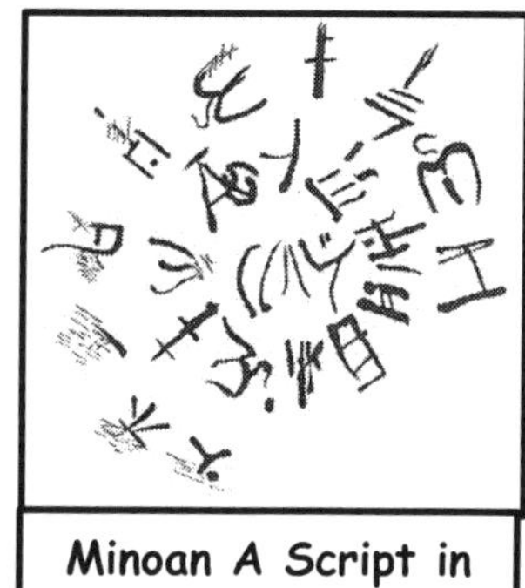

Minoan A Script in a cup

MINOAN CIVILIZATION
CRETE AND PARVAIM
LEAVING SUMER FOR THE MEDITERRANEAN

The Legend of Atlantis
"There is a land called Crete in the midst of the wine dark sea, a fair land and rich, begirt with water, and therein are men innumerable, and ninety cities. ------ And among the cities is the mighty city Cnosus, wherein Minos when he was nine years old began to rule, he held converse with great Zeus." The Odyssey of Homer, Book XIX.

Quote from Lang-Leaf-Myers-Butcher translations of the Iliad and the Odyssey

The Odyssey was written by the ancient Greek, Homer [c. 700 BCE]. He described in mythical terms what was believed to be the emergence of the Minoan civilization. About the only correct information the story contained was the concept of physical beauty combined with the presence of the powerful rulers and beautiful women of Crete.

By 6,500 BCE the core leadership of the Lords had devised long term plans to facilitate lavish, secret palace sanctuaries throughout the Mediterranean area. One of these sanctuaries was the island of Thera [Santorini], known as the mythical **Parvaim**. Parvaim, the Mythical

Paradise of The Great Ones, The Holy Watchers and the Nephilim. Thera was named for its mythical ruler Theri.

During this era the Lords began relocations of their bases of power. The foundation for a slow but progressive civilization had previously been established in Egypt. The Lords relocated their headquarters closer to this developing region to better control the emerging trade in the Mediterranean and Middle East. They developed several small wealthy civilizations on Crete and adjacent islands.

Crete was ruled by a group of powerful, secretive men and women. Most civilizations were founded with the names of the rulers prominently displayed for future generations. However, the Lords obsession with secrecy provides the evidence required to track them through various historical periods. Once again, the faint trail of the Lords emerges.

The primary religion of the Minoans was The Sun God [Mitra]. A Priestess led the ceremonies of labyrinth worship, using a staff which appeared to hold a two-headed axe. This symbol is actually portraying a butterfly on a staff. The butterfly was the symbol for resurrection and eternal life after death in Minoan, Egyptian, Greek, Olmec and Mayan civilizations, and in many others.

When first discovered archaeologists called this symbol "The two-headed axe" from the Greek word for labyrinth, which they insisted meant "home of the two headed axe" and *Academia* never looked further.

The word labyrinth was used in the Greek mythical tales of King Minos for the chamber which housed the Minotaur beast. The definition is; a maze or large building with intricate passages. An underground labyrinth is a grotto with many intricate passages and hidden rooms.

The Labyrinth Priestess was called the "Butterfly Goddess" because of two headed axe interpretation. Minoan Women Priests were held in high regard and led the Sun God rituals in labyrinths. The "Minoan Maze" symbolized the Grotto labyrinth. The "Butterfly Staff" or "Two headed axe" symbols were carved in Stonehenge pillars [2200 BCE], which indicate the introduction of the Minoan Sun God, Labyrinth ceremonies and maze symbols. This was a result of the Minoans establishing trading outposts in the British Isles.

The Minoan civilization was at its peak on Crete and adjacent islands by 3,200 BCE and was spectacular until its sudden ending in 1628 BCE.

The power of the rulers, combined with the absolute beauty of the architectural designs of the palaces, was pervasive in the classical period of ancient Greek Architecture and literature. The lifestyles of the Minoan rulers provided the basis for the mythical Greek stories of Gods who ruled Man on Earth. Crete was the production site for goods and Parvaim [Thera] was the corporate center for trade.

Crete is located in the Mediterranean Sea and to the North the Aegean Sea contains numerous islands extending to the Greek mainland. Thera is in the Aegean and 70 miles north of Crete. Cyprus is 350 miles due east. 110 miles to the northeast is the landmass of Asia Minor, which for this coastline is primarily the country of Turkey. South of Turkey, on the same coastline, is Syria, Lebanon, Israel, and Egypt. Crete is about 700 miles from the coasts of Lebanon and Israel. Crete is 152 miles east to west, and varies in width from 7 to 35 miles. The total landmass is 3,186 square miles and it is the fifth largest island in the Mediterranean Sea.

Crete is rugged and beautiful, with mountain ranges with towering peaks. The highest peaks rise to 8000 feet and are normally covered with snow year-round. The mountain snows support three main rivers and numerous streams that cross upland basins, fertile meadows, and mountain plains. The valleys and hillside slopes of Crete are carpeted in a vast array of colorful wild flowers, which were used in the production of perfumes and spices.

One of the main exports was Saffron, produced from the pollen of the crocus flower. Saffron is used as a spice and a dye, and was more valuable, by weight, than gold. This trade export equaled the trade of black pepper and frankincense.

The island's mountain areas are noted for numerous extremely large caves and narrow ravines bordered by precipitous cliffs. Smaller caverns form extended underground chambers in the solid stone. The mild winters and warm air of the Mediterranean Sea produce ideal conditions for the plant life of the island. The highland areas supported vast stands of Cypress, Oak, and Pine trees. The lowlands produced numerous groves of Chestnut, Olive, Locust, and Juniper trees.

Crete provided more than beauty for the Lords of Sumer; it was a natural sanctuary from the mainland. The Mediterranean Sea provided a natural barrier to invasion from warrior kings. Most importantly, the island prevented the scrutiny of emerging civilizations.

Historians have labeled the entire region, from Crete through the Aegean Sea north to the Greek mainland, the Aegean civilization. The Aegean civilizations are comprised of four main geographical areas: First, the Minoan civilization on Crete; second, the Cyclades islands, which includes Thera; third, the mainland of Greece; and last, the lands and islands of northwest Asia Minor.

As the history of this region developed, historians erroneously concluded a completely separate civilization evolved on the Greek mainland, the Mycenaean. This cultural name was derived from the most ancient city of Greece called Mycenae.

The development of the Greek mainland and adjacent islands by the Lords was underway by 1,900 BCE. The stonework of the area is complex, precise and typical of work around the world. Some stones weighed over 120 tons. The building methods, art and paintings were identical to the Minoans.

Mycenae was strategically located on the Greek mainland in the Argive plain. Its location afforded the shortest route from central Greece to Thera and Crete and the civilization was simply an extension of the Minoan region of control.

The Lords began building four grand palaces on Crete about 3,200 BCE, producing Europe's first civilized metropolis. That conclusion by historians was because the first metropolis, built on Thera was vaporized and buried in 1,628 BCE and the ruins had not been discovered. The architecture of Crete is identical to that excavated on Thera, which was buried under 200 feet of volcanic ash. This inundation protected the ruins from the final explosion of Thera.

Historical suspicion should have been aroused when Crete did not produce one recorded ruler in over 1,600 years. The only King associated with Crete comes from Greek mythology in Homer's Odyssey. Minos is the mythical nine-year-old king who ruled the palace of Knossos. This is fiction, as there is no record or evidence to support this story of a young ruler.

Historians had evidence of a civilization that dominated the area, but there was no evidence of a ruling dynasty. So, they took the name of the fictional king and named an entire civilization after a nonexistent person. Minos became Minoan. A parallel view of this historical oddity can be seen by comparing Minoan history with Egyptian Dynasties.

The Minoan history from 3,200 to 1,600 BCE equates to 1,600 years of an obscure ruling class. The same time period produced Egyptian Dynasties from the First Dynasty of King Mena, centered at Thinis, to the Eighteenth Dynasty of Pharaoh Ahmose I. The Egyptians recorded hundreds of kings, Pharaohs and princes, and numerous lesser-known Hyksos kings of the Fourteen and Fifteenth Dynasties.

The question of who built the Minoan civilization remains a mystery to historians and archaeologists. When the Lords established the Minoan civilization, they were using two written languages. The "Linear A" script of the Minoan rulers has yet to be deciphered, and it disappeared from Crete after the Thera explosion. Linear A is in the same form as the Sumerian and Indus un-deciphered languages, which are "key" type languages. "Linear B" script was used in trading sites throughout the Aegean civilization. Stating the mystery Linear A language is a "Key type language" is probably my first contribution to deciphering anything.

A "Key" symbolic communication is one of the first things taught in Masonic education. I previously stated this, but again, understanding the Key is about understanding veiled allegory.

As a reminder, to prevent tunnel vision, Minoan history runs parallel to the histories of the Sumerian, Indus, Egyptian, and the Americas civilizations.

Beginning in CE 1886 archaeological expeditions constantly investigated the Minoan civilization. The island has been combed by expeditions from England, Italy, America, France, Germany, and Greece. Their archaeological finds provide a wealth of information regarding the progression of the civilization, which has been a puzzle to archaeologists. The archeological reports leave many unanswered questions regarding the progression of this civilization.

The Palace of Knossos has attracted a majority of the attention of archaeologists. One archaeologist spent twenty-five years excavating the palace and grounds trying to solve the mystery of who its builders were. He dug through the main palace courtyard, down twenty-three feet to find the level of the first New Stone Age people to inhabit the site, the Neolithic level.

The archaeologist reported ten levels of habitation that covered about three thousand years. On the lowest level of habitation, he found evidence of Stone Age people who hunted with spears and used sharpened rocks as tools. This group did not build any type of permanent structures.

Above this level, on level nine, the archaeologist found what should not have existed in 3,200 BCE, the remains of houses made of kiln-fired brick, built on stone foundations. Between levels ten and the preceding levels there should have been evidence of a progression of building phases. The houses and palaces built with foundations, fire baked brick and precision measurements should not have existed for another thousand years. Later archaeological finds at the same location and same level produced stone vases from Egypt. The Minoan builders arrived with the skills to produce this magnificent architecture.

The reaction of the archeological community of that time was;

> **"The use of such advanced construction techniques is rather surprising for the cultures of this period." And, "The earliest artifacts which refer to the peoples of the Neolithic culture of the island indicate the group emigrated from a mainland location." Also, "The architectural advancements of these Neolithic Artisans are quite surprising. The houses contained quite large fireplaces, complete with hearths, such an advance in structure is yet to be defined."**

And the classic comment: **"One suspects the Neolithic Artisans were of an advanced Middle Eastern civilization."**

One also suspects the Stone Age people did not have kiln-fired brick. They also did not possess the engineering knowledge to build large sailing ships to bring people from the mainland. Here again, there were no statements that the houses built of kiln fired bricks were totally out of character, or out of sequence for man's natural evolution in this area. Also, the "*Artisans*" installed flush toilets with clay pipes connected to a sewage system, identical to ruins on Thera and in the Indus Valley.

In 3,200 BCE Sumer and the Indus civilization were the only other areas that produced fire baked brick. The houses provide the evidence that Lord Bal began moving his people from the Sumerian region to Crete. Crete and Egypt had farming communities by 5,000

BCE and later the Egyptians in the Delta constructed their buildings of wood and plaster using the same fixed and free mortise and tenon joints used on Thera.

During c. 3,000 BCE archaeologists and historians agree there is clear evidence of trading contact between the Sumerian civilization and Egypt. The continuing movement of craftsmen from Sumer to Crete provides evidence the Lords were aware Sumer was headed for a decline. Instead of wasting the skills of the ancient Masons on a faltering civilization, the craftsmen were moved. Before the overthrow of Sumer in 2,600 BCE, the elite of the Sumerian Lords completed their move to Crete and Thera, with outposts in Egypt and Mycenae. The move included Lords Bal and Yahweh although Yahweh chose the area known as Canaan as his personal sanctuary. He spent a lot of time at his Minoan style villa on one of the "Holy" mountains there.

About 2,600 BCE the Lords on Crete and Thera split into two groups. One group remained at Thera and Knossos to manage trade. The second, and larger group, followers of Bal, began a trans-oceanic move of personnel, equipment and treasure to Central America. The group joined Lords who survived the comet and meteor strike at Tiwanaku and were living with various civilizations, including the Olmec Civilization.

The smaller island of Thera was home to the most elite of the Lords, along with their extended families, priests and craftsmen. This was the mythical Parvaim. The palaces there are said to have rivaled the Palace of Knossos. The main structures had large interior timber frameworks designed to withstand the constant earthquakes of Thera. The timbers were connected using mortise and tenon joints which resisted the earthquake forces.

Thera was the Wall Street of ancient times. Trade and shipments of goods from the known world were brokered by the Lords on Thera and Crete.

Their paradise was short lived, as a volcanic explosion greater than any known would end this retreat. In the 1930s several prominent archaeologists excavated the sites remaining on what was left of Thera. Their conclusions were as stated above except for the timing and size of the catastrophe ending this occupation.

The archaeologists concluded the volcanic explosion occurred about 1,450 BCE, spewing ash over most of Egypt. They also presumed the ash cloud provided Moses with one of his "Plagues," in darkening the skies and blotting out the Egyptian sun. It was also their opinion this explosion ended the Minoan Civilization with devastating Tsunamis along the coast of Crete.

Of course, the main part of Thera was vaporized, and the remains of most of the cities collapsed into the ocean. What remains of Thera resembles a South Pacific atoll. This highly evolved and advanced civilization had "vanished into the sea." This is undoubtedly the event, and "lost civilization," which gave rise to the mythology of "Atlantis." Atlantis was a mythical island in the Greek philosopher Plato's writings about 360 BCE.

Recent scientific explorations and data place the destruction of Thera in 1628 BCE and significantly upgrade the power of the event. Some say Thera was far greater than Krakatoa in volume and intensity. The total volume of material estimated to have been ejected is 14 cubic miles.   The ash fallout from Thera occurred around the world producing several years of global winter. Tsunamis up to 500 feet high and moving close to 450 miles an hour destroyed all lowland island settlements in the Aegean Sea, coastal mainland and on the north side of Crete. The Tsunamis destroyed everything up to and above 500 feet above sea level, killing tens, or hundreds of thousands on Crete. Egypt's Nile River Delta was subjected to ash fallout and Tsunamis which changed river channels in the Delta.

The information gathered from archaeological excavations on Thera provided some interesting facts and conclusions. There were few artifacts gathered from the remaining ruins. All of the important items in the grand palaces that could be moved were absent. This lends to the undeniable conclusion: Thera was subjected to constant earthquakes and eruptions making life there untenable. The Lords knew the island was going to explode and had sufficient time to move valuables and people to Crete. These facts coincide with the final construction phase on Crete, the expansion of the grand palaces between 2,000 and 1,800 BCE.

Another remarkable site is on the southeastern coast of Crete, the Myrtos settlement. The settlement was located on the knoll of a hill and extended outward to cover an area of about fifteen acres. The excavation revealed a community that was occupied between 2,600 and 2,250 BCE.

The people lived in a single stone and brick building containing ninety rooms and working areas.   On nearby slopes were vineyards and orchards of olive trees.   Near the area were large fields of barley. The people managed herds of goats, sheep, cattle, and pigs.   This area also produced an excessive number of potters' wheels, weaving looms, and dyed cloth.

Knossos inscribed clay tablets indicate about 100,000 sheep were grazing in central Crete. The tablets list expected wool for trade and weaving and indicate the expected increase of the flock.   The settlement has been described as a community of cottage industries. Other than the statement; *"the settlement was remarkable,"* there appears to have been no effort to explain the settlement's existence. The community should have been described as a factory producing trade goods.

As the archaeological excavations continued, another two-acre complex of four hundred rooms was found. The historical results of this find were just as before. A simple statement was issued and there was no effort to connect the complexes. The statement issued on this find was, "Evidence is quite lacking as to suggest the purpose of the buildings." There has been sufficient evidence found on Crete to deduce the area was under continual management for the production of trade goods.

The excavations only provide evidence of the activities of the civilization. The excavations do not provide information on how many two-acre warehouse complexes there were, or how many trade item factories there may have been. Certainly, there were more than were found. The important issue is the continuity of a civilized framework from 3,200 BCE to about 1,600 BCE [1,600 years].

The palace building phase on Crete increased near the end of the Indus civilization in 1,900 BCE.   Confirmed by archaeologists and anthropologists, an influx of Hyksos from the East began in Egypt's Delta. I believe the Indus craftsmen [and families] were brought to Crete for construction and to Egypt to colonize the Delta.   The architecture and housing improvements of potable water and sewage systems of Crete are identical to Parvaim [Thera] and the Indus civilization.

Brokers for Mediterranean trading were centered at Parvaim, providing the Aegean colonies with easy access to goods. During this time the Lord's operation was similar to that of a giant corporate structure, trade continued with Sumer and Egypt and empires beyond this area.

The wealth acquired through trade was used for several purposes, to begin the building phase on Crete, support Pharaohs' construction in Egypt, and to finance a large fleet of ships. The Phoenicians dominated the trade routes of the Mediterranean and Aegean Seas.

The primary focus of archaeologists has been on the palaces of Knossos, Phaistos, Mallia, and Zarkros. The palace of Knossos appears to have been the center of power on Crete. This assumption has been made because of its location, splendor and the thousands of clay receipt tablets found stored there.

Knossos was centrally located on the northern side of the island. A metropolis, beginning at the sea, surrounded the palace with a population of approximately eighty thousand residents. The community extended from the mountain valleys to the coastal settlements. The main routes from the coast to the palaces were paved, with guard posts at regular intervals.

The principle interest of historians has been focused on the architecture of the palace estates, described as remarkable monuments of magnificent architectural design. The palaces were all built alike, using the same plan and architectural design, incorporating large interior rectangular courts of identical shape and size. The courts were 168 feet in length and 75 feet in width. They were enclosed with grand pillars or columns like those seen in classic Greek architecture. The entrance to the palace contained a flight of twelve grand sweeping steps, which were 45 feet to 50 feet wide. Due to irregular ground levels, steps were frequently provided to assist in wandering through the terraced palace flower gardens and courtyards.

The palace at Knossos was built on the slope of a small hill that is estimated to be seven acres, providing a commanding view of the lower valley. East of the knoll a river flows to the lower valley and on to the sea. The southern side of the hill drops off into a deep gorge containing another torrent of water that flows into the river.

Prior to constructing the palace, a massive amount of earth was moved. It is estimated that twenty-five to thirty feet of dirt and rock was excavated to produce a level building site. Above this site another level area was constructed. On the first level the Lords built a two-story wing complex of grand apartments. The second story of the apartment complex was joined to the second palace level by a central court forming the base of the central structure of the palace.

The lower apartment complex was built around a magnificent ornate staircase consisting of four flights which was used to enter or exit the complex. Open courtyard gardens along each level served as skylights which illuminated the staircases. This structure has been described as a masterpiece of architecture and engineering design.

The palace consisted of several grand wings of rooms connected by long corridors. The interior halls were wide and decorated with large ornate columns. Each column contained engraved and convex spirals of lutes that began at the foot of the column and wound upwards to the ceiling. The decorative effect was that of a musical vine, spiraling around the column. These columns were the source for later classic Greek architecture.

Archaeologists spent years trying to unravel the secrets of the Minoan civilization and did an excellent job. They provided all the bits and pieces necessary to establish the framework of the civilization. However, they missed the most important clue that had been left for them. The rulers of Crete left several messages for future generations, within the Palace of Knossos, and until this time these messages have been overlooked.

The Palace administrative quarters were located in the western palace wing. Off of this wing a large set of stairs led to an upper great ceremonial hall where business meetings, parties, and communal feasts were held. The walls of the hall were decorated with fresco paintings of bare breasted royal ladies, with coiffure hairstyles and wearing long colorful flounced skirts. Their facial expressions gave them the appearance of being happy, beautiful beguiling women.

An extremely large painting depicts a young king leading a legendary sphinx, which has the body of a lion and the head of an eagle. The young king is surrounded by butterflies, which is the Minoan symbol for eternal life. Other than being large and colorful, this fresco painting has not received attention from the historical or archaeological community. This method of leaving a message is the signature of the historically obscure rulers of Crete, the Lords. The painting provides a veiled allegory, which requires an understanding of the paintings on the lower floors of the palace, to unlock the message.

An eastern wing of the palace contained fifteen hundred rooms of royal apartments. Each apartment was complete with running water and a bathroom connected to the palace sewer system that is as modern as we have today. The walls were decorated with elaborate fresco and mural paintings. The paintings usually depicted the lives and activities of the island residents. Most of the pictures were nature scenes of the island. In other areas of the palace the paintings depict a festival of hundreds of figures singing and dancing. They appear to be carrying gifts to a young man of royalty. All the paintings are of, or relate to, the life styles of the residents of the palace. A message was left in the fresco paintings, beginning in the less important areas of the palace.

The largest fresco, located in the most important area of the palace, is that of a young king, surrounded with butterflies, leading a legendary sphinx [noted as a Griffon]. The lower body of the sphinx is that of a lion, which is symbolic of the power of Egypt. The head is of an eagle, which is symbolic of the Ancient Masonic Lodge. Like the eagle, the Lodge was watchful of everything around it, was fierce, and like the eagle, would strike without warning.

The painting is the foundation for solving another secret found in Egypt. The young king and butterflies are symbolic of the Lords and their extended life spans. The scene depicts the Lords leading the power of Egypt through the Ancient Masonic Lodge, both of which are under the greater power of the Lords.

The symbolic butterflies are a trademark of the vanity of the Lords. The butterflies provided the means to follow the faint historical traces of the Lords. The trail leads to another civilization located in Central America.   The butterfly God of the Olmec and Mayan civilizations was symbolic of resurrection and eternal life.   These civilizations existed during the same time in history.

One more unique clue that remained at the Palace of Knossos was a labyrinth, or maze. This particular maze is known as the Cretan, or seven-circuit maze. A similar maze, a tri-spiral, was found at a site in the British Isles, at the now famous New Grange Megalithic Passage Tomb. The New Grange site is dated to about 3,200 BCE, further evidence of the mining colonies established by the Lords.

The following question is for Historians and Archaeologists who insist Man elevated the arts and sciences without introduced intelligence. What do you think the odds are of two totally different civilizations, existing on separate continents, at the same time, using the same symbolic references to depict resurrection and eternal life? I am sure there is an answer forthcoming. I really would like to hear something other than the lame phrase about the "*perseverance of Neolithic Artisans*," to explain introduced intelligence.

Under the main floor of the palace there was a vast basement area used for storage. Numerous chambers were used to store treasure, metal ingots, grain and vast amounts of food and wine. One basement chamber was filled with large stone vases and vats holding over a thousand gallons of wine and olive oil. Honey was also stored in great quantities.

The areas immediately outside the palace were manicured parks. The parks were complete with raised sidewalks connecting numerous private courtyards.   Open areas of the palace grounds were surrounded by gardens of flowers and shrubs. Outside the palace grounds a residential area of seventy very well-built houses surrounded a large grand house, built as a miniature copy of the palace. Within this area, archaeologists found the remains of a large workshop and numerous tools used for maintenance. This residential community was for palace servants.

Nearby there is a second residential area of grand houses, larger and more elaborate than any other homes on the island. It is believed these houses were for a group of resident priests. The answer to this secret is fairly simple.   The elaborate houses were built for the members of the Lodge. The reasoning for this answer is also simple. If you have an area of servants and a grand palace, the only thing missing would be the master craftsmen who were needed to maintain the structure and administer the business of trade.   Around this entire area was the metropolis spreading across the valley floor to the coastal docks and warehouses.

With Thera [Parvaim] as the center of power the Minoans emerged as a powerful, wealthy nation controlling all trade from the British Isles to India.   Knossos was the administrative center for an efficient trading monopoly.   The administrative records mirror those of the Sumerian civilization, with trade records meticulously recorded on clay tablets. The early language of the "Minoans", linear A, has yet to be deciphered.   The same statement applies to the early languages of Sumer, Indus and of Teotihuacan, Mexico. These original languages of the Lords have yet to be deciphered.

The Lords established trading posts in Greece by 3,000 BCE. One notable outpost was Troy. Colonies such as Mycenae were established in strategic locations in the southern region, providing control of the area. Another group of colonies was established along the coastal areas of Asia Minor, spreading their influence northward and southward.

By 2,600 BCE the Lords had successfully created a vast trading monopoly that consolidated their rule of the entire region. To facilitate trade across these great distances the Lords introduced new and larger cargo ships with engineering technology and designs previously unknown in the area. The Lords had used larger ships in their move to Crete in 3,000 BCE and in their relocation to the Americas. These new larger galleys also enhanced trade between the Americas and Egypt.

The new ships were sleek, trim galleys fitted with sail and twenty or more oars on each side. Some of the upper decks had canopies to shade the traveling elite. With favorable winds the ships could travel more than one hundred miles per day. The ships were built with a keel extending out of the ships bow, specifically built as a ramming device. The ram was fitted with a massive bronze end-piece which became a formidable weapon when needed. The ships ensured continuous Minoan prosperity based on trade from Greece to Egypt and in the regions between Sicily and Syria. These sea routes also extended to the British Isles and Africa.

By 3,000 BCE a new seafaring civilization emerged from the extensive sea trade routes. This new culture was supported by the Minoan trade coalitions as both a transporter and protector of trade goods. These seafarers were known as the **Phoenicians,** which translates as "*The Peoples of the Seas*".

An example of the strength of the Phoenician Civilization is located in present day eastern Lebanon. The site is **Baalbek**, translated as "Lord Baal of the Beqaa Valley", which has an ancient temple dedicated to Lord Bal. The Phoenicians, Greeks and Romans built temples at the same site. The real mystery of the site are ancient, fantastic smooth columns weighing from 100 tons to 900 tons. From the time of the Phoenicians to present day, no one has moved these stone marvels.

During this era of colonization, the most northern settlement was located on the mainland of Greece, where the Lords built another grand palace. This was the Palace of Mycenae, built in an area known as Argolis. Like the palace at Knossos, it served as an administrative center for records of trade. The same architectural design used for Crete was used to build the structure on the mainland. The palace was as elaborate and spacious as the Palace of Knossos, containing the same types of apartment wing complexes. One complex was used strictly for administrative purposes and, like Knossos, an upper complex contained a great ceremonial hall for meetings and feasts.

The Aegean fleets, although primarily used for trade, contained the most powerful navy of the times. A considerable number of their ships were sleek fighting vessels used to destroy pirates or ships that invaded their trading territory. The Mycenaeans were an independent warrior breed who successfully defended their civilization.

These City States were all governed by the extended families of the Lords. Each generation removed from the original Lords lost some of their life span. Even though they lived for only one or two thousand years, they were "Gods" to the local population.

When the Mycenae Palace site was first excavated, archaeologists applied the name to the surrounding villages, creating the Mycenaean Empire.   There were no complete towns along this mainland area although there were numerous settlements, built with a lack of uniformity. As the Minoan influence spread thorough the land, the Lords used the area without attempting to gain regional control. The situation could be described as a royal trading post within a barbarian world. Mycenae was on the verge of emerging into a civilized power.

The combined power projected by the Palace of Knossos, and the trade wealth brought into the region, allowed the Minoans to dominate the area.   The written Mycenaean language [known as Minoan Linear B Script] was developed at Knossos to facilitate trading from the mainland.   Linear B is a hieroglyphic script and is categorized as Archaic Greek and was well understood by the Egyptians.

The prosperity and political power of the Minoans continued to grow. They introduced their Phoenician fleets to even longer trade routes, with one route circling the entire continent of Africa. Along with the extended trade routes, the Lords introduced a new ship class called a *Tarshish*, which was over a hundred feet long, and built with a broad beam. The new ship was a heavy cargo carrier equipped with sails and a double bank of oars enabling it to sail open seas.

The Phoenicians ruled territory from both sides of the Straights of Gibraltar [Tarshish], the north coast of Africa and several

Mediterranean islands with ports in Sidon and Tyre. Ships from Tarshish are well known in Hebrew history.

The Phoenicians sailed another ship of greater size and capacity than the Tarshish class vessel. Little is known of this mighty vessel as it is only mentioned in legends of that time. It has been described as a great sailing ship with three banks of oars capable of long-range voyages. These great ships never surfaced in the history of Phoenician trading. For the areas they sailed, there was no need for three banks of oars. The logical conclusion for the necessity of such power would be to cross the Atlantic Ocean.   These were the ships used to transport groups of the Lords, and their treasure, to their final destinations of Central and South America in the era of 2,250 BCE. Many ancient legends discuss contacts with the great civilization across the Atlantic Ocean, "beyond the pillars of Hercules" [The Strait of Gibraltar].

In 1,628 BCE the Minoan civilization was at its greatest prosperity when it ended abruptly. Overnight the northern coastal towns and ports were devastated by Tsunamis and earthquakes, killing tens of thousands. Most of Parvaim [Thera] had vaporized in a cataclysmic volcanic explosion. Eruptions at Thera continued for centuries.

The rulers of Crete and their Masonic craftsmen vanished from Minoan history. Over the next 200 years the Mycenaean empire took possession of the island and became a power in the region for at least seventy years.   Historians theorized the Mycenaeans from the mainland invaded Crete and overthrew the Minoan rulers.

The theory of Mycenaean conquest was advanced simply because it provided an adequate explanation for the event. The problem with the theory is, there is no evidence to support it. Archaeologists have been unable to locate physical evidence of an invasion, such as discarded weapons, evidence of victims, or burned out boats in the main harbor. Archaeologists continued to search for answers even though historians were satisfied with their explanation for the sudden end to the civilization. During their exploration of the island they made an unusual discovery in the mountains of eastern central Crete; a hidden Minoan sanctuary.

The discovery of the sanctuary is in an area described as a small hidden valley, 3600 feet above sea level. Mountain peaks rising to 7000 feet dominate the valley. One of the peaks is a natural pillar of stone referred to as the *Nail* because of its unusual formation and is accessed from the backside plateau.   The local name for this promontory is Karfi. A settlement of one hundred and fifty rooms is located on this towering pinnacle of rock.

Karfi is located in the Dikti Mountains of eastern Crete. A relatively unexplored aspect of the Nail location is that it provided a line of sight to the various palaces and other "Peak Sanctuaries" across Crete.

These elevated sites provided instant communication across Crete and to Thera by using mirrors to flash code, or signal fires at night. This opens the probability that the Lords developed a "Morris Code" for their language. This could only occur with an advanced written language used by the civilization.

Karfi – The Nail is easily accessed from the backside plateau

Archaeologists found evidence this settlement, and many other "Peak Sanctuaries", was continuously occupied from 1,600 BCE to 1,100 BCE. Instead of finding answers, the archaeologists only added to the mystery of the fall of Crete. To solve the mystery of the settlement's existence, historians produced another unusual theory. They published articles claiming the survivors of the Mycenaean invasion fled to the sanctuary and occupied it until 1,100 BCE. This would mark the beginning of the Greek "Dark Ages".

This explanation is totally without merit. Clearly the story was given to fill an historical gap. The lower valley showed no signs of farming or habitation. During this time in history, the average life span of native Man, under the best conditions, was approximately forty years. The settlement was occupied for 500 years. These years equate to at least eighteen generations of families living on a towering mountain peak. It is ridiculous to believe a normal group of people could live in such a small sanctuary, producing eighteen generations of families over 500 years, without being discovered.

If you are beginning to understand the realities of history, there is a very plausible answer for the sanctuary. There were no settlements of families producing generation after generation of people, until after 1,000 BCE. The hidden sanctuary was used by the Lords to store equipment, probably some wealth, and to provide for their total security, if and when they needed it. Many sanctuaries were built during the early development of Crete, showing their use was anticipated. This leads to the question; how did the Lords arrive and leave the mountain peak?

The Mycenaeans eventually had possession of the entire island, including its only natural harbor. This means they controlled the roads and the access to the sea. For the sanctuary to remain undiscovered there could not have been any roads or paths to it. The only avenue of travel left to enter or exit the site was by air.

When the Minoan civilization came to an end the surviving Lords who wished to leave departed for The Americas. They were led by one who was blond or red headed [Lord Bal], and would be called Kulkukan or The Feathered Serpent in the Americas. In Babylon he was known as the Invincible Sun God and the Feathered Serpent.

The Lords who were allied with Lord Yahweh joined him in Canaan or relocated to Egypt's Delta to deal with an event developing there. Many groups of lesser Lords [renegade groups] remained in areas of Sumer, Iran and central Asia. They left men and machines in hidden sanctuaries in the regions next to Egypt.

Avaris, the capitol of the Hyksos in the Nile Delta, was the site of a large Minoan palace. The Lords there were still allied with the Phoenicians for trade and military backing, supporting the Hyksos battle with the Egyptians.

TL 5 Egyptian Secrets

2000 CE

0 BCE

YEARS BCE

1,180	Setnakht expelled Hyksos in 2nd "Exodus" reclaims looted gold
1,140	Hebrews attack Canaanite Kingdoms
1,450	Yahweh's Temple built on Mt. Gerizim in Samaria
1,533	Ahmose I routs Hyksos in 1st "Exodus" sends Hyksos back to Canaan
1,628	Thera explodes and Crete is decimated – ending support for the Hyksos
1,880	Joseph is appointed to the Temple of On by Pharaoh Sesostris – Amun is the Sun God
1,900	First Hyksos capital at Avaris—Minoan trade routes to the Americas
2,080	Abram journeys to Zoan [Avaris]
2,490 to 2,550	3 Giza pyramids built: Khufu [largest] Khafre [middle] Menkaure [smallest]
3,000	Yahweh builds Minoan Villa in Samaria
4,400	Scorpion Kings of Nagada [The Ka] rule Upper Egypt to 3,200 BCE
6,000	Temples and Cities in Sumer—writing improved from ancient Pre-Deluge Sumer Writings—Egypt's Delta organized into Nomes
7,000	Sphinx Head Monument in place
8,000	Egypt has organized farming villages Sahara is lush savannah and forest
10,000	Gobekli Tepe temple is purposely buried in northern Sumer
10,900	Comet impact of Earth causes Pleistocene Extinction
18,000	Lords establish civilizations in Asian And American Continents

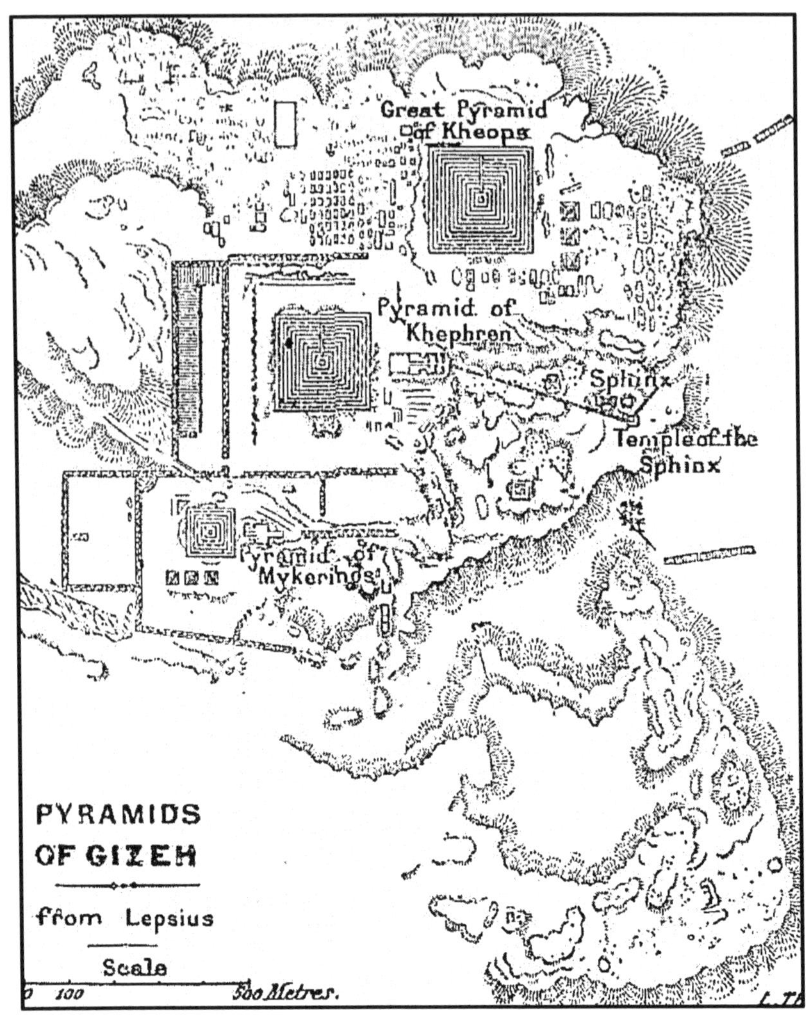

Egypt's Beginning 3,100 BCE

Chapter 7

EGYPTIAN SECRETS

Now King Rameses was a great conqueror and a mighty man of valor, who numbered among his vassals princes of no mean degree. These latter came every year to Naharaina, at the mouth of the Euphrates, to do homage to their overlord and to render tribute to him.
[ANCIENT EGYPTIAN MYTHS AND LEGENDS   -   Author Lewis Spence, Dover Pub.]

Lord Yahweh and Lord Bal were definitely in the leadership circle of the Lords of Sumer. Yahweh's purpose changed from being rescued to having his Tribe worship him as The Great One, that is, "God". He was apparently a narcissist as he constantly invoked new laws and harsh treatment on the Hebrews. In response to his abuse they constantly fell in with their cousins who worshipped Bal.

Lord Bals' Tribes were given free rein to do whatever they wished, and worshipped Bal as the Sun God. This is an obvious key to know who was supporting which civilizations. Yahweh was incensed that Bal drew such great followings and he [Yahweh] had to constantly struggle to keep his followers.

Yahweh, throughout this odyssey we have pursued, has been somewhat of a loser. He was obviously a narcissist and hardcore disciplinarian for his tribe's pursuits of life and pleasure. According to the ancient accounts, he thought little of killing anyone to set an example.

He spent a lot of time at his mountain-top villa in Samaria and built his Palace by 3000 BCE. I think he resented Bal's popularity on Crete and

Bal's mention in the Enuma Elish as the "God of Creation". He compensated with planning for the right time to bring his people together and inflict some long overdue punishment.

Lord Yahweh had different motives than rescue. Rather than leave his People, the Hebrew Tribes, who at times worshipped him as God, and pursue rescue from this planet, he chose to stay in the Middle East as God.

Egyptian history emerged in the Paleolithic period before 8,500 BCE. Egypt began a slow, progressive social advance of developing communities in Upper Egypt and in the Nile Delta.

By 8,000 BCE the Saharan [Future Desert] area of North Africa was covered with lakes, forest and savannah. This lush, warm zone provided vast areas for animal herds and nomadic communities which grew into the North African civilizations. The development along the Nile was typical of other Paleolithic cultures, as the first structures built were one-room mud and reed huts. As the population increased, a series of huts were built close or walled together with plaster, forming the first permanent tribal communities.

The inhabitants of Lower Egypt were non-aggressive farmers dependent on agriculture and fishing to sustain their lives. Their entire focus was on their daily existence. The semi-dependent tribal communities were built along the banks of the Nile River and widespread in the Nile Delta. Their existence depended on the annual floods of the river to fertilize their small farms.

The Nile originates in the Lake Victoria region, which lies far to the south of the Mediterranean Sea coast. During its journey to the sea, smaller tributaries feed the great river. Seasonal rains in the upper regions bring floods to the lowlands each year, carrying fertile silt from Upper Egypt to the Nile Delta. Ancient Man recognized the Delta as an excellent area to farm and hunt. The Delta had many channels leading to the sea, providing shipping lanes to all settlements. The resulting agriculture provided the foundation for one of the worlds' greatest civilizations.

These annual floods often buried existing settlements in several feet of mud, requiring relocation. The inhabitants moved to the edge of the Delta during flood season.

In the Delta, c. 5,500 BCE, structures were made of wood and plaster with very little stonework. The stonework was usually limited to idols of their Gods. The Delta areas [Lower Egypt] were ruled for several thousand years as "Kings" developed in the Pre-Dynastic Period. Eventually Lower Egypt was divided into 20 Nomes [districts], each ruled by a Nomarch during the 2nd Dynasty.

The term of "Dynasty" was given to Kings who ruled Upper and Lower Egypt.

The town of On [Annu], a few miles north of Memphis, founded in pre-historic time, was the seat of power for the 1st and 2nd Dynasties, although the 1st dynasty started at Thinnis. The 3rd Dynasty moved the short distance from On to Memphis.   The Priesthood needed separation from the King.

On is one of the most important cities of Egypt. It was called Beth-Shemesh [house of the sun], an Hyksos name. It produced the Pyramid Texts, [myth of Osiris, Set murdering Osiris] the oldest religious texts of Egypt. On was a temple of the Sun God, Ra, and also Atum, the setting sun, or the sun of the Underworld. On also produced the Book of the Dead, which was being documented for centuries prior to 4,400 BCE.

On was a power base of the Lodge Priests and Kings into the 15th Dynasty when the Hyksos built a defensive wall of fortification in the city. The Giza plateau is located approximately eight miles west and across the Nile from On.

The First Dynasty of Egypt was led by King Menes [3,200 BCE or earlier] who unified upper and lower Egypt. This dynasty was in the Egyptian Archaic Period, when the seat of government was centered at Thinis, located north of Thebes. Menes succeeded the Naqada Scorpion Kings [Ka] of Pre-dynastic Egypt [4,400-3,200 BCE], named for the town of Naqada.

The Second Dynasty of Egypt 2,890 – 2,686 BCE is the latter of the two dynasties of the Archaic Period. Except for the last ruler Khasekhemwy, it has few records in ancient Egyptian history. Its center of power was The Temple of On.

The Third Dynasty, 2,686 to 2,613 BCE, was founded by King Djoser [2,686 to 2,667 BCE] and was located at Memphis. The Third Dynasty is the first dynasty of the Old Kingdom. Other dynasties of the Old Kingdom include the Fourth, Fifth and Sixth. The capital during these dynasties was Memphis, located near the beginning of the Delta and it is the divider of Upper and Lower Egypt.

This was a period of massive stone construction in Egypt. The stonemasons and craftsmen came from Canaan and Sumer, the only civilizations at that time which produced skilled craftsmen. These craftsmen, and their families, were followers of Bal. Not only did they build, they assimilated and became Egyptians.

The craftsmen bolstered the Egyptian civilization by introducing new techniques for crafts and farming. Primarily the new methods focused on metallurgy, pottery, and simple architectural structures. The Masons were bound by their oaths of secrecy not to reveal more knowledge than the Lords allowed.

The massive construction during the next 500 years in Egypt was extremely expensive. The funding for this, the buildup of Egypt's Temples and the Pharaohs power came from the only source available; The trade barons of Thera and Crete. Without this massive influx of finance and technology Egypt would have continued along as mediocre kingdoms. The High Priest of On, the Masonic Grand Master Imhotep, was the driving force for the entire Third Dynasty. He produced a great priestly sect of builders governed by the Lodge.

The Temple of On was dedicated to the Sun God [Lord Bal] and many other Gods [children of the Sun God]. It was known as the College of Annu and was the On of the Holy Writ. The Greeks named it Heliopolis. Due to the religion it is evident Bal was the driving force of the Lords for this business venture. Trade was expanding in the Mediterranean, the Middle East and into Africa by land and sea.

Imhotep was a mathematical genius and great builder of monumental architecture. He and his priests were regarded with great esteem by the royal court of King Djoser [Pharaoh Zoser]. During these years of royal protection, the priests operated openly as the architects and administrators of the Pharaohs.

Imhotep provides us with the first glimpse of early Masonic political power derived from his genius for building elaborate structures. He also appears to be the first known Grand Master of the Ancient Masonic Lodge in Egypt. To give our present-day Blue Lodge members a glimpse into their distant past, it took twenty-two years to pass from an Entered Apprentice to the next Masonic level.

Imhotep and his group designed and built the first Egyptian pyramid for King Djoser. It is known as the Step Pyramid, built south of the Giza plateau in an area called Saqqara. The structure was the first of its kind to be built of stone. It began a new generation of architecture for Egypt. A complex of intricate subsidiary buildings including temples, crypts, and courtyards surrounded the Step Pyramid. Imhotep lived to about 2,620 BCE, into the reign of the Pharaoh Huni, the last king of this dynasty.

Historians and archaeologists argue the stepped pyramid was a "test". They conclude the pyramid was to be built as the following pyramids were constructed, with smooth sloped sides. Further, that the stepped pyramid only came to be after the structure began to fail. The stepped pyramid was built as designed. It had a specific purpose in being a stepped structure. I am certain of this because some pyramids built in Central and South America are also stepped in structure. The coincidence is too great to be ignored. This conclusion of purposeful construction is stated by renowned Egyptologists.

In Lower Egypt archaeologists recently discovered an unusual stone city. The city has remained hidden by sand, twenty to thirty feet below present-day ground level. It has been determined this city was built in 5,500 BCE. It may have been the source of labor for the Temple of Annu [On].

The problem for historians is they believe Neolithic Man did not possess the intelligence or tools to construct the city, they rely on the same story they have for Sumer. The city remains a mystery to archaeologists because it does not present any evidence concerning who built the structures. The stone buildings are conspicuously absent of petroglyphs or hieroglyphic writings, and the area is lacking in the usual broken or discarded pottery. Usually an area such as this contains statues and graves of the former leaders of the civilization, but in this case, there are none.

There are thousands of small tombs for the workers that died, providing evidence they were not slaves, but paid craftsmen.

The craftsmen were sent to the Lower Egyptian region to build boundary markers. The methods used were not unique to Egypt, as these same practices were used in Sumer. The Lords used massive, advanced structures to advertise to any person entering the area, that the ownership of the entire region had been claimed. The stone city informed native Man the region was claimed by a mighty civilization.

Pylon at Karnak

The Great Sphinx of Giza - Photo 1858 of the beginning of excavation of sand covering base.   Note the different rock formation of the head to the sandstone "base".   The Head was sculptured long before the body was created when the surrounding stone was quarried for the Temple and causeway constructions.   The "Khafre" head was re-sculptured when the temple was built.

1800's French Archaeological Team at Giza uncovering Temple Priest's housing

The Giza Plateau is the site of the Great Sphinx. It is 66 feet high, with the head rising about 26 feet above the lion body. The massive lower body is 241 feet in length and 62 feet wide, appearing as a fascinating symbol of the power of ancient Egypt.

Giza is also home to three remaining pyramids. The first built, and largest, was built by Pharaoh Khufu in 2,550 BCE. The second, mid-sized, was built by Pharaoh Khafre in 2,520 BCE. The third and smallest was built by Pharaoh Menkaure in 2,490 BCE.

Archaeologists have discovered a massive complex beneath the Sphinx. Beginning at the Sphinx Temple, underground rooms and tunnels provide secret access to the three pyramids. There are air and light shafts for the underground complex, which also served as a means to lower mummified bodies into the access tunnels.

The Great Sphinx does not appear in any known inscriptions describing its construction or its original purpose. The Sphinx is a monolith carved into the layered bedrock of the plateau, which also served as the quarry for the funeral temples' construction.

In front of the Sphinx is a temple complex on the ancient bank of the Nile River. It was constructed to house priests who prepared kings for burial and to keep the Nile River and surrounding areas under constant observation. The causeway from the Sphinx Temple to Khafre's Great pyramid was built around the Sphinx, indicating the Sphinx was already in place.

Some scientists and archaeologists date the Sphinx to 7,000 BCE; however, these findings are labeled pseudo-archaeology by *Academia* and, of course, they have never been in error.

Many archaeologists have noticed the head of the Sphinx is out of proportion with its massive lion body, appearing to be too small. One theory regarding this feature is that the head was originally constructed in correct proportion to the body but was reconfigured to provide a portrait statue of a ruling king. Historians correctly concluded the reconfiguration was the stone portrait of King Khafre, also known as *Chephren* of the Fourth Dynasty [2,558 to 2,532 BCE]. The original re-sculpture was complete with a sacred cobra head-dress and the braided beard hanging from the chin.

The theory of the head being out of proportion suggests that the Head and body were originally made at the same time. This is not correct; the massive Sphinx head was sculptured aeons before the body was created by the quarry excavation.

Recent geologic investigations of the stone quarry surrounding the Sphinx found the quarried blocks were used to construct the temple in front of the Sphinx. Absolute matches were made between the quarry walls and individual blocks of the temple. It was very well documented and certainly convinced me that the lion body and temples were dated to the Great Pyramid construction, but not the head of the Sphinx. The limestone formation of the head is noted as Member III, which is a much more durable limestone than the lower Member II layers.

The head of the Sphinx was carved from an outcrop of durable limestone which protruded well above the desert sands. There are no remnants from the head carving which have been identified, or any indications this has been investigated. There is no doubt the huge desert carving was chosen to be enlarged and enhanced as part of the overall Pyramid of the Sun construction. Dating of the Sphinx head, to an exact time, has not been accomplished.

Egyptian stelae have been deciphered which state that Khafre found the Sphinx, but the circumstances are unclear and the name "Khafre" was assumed to be the one inscribed. I believe Pharaoh Khufu chose to build his pyramid near the ancient sphinx head and the body was added by the process of excavating the quarry.   The underground access tunnels were added as each pyramid was built.

The original Sphinx head was constructed prior to ruling dynasties, with tools and craftsmanship the Stone Age Egyptians did not possess. The only craftsmen who possessed the tools to sculpt the Sphinx head were from the Sumerian region. The clues to the original features of the head come from the island of Crete and the Minoan civilization.

At the palace of Knossos, in the great ceremonial hall, there is a fresco painting of the original Sphinx. It portrays the Sphinx with the head of an eagle.   These Sphinxes are labeled as Griffons.   The fresco depicting the Sphinx was completed after 2,000 BCE, well after the redesign to complement Khafre.   The redesign of the Sphinx also removed this not so subtle symbol of the Lodge. There is no reason to believe the people who designed this massive structure would portray it in anything other than its original form. A few original small sphinx statues survived and are known as "Falcon Sphinx."

The original form of the sphinx was designed to project a powerful symbolic message.   The Sphinx served the same purpose as the ziggurats in Sumer. The massive eagle head, rising above the sands, projected the strength of the builders.

Some 1906 historians date the first Dynasty at 5,500 BCE, however this date may refer to early Kings and rulers. These historians also correlated Egyptian mythology and beliefs of underworlds and symbolism with Maya mythology and symbolism. I did say at the beginning of this work that nothing in this book is new. I am certain that even my *brilliant* observations have been written before my time.

The first king of the 4th Dynasty [2,613 to 2,494 BCE] was King Sneferu who reigned from 2,613 to 2,589 BCE. He finished the first true pyramid of Egypt, the Red Pyramid, and built more pyramids of all types, than any other Pharaoh.

The second ruler was King Khufu [2,589 – 2,566 BCE]. He was also known as Cheops and during his reign, built the largest of the three pyramids at Giza. The structure is known as the Great Pyramid Cheops, or the Pyramid of Ra [the Sun]. Its height is 481 feet, and the entire structure covers an area of 13.1 acres. It was constructed with 2.3 million stone blocks. Each block weighed at least two and a half tons, with some weighing up to fifteen tons.

On completion, the entire structure was carefully fitted with a shell of white polished stone, as were the other two pyramids. Time and purposeful destruction have since removed the more thinly cut rock, so that at present we see only the basic rough construction phase. In the distant past, the three structures were gleaming white monuments, with the very top of the Pyramid of Ra covered in gold producing a gleaming "be-jewel".

The final phase of construction consisted of a stone wall surrounding the pyramid. The wall formed a courtyard containing several buildings at the pyramid entrance. The largest building was the Mortuary Temple. From the Mortuary Temple an attached raised stone causeway, several thousand feet long, leads to a valley temple. Therefore, the only way to gain entrance to the pyramid was through the valley temple. The temple housed the priests who provided security for the entire complex. Subterranean tunnels were used only by the Temple Priests.

The plans and motivation to build such a massive structure came from the priests. They were well versed in manipulating the Pharaoh's royal vanity to achieve their objectives. The Pharaohs were taught from birth to believe they were divine rulers, second only to the Gods of the land. The priests had only to appeal to their vanity to receive permission to build the pyramids.

They convinced the Pharaoh the royal tomb would mark his passing as the greatest ruler ever to live. He was also persuaded that the great size was necessary to store his possessions for his resurrection journey to the next world. To this day our society follows Egyptian funerary practices, preserving bodies for their eventual "resurrection."

Funding for this project was not a problem as the Minoan civilization was funneling vast amounts of wealth to Egypt. It was an integral part of the Lords' plan to provide the wealth necessary to build the structure. Their objective was a massive structure which would serve as an astrological observatory. It was necessary for this building to last for centuries as they continued with their plan for rescue. The Egyptian civilization, strong and free from the threat of invasion, combined with the pyramids, provided the answer for their needs.

The Giza pyramids were constructed exactly alike with the exception of size. Some astronomers claim the layout of these three pyramids, and their corresponding sizes, mirror the three stars of the constellation Orion in 8,500 BCE. The observation shaft in the great pyramid also aligns with Orion.

The pyramids have been written about for the past several hundred years. To reveal the secrets the structures held, they have been measured, photographed, x-rayed, explored, drilled, tunneled into, climbed over, and dug under. Every possible structural angle has been mapped and investigated. One team of investigators even used sound waves to probe the massive structures.

The fact that each of the pyramids on the Giza plateau is the product of mathematical marvel and genius has been fully explored. These structures have attracted mathematicians since 1638. In 1820 one investigator was surprised when he divided the perimeter of the pyramid by twice its height, the result was identical to the value of pi [π] [3.14159+]. This is the number, that when multiplied by the diameter of a circle, gives its circumference. Pi is a mathematical constant with no ending decimal place, it never changes.

From those days forward, every possible angle has been surveyed. All the conclusions were basically the same. Ancient Man should not have possessed the mathematical knowledge to build the structures.

There have been books written which openly conclude the structures were built and maintained by the Ancient Masonic Lodge in Egypt. It is no longer a secret that ancient astronomers used the grand galleries of the pyramids for celestial observations. The accumulation of information includes a host of multipurpose uses, including charting the stars to obtain precise seasonal changes. The shadow of the pyramids was used as a sundial calendar, indicating the seasons and the length of the year. One mathematician produced evidence the priests charted astrological cycles based on the premise of 3,625-year cycles.

Who was this projection of intelligence intended to impress? It could not have been for ancient Man. They did not possess the ability to recognize the mathematics involved. Also, it took Western civilization until 1820 CE to partially grasp the mathematics involved, a result of French archaeologist Champollion breaking the Egyptian hieroglyph code.

Why bother putting so much effort into impressing people several thousand years in the future? Most of us cannot think that far ahead. This symbol of pure mathematics and advanced intelligence was meant to be seen, and that is the answer. It was to be seen by people who possessed the same level of intelligence and within a specific time frame. This was the reason the Lords expended so much effort providing Egypt with a stable progression of civilization.

The Pyramids were designed to draw attention from the air. A closer inspection would project a representation of Earth ratios, constellations, equations, and pure mathematics that alluded to the advanced intelligence of the designers of the structures. The pyramids would project a message that the Lords were alive and awaiting rescue. In their later history, the Lords produced other images on the ground their rescuers would recognize from the air. This recognition would be based on structures the rescuers were familiar with. Simply stated, the construction was something the rescuers had seen before in a different area of the universe.

The precision of the construction of the pyramids provided an advanced observatory to chart constellations, some of which have only recently been visible with modern observatories. The entrance to the pyramid initially consisted of a long downward sloping passage. By looking up from the lower end, the entrance became a grand gallery to observe the stars. Because of the depth of the passageway the gallery could be used day or night to observe the passing constellations.

The pyramids were built to an exact north-south meridian providing the priests with a precise mathematical baseline to chart the stars. This baseline was used to chart the movements of various constellations in exact times. As a star passed the meridian line, it was timed until it reached another fixed point or meridian line. The time between the points was then applied to a mathematical formula. The formula established time and distance from one star to another, and the time and distance from the star to the Earth. This method is used in modern observatories.

One scientific study provided information that the descending angle of the passageway was precisely constructed at twenty-six degrees and seventeen minutes. This allowed for the observation of specific constellations, such as Alpha Draconis. The priests appeared to be obsessed with the study and charting of the stars within various constellations. The secret of the observations, under the direction of the Lords of Sumer, was the priests were using the observatory as a giant sextant. This practice is the same as ship captains used to chart their location on open seas. They were using the stars and planets to establish the time of their rescue, based on universal time and distance. Another way of explaining this is, *they were using the universe as we use a clock and a map.*

Another facet of charting the stars added to the power of the priests. This power was the introduction of astrology. Astrology is pseudo-science [fake] claiming to foretell the future by studying the influence of celestial bodies on the affairs of individuals. This practice of foretelling royal futures added to the priests' stature in the royal court. The priests could directly influence the decisions of the Pharaoh and other individuals of importance. Because of the wealth and power derived from its use, astrology quickly spread throughout all civilizations.

The priests used a simple system to reinforce their predictions. They used everyone from slaves, handmaids, guards, and others as social spies. They usually knew beforehand what royalty wanted to hear. If the prediction was within their means, the priests supported or made the event happen. The priests were also taught the arts of "magic." As will be later documented, some priests studied for 40 years to master techniques provided by the Lords.

A structure in Upper Egypt, constructed by workmen about 2,200 BCE, was a monumental labyrinth of multiple connected maze features. The structure, in total, was equal to or greater than the buildings and structures of the Giza plateau. This site, although destroyed for its materials in later times was a center for teaching the mysteries of the Lodge, conducting rituals for the Sun God and a proving ground for priests.

The most notable member of 6th dynasty was Pepi II, who is credited with a reign of 94 years. During this time the Egyptian nobility grew in power and usurped the Kings, bringing the end of the Old Kingdom and an overall decline of Egypt. Pharaohs continued to build pyramids as tombs, and the tombs continued to be looted [by the next king].

Because of what I will present to you concerning the OT Holy Writ, this Egyptian history was necessary to establish a factual foundation. Egypt continued a decline into the 11th Dynasty [2,000 BCE] and the coming of The Hyksos. The 12th Dynasty constructed 9 pyramids from 1,990 to 1,800 BCE, with 7 Kings and 1 Queen.

The Lords established trade routes between Egypt and the Americas prior to 2,000 BCE, bringing such items as cocaine and tobacco to the ruling class of Egypt. This trade was validated by testing performed on hair samples removed from Egyptian mummies. The testing used gas chromatograph technology, which positively identified the presence of nicotine and cocaine residue. The fact that the residual chemicals were found in hair samples is irrefutable evidence that living people ingested the drugs. The drugs were not a result of later contamination.

At that time in our history, the Americas were the only source of these compounds. What better way could there be to control the ruling class of any country? Note: The Lady Scientist who discovered the ingestion of Cocaine and Nicotine by the Egyptian Royalty rocked the scientific world with her news. Although I had heard rumors of this possibility as far back as the 1950s, no one with academic tenure would dare openly express the thought. Guess who fell before the "slings and arrows" of her peers? Remember, history and religion has been set in stone. Let not the unwashed change the thought processes that produced "*The perseverance of Neolithic Artisans.*"

The history of the Hebrew people was skillfully merged with the history of Sumer and the Egyptian civilization to produce absolute fantasy. These fables, interspersed with their genealogy would be the story of the Nation of Israel. The laws and edicts of Lord Yahweh in the Hebrew OT were an attempt to unify his legacy and were included in the "history".

To this point we have set the stage of "THE BEGINNING" of this epic time of the Lords not only surviving on Earth but establishing entire civilizations with their own "Gods" and histories. These Gods and histories have evolved as the survival of the fittest in true form. Even with the guidance and interference of the various factions of Lords, a natural selection evolved as Man chose which Gods and which cultures suited him best. This is Evolution at its finest.

Other than Lord Yahweh, the Lords had no problems with the people under their control worshiping all manner of Gods and idols. Lord Yahweh, however, was worshipped as a God, and intended to maintain that status. He was a jealous, harsh and vengeful God, and would not tolerate his People paying homage to any other form of Gods. All of the Lords, including Lord Yahweh, approved of Human sacrifice. This is documented in archaeological excavations and in the history recorded in the "Old Testament" portion of The Holy Writ.

YEARS BCE | 70 CE | TL 7 Yahweh and Torah

300	Torah mostly complete— is finished 70 CE
700	Age of Prophets 750—600 Hebrews exiled Torah is beginning to form
922	King Solomon dies and the kingdom splits
950	Lord Yahweh dies and kingdom declines
1,020	King Saul 1st King of United Hebrew Kingdom
1,180	Setnakht expelled Hyksos in 2nd "Exodus" reclaims looted gold
1,400	Hebrews conquer Canaanite Kingdoms and invade Egypt's Delta
1,450	Yahweh's Temple built on Mt. Gerizim in Samaria
1,533	Pharaoh Ahmose I routs Hyksos in 1st "Exodus" chases Hyksos back to Canaan
1,628	Thera explodes, Crete, N. Egypt and Med area destroyed By Tsunamis and volcanic ash - Hyksos support ends from Lord Bal
1,850	Pharaoh rewards Joseph with land in Canaan [includes Judah and Samaria]
1,880	Joseph rules as "The Minister of Egypt" from the Temple of On by Pharaoh Sesostris - Amun is the Sun God
2,080	Abram travels to "Zoan" [Avaris] in 11th Dynasty
3,000	Yahweh builds Minoan Palace at Mt. Gerizim [Samaria]
3,200	King Menes 1st Egyptian dynasty [some date at 5,867 BCE?]
10,000	First Holy Writ — Enuma Elish develops

Book II

The Holy Land Chronicles

God Anu in his winged sky-disc

Chapter

1

God Enki creating the
world - Enuma Elish

HOLY WRITS and GENESIS
In The Beginning Man Discovered Earth

"After the kingship descended from heaven, the kingship was in Eridug. In Eridug, Alulim became king; he ruled for 28,800 years."

[From the Sumerian Kings List for the first known God of Sumer, King Alulim - 254,000 years ago]

[OT] Genesis Chapter 6 vs. 1-4
"And it came to pass, when men began to multiply on the face of the earth, and daughters were born unto them, That the sons of God saw the daughters of men that they were fair; and they took them wives of all which they chose. And the Lord said, my spirit shall not always strive with man, for that he also is flesh: yet his days shall be an hundred and twenty years. There were giants in the earth in those days; and also after that, when the sons of God came into the daughters of men, and they bare children to them, the same became mighty men which were of old, men of renown."

This ancient history has been muddled by religious and social tunnel vision, mythology and superstition. These formidable forces have merged into concepts of spiritual fear. Most people believe if they dare to think beyond what was written by ancient scribes, they will suffer an irreversible punishment, the damnation of their souls. The purpose of this exploration is to challenge social and religious superstitions. It is time to re-think our concept of the ancient Gods, especially Yahweh.

Most of us appreciate mythology and epic tales of old. We also realize most ancient tales have some factual basis of beginnings. We have the ability to think, reason and make judgments based on reality and common sense. *Western Teaching*, that we are the only humans in this universe, is a limiting concept that affects our perspective of reality. The existence of humans in other galaxies does not equate to weird alien beings, as they are people like us. The term alien is applied to anyone not a citizen of a particular country. It has been mutated to mean something weird and sci-fi.

If you can clear your mind of Western Theology, superstitions, and other religious mysticism, you will begin to understand Biblical history as never before.

The "Masoretic Text" and the "Samarian Pentateuch" were first assembled from about 700 to 486 BCE and became the foundation for *The Holy Writ*. This was about 1,000 years after the fabled "Exodus". It contains names and genealogy which can help establish some true history. The fables glorify Lord Yahweh when Lord Bal was the true power of the region and civilizations. In Sumer Bal was called *Anu*, "The King of Gods".

The Torah [Old Testament] was assembled from several sources. Four of these are titled; the Yahwist, "J", Deuteronomist, "D", Elohist "E" and the Priestly, "P". These four main sources were combined to produce the Pentateuch, the five books of "Moses": Genesis, Exodus, Leviticus, Numbers and Deuteronomy. Revisions continued into the First Century CE and outright censorship came from the Vatican in the 1500s CE.

While exploring the Holy Writs we must consider the Enuma Elish. The Enuma Elish contains stories [records?] of the first Gods, their lives, struggles and battles. There are tales of making First Man from the blood of Gods, of the great flood and an "Ark" and the building of empires. The Enuma Elish was written by the Sumerians, Akkadians and Babylonians with changes through time. This Holy Writ Epic was sung, read and recited at religious festivals during these empires, as homage and reverence to the Gods. In each kingdom the favorite God is recorded as living there and was added to the Epic. With this consideration, and having read many of the ancient records, it is apparent the Enuma Elish was the **First Holy Writ** known to Man.

In several Semitic languages, *Elohim* referred to a pantheon of seven Gods. *Elohim* translates as "*The children of El*", *El* being the "Most High" of the Gods. The listings for the Hebrew and Canaanite Gods are considerable. These lists contain Assyrian, Babylonian and Egyptian Gods as well as Yahweh [Elohim]. Yahweh's vision for his Tribe was for it to be a theocracy with himself as the Lord of the land. Many of these "God" names are the same God with names changed due to different civilizations and languages.

The Pentateuch is in the same category as the legends of some Egyptian Pharaohs who actually got their asses kicked, but the scribes knew how to show them as heroes. The "historical" writings were skewed to portray the writer's leaders as heroes. This assured the scribes would be around to record the next epic deeds of the king.

What follows is the best I could do with actual deciphered ancient text and the genealogy of the Holy Writ. I can tell you now that "Joseph ruled over Egypt" and "Moses and the Exodus" did not occur as portrayed.

I recited so much Egyptian history hoping to establish a base of reality. So, the story will be as entertaining as possible, while including the Biblical characters and fables. We will explore in detail "Moses and the Exodus" beginning with the formation of Genesis. Once we get to Ibrahim's [Abraham's] Journey from Ur, in Sumer, to Egypt's Delta you will understand this entire fable.

Genesis begins a spiritual journey through history written for the Hebrew Tribes by Enoch. Lord Yahweh is recorded as God, savior and guiding force who saved and protected his tribe. He finally established his Theocracy in Samaria after the Hyksos were defeated and run out of Egypt by Kamose and Ahmose I in 1533 BCE.

The Egyptian name for the Hebrews, Canaanites and southern Sumerians was the Aanu, meaning followers of "Anu". Anu was the supreme Sumerian God known as the "King of the Gods" and "Supreme Ruler of the Kingdom of Heaven". They were also known as **Hyksos**, which meant "*Shepard Kings*", or "Rulers of Foreign Nations".

The social difficulties in disclosing this history lie within the religious scotomas of our society. In our search for spirituality, we often leave reality behind. We rely on acceptance of mythology to arrive at what we believe to be a spiritual existence. This mythology, having been taught to most of us from birth as truth, is extremely difficult, mentally, to perceive as anything else.

An example of these mythological attitudes and/or beliefs is that it took six days to create the Earth, yet the planet is billions of years old. These interpretations allude to placing time limitations on the creation of our Universe. We really do not need mythology to begin to understand the power and infinity of the Universe. What we do need, to overcome these mythological attitudes, is a platform of reality, which is, the universe is infinite, and continues to recreate itself, without any limitation of time or distance.

This research may appear as an attack on the validity of the many *Holy Writs* and *Organized Religions*. **It is**. It did not start that way, but the more fairy-tales I found over the last 40 years, the more truth oriented this research became. I will let the truth of history, logic and reasoning, and your good common sense be the judge of any validity issues of the various Holy Writs.

What is in question are the fairy tale transliterations, which obscure the real truths and secrets contained in these most valuable books. A noted philosopher of the Holy Writ stated, "Theology is the use of philosophy to try to understand God so it [the premise] is believable and understandable. What is not understandable is covered under Faith".

Pope Leo X, born Giovanni di Lorenzo de' Medici, was Pope from 9 March 1513 to his death in 1521. He remarked, "This myth of Christ has served us well". This quote is widely disputed by church historians and devotees of the Pope yet it appeared in the journals of his "Cabin Boys", that is, his Bishops. Note his family name "Medici" as you will read more about this family later and their censoring of the Jewish Torah. The Medicis' controlled the Vatican and most of Europe in the late 1400's and 1,500's. Modern Vatican apologists' view of anyone giving credence to this quote render the following opinion; "This quote is used mostly by skeptics of the intellectual low rent district." When you cannot debate facts, attack the messenger! It is time to separate mythology from fact and get a grip on reality.

The Genesis epic derives its name from the first phrase in the ancient Hebrew Holy Writ account of creation. This was the ancient method of tracking stories and epic tales. The title, Genesis, is a derivation of the Greek **geneseos**, which can translate as history, origin, birth, genealogy and several other similar meanings. The epic starts in

Hebrew text with **bereshith**, or "In beginning." After this lead-in is the primeval history of creation.

Today we can all understand that simple statement about creation. However, if you were relating a story to an uneducated audience in 1,000 BCE, you needed to use symbolic language and graphic folk tales to achieve understanding. It was known as oral law.

Symbolic language established the premise of how Man came to be, in very simple understandable terms. When a religious leader lectured his followers, it was easy for the group to understand terms like "on the second day's work" and "Let the land produce living creatures". This continued on and on with the creation of each element of their world. When, or if, questioned how this could be, the answer was simple, "God spoke and it was so."

The Genesis we have become accustomed to was assembled by Hebrew leaders 7,000 years after the "Garden Event" and about 3,000 years after the creation story was recorded in the Elba Tablets and in the Enuma Elish. The original composition included instructions on strict social customs and behavior provided to prevent widespread disease, social and religious unrest, and a foundation for legal redress of individual complaints. Most of these instructions were derived from the Hammurabi Codes.

These codes of civil and penal justice were established by the King Hammurabi of Babylonia in 1,754 BCE. The Code established 282 laws for justice and moral conduct throughout his empire of Mesopotamia.

Translations of the Hammurabi Stelae:

"Hammurabi, the prince, called of Bel am I, making riches and increase, enriching Nippur and Dur-ilu beyond compare, sublime patron of E-kur; who reestablished Eridu and purified the worship of E-apsu who conquered the four quarters of the world, made great the name of Babylon, rejoiced the heart of Marduk, his lord......When the deities of old who allot the destinies of the world, Gave the rule of human beings to Marduk, set him over all other deities, made Babylon the foremost city state in all the earth and the capital of an everlasting kingdom, with foundations laid strong as those of heaven and earth........I, Hammurabi"....."*To prevent the strong from oppressing the*

> **weak and to see that justice is done to widows and orphans……."**

I included these translations to leave no doubt as to which Lord [Bal, Baal or Bel] ruled Sumer at that time. The last quote openly professes support for cornerstone practices of the Ancient Lodge.

Genesis chapters 1 through 38 retell Sumerian tales of primeval history, some of which have been dated on clay tablets from the 4th Millennium BCE, predating "Genesis" by several thousand years. These epic tales describe Creation, the Great War of the Heavens, Man's rebellion against The Almighty, and that He flooded the world leaving one lineage to populate and rehabilitate the Earth. The "Flood Epic" provides the religious platform to establish "God's chosen people." These first chapters also provide the all-important lineages of Yahweh's Prophets from Adam to Noah and from Noah to Abram [Ibrim]. Curiously, all detailed lineages cease at this point in the Hebrew Holy Writ.

The balance of Genesis has definite Egyptian influence and reflects education from the Egyptian Temples. It contains the rites, social customs, laws, birthright obligations for the Semitic Tribes to follow. Many of the laws and customs are rooted in ancient Sumerian customs [Hammurabi]. The balance of the customs and laws are derived or come directly from Egyptian influence.

A host of religious scholars, referred to as *theologians*, have attempted to uncover and reveal the innermost secrets of Biblical text. Their interpretations expand and raise the spiritual plane of a given subject, yet they fail to establish a foundation of physical reality. The theologians usually present their interpretations to their own religious elite, as human nature drives them to find psychological safety in a group with similar beliefs. The audience in this case serves as a conduit for mythology. As a modern saying goes "You can put lipstick on a pig, but it is still a pig". You can try to prove a fable with another fable, but it is still a fable.

Individual concepts of the meaning of life are unique to Man, known as intelligence and the ability to reason. More simply put, we all have the power to think in abstract concepts. It is from this gift we evolve our individual beliefs. To arrive on a plane of historical understanding, it is important to avoid debating conflicting beliefs. We can leave the interpretation of the spirituality of Genesis to the ministers of religious assemblies and focus on logic and historical fact.

One of the first messages of Genesis was in symbolic terms for ancient people. "Let there be light," was a message sent from a time of antiquity to modern Man as a symbolic term for intelligence. The message is: Let there be intelligence, and independent thought about the universe. Look within yourself as you pursue the answers to the mysteries of the Universe. This teaching was labeled as Gnostic by the Catholic Church for not conforming to organized religion. Gnostics were deemed heretics and banished or killed, beginning in the early Christian era into the 1700s CE.

It is physical reality that our world and solar system was "created" along with billions of other stars and planets. This is the first message of Genesis.   The message was sent to enable modern Man to understand the physical power of the entire universe. The scientific community continues to reinforce this message, providing us with extensive information regarding the formation of the galaxies within the universe. It is unfortunate the creation of the universe is often viewed as a separate entity of our history.

We will most likely never grasp the meaning of the infinite depth of the universe. It is mathematically represented by the symbol for infinity [∞], in all directions of time and distance scales. Psychologically, Man must be able to understand time and distance in measurable quantities. The Biblical Alpha and Omega, the beginning and the end, are the mental symbolic meanings applied to the infinity of time and distance.

This symbolism was provided as an absolute, measurable mental reference when we contemplate our place in time and space. In truth, if we were to even approach absolute understanding of the Alpha and Omega reference, our brains would overload, as the concept of infinity has no real solution, mentally or mathematically. There is no beginning, or end.

There are many names for Bal's "firstborn sons" such as Marduk, Ba'al, Merodakh and so on. These firstborns became "Gods" just like their father, confusing history with the names. The same can be said for Lord Yahweh's "firstborn sons", such as "Enoch" supporting and taking on the role of their father.

The early Hebrew text was pure mathematics. The language symbols not only depicted sounds, they also represented numerical values. Hidden within the religious messages and family lineage was a mathematical "key." A "key" is a series of numbers or letters, which allowed a priest or prophet to quote ancient tales and secrets of the Universe verbatim.

An example of a key is the letters **ITB,** converted to the corresponding numerical value of our alphabet each letter would read, **9, 20, 2.**   Once memorized, this "key" could then be quoted alphabetically as "***In the beginning, [ITB]***" or numerically establish a date of ***9th month, 20th day, 2nd year.*** This ability was developed over decades of training with Lodge Masters, usually in a temple setting. In antiquity, a Mason who entered this training would take twenty years or more to master the first level of development.

The personal scribe of Lord Yahweh, Enoch, compiled the genealogy and stories for Yahweh's Tribe's development and growth into a nation. When translated to the original Hebrew language, it maintained the secret keys of the Lodge in the text. Most of these keys were later lost, as the original documents were translated into other text, or other languages, or the story was embellished by scribes. The ancient script used by serious translators is the *Samarian Pentateuch.*

The Hebrew Tribes were led by priests until Saul was appointed the first King of the united kingdoms of Judah and Israel [Samaria] from about 1020 to 1000 BCE. He was followed by David, 1000 to 961 BCE and then by Solomon, 961 to 922 BCE.

Yahweh's life ended about 950 BCE after he successfully united the Hebrew Nation. His death occurred during the reign of King Solomon. The reason I believe Lord Yahweh died during Solomon's reign is it fits the time of the Hebrew disintegration as a Nation.

The phrase "Ruach ha' Kodesh" is recorded in the Hebrew Religion to define Yahweh's "spirit", clearly indicating he died. Also, Solomon departed the ways of Yahweh, and followed the lifestyle of Bal in his declining years. Stories of his wizardry abound in ancient tales.

Yahweh spent his life in his Samarian palace without interference because of his position on the Council of Lords. Bal ordered no harm must come to Yahweh and this decree was passed on to his offspring Gods, such as Marduk. Without Yahweh's protection invasions from the Akkad led to the capture and exile of most of the Hebrews.

In 922 BCE King Solomon died, and the Kingdom split again into the Northern [Samaria or Israel] and Southern [Judah] Kingdoms. In 721 BCE, the Assyrian civilization was located in Mesopotamia, the same region of the old Sumerian civilization, and in that year the Assyrians captured the Northern Hebrew Kingdom of Samaria and exiled the captives. King Nebuchadnezzar of Babylonia captured the Southern Kingdom of Judah in 600 BCE and did the same, sending the Hebrews to Babylon.

During the decline of the Hebrew nation and the exiles, the people passed through a religious period known as the Age of the Prophets. This period lasted from about 750 BCE through 600 BCE. The Hebrew prophets were attempting to refine the concept of their God Yahweh.

Lord Yahweh existed in the Hebrew religion as a cruel and harsh God, and generally speaking, the Hebrew people had enough of Lord Yahweh. The people refused to listen to the threats of their prophets to return to living under the laws of Yahweh. Instead, they continued their lives using the basic doctrines of Lord Yahweh and worshiping every God they had brought from Egypt or had followed in the past.

Samaria was the name of the ancient capital and of the district of the first Kingdom of Israel [922 – 722 BCE]. [this compares to the 22nd Dynasty of Egypt, 945 -720 BCE].   It extended from the Mediterranean to the Jordan Valley and beyond. This area was previously captured from the Canaanites by the Egyptians and given to the Tribe of Joseph when he was "The Minister of Egypt". The city of Samaria had several large square and round towers combined with large walls. Some towers were about 40 feet across. In the Hebrew language the city name was Shomron, which meant "watch tower". In the later Philistine language, a tower would be called "Magdala".

I believe Samaria was the "Home", The Promised Land where Yahweh spent most of his time away from Parvaim, in his villa. This is where he wanted his vassals to prosper and live.

Yahweh clearly had residence in the area as remains of furniture of Minoan design, inlaid with ivory were found in the ruins of a "Minoan Palace". Yahweh loved his luxury; ivory carvings from 1,000 BCE were discovered at this site.

King Omri [876 to 869 BCE] was the 6th king of divided Israel and ruled from the city of Samaria. It was Omri who named the city Shomron.   He allowed Aramean merchants to trade in his city. Arameans were a Semitic tribal people from Syria who spoke Aramaic. The Aram tribes established kingdoms from the Mediterranean to Babylon about 1,000 BCE. Omri's son, King Ahab ruled from about 869– 850 BCE.

Ahab is important in that he married the daughter of the King of Tyre, Jezebel of Sidon. Jezebel worshipped Baal and brought Ahab in line to do the same. Ahab was known as an evil King, murdering one of his subjects to steal a vineyard. Ahab spread the idol worship of Baal throughout Israel causing many Prophets to denounce him for not worshipping Yahweh. Ahab was killed in a battle in 850 BCE and his two sons ruled until 843 BCE.

A new Hebrew King, King Jehu took over, threw Jezebel off of a tower, got rid of Ahab's sons and restored the worship of Yahweh.

The Samaritans were The Kingdom of Israel. They later worshipped Yahweh under "Abrahamic Law", which has slightly different interpretations of Yahweh's directives than Masoretic Law, as their religious basics. The Samaritan Hebrews use the Samaritan Torah for worship. They built their temple to Yahweh at Mount Gerizim in 450 BCE. Samaritan is translated as "Guardians/Keepers/Watchers [of the Torah]".

Hebrew scribes from succeeding generations [to about 200 BCE] translated the text of the Samaritan and Masoretic Torahs to fit their current political needs. Both Torahs are essentially the same story. Each generation had their own special interests, and these were filled by a new interpretation raising the spiritual plane of events to a religious and mystical event. The result of these interpretations is a present-day Hebrew Holy Writ without a foundation of reality. This provides a fairy tale atmosphere instead of reality based on history. You might say God was evolving by Local Selection.

The Hebrew Holy Writ was developed in three stages. The oldest, the Torah [Law], began with "Moses" and was mostly complete by 300 BCE. The second part, the Neblim [Prophets] was added by 200 BCE. The third and final segment, the Ketubim [Writings] completed the Hebrew Holy Writ by CE 70. Since Jews no longer understood, or spoke ancient Hebrew, their Holy Writ was translated into Aramaic and Greek.

Ruins of Ancient City of Samaria [Shomron] in the Kingdom of Israel, built by King Omri in the 870's BCE. Photo from 1925.

The Israelites did not have the guidance of a "Holy Writ" [partial] until 300 BCE to 70 CE when the first version was completed. They did not have the Torah during the fabled Exodus, or during their captivity as alluded to in modern Holy Writs.

When composing the Torah, the fable of the "Tower of Babel" was developed to cover the reason for all of the different languages of the Earth. The reason it must be taught is because the fable of "Noah's Ark" and the Deluge was taught from ancient tales of Gods, and of course the survivors spoke the same language. The "Tower fable" occurs right after the flood. Man did a lot of "begetting" in a hurry because Mesopotamia was overrun with people. Each ziggurat temple was named after the local God or Gods, and they were all known as "Staircases to the Gods [or Heaven]". The main ziggurat of Babylon was named after lord Bal as the Temple of the "Feathered Serpent".

Ancient Sumerian was the language of the Lords and their descendants. This lost language is alluded to in the Biblical fable of *The Tower of Babel*. When the Lords left the area, they instructed the Masonic Priests to never use the language outside of the Lodge. I suspect it remained in the Lodge for several thousand years.

The word, which we have been taught means "confusion," is "Ba-Bel". "The Tower of Confusion" as it is known in liturgy was mis-translated from the Akkad word "Ba-Bel," which translates as "Gateway to the Gods"." The ancient Hebrew word for "Confusion" is "Ba-Lal" and only sounds similar to "Ba-Bel." Although early and modern Biblical scholars were aware of the distinct difference of "Ba-Bel" and "Ba-Lal" they refused to break the liturgy of the fable.

If the ancient text were properly translated this and other fables would vanish. The hidden reason for the fable was to secretly pass on Masonic knowledge in veiled allegory. For what was "lost," Masonically, was the true name for "The Supreme Architect of The Universe" in correct pronunciation in the extinct Sumerian language. Even though Hebrew was reborn by scholars after becoming extinct, there is no way to establish if the two languages sounded alike. The same would be true if scholars brought back the extinct Sumerian language.

The Maya also used the same staircase to the Gods descriptions for their ziggurat temples. Babylon's temple name is translated as "The House of the Foundation-Platform [Creator God] of Heaven and Earth." Others are dedicated to "The God of the Mountain," "The Seven Guides of Heaven and Earth" and so on. These "Seven Guides" were honored in the Temple of Anu [On] in Egypt.

The Maya had a fable similar to the Babylonian "Tower of Ba'Bel". The largest remaining pyramid in the world is one built by the Maya. According to the Maya fable the pyramid was built as a refuge by the Seven Gods who survived the great flood. The pyramid's height finally reached into the heavens and angered the Sky Gods. The Gods rained down fire on the towering construction, killing or scattering all of the workmen. You have not heard a lot about this fable, or the pyramid, because the Vatican built a Church on top of it in the 1500's. The fable, if published, would have embarrassed the Vatican and brought doubt on the Holy Writ.

By order of the Vatican, the ancient Hebrew [an extinct language] of the Hebrew Holy Writ was translated into Greek by "72 translators" in Alexandria in CE 300, hence the title *Septuagint*, that is, 70 in Greek. Because of a lack of understanding of ancient Hebrew, a considerable amount of the original Hebrew was not translatable into Greek. This resulted in many mis-translations, added stories and distortions of the original meanings.

Other translated versions include: The Masorah [Margin notes and critic of the Hebrew Holy Writ c. 6th to 10th centuries CE]; The Aquila

[2nd century CE Greek Old Testament]; The Symmachus and Theodotion [early church fragments of transliterated Greek]; The Vulgate [Latin Bible CE 1592 commissioned by the Vatican Council of Trent CE 1545-1563]; The Syriac Peschitta [1st century Old Latin transliterated from the Septuagint]; The Targums [Aramaic paraphrase of the Old Testament]; The Juxta Hebraica, Sanhedrin Council [Jewish Supreme Council of 71 Priests during early Christian era]; and interpretations from The Dead Sea Scrolls. And of course, the King James Version of CE 1611. The provenance of the King James Holy Writ will be discussed in "*CHRISTIANITY*".

The current publications of the Holy Writ, for the Western World, have been carefully crafted to reflect a narrow view of religion and history. Contained in that history are strict views of the order of people. By this I mean we have been taught our "places" as citizens, men or women, priest or parishioner, laborer or boss, skin color or cultural status - ad infinitum.

These narrow views have not changed. The "new translations" of the Holy Writ follow the outline of the 1611 and earlier versions, even when the modern translators know better. A simple example of this is the reference to an ancient widespread personal affliction as "a noisome spirit," rather than accurately translating "the Pharaoh and his family had gonorrhea."

In the current "Bible", in Genesis, the Creator God is YHWH [Yahweh], and the polytheistic God is Elohim. In chapters 2 and 3, the "Adam and Eve" story, the deities are combined as *YHWH Elohim*. *YHWH* [Hebrew, Yahweh] is referred to as the Tetragrammaton and is translated as *Lord*. There are several other Hebrew words that translate as some form of lesser *Lords*. Some original phrases translate as "the Lord of Hosts" and "God of Hosts."

Early Christian translators did not feel these phrases conveyed proper emphasis so they used "Almighty God" as a general translation, distorting the original meanings. There are more than four different, distinct, original Hebrew words translated as "God" in modern Bibles. Finally, in Chapter 4 the deity becomes simply Yahweh, or *Lord*.

The Old Testament book of Genesis provides positive traces of the Lords' existence. Although lineage dating in Genesis [King James Version of The Holy Writ] sets the time for "Adam" at about 4,200 BCE [with numerous date gaps], the historical information of Genesis was first assembled about 1,000 BCE from oral tradition.

The first "Garden" incident of Genesis history, with Lilith as the bride, occurred prior to the comet impact of 10,900 BCE. According to descriptions of the location of "The Garden of Eden" in ancient texts, the site is under water. Satellite imagery has revealed the ancient river channels of the four rivers confluence, which marked the garden site, are under water in the Persian Gulf. The second "garden story", with Eve, was located near Eridu, a few miles southwest of Ur, around 6,400 BCE. Most convincing for this date is the Biblical lineage of Yahweh recorded in Genesis and correlations of other ancient text.

The numerical computations of the years of family lineage, based on the King James Version of 1611 [ANNO DOMINI; in the year of the Christian era.] establishes the "creation" of Adam at about 4,214 BCE. Assuming Adam was +/- 100 years old in the *Garden of Eden* it is easy to compute a separate date for the Garden Fable. However, there are numerous lineage omissions and mistaken translations. One important missed translation is the similarity of the old Hebrew language between *father* and *ancestor*.

The older the history, the more errors occur in maintaining chronology. The era of Noah is an absolute mess. Relying on other versions of The Holy Writ, there are dozens of breaks in the lineages of the Firstborn Sons. From Noah to Shelah there are at least three lineage breaks. One of these breaks in chronology is 130 years. Overall, about half of the genealogy is missing.

In the 2,100 years listed from Adam to Abram the omission error is over fifty percent. Using correlations of other ancient text and history, Adam's birth [creation] occurred about 6,500 BCE. Assuming Adam was about 100 years old when he was presented with "a suitable helper" would date the "Garden Fable" at about 6,400 BCE. This correlates with the large estates of the Lords existing in Sumer.

Using the same error rates for genealogy, Noah's birth occurred about 4,400 BCE. This would date the *Great Flood Fable* to about 3,800 BCE.

Genesis provides positive traces of the Lords of Sumer's existence; the following is a Genesis excerpt:

> **And the Sons of God saw the daughters of men were fair;**
> **and they took them wives of all which they chose.**

This is evidencing the Lords recognized beauty and enjoyed the comfort of female companionship. This information also indicates they took women as wives with or without their consent, or the consent of their families. The Lords each produced their own large extended families, or tribes. Sumerian history indicates the Lords treated women as mere chattel. Some were taken as wives while others were housed in separate temples as sources of pleasure for their new masters.

It is interesting to note that an ancient historian was able to differentiate between their God of the Universe [Lord Yahweh] and the men who posed as Gods. *"The sons of God'* [Genesis 6:2] was derived from the original Hebrew *n-ph-l* and translated as *"Nephilim,"* and is also translated as *"fallen angels,"* or, *"Those [who came] from above"* and, *"The Mighty Ones."* They were also described as *"Giants from the Holy Watchers."* These descriptions of a variety of Gods and God-like people verify independent thought and judgment by the Hebrew historians. These tales of supernatural beings were later incorporated into the *Holy Writ* of the tribes.

There are significant Biblical histories omitted between chapters 1 and 2 of Genesis. The logic of this is that right after creation we have an epic tale beginning with Adam and Eve, and an evil Lord Marduk [Bal]. Lord Marduk was the son of god Enlil [Bal] and was known simply as "Bal," that is *Lord*, in Babylon. Lord Marduk used the same symbol as his father; a "Feathered serpent" emblazoned on city gates and temples.

In the second Garden story it is obvious that Lord Bal was not in a subservient position to Lord Yahweh when he was banished from Eden. They were "equals" in a council. This council was formed after the Great War of the Heavens, as described in the Old and New Testaments of the Holy Writ. This war is also described in great detail and recorded in those 4th to 2nd Millennium BCE Sumerian epics previously mentioned. It is possible the principles of the opposing groups had a peace agreement and council in place.

A Biblical fable which is out of place is the account of Noah and the Great Flood of 3,800 BCE. Compared to the Garden of Eden *"Story,"* The *"Story'* about Noah is the second greatest fantasy misrepresented as religious experiences.

There are geologic records of floods in many parts of the world over epic times. This is obvious when ancient ruins are under many feet of flood sediment. There are no indications that a primeval epic world flood occurred during this time, which resulted in one lineage [family] remaining. Even the last theological conclusion is at odds with its premise. According to Noah's lineage, he started every Race of people on Earth by sending his firstborn sons, of different wives, out to populate the world.

A recent theory about the "Ark", from Vatican sources, is the Ark was not large enough to house "two of every living-thing". Instead it must have been an Ark of safety for DNA storage for every living-thing. I only mention this because like past excuses for finding fallibility with the Holy Writ, this is truly absurd and laughable.

"Adam, The Woman and The Garden Party"

Who was Adam and where were the Gardens of Eden? In the Hebrew language "Adam" means Man as a Species. An "Adam" was a firstborn son in a Genesis lineage. "Adam" [Mankind] was the firstborn of Lord Yahweh's Tribe and you will see this as we pursue the Garden of Eden story. As the firstborn son, Adam would have control of all of the estates and livestock of his father under Sumerian law. The Genesis phrase of "gave names to all the livestock…." correctly translated from the original language is, "*took, or had, ownership of all the animals on the estate.*"

At the time of the Second "Eden" account Sumer was the best-known civilization to have writing skills. It logically follows that Sumer, and more specifically the area from south of Babylon to Eridu was the area of the fabled Garden of Eden. The Biblical description is not complicated to follow.

The First Eden was near the junction of four major rivers. The Tigris and Euphrates Rivers are still identifiable and the other two rivers were located by satellite. They were found under the Persian Gulf in the ancient Euphrates River Valley.

The second "Eden" was at Eridu, 7.5 miles southwest of Ur, and was irrigated from the Euphrates River. This is close enough for history. Further reasoning for this is that 6,400 BCE coincides with both the Biblical account and with archaeological evidence of the area.

Abraham's family is well established as being direct descendants of Adam. His family originally lived in the city of Ur, which was located in southern Sumer.   Terah, his father, was the Master Architect [builder] and Grand Master of Ur. His ancestors all lived in this region, as fathers passed their estates on to their firstborn sons. Lord Bal was establishing his power base and primary following in Babylon. With Bal frequenting the estate on a regular basis, it is very likely it was in the vicinity of Ur.

It is very probable we will never know the exact location of the Gardens but this is not an important issue of history. The important issue is that the detailed lineage of Adam was specifically intended to create and exert great influence on man's evolving history in this area. This influence was intended to provide a balance of power between the forces of good [Lord Yahweh's descendants] and the forces of evil [Lord Bal's descendants].

This history served several purposes. First, it provided the early Hebrew Tribes with a "record" of their direct lineage from Lord Yahweh, and a connection to ancient history. Next and most important it established religious law and social form for tribal and family organization.

It is a curious turn of events that Lord Yahweh established "Eden" as the original "Holy Land" for his tribe, and millennia later abandoned this area for Canaan as the "Holy Land." As you will discover, Eden was established to form a coalition of the two major powers in the council of Lords. When this attempted coalition failed, Yahweh abandoned his plan for Eden as his "Holy Land".

The Island of Thera was being developed as a center of power for the Lords by 6,500 BCE and would become known as "Parvaim". That is "Paradise" in ancient civilizations. I believe this is the reason Yahweh was not living in "The Garden" where his new son, "Adam", was born. He came to visit occasionally to check on his family's progress and maybe a booty call.

To preserve some balance with Sumerian epic history and fables, we need to include a bit of history omitted from the **King James** story. Sumerian epics describe the first marriage in "Eden" as a bit of failed diplomacy. I have concluded that this marriage was set to politically unite the tribes of Lord Yahweh and Lord Bal, or to at least bring peace between them. The date for the first "Eden" was prior to the comet impact of 10,900 BCE. An "Adam" was the groom, a son of Yahweh, and the bride was Lillith, a daughter of Lord Bal.

The need for this diplomatic marriage was brought about by friction between factions of the Lords. Lord Yahweh had a first-born son who was destined to rule from Yahweh's position of power. An heir to the Throne, as Lord High God, if you will. For this to come to be, Yahweh ordered all of the council of Lords [The Angels] to bow and subjugate themselves to this heir apparent, as they apparently did to Yahweh.

According to ancient text, Lord Bal [Lord Bel, Lucifer, Bal, etc.] was livid. He and his followers informed Yahweh that his Son was of the Earth, not even close to their own cosmic stature and they would certainly not debase themselves by showing any deference to any mortal man, even his son. Also, if any homage was to be shown it would be from the Son to the Lords.

So, Adam and Lillith would bond and everyone would live happily at the ranch. I don't think anyone interviewed Lillith about her lifestyle. From the Sumerian epics it appears the Lords of Sumer had a substance, or source of a substance which prolonged their life-spans: Made them Gods, life eternal, as it were. The Lords did not want common man to possess this "substance", referred to in Sumerian epics as "the Hulluppu Tree", a tree of life. It is evident that the reference to a tree of life is allegorical and is used for the purpose of storytelling. The story also explained the source of the "Gods" extended life spans and advanced knowledge.

Lilith, like her father Bal, was a free spirit and would neither submit nor subjugate her life to anyone, especially to her new husband. Lillith led Adam to partake of what would be described as deviant sexual practices and worship of other Gods. Yahweh would have disapproved of any rites performed for Bal's festivities, in his Son's household.

Lillith would not sit quietly in the tent, darning Adam's underwear and praying to Adam's God, Yahweh. Lillith subsequently took the kids, checkbook and camels and moved back to Mother. Her new home was where Cain eventually fled, the Land of Nod, East of Eden and is present day Iran. Lillith is still celebrated as an evil force in Jewish mythology. If this was the true story or not, this first Eden came to an end with the Comet strike and the destructive global aftermath.

With this insertion of pre-second Garden of Eden history, it is easy to understand why Lord Yahweh provided his next "Adam" son with a wife from his own bloodline. "Made him a woman from his own rib" means a woman from his own tribe. This wife would submit to her husband and would uphold tribal traditions. It is also easy to understand why Yahweh was livid when Bal interfered once again in his son's marriage. We return to the Garden Party.

I place the entire "Garden" episode of Genesis in the same category as "Noah and the Flood", a little fact and a lot of BS. I will attempt to pick out some traces of history. The rest is Yahweh's religious fable to subjugate women to property status and elevate his role as "God". The portions I comment on are solely to illustrate how religion was, and is, used to control entire populations.

In the Epic of Gilgamesh, the Sumerian creation story [labeled a myth by Academia] relates the creation of Man to provide labor for the Gods: The Gods came to Earth and mined for metals and planted their trees and food crops in Eden. The "toil was too great" for the Gods and they complained to the highest God, Anu. The solution was to kill one of the Gods and mix his body and blood with clay and produce Man to toil for the Gods.

This all took place in the Gods garden, Eden. This first Man was named Adapa. Adapa could not reproduce on his own so Gods Enki and Ninki modified Man so he could reproduce. Enki's brother Enlil was enraged by this change to elevate Man and became an adversary to Enki and Man. He set the stage for a hearing by Anu [Chief God] of Adapa's knowledge and ability to oversee the Garden. When Adapa failed to properly answer questions from Anu he was expelled from Eden.

I believe these adversaries equate to Bal and Yahweh. It is also very apparent where the stories in Genesis came from.

In the Hebrew Bible Yahweh planted the garden with all sort of trees. The famous tree partaken of was "The Tree of Knowledge". When Yahweh evicted his kids, he commented:

<u>Hebrew Bible</u>
Genesis 3,22 And the LORD God said: 'Behold, the man is become as one of us, to know good and evil; and now, lest he put forth his hand, and take also of the tree of life, and eat, and live for ever.'

Note the context of "as one of us" and "also of the tree of life". Who were "us"? This "tree of life" is most likely a genetic modification, or serum, which slows the ageing process. But who knows the purpose of three-thousand-year-old commentary?

The "Tree of Life" is a constant throughout the balance of history occurring in the Sumerian Religion, The Hebrew Religion, the Christian Religion and the Religions of the Americas. Another symbolic religious image which occurs with these religions is the candelabra. The Tree of Life and the candelabra are included in the geoglyphs in the Nazca Desert.

In the Second Garden Fable, it is important to identify the characters. First in the Garden, is God [Lord Yahweh], then his favorite "Adam", Adam's "Suitable helper", and Satan [Lord Bal]. Satan is mentioned by several different names in the Holy Writ. Bal and his cult following are rebuked throughout the Old Testament. This cult was also identified as "The Dark [evil] Lodge," and "The Lodge of the North" in the Dead Sea Scrolls. I believe the recent discovery of Gobekli Tepe reveals one of Lord Bal's "Lodges." As recorded, the "Garden Incident" provides some unintended insight to the personality of Lord Yahweh, and how this attitude was portrayed as divine inspiration.

Yahweh's emotional responses are of an older, narcissistic mortal Man, certainly not the responses expected of an all-knowing God. Yahweh expresses anger, confusion and ignorance about the events in the Garden. These emotions show that Yahweh was a very jealous person.

The second person in the Garden was Adam. He was Yahweh's favorite. Adam was the first something in Genesis, certainly not the first Man on Earth. He was one of Lord Yahweh's Firstborn Sons, *"created"* in Yahweh's image. Yahweh always called out to Adam first when he returned to the Eden. Adam's position of superiority is clearly established as he was the sole person to *name* [take ownership of] every living creature upon the "Earth". The "Earth", or Adam's world at this time, was the *Eden* [translates as *a beautiful plain*] portion of Sumer.

The next person revealed in the Garden was the woman "helper". In today's world She would be described as a sad case. Her role in life was totally subservient. Genesis describes her position as *"an help meet,"* which is defined as "an appropriate domestic servant." She would have been the perfect specimen of a woman. There is a veiled reference that She was not the first choice as a mate for Adam. Just before "creating" the woman the Holy Writ states "But for Adam no suitable helper was found". It does not say there were no helpers available, just there were no suitable ones found.

After the spectacle with Lillith, Yahweh would not have allowed imperfection to be introduced to his lineage. After her *creation* [introduction to the Garden of Eden] Adam simply called her *Woman*. If you read Genesis Chapter three very closely, you will see that She did not receive her name until her last day in the Garden. Even then it was Adam who gave her a name. The Woman's status went from an unnamed domestic servant, to the root cause of all of mankind's woes in one garden party, if you believe popular western theology. Women were to be punished all their lives for causing "Adam" to get laid, thereby spreading "The Sin Virus" through all of Mankind.

The last person in the Garden spectacle was Lord Bal [Satan]. Ancient scribes used symbolic terms to describe the personality and character of Bal. Other than great shining beauty, there has not been a good physical description given for him in western literature, except as a comic-book character. Bal's personality is described as crafty and subtle [a serpent]. The primary reason for the "serpent" description is that Lord Bal was also known as the "feathered serpent" by his followers, with the feathered serpent symbol on city gates where he was worshipped.

These symbolic descriptions have confused followers for centuries, and have been taken as a literal, physical description. As soon as the word serpent is used, the mind produces the image of a snake. This problem is further compounded by a mystical spiritual attitude regarding Bal. The symbolic word *serpent* alludes to a character that is silent, swift, and deadly. The use of the word *subtle* means Bal was a very clever and deceptive person. Prior to his personal war with Yahweh he was known as the Angel of Light, the bearer of great knowledge and the *most beautiful* of all beings.

Time is condensed in this fable, producing the illusion that events occur in the period of a few days. This entire garden party probably occurred over several years.

The term *Eden* alludes to a beautiful garden estate. The crowning achievement of this place of serenity and beauty was its principal occupants, Adam and his woman helper. Yahweh consummated this arrangement with a marriage and she is referred to as Adam's wife. They set the standards for physical perfection. This can be described as physical beauty without blemish, and yet, there were only human. They are described as being "both naked." The ancient Hebrew phrase actually translates as "morally innocent" and they lived in almost total seclusion with their servants.

The *fruit of the Tree of Knowledge* fable was told to enhance the beginnings of Yahweh's Tribe and to set standards for women's roles in life. This "Tree" was taken from the Elba Tablets and the Enuma Elish mythology. All of the references to the tree and fruit were veiled sexual references to Bal fathering Cain with Adam's wife. This was obvious when the boy was born with light skin and blue eyes. This story has been used over the millennia to keep women in their "place" and to explain the difficulties of childbirth. And the sexual references were really not all that veiled to anyone over the age of ten.

Genesis Chapter 4 vs. 1-2
And Adam knew his wife; and she conceived, and bare Cain, and said, I have gotten a Man from the Lord. And she again bare his brother Abel. And Abel was a keeper of sheep but Cain was a tiller of the ground.

"I have gotten a man from the Lord" was the ancient scribe's way of telling the hidden story. Cain was not treated as a firstborn; he was eventually cast out of the family and left with a very distinguished "mark'" to all who saw him. He went to the area of Bal's tribe and lived happily ever after.

In all Hebrew families, the firstborn son held the authority of the family, second only to his father. This tenant of religious practice did not allow a father to pick his "Firstborn" from his favorite wife but could reject a child fathered by someone else. The firstborn son was the sole heir of the family wealth and his father's position within the tribe. He was placed in the position of guarding the family wealth and doing the least amount of physical labor. Wealth in these ancient days was equated to land and herds of domestic animals.

In the absence of his father, the eldest son was automatically regarded as the authority figure of the family. This custom applied to almost all civilizations, from antiquity into the history of the Middle Ages. There are civilizations where this practice continues even today.

The "Cain and Able" fable was recorded as a way to explain the superiority of the Hebrew race to inferior cultures. There were probably some other cultural lessons, but I gave up trying to decipher them.

The story could be an attempt to explain the intermarriage of Yahweh's tribe and Bal's tribe. Lord Bal was described as Great Beauty and Light, he was light skinned, Blue-eyed and Blond or Red haired, and so was Cain. Yahweh was darker skinned with dark hair and eyes. Cain's linage was very evident; he was one of the "White Boys", the Canaanites.

A final note supporting the premise that Adam did not father Cain comes from Adam's continued lineage with his next recorded son:

> **Genesis 5,3: And Adam lived a hundred and thirty years, and begot a son in his own likeness, after his image; and called his name Seth.**

The ancient scribes make the point of this son being true lineage of Adam. Also, in Hebrew "Adam" means Man as a Species. And once again, these lineages and stories in Genesis are so mixed-up it is obvious they were established between 1000 and 200 BCE from mostly oral tradition and from the Canaanite-Akkadian Cuneiform writings of the Babylonian Enuma Elish.

Next – A famous "Story" of The Deluge

Chapter
2

**Mitra Gods of Noah's
time near Gobekli
Tepe**

NOAH
[Veiled Allegory]

The accounts of Noah are the most mistranslated, misrepresented account of history produced in the archives of the Hebrew Tribes. Through this veiled allegory of history, we have been taught that Noah was a "Godly" person, escaped the flood of destruction with his immediate family and re-populated the world with different races.

An allegory is by definition *"A work of art in which a deeper meaning underlies the superficial or literal meaning."* A Veiled Allegory is one in which you would not normally suspect as a bogus story, without extensive research.

Old Testament scribes plagiarized The Akkadian Epic of Atra-Hasis [c. 1800 BCE] to create the "Noah Flood Story". The Babylonian God Enki was going to bring a flood to destroy all Mankind. One person, Atra-Hasis, whose name meant "very intelligent" was warned by the Gods and told to tear down his house and build a raft to survive the coming seven-day flood.

After the storm abated the Sun God appeared and a character named Zi-ud-sura opened the craft and sacrificed sheep and oxen. When the flood abated the Gods Utu [Sun God] and Enlil [Leader of the Gods] gave Zi-ud-sura eternal life and placed him in Dilmun so he could "preserve the animals and mankind".

If you study the related portion of Genesis closely, along with related translations of The Dead Sea Scrolls and other ancient documents, you can discern some truths of this period of Noah's life. Noah was the 9th or 10th generation from Adam through the lineage of Seth, Adam's third recorded son, and the 8th or 9th generation from Adam through the lineage of Cain [Bal], Adam's first recorded son. Noah was a descendant of both Yahweh and Bal, if the lineage is correct.

So, most of this is entertainment except to ardent "Believers". The genealogies presented in Genesis for Cain and Seth are extremely similar in names, and both arrive at a "Lamech". One Lamech has a son named Tubal-Cain [an important name in Masonic teachings] and the other Lamech has a son named Noah [very important to "Yahweh is God" believers].

Yahweh referred to his own lineage as "The Sons [children] of Light [God]," and to Bal's [Marduk's, Belial's] lineage [from Cain] as "The Sons of Darkness [man]."   To condense this last statement, Yahweh referred to his lineage as being from "God," and Bal's lineage as being from "Man."

These definitions are keys to determining what the real subjects are in the Holy Writ and in The Dead Sea Scrolls. In the "Scrolls" an entire book is about the war between The Sons of Light and The Sons of Darkness. These scripts both originated from the same priests.

Most references to Yahweh's or Marduk's early lineages would fit into the following descriptions; Yahweh's group is referred to as Heavenly Watchers, Emissaries [angels] and Messengers, and Bal's group was known as fallen angels, mighty ones and Nephilim.

In the 1611 version of the Holy Writ, what was mis-translated as Godly "giants', "mighty men" and "men of renown" [see opening vs. 1-4] would have been more properly translated as, fallen [sinful] ones, or morally corrupt men. Although Yahweh tried to maintain separation of the lineages of Seth and Cain, ancient documents clearly show that intermarriage was common.

About 4,400 BCE, Lamech, Noah's father, while traveling his domain came upon a strange happening in one of his wives' home. He arrived at night and his house [one of many] was lit with "a light like the sun," along with "Holy Beings" [Watchers] attending his wife Bath-Enosh. His wife came to be with child and he was livid when he questioned her about the timing of the conception and the visitors. This implies he certainly had no reason to suspect the child was his. His wife [a cousin or close kinsman of the lineage of Seth] assured him the child was his and was not conceived during the visit of the "Holy and Great One, The

Sovereign of Heaven and Earth." Her statement indicates it was Lord Yahweh in person who visited her. Lord Yahweh, with a security detail, had come for a booty call.

Lamech is described as "the embodiment of evil" in ancient writings, he was a follower of [and lineage of] Lord Marduk [The Sun God] and worshipped his many other Gods. Lamech did not believe his wife's story and beset his father, Methuselah, with the story of the "Heavenly Watchers" in his home, the bright lights, and the birth of Noah. The "Watchers" had returned to witness the birth, as it was reported his house was again illuminated with lights "as the Sun" at the birth of Noah.

This illumination during the birth of certain "Holy Men" was accredited by scribes as a "Heavenly" illumination or aura emanating from the child at the time of delivery. These "Holy" births, with illuminated children, are attributed to Noah, Abram, Moses, Buddha, Greek Gods, Christ and on into Christian Saints.

Lamech asked Methuselah to counsel with his father, Enoch, [not to be confused with Cain's firstborn son named Enoch] about the matter and ascertain the truth of the entire account. Enoch is said to have been a favorite of the "Watchers" and they constantly held discussions [reported as "gossip" in the ancient writings] with him. This is why Lamech asked Methuselah to find his grandfather Enoch, and to determine the truth. According to legend, Enoch was carried off to "The ends of the earth" by God, thereby going directly to Parvaim, "Heaven" without having to die.

Methuselah set out to travel to a place known only as "Parvaim" to locate Enoch. Parvaim was a mythical, mystical place not visited by many mortal men. I call it mythical only because it is not specifically located in any writings. I suspect it was the island of Thera in the Mediterranean. Enoch was found at Parvaim and when questioned about the affair admitted these Heavenly beings "used to" come down and seduce the local women. However, Enoch sent assurances to Lamech that Noah was certainly his child. Enoch was not about to give away Lord Yahweh's secret and ruin his good standing with the Lords. Enoch was reported to "sit at the right hand of God" and was his personal scribe. He was the only mortal known to sit in the presence of "God".

Lamech was evil. Methuselah was his father, and his mother was of direct lineage to Cain [Caucasian]. Apparently, Yahweh did not like

Lamech but found it difficult to remove him from his tribal position. One reason could have been the laws of the times established the firstborn son as the heir and leader, therefore Lamech could not be denied his inheritance and tribal position.

Lamech's wife, Bath-Enosh, was a direct descendant of Seth, and provided Lord Yahweh the perfect opportunity to correct the damage to his lineage caused by Methuselah. Yahweh gave Lamech a firstborn son [with this wife], with a pure Semitic lineage by visiting Bath-Enosh. I suspect Lamech figured out what happened but did not want to mess with "The Watchers."

The time of Noah's birth was about 4,400 BCE. 600 years later, in 3,800 BCE, the Biblical disaster myth befell the neighborhood of Noah. I believe, with a reasonable certainty, that Noah was a son of Lord Yahweh, and was in great favor. What is clear, from the records, is the lineage and worship of Marduk [Belial] was rampant in the area where Noah was living. This was most likely the area of Southern Iraq near the city of Ur, inherited from his father Lamech. Noah was the patriarch, as Lamech had died five years earlier at the age of 777 [a very curious number].

The story of the Great Flood is a parallel to the story of Lot and Sodom. Patriarch Noah's tribe and sub-tribes were exceedingly evil by worshipping Marduk instead of Yahweh and doing various nasty things in the village. The difference, from the destruction of Sodom, is the story of the flood resulted in a covenant from God not to kill everyone on Earth again by sending a natural disaster. In both cases Yahweh sent emissaries to the patriarch he wished to save, with a warning to gather his family and prepare for total destruction of the "sinners."

In this destruction of Marduk's stronghold, Yahweh recorded a flood and established a covenant with Noah's descendants never to flood the Earth again and gave them a rainbow to prove it. Good choice, since Yahweh could not live up to the story if anyone asked him to flood the Earth again, and everyone could see his rainbow quite often and be thankful "God" didn't drown them for their sins.

I believe the ancient scribes of the Torah attributed the destruction of Noah's neighborhood to a great flood, by God, to counter the existing account of a worldwide flood recorded in third millennium Sumerian text. The Epic of Gilgamesh relates the story of a half-God, Gilgemesh, surviving a flood by building a raft and saving his immediate family and animals. The epic story is very close to and pre-dates the saga of Noah, even with Gilgamesh sending a raven out to find dry land, and the bird returning with twigs and leaves. The Akkadian Epic of Atra-Hasis is another ancient flood survival epic. These flood stories most likely are stories of the aftermath of the comet strike.

Wouldn't you think if "God" were going to clean up the world, flush all the bad things down the drain, he would not allow the unclean of the animal world and the evil descendants of Lord Bal [Canaanites, the White Boys] on the Ark?

If any destruction actually occurred, the "Ark" was nothing more than a place of safety for Noah and his chosen few to wait out the destruction of the neighborhood. Most of these stories are nothing more than fairy tales intermingled with tribal history to instill some perceived virtue. These fables are also necessary to document the lives of "important" Prophets.

After the great disaster abated, Noah set off to live in a far place and tended his garden. As with Lot, Noah was also guilty of incest, but not with his daughters. Noah's garden eventually was his moral undoing. He planted grapes and celebrated his crop with wine. He celebrated quite often it appears, or his drunkenness would not have been recorded. A man can mess up once, or twice, and not get "written up."

Although some of the details are omitted in the 1611 Holy Writ, the results of an incident with his grandson were recorded in a variety of ancient text. It seems Noah was caught drunk and naked in his tent, with his grandson Canaan, playing some version of "hide the sausage."

Canaan's father, Ham, discovered the drunken interlude and told his brothers, who in turn went to the tent and "cleaned up" the mess. After he sobered from his wine, Noah cursed and banished Canaan "for what had happened." Canaan and his descendants were cursed to become slaves to Noah's other sons.

Modern theologians hold that "either the son [Canaan] was punished for his father's sin, of viewing his father's 'nakedness', or Canaan was punished for the future sins his lineage [the Caucasians] would commit". By the way, modern Theologians, it was Granpa messing with the boy, not the boy's daddy.

When compared to the laws and customs of the time, neither theory is correct. Banishment by a Patriarch was allowed only for *"those who despise me."* Banishment was a personal punishment, not a group decree. This proves the punishment was for something Canaan was personally involved in, in the tent, while he and Granpa were drunk and naked.

In closing this dissertation on "The Great Flood", the Dynasties of the Egyptians during this period [3,800 BCE] did not record any major disasters and continued with an unbroken lineage. Someone did not think ahead, in 1611, when they translated this fable into the Holy Writ. Of course, they only translated the Latin versions provided by brother Pope. I should not be too hard on the boys from 1611 for this translation, since they had recently found out the Earth was round. This entire episode is meant to explain the reason for the different races of the world.

This story was also used by the "Church" to continue slavery as a right from God. Different skin colors, or lack of cultural development [no intellectual ability] to church standards, was "God's Message" that these people were for the taking.

A curious oversight to this entire episode is the inheritance of property by "firstborn sons". Noah's neighborhood was in the area of Ur. After the "flood" he went off to some distant land. But his descendants were all recorded as being on the family estates at Ur. Someone did not research the "story" enough.

ENOCH and PARVAIM

A very interesting character, and place, in the Noah Fable is Enoch, the grandfather of Noah, and the mythical paradise Parvaim. Attaining a true understanding of the importance of this ancient character and place would require a tremendous amount of writing. I will attempt to give you some concept of it in a few pages.

Enoch was the 6th recorded Firstborn Son [Yahweh's] from Adam, roughly 1150 years from Adam's birth [6,500 BCE]. Adam lived for 930 years. Enoch was born in 5,350 BCE. Enoch was 950 years old when his great-grandson Noah was born [4,400 BCE]. This is boring but necessary, now comes the mystery of the ages.

Previously you read about Lamech pleading with his father, Methuselah, to go to Enoch at Parvaim to determine if Noah was Lamech's son, or the son of Lord Yahweh. Methuselah reported back, after an extended journey, that Noah was indeed Lamech's son.

Enoch was also known as the Angel Metatron [the Angel which communicates God's word], and by his own description, he was the "Lesser Yahweh". He is said to have assumed the duties of "Prince of the World" from the Angel Michael and was a favorite of Yahweh. The ancient records state that when he was 365 years old [about 5,000 BCE], God took him away and he was no more. [known as **"Metatron"** in Greek; and **Mitra** in Hebrew] [From the Sumerian Kings List, about 5,000 BCE **Etana** is noted as *"the shepherd, who ascended to heaven and consolidated all the foreign countries"*]

Yet it is recorded by Prophets who visited and walked in Paradise [Parvaim] that he sat next to Yahweh and was the scribe of the deeds of the Hebrews. This act of sitting in the presence of God bestowed the title of a "lesser Yahweh" on him because no one was allowed to sit in the presence of God. Enoch advised the "Heavenly Watchers" and Lord Yahweh himself. According to one traveler to Paradise, Enoch took him on a tour and explained all the wonders before him. Parvaim is derived from a Persian word meaning "enclosed garden".

This is a bit of conjecture, but if Yahweh's crew picked up some goat-herder and flew him to a Mediterranean paradise, brought him before the Almighty Yahweh and returned him to his tribe with a message from God, what a Prophet he would be!

Enoch was full of himself, and rightfully so. He held tremendous power in giving his reports directly to Yahweh. He could shape the politics and favors given various leaders. Yahweh must have provided Enoch with the serum, or whatever medical miracle the Lords used to live their extended life-spans. Of course, being the son of Yahweh would provide an extended life span. The secret of the Gods' extended life spans will be explored in-depth later on in this work.

Have you sorted out the mystery of Enoch and Parvaim? Here it is - boiled down to the nut. Enoch went to Heaven [Paradise] when he was 365 years old and "was no more." His Grandson traveled to Parvaim [Paradise] when Enoch was 950 years old and found him. I believe Parvaim was the Mediterranean Island of Thera [present day Santorini]. This was indeed a Paradise for the original **LORDS OF SUMER** and chosen family members. It was established about 6,500 BCE. This was where the governing board made the decisions concerning all of the nations of this part of the world, so far as their influence would carry.

Parvaim was reported as the actual Paradise [Heaven] to all followers and believers. Lord Yahweh was Almighty God who ruled in Paradise. Great religions have grown from a far less glorious beginning.

Enoch legends include providing the Lodge with rituals and instructions and providing King Solomon with guidance and wisdom [Enoch would have been over 4,000 years old]. One legend is that Enoch hid some gold tablets, with inscribed instructions, in Solomon's Temple. This legend is still reenacted in some Lodge rituals. Joseph Smith would utilize this Masonic myth to begin his "religion" thousands of years later.

Lord Yahweh did not continuously oversee the development of his people. It is quite apparent when he is around and when he is not. When he was gone his descendants turned to worshipping Gods that were not so harsh, the Sun God [Marduk] and the Moon Goddess.

Next, we follow the travels of Abram.

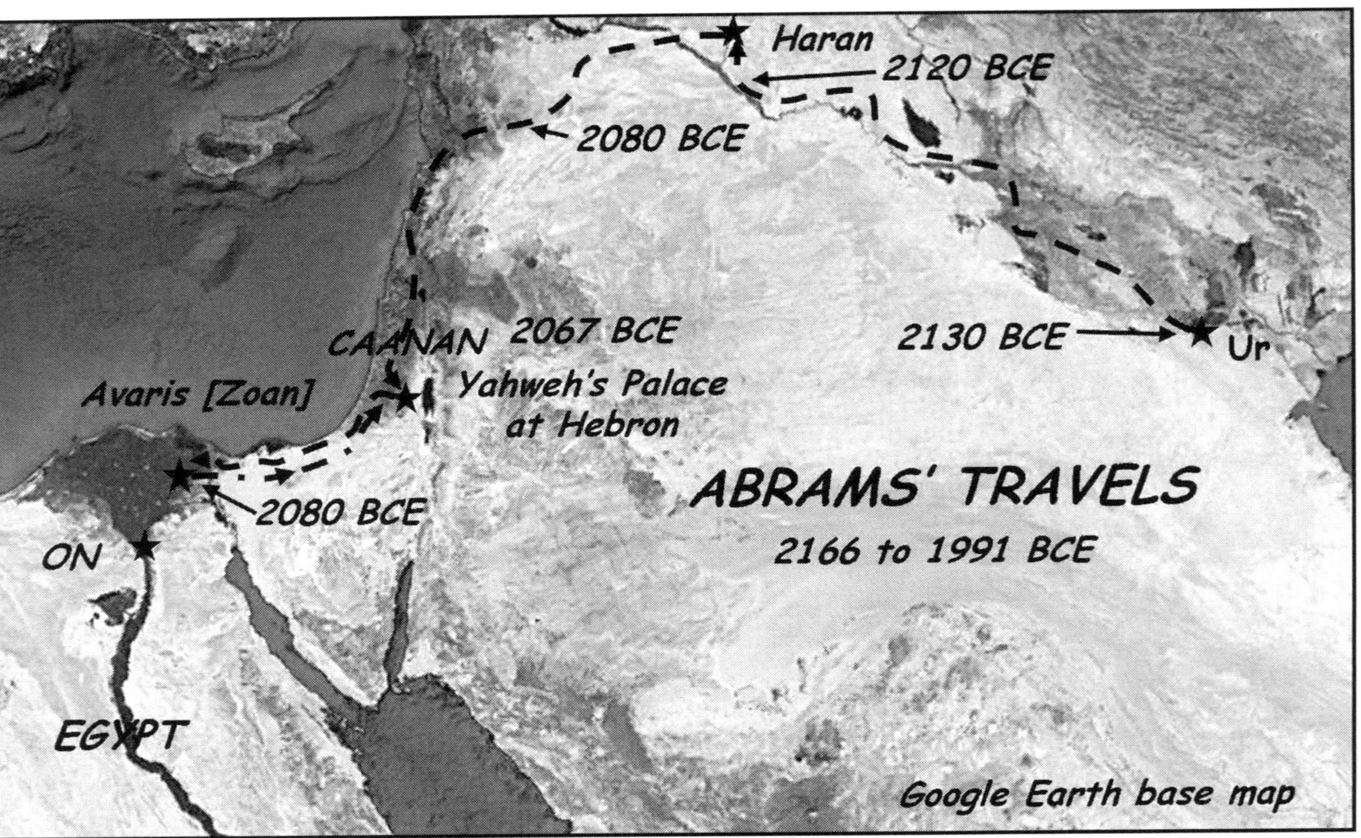
Haran
2120 BCE
2080 BCE
2130 BCE
Ur
CAANAN
2067 BCE
Avaris [Zoan]
Yahweh's Palace
at Hebron
ABRAMS' TRAVELS
2166 to 1991 BCE
2080 BCE
ON
EGYPT
Google Earth base map

Chapter
3

**Having a brew in an old
Egyptian roadhouse**

ABRAM [IBRIM]
[2166 to 1991 BCE]

Genesis Chapter 12 vs. 1
*Now the Lord had said unto Abram, Get thee out of thy
country, and from thy kindred, and from thy father's house,
unto a land that I will shew thee:*

It should be apparent by now that Lord Yahweh was instrumental in
nurturing the development of the Semitic Tribes as his lineage and
descendants, and he as their God. As one of the council leaders of the
Lords of Sumer, and the father of Adam, he had an obligation to
nurture these movements while waiting for his own rescue.

The Old Testament contains many examples of "divine interventions",
which supposedly altered the course of history. These interventions
were recorded by men to impress a following who would believe what
their Prophet told them.

The ancient scribes who put together the myth of the Exodus believed
they were recording acts of God's spiritual mysticism. These myths
provided a view of God, Lord Yahweh, as a deity who would provide
punishments of instant heinous death and destruction for failing to
comply with religious or social law.

It is apparent, in their memoirs, that the Patriarchs of the Hebrews knew of Lord Yahweh long before the famous name game of "*I AM WHO I AM*," that is, Yahweh. This was supposed to be the first revelation of the name of the Hebrew God. It is clearly an untruth, a lie. The Patriarchs knew of Yahweh but could not decide where he fit in the hierarchy of Gods. They clearly knew he was associated with *Elohim*, the pantheon of seven Gods dealing death and destruction for millennia.

In the ancient Grand Lodge, high ranking members held the power of life or death over members of lesser degrees. What has been overlooked in biblical history is that Abram was subservient to dual authorities. The first authority being Yahweh, and the second was the Grand Lodge, subservient to the Lords of the kingdom. When Abram encountered Grand Lodge members in his travels, he was able to immediately identify them by their use of secret signs. These signs would communicate that the approaching person was a Masonic brother. The body stance would inform the Lodge member that he was looking at a person of specific authority. At this point the subservient member would address the visitor as *My Lord*. If this sounds unrealistic, read Genesis Chapter 18 verses 1-3.

A common overuse/mistranslation of a word, or phrase, is *angel*. One original phrase which translated as angel was *mal a'khim*. A more correct translation is emissary or messenger. Depending on the context in which it was used, the word had different meanings. The 1611 CE translators disregarded any meaning less than spiritual and used the word angel. By doing this, the stories were raised to a higher religious plane, creating spiritual beings in the place of quite ordinary men.

[*The following commentary is from* **THE DEAD SEA SCROLLS DECEPTION** *addressing the existing King James translation*]. *Author acknowledged.*

The King James Version translated the following phrases to Angel(s); the righteous, the upright, the blameless, the saintly, the penitent, school children, the pious, those who held true knowledge, those who possessed the wisdom of the *Sons of Heaven*. Also accorded the angelic titles were certain members of nobility who demonstrated the proper moral foundation. Each of these examples was originally written using ancient Hebrew phrases.

When a member of the Grand Lodge sent a message through a *mal a'khim*, a messenger or emissary, to Abram, the ancient text would later be translated to, "And the Lord sent an angel to Abram." The result of the translations obscured the physical realities that Abram dealt with authorities other than Lord Yahweh.

If you are wondering, "What ancient text would be translated?" you are beginning to apply free-thinking. The only "ancient texts" available at this time were prepared by the priests and scribes of the Ancient Lodge. In this instance the text would be the daily Lodge records. All Lodge business and communications were meticulously recorded for the secret records of the Grand Lodge. The Lodge records of importance were communicated to Enoch. There was a very detailed record kept of Yahweh's descendants at Parvaim, by Enoch. The objective of this explanation is to widen our view of Abram as a real person. Although he followed the tenets and commandments of his Gods, he also dealt with everyday problems.

This epic tale of Abram's travels and interactions with Lord Yahweh should be viewed with the same candor as other epics, such as Noah. Abram was most likely a real person and the name was very common at the time. There are independent accounts of his life which bear out times and locations of his travels. Again, I must use considerable unverified Holy Writ information to put together any meaningful storyline.

Abram was about 35 years old and was living in his ancestral town of Ur with his father's [Terah] family in the southern region of Mesopotamia. This history is well known with every aspect of the religious significance of the revelation and subsequent journey written about or discussed. Scholars usually dote upon the spirituality of the event. This causes everyone to overlook the physical reality that motivated the event.

Lord Yahweh communicated directly with Abram because of an immediate necessity. Terah's family, including Abram, was in physical danger because of his direct lineage from Adam. Marduk's cult was under orders to murder all of them. In the book of Genesis, Chapter 12, verse 1, Yahweh commands Abram, *"Get thee out of thy country, and from thy kindred, and from thy father's house."* Yahweh usually only openly communicated with his "firstborns".

Abram did travel from Ur, eventually reaching Egypt's Nile Delta after a visit with Yahweh at his Samarian villa. I believe this palace was located on Mount Gerizim.

Abram's recorded odyssey began in southern Sumer about 2,130 BCE. Lord Yahweh revealed himself to the Prophet Abraham's family. Abram was living in the old Sumerian city of Ur when his father, Terah, was instructed to leave the city and move to a place of safety.

The exact year of Abram's departure from the city of Ur is unknown. Historians generally conclude it occurred around 2130 BCE. Some Biblical scholars place Abram's life from 2166 to 1991 BCE, however, the exact date is not that important in establishing his history. Abram's travels began when his father, Terah, took the family from their inherited, native homeland, the city of Ur in Sumer, and moved them to the city of Haran. If the pending danger was to Abram alone, there was no reason for the entire family leaving their inherited lands and homes.

Haran was situated in northwest Mesopotamia, about 600 miles north of Ur. The town was located at the foothills of the Taurus Mountains, where several caravan routes merged. This area was a major crossroads for trade to and from Asia Minor. The established God of Haran was the Moon Goddess, which was the favorite god of Abram's mother.

The forces that motivated Abram's father to leave the city of Ur have been obscured in biblical history. Rather than researching this era, historians focused on the spirituality of Yahweh's revelation to Abram. Had anyone reviewed other data of that area, an intriguing scenario of serious physical realities would have emerged.

Lord Yahweh had lost his battle for supremacy of the southern part of Iraq to Lord Marduk [Baal]. Marduk continuously beat up on Yahweh and his tribes, and actually had more followers from Yahweh's tribes than Yahweh had.

Yahweh decided to abandon this area and move his most ardent followers to a safe distant area where his people could grow without the interference of Marduk. That place was Canaan and the Delta of Egypt.

The history before Abram's command to move provides some additional, very interesting and unusual information. Prior to Abram's family moving to Haran a powerful cult emerged, whose origins remain unknown. The cult arrived from an undisclosed region of the northern area of the Fertile Crescent and established itself in the most northern city-states of Mesopotamia. Although the cult left no known written history of its existence, historical traces of the cult can be found. Ancient Assyrian cuneiform text provides some of the clearest views of the cult of Marduk and refers to him by the name Merodakh.

The name Marduk, in the early Assyrian language, translates to *Son of the Storm.*   Marduk was recorded in the Assyrian and Sumerian histories with 50 different names. He was always portrayed in his "weaponized Sky Disk", often shown hovering above palm trees. The Assyrians described Marduk as, *the joyous devourer, the terror of merciless inexplicable and unpredictable death.* In later history he is referred to under the ancient Semitic name of Molech, as referred to in Leviticus.

Leviticus Chapter 20 vs. 1-6
And the Lord spake unto Moses, saying, Again, thou shalt say to the children of Israel, Whosoever he be of the children of Israel, or of the strangers that sojourn in Israel, that giveth any of his seed unto Molech; he shall surely be put to death: the people of the land shall stone him with stones. And I will set my face against that Man, and will cut him off from among his people; because he hath given of his seed unto Molech, to defile my sanctuary, and to profane my holy name. And if people of the land do any ways hide their eyes from the Man, when he giveth of his seed unto Molech, and kill him not: Then I will set my face against that Man, and against his family, and will cut him off, and all that go a-whoring after him, to commit whoredom with Molech, from among their people.   And the soul that turneth after such as have familiar spirits, and after wizards, to go a-whoring after them, I will even set my face against that soul, and will cut him off from among his people.

The Biblical use of the word *seed* is symbolic of having sexual intercourse with cult members during the rituals performed at festivals. The symbolic use also refers to providing an infant child for ritual sacrifice at cult festivals. These festivals were held to honor the Sun God, Moon Goddess, the solstices and equinoxes among many lesser Gods.

The cult established itself in the northern city-states by adapting drama rituals to ancient man's religious festivals.   The festivals celebrated the planting and harvest of agricultural produce, on which the communities survived. During this time Man had invented Gods to govern every aspect of nature. There were also Gods to protect or intervene in all aspects of their daily existence. The cult simply exploited this belief in numerous God figures. Ancient Man was led to believe cult drama would result in improved relations with these God figures, and prosperity would be ensured.

As the power of the cult grew, they became the orchestrators of all the religious festivals. The festival of the date palms was first practiced in the northern city-states of Sumer and centered on a cult drama known as the **Sacred Marriage**. In this celebration, the cult reenacted the wedding of The Sun God with the Moon Goddess beneath a date palm. The priest depicted himself in the drama as the Sun God and performed with the local Moon Priestess. This supposed joining provided the means that caused the date palms to bear fruit. The priest not only acted as, but actually became a God. His sexual union with a Goddess of nature provided the power to fertilize all of nature. Similar Gods were in place in Egypt at this time, of course with Egyptian names.

The Sacred Marriage ceremony was depicted throughout the Sumerian empires in terra cotta, carved stone images and in paintings. It was the staple event to celebrate the Spring Equinox, guarantying fertile crops, particularly dates and for the population. It was an extravagant and well attended religious annual ceremony. The Spring Equinox continues to be a time for religious celebration. [I cannot include an image of these depictions, as it would require a classification as pornographic material.]

After portraying himself as able to influence the forces of nature, the priest became a powerful figure in the community. As this cult spread, it was entrenched in every facet of daily life able to influence decisive political victories, battles against enemies, the planting of fields, and even successful journeys.

To induce the priest and the cult to remain in their communities, the population provided them with temples. The temples were complete with servants, handmaidens, musicians, and other personnel to ensure their comfort. The ancient Assyrian texts relate the priest was treated as God, and was a great landowner. His daily needs were met regardless of what they were.

When the cult held the prospering economy in their power, the venue of the celebrations and festivals expanded to include active participation of the local population. This became a forum for sexual debauchery, and ultimately, the sacrifice of children. The sacrifices were disguised as gifts of fertility to the Gods. In realistic terms, the sacrifice of children symbolized the total control of power over a human population. The complete terror of innocence victims was the perverted power that fed the cult.

Marduk was firmly entrenched in the Babylonian civilization. Marduk, or someone representing Marduk, became the city God and later attained national status as the primary God of Assyria. After establishing itself in the northern-most city-states of Sumer [Mesopotamia], its influence spread southward. During this time the kings of the city-states were in constant conflict with each other. The cult was unable to persuade many of the kings to share their power over the local populations. Apparently, they had more important matters to contend with, such as retaining their status as rulers.

Terah is recorded as "The Master Builder of Ur," he was also a polytheist. Along with his belief in Lord Yahweh, he worshipped lesser Gods, with the Moon Goddess being the family favorite. The Sun God and Moon Goddess were favorites of the Assyrians centered in the northern city of Haran. It was not unusual for a man to take new "lesser Gods" into his home every time he brought in a new wife. Terah had two first-born sons of importance born in Ur. He had several wives, as was custom, and his favorite wives bare Abram and Haran.

His sons each married at the age of about 30 years, which was custom, and Haran fathered a son, Lot, Abram's nephew. Abram's wife Sari was barren and bore no children, his other wives gave him sons and daughters. Haran was murdered by a cult of "Chaldeans" which was gaining power in Ur. The threat to Terah's family was so great that he moved from his ancestral homeland to the city of Haran. *[No connection to his son's name, just different ancient names translated to the same word].*

The city of Haran provided security and was well established in the worship of the Moon Goddess. The reason Abram's nephew Lot stayed with him through his journeys was, it was the custom for a brother to take his widowed sister-in-law and children into his home. She became his wife, and Lot his son. Terah most likely left Ur about 2,130 BCE, and his extended family lived in Haran for about forty years, until 2090 BCE, before Abram decided to leave.

Assyrian texts describe Marduk as *wandering* during this period and sending supplies and emissaries through Haran. The translation of the ancient writings should have been *searching*. I believe this was the case; that Marduk was searching, not wandering.

The journey from Ur to Haran, along the Euphrates River, was about 600 miles. Consider the effort to move an extended family, herds and possessions in wagons. If the group averaged 10 miles a day on days they actually traveled, the journey took months to complete. More like several years. Terah did not sneak out of Ur in the middle of the night. Marduk's cult knew very well that Terah was leaving and where he was going. I suspect all was negotiated, with Lord Yahweh, allowing Terah to safely depart.

After about forty years, Marduk's emissaries entered the area of Haran and Abram decided to move on. Interesting enough, his father lived there with his extended family for another 60 years before dying at the age of 205 years.

Abram was in the direct family lineage of Adam, and Biblical history indicates this lineage worshipped one Supreme God, although they did often favor a great number of "lesser Gods." At the time of the revelation, Abram was in serious physical danger in the city of Ur, at age 35, not at age 75 in the city of Haran. The reason for this explanation is most theologians teach the latter version. Ancient text indicates the discourse from Yahweh occurred prior to the move to Haran.

Genesis Chapter 12 vs. 1
Now the Lord had said unto Abram, Get thee out of thy country, and from thy kindred, and from thy father's house, unto a land that I will shew thee:

This command carried a message of urgency; instructing Abram to *get out of the country, get away or apart from all your relatives*. This instruction was because the family relatives usually knew the business and location of other family members. The part of the message which states, *from thy father's house,* means, do not identify yourself as being part of your father's household. Abram was to immediately leave and sever all ties that would identify him to anyone searching for him.

This urgent message was either ignored or moving to Haran with his extended family was part of Yahweh's plan. Or, maybe the translations over the years were more "Religious" with pieces of this history omitted. Moving a large extended family, with herds and possessions was not a stealthy thing to do. Possibly, Terah gave up family estates and promised homage to the "Moon Goddess" in Haran. However, it happened, they made the journey and prospered for "forty years." Abram began his travels toward Egypt at the age of 75 years, in 2091 BCE. You may notice the number "40" preceding times of days or years in biblical history. These are often not exact spans of time in a true translation; just really mean "a very long time" counted in either days or years.

ABRAM'S [IBRIM'S] JOURNEY TO EGYPT

[2080 BCE – approx.]

[The following stories about The Prophet Abraham's journey and contacts in Egypt are taken from *Memoirs of the Patriarchs, Dead Sea Scrolls*] [*Author acknowledged*] and the Kings of The Book of The Dead.]

This is the beginning of the political interaction of the Hebrews with Egypt in Biblical folklore. It is important to establish as much factual data about the rulers and politics of Egypt to understand the depth of the fables in the Holy Writ.

There are several versions of the Egyptian records called *THE BOOK OF THE DEAD*, each with differences depending on the politics and preferences at the time of writing. Some King's dates vary by 1,000 years, depending on the researcher, others are omitted. So, don't let some date discrepancies distract you.

The earliest compilations of Egyptian Dynasty Kings dates are 5,867 BCE and were heavily edited in later versions. These listings did not include per-dynasty kings.   There were apparently problems of deciphering earlier listings due to language and writing changes.

The Heliopolitan [On, or Annu] version is compiled from inscriptions found in pyramids of the 5th and 6th dynasties at Saqqara. These were inscribed by Priests of Annu [On of the OT]. One of the inscriptions in the pyramid of Pepi II addressed the "great nine Gods who dwell in Annu".

The 18th, 19th and 20th Dynasties compiled The Theban Version, at Thebes. They used papyrus scrolls and hieroglyphics listing kings in chapters.

Some archaeologists have dated King Menes of the 1st Dynasty to 5867 BCE. He is commonly dated to 3150 BCE. This shows the difficulty in dating early dynasties.

When Abram left Haran, about 2090 BCE, he took his extended tribe, which included the sub-tribe of Lot.   Lord Yahweh knew of his departure and delegated a group of Lords to monitor and protect him. Yahweh *appeared* to Abram in Canaan and promised him all the lands for his descendants. Yahweh apparently despised the religious practices of Crete where the other Lords promoted the worship of The Sun God as primary.

At this time all of Canaan was part of Egypt and the Pharaoh was most likely Intef II, based at Thebes. The boundaries of Egypt extended east of the Nile Delta and north beyond Damascus. All of present-day Israel and most of Syria was in fact, Egypt. At times Egypt extended to Sumer. The tracking of Gods in Egypt was quite a task. The Theban Book of The Dead [a version] listed over five hundred Gods. The Primary God was the Sun God, Geb.

Abram was about to settle in Canaan and worship the local Gods, to get along with the Canaanites, but Yahweh intervened in his usual bluster and Abram built an altar to worship him at Beth-el.

Abram settled in Hebron, which is about 30 miles west of the Dead Sea and stayed there for two years. When a famine swept the land, he headed for the Nile Delta, hearing there was plenty of food and grazing there. Before he left, Lord Yahweh devised a plan for Abram to meet "Pharaoh" and get rich and promised him it would work. Abram said "let's get to it". The OT version of this encounter says "The Pharaoh of Zoan". Zoan was a Nile Delta city, later named Tanis, which was built about 1075 BCE, about 1,000 years after Abram's time. Most scholars believe the city of Abram's encounter was Avaris, which housed the Nomarch of this Nome. The Delta was divided into 20 Nomes, each administered by a Nomarch.

When Abram arrived in Egypt's Delta, he set Yahweh's plan in motion. He told his wife Sarai that the Pharaoh of Zoan's [the Nomarch of Avaris] men would come for her, to become one of his wives. He told her that if she divulged she was his wife, they would kill him, and take her anyway. He instructed Sarai to tell Pharaoh that he was just a "kinsman." The Hebrew word used was 'ah usually denoting the feminine noun for a relative and is ambiguous as to the extent of kinship. Abram reinforced this warning to Sarai telling her he had a dream from God that this was so.

Abram settled in the Nile Delta and lived there for five years when three Egyptian nobles arrived and confronted *Abram and Sarai* on orders of the Nomarch. The nobles had orders to find out who was living in the land without permission. They found Abram's and Lot's tribes camped, and their herds grazing. The families were tending crops and herds. Abram told the nobles he was only there to wait out the famine that was in Canaan.

The Nobles returned and reported on the homesteaders and also that there was an absolute beauty living there. They described her from head to toe, the form and color of her breasts, thighs, and complexion. They had been provided a good look at her. This was extremely unusual, actually unheard-of, for the Patriarch of a tribe to receive royal visitors with his women in apparent skimpy dress, in view of anyone.

The Nomarch immediately sent his men to bring this beauty to him. As soon as he saw her, he "took her to wife." He then instructed his men to kill Abram because it would have been against custom to steal another man's wife. Sarai told the men that he was only some relative and not to worry. The Nomarch compensated Abram with lavish gifts of herds and jewels for the loss of his kinsman to marriage. As the ancient texts say, "...and Abram prospered from the gifts".

Two years passed and the entire population of the Nomarch's household had contracted "a noisome spirit." The actual translation is, they contracted the **Spirit of Gleet**, that is, gonorrhea. A full-blown epidemic had rendered the male population impotent and the women sterile. The ancient text states "**In the Royal household not a man could function and all of the women were sterile**". The Nomarch appealed to his physicians, but not only did they not cure him, they were infected.

The Nomarch learned that Abram was not infected with this disease and wanted him to come to the city and heal his household with Abram's God's powers. Lord Yahweh put the rest of the plan in motion. Instead of Abram, Lot went to the Nomarch and told him this plague was a curse from God because he had Abram's wife and that no cure was possible as long as he held Abram's wife as his own. The Noble was stunned. His words to Abram, "**What have you done to me? Take your wife and get out of Egypt! But first, cure this plague,**" shows his state of mind. So, Abram provided the cure for gonorrhea and when the Nomarch and his household were finally cured, he released Sarai.

Abram now had the man in a moral and legal dilemma along with the backing of an all-powerful God. The Noble had given Sarai a formal marriage contract, and under Hebrew custom a formal divorce decree would have to be granted before Abram would accept her back as his wife. The divorce settlement was just like some of today, an absolute killer. All of the gold and silver, clothing, jewels, servants and herds she could travel with. Lot also received huge herds and wives from the Royal lineage of Egypt. The Nomarch then escorted the entire tribe of Abram out of the country.

Could it be that Sarai was always barren due to a gonorrhea infection? I think Lord Yahweh invented *The Trojan Horse* scam.

I included this ancient tale because it was humorous and to show how ancient "war stories" were turned, and twisted, into a supposed religious experience.

During the next two years, Abram returned to Beth-el, built a second altar and worshipped, providing burnt offerings to Yahweh. Soon after Abram built the altar, Lot and Abram parted company because of feuds between their camps. I suspect the feuds were religious in nature, as Lot brought Egyptian wives and their Gods out of Egypt. However, Abram did the same, as was the custom of that time. The grazing issue was the face-saving issue to allow both to part company. Whatever the reasons for the breakup of the family, Abram was not pleased with Lot leaving. Abram added "lavishly" to Lot's herds and wealth when he left. Such a separation of the family would have been a very serious matter. The result was a division of their wealth, power, and most important, personal security. It is easy to conclude Abram was avoiding an even more serious conflict between them.

The continuation of this story shows the downfall of good people who move to big cities, drink and party too much. Other than a few interesting points preserved for history, I do not intend to use obvious fables to fill pages with commentary.

The story continues as Lot moves to the evil city, God bombs the town, Lot becomes a drunk and performs incest with his daughters and dies an asshole. Have you ever thought about how many people have made their career about proving the "Sodom and Gomorrah" story?

The cities were destroyed as many others in the area were destroyed, wars, earthquakes, droughts and floods. The destruction was incorporated with religious fables which were widely promoted, as was "Noah's flood".

Homosexuality existed then, and today, in every culture on Earth. I am not an advocate or defender of anyone's sexual conduct. I don't care. If God were going to destroy humans for their social conduct, he would have started with the groups engaging in human sacrifice. That would have been Lord Yahweh and Lord Bal [Marduk] and all of their followers.

Abram remained on Beth-el Mountain for a time and eventually traveled to the plains of Mamre, near Hebron. There he allied with three Amorite brothers, Mamre, Aneram, and Eshcol, Grand Masters all.

Abram was also identified as part of The Grand Lodge, as Grand Master Melchizedek, King of Jerusalem, prepared a feast and blessing ceremony for him. After receiving this *blessing*, or Lodge honor, Abram donated "a great amount" to High Priest Melchizedek.

A Lodge ceremony recorded at this meeting indicates an ancient Masonic ritual. The members, swearing allegiance to each other and to the Grand Lodge of Melchizedek, arraigned the parts of slaughtered animals hanging in two rows. They then raised their hands in a particular manner and walked between the rows stating "**May it be so done to me if I do not keep my oath and pledge.**"

Following Yahweh's revelation that Canaan would become the homeland of the Hebrews, Abram entered into the covenant of circumcision. He changed his name to Abraham, and Sari's name to Sarah. Although the English translation of changing Abram to Abraham does not appear significant, it was a considerable change. The original title was of royalty, a great leader, specifically "Exalted Father." When changed, the name translated "Father of many". Abraham was 99 years old. The year was 2,067 BCE.

Lord Yahweh promoted this "covenant", the ritual of genital mutilation as one of many attempts to control rampant sexually transmitted diseases in the tribes. Usually the victors of any battle would take the women as their own concubines, spreading any disease through the tribe. Circumcision also was a means of identifying members of his tribe. Lord Yahweh always disguised social constraints and the building of leaders with religious overtones. It is difficult for me to attach any religious meaning to the mutilation of one's genitalia. Of course, that depends on who has the knife.

These series of events; Abram's army defeating the forces threatening a number of important cities, the Grand Lodge's blessing of Abram, the covenant of circumcision, and Abram's name change, were all overshadowed by the story of Lot.

Abraham continued uninterrupted into history, emerging as a prophet and the patriarch of several great religions. He lived another 75 years, dying in 1993 BCE. As recorded by scribes; Abraham continued to allow his wife to be taken by kings when he passed through their kingdoms. The story is the same as with the Egyptian, the various king's entire household became so infected with gonorrhea that no children were born, and "not a man could function." After paying a great ransom to Abraham and Sarah, the king's household was cured and everyone lived happily ever after.

One of Abraham's medicinal cures was nitrated silver. There were several other "cures" of salts of certain metals and various Sulphur compounds which were known from pre-deluge times. These discoveries led to the term alchemy, as the Lodge Priests continued scientific experiments.

The Hebrews needed a place where they could multiply and prosper without famines and without constant battles with Assyrian forces. Egypt was perfect for this purpose, isolated and easily defended. Abraham was the "Father of Israel" and the first recorded Hyksos leader to journey to the Delta area.

A final comment on the "religious" history we have slogged through. We, in Western theology, have been taught that "God" put a "Mark" on Cain so no one would slay him. We were also taught this "Mark" was the religious coloring of his skin, creating "the dark people." Adam knew Cain was not of his lineage as soon as he was born because of his very light skin and red hair. Adam was of Semitic origin, dark skinned. Cain was of Caucasian descent, that of Marduk.

There was no reason, or way, to change the color of his skin. It is recorded that he was given a "Mark" to protect him. In the Hebrew Bible it states "And the LORD set a sign for Cain", which is more definitive than the translation of "a mark".

The only protective sign or mark of this time was later to become the "**Taw**," the last letter of the Hebrew alphabet, the Masonic hooked **X** of protection. This was also the symbol of worshippers of Lord Bal, **The Sun God**, and later of **Mitra** [Sun God] in Roman times. Yahweh did not give Cain the mark [sign] of Lodge protection, Bal gave it to him.

Moses having a brew in an old Egyptian Roadhouse
[Image from carved and painted stelae]

TL 6 Hyksos & Exodus

YEARS BCE

2000 CE
0 BCE

Years BCE	Event
1,180	Setnakht expelled Hyksos in 2nd "Exodus" reclaims looted gold
1,140	Hebrews attack Canaanite Kingdoms
1,450	Yahweh's Temple built on Mt. Gerizim in Samaria
1,533	Ahmose I routs Hyksos in 1st "Exodus" sends Hyksos back to Canaan
1,628	Thera explodes and Crete is decimated – ending support for the Hyksos
1,880	Joseph is appointed to the Temple of On by Pharaoh - Amun is the Sun God
1,900	First Hyksos capital at Avaris
2,080	Abram aligns with Yahweh and journeys to Egypt's Delta– this begins the Hebrews' journeys to Egypt
5,500	Enuma Elish describes Eden and making First Man - Chief God is the Sun God El— first "Holy Writ" expanded from ancient Sumer
6,000	Temples and Cities in Sumer—writing Developed from ancient Pre-Deluge Sumer
8,000	Egypt has organized farming villages
10,000	Gobekli Tepe temple is purposely buried in northern Sumer
10,900	Comet impact of Earth causes Pleistocene Extinction
18,000	Lords establish civilizations in Asian And American Continents

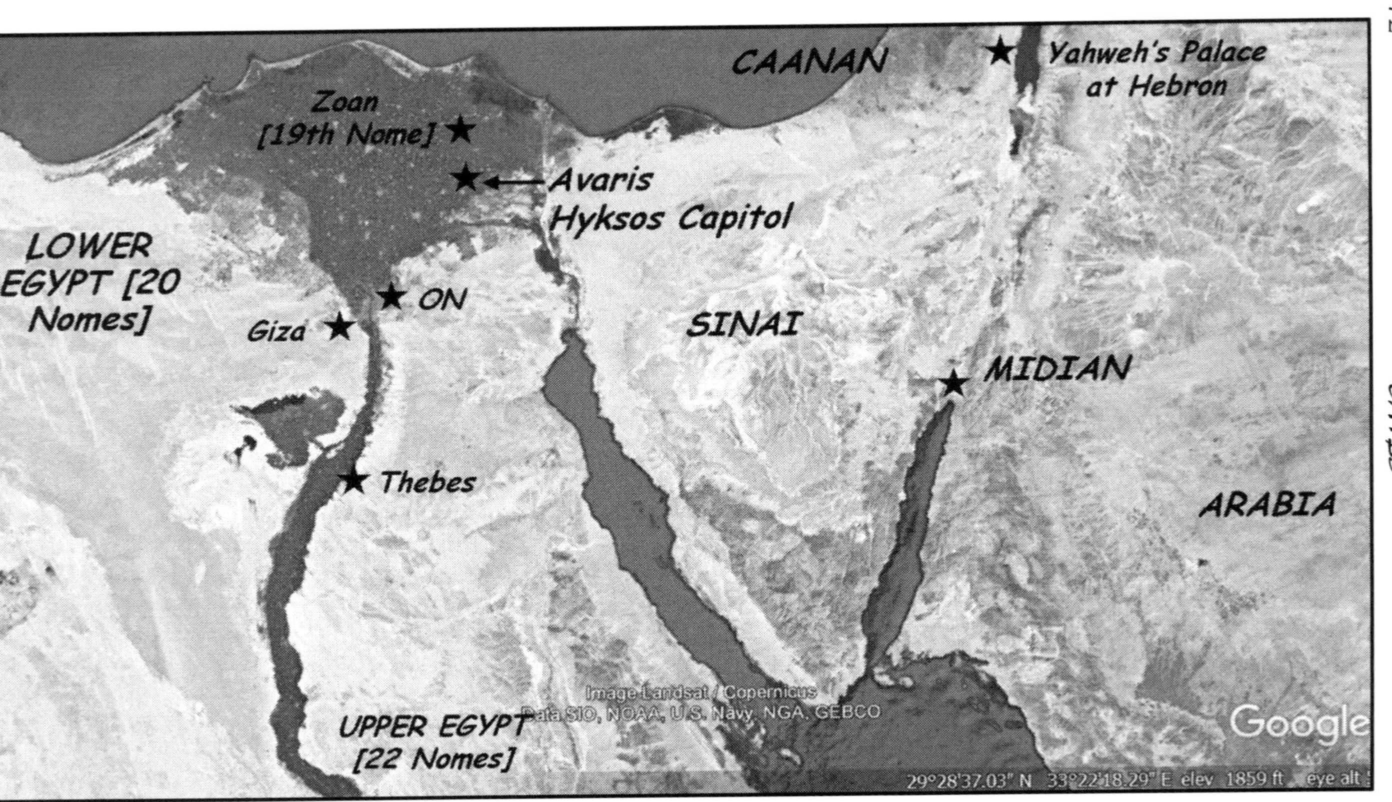

CAANAN
Yahweh's Palace
at Hebron
Zoan
[19th Nome]
Avaris
Hyksos Capitol
LOWER
EGYPT [20
Nomes]
ON
Giza
SINAI
MIDIAN
Thebes
ARABIA
UPPER EGYPT
[22 Nomes]
Image Landsat / Copernicus
Data SIO, NOAA, U.S. Navy, NGA, GEBCO
29°28'37.03" N 33°22'18.29" E elev 1859 ft   eye alt
Google

Chapter
4

THE HYKSOS
[Shepard Rulers from Canaan]

Exodus Chapter 1 vs. 8-10
Now there rose up a new king over Egypt, which knew not Joseph. And he said unto his people, Behold, the people of the children of Israel are more and mightier than we: Come on, let us deal wisely with them: lest they multiply, and it come to pass, that, when there falleth out any war, they join also unto our enemies, and fight against us, and so get them up out of the Land.

The true history of the Hebrew Tribes prior to, and after the "Exodus Fable", has been distorted and hidden by religious zealots for thousands of years. The actual events were rearranged and enriched with spiritual mythology. The Hebrew culture coined the phrase "God's Chosen People" and fabricated the story of "Moses and the Exodus" in the Torah.

Around 700 BCE Hebrew scribes used a combination of customs, laws, legends, superstitions, and spirituality to enrich historical events. Yahweh provided the strict religious laws to maintain and control his tribes as a unified People. As religious history was recorded, spiritual mythology replaced physical realities. This continued and compounded with each translation from one language to another, and from generation to generation.

The Old Testament only existed for the Hebrew culture and only after about 300 BCE. The outline for this ancient history was first recorded by the angel Metatron [Prophet Enoch], while serving as Lord Yahweh's personal scribe. This recorded history excludes most civilizations outside of a physical area of about 1,200 hundred miles square. According to Biblical history this area was the total land-mass of the world. A fact of the knowledge of the world is recorded by the Hebrews describing the Phoenicians territory as being to the Straits of Gibraltar and the north coast of Africa.

In reality the OT recorded the lineage and movement of Yahweh's descendants. This record was inserted into the framework of the Sumerian Enuma Elish, with the Elba Tablets providing much of the narrative for creation, cloaking centuries of natural disasters and wars as miracles from God. Years of wars in Egypt were cloaked as miraculous events of a Hebrew leader bringing his people out of Egypt, to the "Promised Land" of Canaan.

The Elba Tablets [Enuma Elish copies] were created about 2,500 BCE and the epic was well known in ancient times. You will be amazed at the similarities of the epic stories compared with "Genesis" of the OT. The Elba tablets along with thousands more were amassed at Ashurbanipal's Library at Nineveh about 650 BCE.

The True History of Hebrews, Moses and The Exodus

Biblical history, reviewed in a perception of reality, is even more difficult every time we see a film version of religious history. Many individuals identify with and subsequently believe these film portrayals are true and correct depictions of historical and spiritual fact.

History provides a very different version of these events. Other than the Holy Writ there is little evidence "Moses" existed, or that an "*EXODUS*" occurred as taught. Another clue that the "Moses" was plagiarized from the Enuma Elish and other ancient tales is the epic Sargon Legend. Sargon The Great is recorded as being rescued as an infant from a reed basket floating in a river. The time was about 2330 BCE, a thousand years before "Moses". But it was a good story! Sort of like "It was a dark and stormy night" opening for a mystery novel.

I will attempt to bring some clarity using the most recently deciphered Egyptian records. This will require considerable speculation on my part. I now believe I have a truer account of "The Tribes of Israel" through recent discoveries and deciphered ancient script. Most of the history was recorded by the Egyptian Priest and historian Manetho. The balance was deciphered fragments of writings and hieroglyphics. Archaeology has made tremendous strides in exposing the Minoan connection to the influx of Hyksos craftsmen into the Delta area.

The massive population influx of Lower Egypt [the Delta] by Hebrews did occur. The Egyptians used the Hebrews as a resource for building monuments, domestic and field labor, and at times the situation was reversed.

The Hebrew Tribes were fractured politically and varied greatly in religious practices. They would need motivation and strong leadership to come together as a people and eventually as a nation under one God. Yahweh and the Hebrew Priests eventually solved these problems with a "Moses" leader but at a much later time and place.

I researched for years trying to support something of a Biblical version of this story. I overlooked my own advice to remove the mental scotomas created by religious indoctrination. I failed to do that. I did not want to give up the "cute" story I had concocted in my mind and in my previous book.

Lord Yahweh did not orchestrate the growth and prosperity of the Israelites in Egypt. Yahweh's grand plan was to defeat Lord Marduk's nations and settle his [Yahweh's] descendants firmly in the land of Canaan. Yahweh had no support from the Council of Lords for an incursion into Egypt. It appears he was in near exile in his Samarian Palace.

The Lords of Crete supported the Hyksos for over four hundred years in Lower Egypt. These were Lords allied with Bal, as Yahweh removed himself to live in Samaria. Bal carefully orchestrated and guided the power and prosperity of the Israelites and the Lodge in Egypt. This power was centered with the Priesthood of Annu [On], worshipping the Sun God and Egyptian Gods. The "Seven Heavenly Beings" were worshipped at Annu.

The Seven Gods have been a cornerstone for religious worship since antiquity. The Ancient Hebrews worshipped seven Gods, represented by seven flaming candlesticks and had many lesser Gods. Babylon had seven Gods representing the Sun, Moon and the five planets and many lesser Gods. The Israelites have seven Archangels and many lesser angels. The Christians have the seven angels of the seven churches and thousands of lesser Gods. Roman Mitra worshippers had the Triad of Mitra, Ahura and Anahita and a myriad of lesser Gods.

The Tribes of Israel

The Temple of On [college of Annu] referred to in the Christian Bible is about 20 miles north of the site of Memphis. On began about 4,000 BCE as a religious center for worshipping the Sun and Moon Gods and the "Seven Holy Beings" which formed the pantheon of Gods that ruled Earth, also known as Elohim. Archaeologists state that On stood for over 4,000 years before its destruction in 525 BCE.

The Dynastic Period of Egypt began when Upper and Lower Egypt were first united under one ruler. Upper Egypt is the southern region and Lower Egypt is the northern region. The city of Thinnis in Upper Egypt was the seat of King Mena's 1st Dynasty [3,150-2,890 BCE] but the seat of the 2nd Dynasty [2,890 – 2,686 BCE] was located at Memphis.

Lord Bal was the influence for developing the Delta and bringing the Pharaoh's power there. Lord Yahweh had built his Minoan style Palace in Canaan by 3,000 BCE and held great resentment for the Hebrews following Lord Bal.

The 3rd Dynasty, of King Djoser 2,686 to 2,613 BCE, was also at Memphis. This location was chosen for the power of the Priesthood located in On.   Memphis was the seat for pharaohs thru the 6th Dynasty [2,345 – 2,181 BCE]

At the end of the 6th Dynasty, King Pepi II had reigned for 94 Years. In 2,181 BCE, the Egyptian Royalty moved back to Upper Egypt, leaving the Temple of Annu as an outpost.

The Royal family of Egypt gained enough power to overrule the Old Kingdom Pharaohs and move the seat of power back to Upper Egypt. The seat of power for Pharaohs moved to Thebes in the 7th dynasty, leaving the Delta to be administered by Twenty Nomarchs. During this time Hyksos craftsmen, laborers and their families moved into the Delta to support the massive building programs in Lower Egypt.

Pharaoh Intef the Elder [reign ending 2,134 BCE], son of Iku, was the first ruler of the 11th Dynasty. Upper and Lower Egypt were united under the Middle Kingdom based at Thebes.

During the 11th Egyptian Dynasty of Pharaoh Intef II, based at Thebes, [2,118 to 2,069 BCE] the first records of a Hyksos [Hebrew] migration into the eastern Nile Delta appear. The date was about 2090 BCE. This is when Abram traveled to "Zoan" [Avaris]. Egypt was in decline for almost 100 years before this event. As the Hebrew population increased Avaris became the center of power for the Hyksos and they followed the Egyptian King of Gods, Amun, with his spouse Mut and their Son Khunsu, the Moon God. These formed the "first Trinity Godhead" in Egypt. This trinity would be advance thru history as the Sun God Mitra and into Christianity.

The 11th through the 14th Dynasties are combined as the "Middle Kingdom", 2,134 to 1,690 BCE [444 years]. The home of these Pharaohs changed often from Lower to Upper Egypt.

During the 12th Dynasty of Egypt [approx. 1,880 BCE], Pharaoh Sesostris III ended a peaceful coexistence with Theban rulers and neighbors to the north by conquering Egypt south to the 3rd cataract and north into Canaan. It was this pharaoh who granted lands in the eastern Delta to "Joseph and his brothers". This must have been a political agreement with the rulers of Canaan. Canaanite migrants [Hyksos] steadily moved into the Delta as labor for the construction of monuments.

Sesostris III established trade with the Mediterranean nations from Greece to Canaan, which was coordinated by the Minoans.

In 1,880 BCE Israel's [Jacob's] son Joseph, at age twenty, and his brothers were sent from Canaan to Egypt to become the ruling class of the Hyksos. He was tutored by the High Priest of the Temple of On, while living with the Pharaoh's Captain of the Guard. The High Priest of On, Potiphera, was second only to Pharaoh Sesostris III [Senusret III, 1,878 – 1,839 BCE]. Joseph apparently married into Potiphera's family.

Joseph ruled as "The Minister of Egypt" from On for the Twelfth dynasty Pharaoh Sesostris III who lived near El Fayum, south of Memphis. Joseph worshipped the Sun God and other Egyptian Gods. His power may have been limited to Lower Egypt, as the Royal families of Upper Egypt despised the Hyksos as "irreligious and a plague on Egypt."

There was widespread famine and plagues from Canaan into Egypt for about a hundred years. The Delta was a good place to be and the Hyksos provided field and building labor. They also brought building skills and new weapons into Egypt.

13th Dynasty Pharaohs [1,803-1,649 BCE] reigned from Memphis over Middle and Upper Egypt to the second cataract to the south. There are 58 known Kings of this dynasty with the first 30 ruling from Memphis. Their power diminished over the next 150 years and ended when Hyksos rulers of the 15th dynasty overran Memphis in 1,650 BCE. The Hyksos 14th Dynasty began during the 13th Egyptian dynasty about 1,700 BCE.

The Canaanite migrants became many and mighty and formed an independent Dynasty 14 in the Delta and reigned from Avaris. They introduced new weapons and farming techniques to Egypt. Native Egyptians were hired to do the field work and herding of livestock. The Hyksos openly defied the authority of Thebes, charging them duty on ships passing the port of Avaris. Grazing fee agreements were made for the Pharaoh's cattle in the Delta.

The Egyptians recorded the Hyksos were supported by "foreign governments, their ships and army". The support came from the Minoans and their Phoenician fleet of warriors.

Archaeologists discovered ruins of a great Minoan palace at Avaris. Furnishings, frescos and other artifacts show occupation by Minoans. The Lords of Crete had put their full support and power behind the Hyksos. At this time Yahweh was residing in Samaria, at his mountaintop villa. He was not happy with his tribe following Lord Bal as the primary God.

The Hyksos served the 13th Dynasty as shepherds and labor to about 1,650 BCE when the 15th Hyksos Dynasty is recorded as defeating both the 13th and 14th Egyptian Dynasties. With the Hyksos in power, the Egyptians served them as laborers and shepherds. This arrangement infuriated the royal families. The various dynasties were not as concurrent as the dates imply. Many of the dynasties overlapped as they controlled different areas of Egypt at the same time.

In 1,628 BCE an event occurred which changed the world. The island of Thera [Parvaim] erupted and exploded, ending the Lords' sanctuaries on Thera and Crete. The fallout of ash caused widespread crop failures and famine through Egypt and Canaan, although the Delta recovered quickly. The power behind the Hyksos vanished overnight, changing the course of history again by natural calamity.   It took almost 50 years for the full effect of this disaster to catch up with the Hyksos rulers.

The 16th Egyptian Dynasty rulers, when Thera vaporized, were Neferhotep III [1,629-1,628 BCE] and Mentuhotepi [1,628-1,627 BCE].

The Egyptians regrouped at Thebes as the Hyksos-Abydos Dynasty gained strength for the next 50 years, listing 16 kings during this time. The Hyksos King Khyan conquered Egypt south to Thebes for a short period in 1,582 BCE before halting his advance. The Hyksos made a peace agreement with the Theban Kings of the 16th and 17th Dynasties [1,660-1,550 BCE]. The Theban Dynasties were most likely ruled by Royal Egyptian families living in an area north of Thebes.

Pharaoh Tutankhamun and his father Pharaoh Akhenaten displaying the Tau sign, or "Mark"

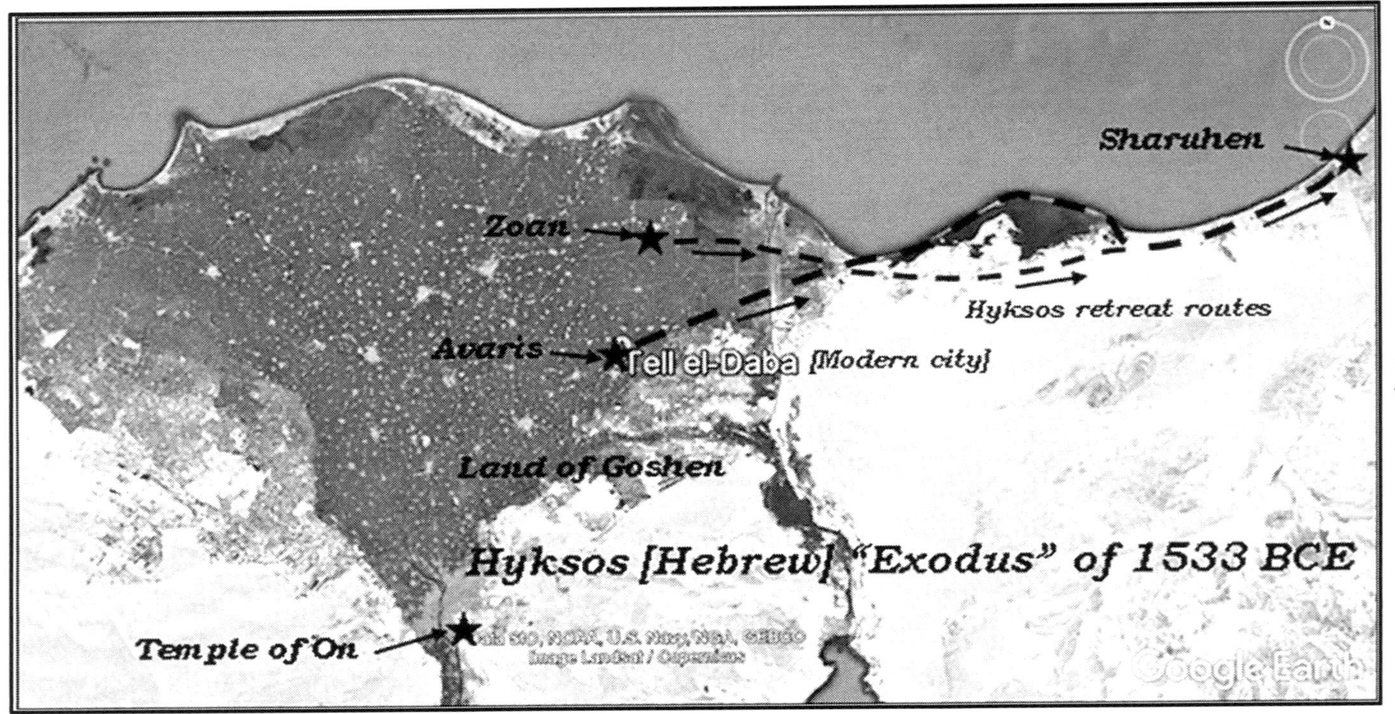
Sharuhen
Zoan
Hyksos retreat routes
Avaris
Tell el-Daba [Modern city]
Land of Goshen
Hyksos [Hebrew] "Exodus" of 1533 BCE
Temple of On
Google Earth

THE TRUE EXODUS

[Derived from translations of Period Hieroglyphs and cuneiform messages to and from Kings and Pharaohs. Other information is from archaeological published findings.]

Theban Pharaoh Seqenenre Tao [1,560-1,555 BCE] began skirmishes against the Hyksos Pharaoh Apepi [1,595-1,555 BCE] and was killed in battle. His son Kamose raised the hostilities to war at the prompting of the royal families. The Hyksos were showing weakness by this time and Thebes pressed the war.

Pharaoh Kamose was the last of 7 kings of the 17th dynasty and ruled for 5 years [1,555-1,550 BCE]. He began the war against the Hyksos King Khamudi [1,555-1,545 BCE] in 1,552 BCE by sailing north in a surprise attack. His campaign advanced close to the Hyksos Capitol Avaris, destroying crops and storage areas. He returned to Thebes a victor but died from wounds.

Pharaoh Ahmose I, [1,549 – 1,524 BCE] Kamose's brother, first king of the 18th Dynasty continued to push the Hyksos south. He overran Avaris and pursued the Hyksos across the Sinai desert to the town of Sharuhen, near Gaza. After a three-year siege the town was destroyed and the Hyksos fled into Canaan and safety in Jerusalem. The year was 1533 BCE.

This was the true "Exodus". 480,000 Hebrews [Hyksos], also known as "Shepherd Kings" were driven from Egypt after a commanding and prosperous presence which lasted about 400 years.

In the true "Exodus" there was no bondage, no killing of infant males, no "Moses" raised by Egyptians, no plagues from God, no killing of the Egyptian firstborn sons, no making the ocean open to dry ground, no drowning the Pharaoh and his army, no wandering the Sinai wilderness, no great displays from "God", no rocks with commandments chiseled into them. I may have missed a few points. No Hatshepsut raising "Moses" because she became Pharaoh [1,479 – 1,458 BCE] about 54 years later.

And the question of building the Ark of the Testimony and of building the tabernacle? That probably occurred in Samaria after Yahweh rounded up his tribes following the 2nd Exodus.

After Pharaoh Ahmose I defeated the Hyksos in 1,533 BCE the God Amun became the primary God of Egypt. Temples were erected at Karnak and the Priests of Amun would become a major ruling power in the land.

18th Dynasty Pharaoh Amenhotep IV [1,353 – 1,336 BCE] and his Queen, Nefertiti despised the power of the priests, changed his name to Akhenaten and moved to Amarna. He built a temple for the Aten, the Sun Disk, and declared this to be the state religion. The Priests of Amun were left without power but would reclaim their power at the end of Akhennaten's reign. He would be known as the "Heretic King" and his statues would be destroyed. The Priests of Amun would regain power and rule Egypt thru the 20th Dynasty.

The Hyksos [Hebrews] Regroup in Canaan

Having been "beaten mightily" by the Pharaoh the Hebrews began to organize and create a large formidable army. By 1,400 BCE the Hebrews were following Lord Yahweh and systematically conquering Canaan. This era was later recorded as being immediately after "Moses". The "Armana Tablets" contained many requests from the Canaanite Kings for assistance in fighting the "Habiru" [Hyksos] before their kingdoms were lost. The various Kings begged Pharaoh to "send his archers" to defend against the Hebrews. Pharaoh realized the Hyksos were now a formidable force and declined to engage them.

Modern Hebrew scholars correlate these battles to their Biblical Joshua conquering Canaan, which resulted in the formation of Judah and Samaria.

After conquering Canaan, the Hebrews again set their sights on occupying the Nile Delta. They allied with the Phoenicians and moved into the Delta around 1,200 BCE.

THE SECOND EXODUS

Ramesses I, [1,292 – 1,290 BCE] was the first pharaoh of the 19th Dynasty, which lasted about 110 years. This dynasty was full of overthrows and civil war. On the death of last pharaoh, Queen Twosret, [1,191 - 1,189 BCE] Egypt continued its civil and regional wars. Due to perceived weakness Egypt was constantly invaded by various neighboring countries. One of the invading coalitions was called "The Sea Peoples". These were the Phoenicians and Canaanites [Hyksos].

These invaders joined the Hyksos laborers already living in the Delta in looting many areas and seizing the Eastern Delta. Pharaoh Setnakht, [1,189 – 1,186 BCE] first king of the 20th Dynasty defeated "a large force of Hyksos" who had invaded the Delta. Records show he returned with most of the stolen gold, silver and gems, and paraded captives for the Egyptians to view. The captive invaders were removed to "strongholds" in Canaan and Samaria. A debated Egyptian stele refers to these people as "Israelites".

These and other stories of the past 800 years were added to the Sumerian Enuma Elish to create the Hebrew "Holy Writ", enriching Yahweh's power and his determination for the Hebrews to form a nation. The second exodus came about 350 years after the first. The date was about 1,180 BCE. This could be the part of the "Exodus" fable where the Hebrews "borrowed" all of the gold, silver and valuables from their Egyptian neighbors and hoofed it into the Sinai. They left out the part about getting caught and getting an ass whipping.

Based on Greek mythology, I am certain not all of the Lords chose to leave the Mediterranean area. They apparently enjoyed their families and lifestyles enough to leave the group and finish their extended lives in familiar surroundings. It is very clear the Hyksos no longer enjoyed the support and protection of Lord Bal. He had long since packed his bags and "got out of Dodge". Lord Yahweh finally had a captive audience to mold into his legacy religion.

YEARS BCE	70 CE	TL 7 Yahweh and Torah
300		Torah mostly complete— is finished 70 CE
700		Age of Prophets 750—600 Hebrews exiled Torah is beginning to form
922		King Solomon dies and the kingdom splits
950		Lord Yahweh dies and kingdom declines
1,020		King Saul 1st King of United Hebrew Kingdom
1,180		Setnakht expelled Hyksos in 2nd "Exodus" reclaims looted gold
1,400		Hebrews conquer Canaanite Kingdoms and invade Egypt's Delta
1,450		Yahweh's Temple built on Mt. Gerizim in Samaria
1,533		Pharaoh Ahmose I routs Hyksos in 1st "Exodus" chases Hyksos back to Canaan
1,628		Thera explodes, Crete, N. Egypt and Med area destroyed By Tsunamis and volcanic ash - Hyksos support ends from Lord Bal
1,850		Pharaoh rewards Joseph with land in Canaan [includes Judah and Samaria]
1,880		Joseph rules as "The Minister of Egypt" from the Temple of On by Pharaoh Sesostris - Amun is the Sun God
2,080		Abram travels to "Zoan" [Avaris] in 11th Dynasty
3,000		Yahweh builds Minoan Palace at Mt. Gerizim [Samaria]
3,200		King Menes 1st Egyptian dynasty [some date at 5,867 BCE?]
10,000		First Holy Writ — Enuma Elish develops

Chapter 5

Lord Yahweh's Tent

YAHWEH'S RULES

In 1533 BCE the Hyksos were driven from the Delta in the First "Exodus" and settled in parts of Canaan. By 1400 BCE the Tribes were formed and Yahweh found a Prophet to lead the Hebrews in conquering Canaan. I believe this is when the Hebrew prophets persuaded their people to listen to Yahweh's rules for life as dictated by a very irate, jealous and vindictive God. Yahweh was all they had and he promised them a nation in Canaan.

The Hebrew Nation was formed by the united Kingdoms of Samaria and Judah and Saul was appointed their first King in 1020 BCE, 160 years after the "2nd Exodus. Lord Yahweh died about 950 BCE during the reign of King Solomon [961 – 922 BCE] and Solomon turned to worshipping the Elohim [seven Gods]. When Solomon died the Nation disintegrated, separating into Judah and Samaria.

This sets the stage for presenting "Yahweh's Rules". The best research I could come up with about this part of "The Exodus" story is that all of the rules and commandments, displays of power, and rants occurred in Samaria. Of course, the finished product would make everyone a hero, especially Lord Yahweh.

I am a bit skeptical of using this history, but it is the only record available. So, take it for what it is, glorifying Yahweh as God.

The Tabernacle tent was a portable temple and would have been put together near Mount Gerizim in Samaria so Yahweh could keep close watch on "his people". He would not live in just any tent, it would be lavish. Yahweh's Mount Gerizim Palace was located nearby and its' remains were discovered by archaeologists and identified as a "Minoan Palace".

The Temple was designed to be easily taken down and erected at will. The structure was designed to fit the needs of a nomadic people. The principle builders of the tabernacle were Be-zal'e-el, and A-ho'liab, master workers and artificers. Although portable I doubt it was dismantled on a regular basis.

There is an intriguing point about the principle builders of the tabernacle, and Yahweh's obsession of destroying the lineage of Cain [Lord Marduk]. Be-zal'e-el was a direct descendant of Terah, Master builder of Ur and Abram's father. A-ho'liab was a descendant of Terah and of Tubal-Cain who was from the lineage of Cain. This is evidencing the tribes were made up of both Yahweh's and Marduk's lineages. This may be the deep psychological reason for Yahweh's fears while living in the midst of the tribes. Yahweh was nearing the end of his days, the glory of Parvaim was a distant memory.

Yahweh gave detailed instructions on the preparation and serving of his food. If you read through the OT you will see he liked his wine, a *hin* [about one gallon] at every meal and brandy afterward.

The tabernacle was a large rectangular court with the rear half of the court occupied by the tent. Under the tent were two distinct chambers, the Holy Chamber and the Most Holy Place. The court was 200 feet by 100 feet, enclosed by a curtain wall ten feet high, which surrounded the entire structure.

The Holy Place was an interior room 40 feet by 20 feet and 20 feet in height. The Most Holy Place was a second room 20 feet by 20 feet and twenty feet in height. The entrance to the room consisted of a veil of fine twined linen of blue, purple and scarlet. It was embroidered and ornamented with figures of angelic beings. The room contained the Ark of the Covenant, which was a chest five feet by three feet, and three feet in depth. At times, Yahweh's voice was projected from the Ark. Yahweh would communicate with his Priests from his palace using this device.

The Torah provides an excellent description of the construction of the tabernacle. It also tells of the wealth of gold, silver, and the richness of the fabrics used in its construction. The tabernacle has been described as an architectural gem. This tent was an engineering genius using hardened supports, combined with curtains, to achieve specific construction requirements.

The details of the construction are very exact. That is with one exception, and that exception holds the key to the secret of the tabernacle. The following verses describe the exception to an otherwise exact construction design.

Exodus Chapter 26 vs. 2-4
The length of one curtain shall be eight and twenty cubits, and the breadth of one curtain four cubits: and every one of the curtains shall have one measure. The five curtains shall be coupled together one to another; and other five curtains shall be coupled one to another. And thou shalt make loops of blue upon the edge of the one curtain from selvedge in the couplings; and likewise shalt thou make in the uttermost edge of another curtain, in the coupling of the second.

The blue loops on the edges of the curtains were to facilitate lacing them together to form a wall. A covering of animal skins kept out the weather and more importantly darkened the interior of the tent.

Exodus Chapter 26 vs. 12
And that remnant that remaineth of the curtains of the tent, the half curtain that remaineth, shall be over the backside of the tabernacle.

The half curtain that remained was twenty-eight feet in length. It was located on the rear wall of the room that was the Most Holy Place, with an eight-foot overlap. With the exactness of the detailed construction, the curtains being joined at the edges, why would there be an eight-foot overlap? The secret of the overlap was it contained an exit from the Most Holy room. The room was located at the rear of the tabernacle providing the means to enter or leave the tabernacle unobserved.

The interior of the tabernacle, the room called the Holy Place, consisted of beautiful tapestry, wood overlaid with gold and five pillars overlaid with gold and topped with silver crowns which supported the ceiling. Above this, forming the ceiling, was a brilliant colored linen covering. The north and south walls were boards, overlaid with highly polished gold, which reflected the splendor of the room. The beauty of the room had a purpose other than offering comfort for Yahweh. The room had poor lighting and was without windows.

When the High priest [Moses or Aaron] entered the Holy room to speak with Yahweh, he had to look through a multicolored, ornate veil into the Most Holy room. The veil produced a camouflage effect, the same as camouflaged clothing in a forest. When Yahweh spoke, it was always behind the veil and through a pillar of smoke. The reflecting light from the lamps, against polished gold walls, produced an eerie mystical effect in the room. The voice and the special effects produced the necessary spirituality for Yahweh.

Exodus Chapter 40 vs. 34-38
Then a cloud covered the tent of the congregation, and the glory of the Lord filled the tabernacle. And Moses was not able to enter into the tent of the congregation, because the cloud abode thereon, and the glory of the Lord filled the tabernacle. And when the cloud was taken up from over the tabernacle, the children of Israel went onward in all their journeys. But if the cloud were not taken up, then they journeyed not till the day that it was up. For the cloud of the Lord was upon the tabernacle by day, and fire was on it by night, in the sight of all the house of Israel, throughout all their journeys.

After the completion of the tabernacle, social reform and the levee of taxes, in the form of offerings, began in earnest. For social reform to be successful, it was necessary to take the wealth of gold, silver, and jewels from the tribes. As long as the people possessed wealth, they would consider returning to Egypt or traveling to adjacent kingdoms where they could live in comfort. Without wealth, the tribes were more inclined or motivated to continue to build their Nation of Israel.

At this time in the history of the tribes, restitution to Yahweh for sins of the tribes intensified. An example of this reaching to extreme limits is given in the following excerpt. In this example the people are paying for what Yahweh describes as a ransom for a person's soul.

Exodus Chapter 30 vs. 11-15
And the Lord spake unto Moses, saying, When thou takest the sum of the children of Israel after their number, then shall they give every Man a ransom for his soul unto the Lord, when thou numberest them; that there be no plague among them, when thou numberest them. This they shall give, every one that passeth among them that are numbered, half a shekel after the shekel of the sanctuary: [a shekel is twenty gerahs] a half shekel shall be the offering of the Lord. Every one that passeth among them that are numbered, from twenty years old and above, shall give an offering unto the Lord. The rich shall not give more, and the poor shall not give less than half a shekel, when they give an offering

*unto the Lord, to make an atonement for your souls. And thou
shalt take the atonement money of the children of Israel, and
shalt appoint it for the service of the tabernacle of the
congregation; that it may be a memorial unto the children of Israel
before the Lord, to make an atonement for your souls.*

The use of the term, "*that there be no plague among them*" was an
open threat to all the members of the tribes. The threat was made
to ensure everyone gave an offering. The Priests would ensure
everyone gave an offering to keep the threat of a plague from the
entire tribe.

As the social reform of the tribes continued, Yahweh began to focus
the tribal members on the concept of absolute discipline and
obedience. Obedience was to be maintained, devoid of individual
initiative or freedom of choice. Any deviation from the imposed
principles resulted in a punishment of immediate death.

One of the first examples of punishment for independent thought
occurred a short time after the tabernacle had been raised. Yahweh
had established the duties and rituals of tabernacle priests. It was
time for Yahweh to reinforce his power over the tribal members.

The entire multitude gathered before the tabernacle to witness an
offering [lunch] The High Priest Aaron prepared for Yahweh. The
entire scenario was to impress the people with the awesome power
that lived inside the tabernacle tent. The display was also intended to
induce absolute fear into those who may have wanted to see the inside
of the tabernacle.

Leviticus Chapter 8 vs. 1-4
*And the Lord spake unto Moses, saying, Take Aaron and his sons
with him, and the garments, and the anointing oil, and a bullock
for the sin offering, and two rams, and a basket of unleavened
bread. And gather thou all the congregation together unto the
door of the tabernacle of the congregation.*

The door to the tabernacle was the front entrance of the wall that
formed the outer courtyard. The tent structure was located at the
rear of the court. Tribal members were located outside and in front
of the compound.

Aaron completed three ritual offerings in front of the people, which
were the sin offering, the burnt offering, and the peace offerings.

After completing the rituals, Aaron blessed the tribes. He and Moses then entered the tabernacle. A short time later they reappeared and again blessed the people. After the second blessing, a stream of fire came out of the entrance of the tabernacle and fell upon the altar used for burnt offerings.

Leviticus Chapter 9 vs. 23-24
And Moses and Aaron went into the tabernacle of the congregation, and came out, and blessed the people: and the glory of the Lord appeared unto all the people. And there came a fire out from before the Lord, and consumed upon the altar the burnt offering and the fat: which when all the people saw, they shouted, and fell on their faces.

With his display of fire, Yahweh instilled absolute terror in the people. He proved that his threats could be supported by physical destruction.

Two of Aaron's elder sons were priests who ministered at the tabernacle. They were clothed in tabernacle garments and felt safe from any harm from Yahweh. After the display of fire, the two priests, out of admiration for the power they had just observed, used independent thought and made an offering back to Yahweh.

They took incense censers and gathered up some of the burning material from the ground. They added incense on top of the fire and walked toward the tabernacle entrance. Their actions were a gesture of recognition of the power of their living God. As they approached the entrance, a second stream of fire spewed from the tabernacle and engulfed them. They were incinerated on the spot.

Leviticus Chapter 10 vs. 1-2
And Nadab and Abihu, the sons of Aaron, took either of them his censer, and put fire therein, and put incense thereon and offered strange fire before the Lord, which he commanded them not. And there went out fire from the Lord, and devoured them, and they died before the Lord.

Offered strange fire also translates as an *unapproved* or *unauthorized offering.* Yahweh would not take the chance of any breach of security going unpunished.

Was this a spiritual event, or was it an act of murder? The evidence that indicates the event was not a product of the mystical, is in the composition of the fire. The fire left a chemical residue, which continued to burn on the ground. A chemical residue constitutes physical properties, not spiritual mysticism. Evidence indicates the fire was a product of a weapon, such as a flamethrower.

Considering the technology that brought the Lords to Earth, one would assume they could have used another type of weapon. The weapon should have been something similar to what we possess today, a laser beam. The use of a flamethrower indicates they were users of technology, not builders with technological skills. They were in the worlds' richest oil reserve, where in many places the oil surfaced. With a little knowledge and work, the Lords produced a variety of petroleum products.

The death of Aaron's elder sons produced an emotional situation that has been overlooked in Biblical history. With these deaths, Yahweh demonstrated an attitude of subtle distrust of Aaron.

The Prophets lectured Aaron about the rules for approaching Yahweh and the consequences of disobeying the rules. Aaron was seething with anger and stood speechless. Aaron and his remaining sons were warned not to show any emotion, not to mess with their hair or tear their clothing. Above all, Aaron was not to leave his place at the front of the Tabernacle or Yahweh would kill the entire family. Aaron's nephews removed the burnt bodies and took them out of sight, out of the camp. Yahweh told Aaron and his sons they could not mourn the deaths, but their relatives could.

The religious laws were so numerous people could not remember them. Living conditions were so harsh that many people complained. Both situations were viewed as sins. When sickness entered the camps, Yahweh stated it was punishment for the sins of the people. When the sickness abated, Yahweh claimed it was because he had forgiven the sins and charged a head tax on the tribes.

Although I limited the "Tabernacle" dissertation, I need to show a bit of religious turmoil between the Priests and how Yahweh used "Leprosy" to end it.

Sometime after the completion of the tabernacle, Aaron decided to establish himself as a religious leader, equal to Moses. He had recovered from seeing his two sons fried in the holy courtyard by Yahweh. His wife, Miriam, aided him in this venture. To rise to this position of equal religious authority, Aaron and Miriam began to speak against Moses. They used the marriage of Moses to an Ethiopian woman as a basis to address complaints against him.

Under the customs of the Hebrew tribes it was only socially correct to take a wife from within the various tribes. Therefore, based on custom, Aaron had a valid complaint against Moses as a religious leader. To further his argument, Aaron stressed that Yahweh also spoke to him.

Inside the tabernacle, Moses, Aaron and his wife Miriam addressed the problem of Moses' marriage to Yahweh. After hearing the problem, Yahweh instructs the three to move to the tabernacle of the congregation. This area was the walled curtained courtyard of the tabernacle. It was located directly in front of the entrance to the tent. From the entrance of the tent, in a pillar of smoke, Yahweh commanded Aaron and Miriam to come near the entrance. After giving them an angry verbal rebuke for their attitude and comments, Miriam appeared to become leprous.

Numbers Chapter 12 vs. 4-5
And the Lord spake suddenly unto Moses, and unto Aaron, and unto Miriam, Come out ye three unto the tabernacle of the congregation. And they three came out. And the Lord came down in the pillar of the cloud, and stood in the door of the tabernacle, and called Aaron and Miriam: and they both came forth.

Numbers Chapter 12 vs. 9-10
And the anger of the Lord was kindled against them; and he departed. And the cloud departed from off the tabernacle; and, behold, Miriam became leprous, white as snow: and Aaron looked upon Miriam, and behold, she was leprous.

Aaron then pleaded with Moses to have Miriam restored to her normal self. Aaron was successful, and seven days later Miriam was fully healed. With this event, the terror of the disease quelled any further challenges to Moses' authority.

The weapon that was used was never seen. We can conclude that because Aaron and Miriam were called forward to the entrance of tabernacle, they were in close proximity to the smoke pouring out of the tent. The weapon, therefore, had a very limited range. From behind the smoke, Miriam received a potent dose of a dry chemical spray. It had an immediate effect upon her skin, which turned white.

Aaron did not make any further challenges to the position Moses held. However, his exhibition of self-worth was recognized by Yahweh as a subdued current of dissatisfaction.   Whatever Aaron's future aspirations were, he had sealed his fate. Sometime later, on the orders of Yahweh, he was taken to a mountaintop, stripped of his priestly garments, and killed.

Leprosy was the most dreaded disease of all. It was a disease of incurable disfigurement and mutilation of the human body. Infected people were rejected and excluded from society, this could mean death by starvation. However, the Hebrews cared for their lepers and other diseased people. This is a sign of a truly compassionate people.

Yahweh not only used the threat of inflicting leprosy on people who displeased him; he used a ruse to make the people believe he had the power to inflict the dreaded disease. But Yahweh himself, or those Lords acting as Yahweh, had a secret. He, or they, also had a fear of contracting the disease. To prove this assertion, we need to examine some of the characteristics of the disease.

Leprosy results from acid-fast bacilli, which cause skin lesions. It is a chronic infectious disease and the onset is insidious. There are two distinct types, lepromatous and tuberculoid. The lepromatous type occurs in people with defective immune systems. The course of the disease is progressive and malignant. It produces skin lesions that usually appear as pale trophic ulcers. The disease attacks the skin, superficial nerves, nose, pharynx, eyes, and testicles. It also causes bone resorption and disfigurement. When the disease spreads to the eyes, the victim becomes blind.

Yahweh did not allow disfigured people, or persons who were blind, or with blemishes to make offerings at the tabernacle. *The reason was that the majority of people described in Leviticus had the symptoms of leprosy.* Here is the Biblical text to compare the verses to the characteristics of leprosy.

Leviticus Chapter 21 vs. 16-23
And the Lord spake unto Moses, saying, Speak unto Aaron, saying, Whosoever he be of thy seed in their generations that hath any blemish, let him not approach to offer the bread of his God. For whatsoever Man he be that hath a blemish, he shall not approach: a blind Man or lame, or he that hath a flat nose, or any thing superfluous, Or a Man that is brokenfooted, or brokenhanded, Or crookbackt, or a dwarf, or that hath a blemish in his eye, or be scurvy, or scabbed, or hath his stones broken; No Man that hath a blemish of the seed of Aaron the priest shall come nigh to offer the offerings of the Lord made by fire: he hath a blemish; he

shall not come nigh to offer the bread of his God. He shall eat the bread of his God, both of the most holy, and of the holy. Only he shall not go in unto the veil, nor come nigh unto the altar, because he hath a blemish; that he profane not my sanctuaries: for I the Lord do sanctify them.

The phrase, *hath his stones broken,* refers to a man's testicles. The phrase, *the offering made by fire,* refers to cooked foods. If you continue to follow this avenue of thought to its end, you can come to another conclusion.

The men cooking the offering were wearing clothing, and Yahweh could only see their face, arms, and hands, and part of the legs and the feet. If a person had a blemish on any of these body parts, it was possible he had other more definite signs of leprosy hidden by his clothing. If he had a leprous hand, he could wrap it in cloth and simply state he had broken his hand.

Yahweh did not take any chances of receiving food from a leper. He banned people with physical imperfections from the tabernacle. The conclusion from these clothing rules is, *he could not see through clothing.* That is really a shortcoming for a person who is selling himself as God.

Yahweh did use the disease as a resource for the embellishment of his power over the tribes. He ordered the priests to inspect suspected people for the symptoms or signs of the disease. The entire Chapter 13 of Leviticus pertains to this inspection. Following the inspection by the priests, every leper was put out of the camp.

Numbers Chapter 5 vs. 1-3
And the Lord spake unto Moses, saying, Command the children of Israel, that they put out of the camp every leper, and every one that hath an issue, and whosoever is defiled by the dead: Both male and female shall ye put out, without the camp shall ye put them; that they defile not their camps, in the midst whereof I dwell.

After Yahweh rid the general population of lepers, he devised a ritual, which would cure the disease. Tribal priests, through the power of Yahweh, would perform the ritual on members who exhibited the symptoms. After the ritual, the person would be shut up seven days to completely heal.

To understand this performance, you must envision the total terror of a suspected leper. If the ritual failed to cleanse this person, the result was loss of their family, coupled with tribal banishment. The ritual miraculously healed the person by the power of Yahweh, after seven days of terror. Now, what would your attitude be? The answer is simple; you would be shouting the joys of being saved by Yahweh. After being saved from a horrible death, your loyalty would be absolute.

The performance would be an astounding exhibition of power to all members of the tribes. Of course, you probably would not consider why Yahweh previously had all the lepers expelled from the tribes. Or, you probably would not consider why Yahweh did not use the ritual to cure them. The secret to Yahweh's power to cure leprosy lies in the world of reality. The reality is he could not cure the disease, not in seven days, or seven months, or seven years.

How did Yahweh pull off such a performance? Actually, it was fairly simple and Biblical text provides the clues to the answer. First, you need to sift through the maze of rituals and Yahweh's instructions pertaining to the inspections for the symptoms of leprosy. The entire Chapter 13 of Leviticus specifically dictates how the inspections were to be made.

To begin, the priests' instructions would separate a real case of leprosy from that of a *chemical burn, which produced very similar symptoms of the disease.*

Leviticus Chapter 13 vs. 42-46
And if there be in the bald head, or bald forehead, a white reddish sore; it is a leprosy sprung up in his bald head, or his bald forehead. Then the priest shall look upon it: and behold if the rising of the sore be white reddish in his bald head, or in his bald forehead, as the leprosy appeareth in the skin of the flesh; He is a leprous Man, he is unclean: the priest shall pronounce him utterly unclean; his plague is in his head. And the leper in whom the plague is, his clothes shall be rent, and his head bare, and he shall put a covering upon his upper lip, and shall cry, Unclean, unclean. All the days wherein the plagues shall be in him he shall be defiled; he is unclean: he shall dwell alone; without the camp shall his habitation be.

This indicates a "Shanty Town" of Lepers and other disease carriers, close but outside of the settlement. They would have survived on the leavings of the people as Yahweh had commanded, they could "eat the bread but only away from the Tabernacle". The next set of verses contains the first clues to the chemical that produces a burn, which appears to be leprosy. The bacteria do not thrive in clothing. This is not to say a leper's clothing does not carry the bacteria. However, the bacteria do not proliferate to change the color of garments. But a chemical induced into or upon clothing could cause a change in the color of the material.

Leviticus Chapter 13 vs. 49-50
And if the plague be greenish or reddish in the garment, or in the skin, either in the warp, or in the woof, or in any thing of skin; it is a plague of leprosy, and shall be shewed unto the priest: And the priest shall look upon the plague, and shut up it that hath the plague seven days:

Leviticus Chapter 13 vs. 53
And if the priest shall look, and, behold, the plague be not spread in the garment, either in the warp, or in the woof, or in any thing of skin;

The verses continue with a series of inspections of the clothing, and subsequent washing to remove the imposed colors. If the colors of greenish or reddish can be washed out, then the garment is saved. But if the material is of such, that the colors cannot be removed, the clothing is burned. The reason so much attention is paid to the clothing is, after a person has gone through ritual cleansing, they will want their clothes back. If the clothing still contained the chemicals, the person's body would again react to them.

After seven days, the clothing was either cleaned or burned, and the priest would again inspect the person to see if they had healed. If the person appeared to be healed, the priest would begin a very lengthy ritual that culminated at the front of the tabernacle, in full view of the tribes. Before being allowed near the tabernacle, part of the ritual ensured that he would be absolutely free of the chemicals.

Leviticus Chapter 14 vs. 8-9
And he is that is to be cleansed shall wash his clothes, and shave off all his hair, and wash himself in water, that he may be clean: and after that he shall come into the camp, and tarry abroad out of his tent seven days. But it shall be on the seventh day, that he shall shave all his hair off his head and his beard and his eyebrows, even all his hair he shall shave off: and he shall wash

his clothes, also he shall wash his flesh in water, and he shall be clean.

To reinforce the assertion that chemicals were used to induce the symptoms of leprosy, the final verses are provided.

Leviticus Chapter 14 vs. 33-38
And the Lord spake unto Moses and Aaron, saying, When ye come into the land of Canaan, which I give to you for a possession, and I put the plague of leprosy in a house of the land of your possession; And he that owneth the house shall come and tell the priest, saying, It seemeth to me there is as it were a plague in the house: Then the priest shall command that they empty the house, before the priest go into it to see the plague, that all that is in the house be not made unclean: and afterward the priest shall go in to see the house: And he shall look on the plague, and behold, if the plague be in the walls of the house with hollow strakes, greenish or reddish, which in sight are lower than the wall; Then the priest shall go out of the house, and shut up the house seven days:

These verses are followed by instructions to scrape the walls, remove stones, and carry all the mortar and dust to outside any city limits. The important thing to remember is the colors of the chemicals and the instructions to clean the house. The instructions were a physical remedy to a problem, not a spiritual remedy. If you disregard the ritual involved in the cleansing of the person near the tabernacle, the remedies to both situations are exactly the same. Get rid of the chemicals by cleaning.

This last paragraph should have tugged a bit on your memory: If the people lived in "houses" they were certainly not trekking through the Sinai wilderness on an Exodus.

Last, from the world of reality, leprosy is a chronic infectious disease caused by the acid-fast, nonmotile, aerobic, gram-positive rod Mycobacterium leprae. The mode of transmission is respiratory and involves prolonged exposure in childhood. Only rarely have adults become infected. Because of the tendency for relapse, treatment must be continued for years.

The previous examples of suspected cases of leprosy were given to lead into a final example of the dreaded disease. This example demonstrates how Yahweh employed the fear of the disease to quell problems that threatened his authority.

For those who are totally enthralled with the spirituality of Yahweh, it should be considered that he did not condemn the buying and selling of children. And this was within the Hebrew Tribes. Nor did he condemn the buying and selling of men and women. He ordered the killing of all captured male children but kept the unspoiled females for breeding. This was part of the commerce within the tribes and with other nations. This was slavery masked by religious authority.

Exodus Chapter 21 vs. 1-6
Now these are the judgments which thou shalt set before them. If thou buy an Hebrew servant, six years he shall serve: and in the seventh he shall go free for nothing. If he came in by himself, he shall go out by himself: if he were married, then his wife shall go out with him. If his master have given him a wife, and she have borne him sons or daughters; the wife and her children shall be her master's, and he shall go out by himself. And if the servant shall plainly say, I love my master, my wife, and my children; I will not go out free: Then his master shall bring him unto the judges; he shall also bring him to the door, or unto the door post; and his master shall bore his ear through with an awl; and he shall serve him for ever.

Leviticus Chapter 25 vs. 45-46
Moreover of the children of the strangers that do sojourn among you, of them shall ye buy, and of their families that are with you, which they begat in your land: and they shall be your possession. And ye shall take them as an inheritance for your children after you, to inherit them for a possession; they shall be your bondmen for ever: but over your brethren the children of Israel, ye shall not rule one over another with rigour.

The tribes were taught a very primitive form of religion by Yahweh. He had them build a great stone altar, decorated with the horns of cattle, similar to the Sun God altars. On this altar, thousands of cattle, sheep and birds, were slaughtered in rituals. The rituals included the burning of the bodies of the animals as an offering to the power of Yahweh. There are also documented human sacrifice rituals to Yahweh.

This human sacrifice occurred about 900 BCE.

Judges Chapter 11, vs. 30-31, 34, 39

And Jephthah vowed a vow unto the Lord, and said, If thou shalt without fail deliver the children of Ammon into mine hands, Then it shall be, that whatsoever cometh forth of the doors of my house to meet me, when I return in peace from the children of Ammon, shall surely be the Lord's, and I will offer it up for a burnt offering.
34: And Jephthah came to Mizpeh unto his house, and behold, his daughter came out to meet him with timbrels and with dances: and she was his only child; beside her he had neither son nor daughter.
39:   And it came to pass at the end of two months, that she returned unto her father, who did with her according to his vow which he had vowed: and she knew no man. And it was a custom in Israel.

The human sacrifice of burnt body parts is celebrated as a custom in Yahweh's religion. This father cut up his daughter, and burned the pieces in ritual sacrifice, on a pile of rocks. This was not, and is not, a religious experience.

The tabernacle priests were led into *blood rituals that promoted a belief in the mystical powers of the sacrifices.* The more complicated the ritual, the more mystical it became. The Old Testament contains numerous examples of the practices.   The following example is provided to illustrate these points.

Exodus Chapter 29 vs. 18-21
And thou shalt burn the whole ram upon the altar: it is a burnt offering unto the Lord: it is a sweet savour, an offering made by fire unto the Lord. And thou shalt take the other ram; and Aaron and his sons shall put their hand upon the head of the ram. Then shalt thou kill the ram, and take of his blood, and put it upon the tip of the right ear of Aaron, and upon the tip of the right ear of his sons, and upon the thumb of their right hand, and upon the great toe of their right foot, and sprinkle the blood upon the altar round about. And thou shalt take of the blood that is upon the altar, and of the anointing oil, and sprinkle it upon Aaron, and upon his garments, and upon his sons, and upon the garments of his sons with him: and he shall be hallowed, and his garments, and his sons, and his son's garments with him.

How is this for an uplifting spiritual occurrence: After defeating a city or kingdom, and killing all of the men, the Hebrews were instructed to **"kill every male among the little ones, and kill every woman that has known Man."** The reasons for this "religious" order were:

1. The cities were infected with gonorrhea and other sexually transmitted diseases and
2. To stop any claims of inheritance by captive sons, over the inheritance rights of Hebrew men. Under Hebrew law, even captive sons held absolute claim to the estates of their fathers. This could not be denied the captive survivors of war. The solution to this legal dilemma was to commit murder. Another great religious experience.

The Hebrew leader Joshua [refined as Yeshua] was first named Hoshea [Salvation], then Yahweh changed it to Joshua [The Lord gives victory].   The Greek translation is "Jesus" and according to NT writings this was the name "Angels" instructed "Joseph and Mary" to give their newborn son, Joshua, or Yeshua.

The Hebrews left a faint Masonic clue for future generations. The clue to the heritage of Yahweh is in the following verses:

Exodus Chapter 22 vs. 22-23 Ye shall not afflict any widow, or fatherless child. If thou afflict them in any wise, and they cry at all unto me, I will surely hear their cry; And my wrath shall wax hot, and I will kill you with the sword; and your wives shall be widows and your children fatherless.

I think this was added from the Enuma Elish, as Yahweh had young males killed and young females taken into bondage.

883 to 859 BCE. Ashurnasirpal II
Note the winged God with a hand basket

Chapter 6

THE PROPHET EZEKIEL
593 BCE

[Author: Most of this Ezekiel presentation has circulated for at least the last century, I have added to the script]

Preachers and UFO chasers have prominently published their interpretations of the unusual events recorded in The Book of Ezekiel. The resulting confusion created by these authors has caused most readers to lose interest in the subject. Some have used Ezekiel in superficial attempts to bolster scripts they were writing. Others attempted to use a single recorded event to create a complete story. Those stories usually lacked credible explanations. The stories created a theme of spaceships landing among ancient Man, which very few people find believable, or that it was a dream from God.

The Book of Ezekiel presents one of the few, and best, descriptions of a group of the Lords from Sumer. It also contains the best descriptions of the aircraft the Lords used. Similar aircraft was used for the original explorations of the planet; however, they have disappeared over the millennia.

There are many monuments to the ancient Gods of Sumer with their "Sky Disks" of war, and tales of the **God Anu** *"The alien father of the Gods"* in his "winged sky disc with weapons". The Sumerian Kings List records these rulers from 254,000 years ago to Marduk in Babylon. Records of Marduk's son, **God Ashur**, in 700 BCE tell of his "flying machines of destruction" defending Babylon from invasions.

Symbolic language was used in the Torah to express descriptions and events. Symbolic language produces a scotoma, a false perception of reality.   Ezekiel's descriptions have confused people for centuries because of these effects.

After Yahweh's death the lesser Lords were left without a sanctuary and fled to hidden areas.   The Prophet Ezekiel clearly had close contact with a faction or group of these Lords around the year 593 BCE. Based on what Ezekiel observed, they were clearly few in number. There is no evidence the remaining Lords were successful in creating another civilization in this area.   This could be the last remnant of Yahweh's group after he died.

Ezekiel lived near the end of the Age of the Prophets. In the year 600 BCE Ezekiel was captured during the fall of the Southern Hebrew Kingdom of Judah and exiled to the old Sumerian region. The entire Hebrew nation no longer existed. Ezekiel's experience produced a mystery hidden in Biblical history. This event has served to confuse people for centuries. What contributed to this history was a group of Yahweh's Lords surviving as best they could, as raiders. Ezekiel believed God was part of this group of men.

There is enough information from Ezekiel's encounter to indicate a small group of Lords was operating from a hidden sanctuary. Yahweh's passing left them leaderless.

This group was a band of outlaws extorting tribute from villages located in remote areas, using fear and murder to accomplish their extortion. The group was relying on old fears of Lord Yahweh for additional psychological support in extorting the villagers. In previous history the Hebrew people were required to support Lord Yahweh with food, wealth, and family members. This support was encouraged by acts of cruelty and punishments of death.

The event Ezekiel witnessed was one of a series of orchestrated spectacles.   Simply stated, it was a display of awesome power producing mind-shocking fear in the local inhabitants. By today's standards, the event was neither mystical, nor spiritual.

Ezekiel's experience began while he was among a group of captives by the river Che'bar, in the land of the Chaldeans. Chaldea was located in the southeastern section of the Fertile Crescent. This area is the southern region of the old Sumerian civilization, and can also be described today as north of the city of Basra in southern Iraq.

Ezekiel looked out into the desert and saw what appeared to be a giant whirlwind traveling towards him. The whirlwind was a great cloud of swirling dust, filled with flashes of light and fire. The event Ezekiel was witnessing was an airborne raiding party consisting of eight machines.

Four helicopters [flying disks] flew in a column, one over the other and low to the ground. The wind from the rotor blades beat dust upwards and outwards, creating a large whirlwind of dust. The dust was raised to greater heights and spread outward by the second, third, and fourth helicopter. This formation created the effect of a giant whirlwind.

The first four aircraft to come out of the dust cloud appear to be small one-man ultra-light fixed bi-wing vehicles. Each aircraft had double wings and an open windshield-like canopy. The double wings were similar to the old crop duster aircraft known as biplanes. The double wings provide great stability for slow flying aircraft. The flight controls were handgrips under the forward wings. The machines were built like motorized hang-gliders and fitted with metal landing skids. With this type of aircraft, the operator lies down on the frame, arms outward to reach the hand controls with his head protected by the windshield canopy.

The small aircraft flew out of the dust cloud to find a suitable landing site for the next four aircraft that remained hidden. On landing the ultra-light aircraft, four men quickly marked a landing site with what apparently were strobe lights.

The poor visibility created a problem for the aircraft remaining inside the whirlwind column of dust. The lack of visibility caused the pilots to use interior lights and exterior landing lights. The lights reflected off the dust particles and created the appearance of flashes of fire from within the cloud.

With the landing site clearly marked, the first of four large helicopters landed. As the other three aircraft landed, the dust cloud dissipated. It was at this time Ezekiel heard what he assumed was the voice of God. The operation was very simple, very military in discipline, and most of all very effective, as it was intended to be. It produced "Fear, Shock and Awe" to all who witnessed the landing.

The following OT text will substantiate how this event was explained.

Ezekiel Chapter 1 vs. 1-5:

Now it came to pass in the thirtieth year, in the fourth month, in the fifth day of the month, as I was among the captives by the river of Che'bar, that the heavens were opened, and I saw visions of God. In the fifth day of the month, which was the fifth of King Je-hoi'a-chin's captivity, the word of the Lord came expressly unto E-ze'ki-el the priest, the son of Bu'zi, in the land of the Chal-de'ans by the river Che'bar, and the hand of the Lord was there upon him. And I looked, and, behold, a whirlwind came out of the north, a great cloud, and a fire enfolding itself, and a brightness was about it, and out of the midst thereof as the colour of amber, out of the midst of the fire. Also out of the midst thereof came the likeness of four living creatures. And this was their appearance; they had the likeness of a Man.

Because Ezekiel had never seen a flying machine, he assumed anything with wings and a body had to be a *living creature*, part of which he recognized as the body of a Man. That is why he is trying to explain *the likeness of a Man.*

Ezekiel Chapter 1 vs. 6:
And everyone had four faces and every one had four wings.

The four wings were the wings of the aircraft. The four faces describe the windshield canopy, which may have had decoration on it.

Ezekiel Chapter 1 vs. 7:
And their feet were straight feet; the sole of their feet was like the sole of a calf's foot: and they sparkled like the colour of burnished brass.

Ezekiel believes the machines are alive. The straight feet were the landing skids; the part about the calf's foot is symbolic of the hardness of metal, hard like a calf's foot, not soft like a human foot. The reason they sparkled like burnished brass was, that is what they were, brass landing skids polished by landing and sliding through desert sand.

Ezekiel Chapter 1 vs. 8:
And they had the hands of a Man under their wings on their four sides; and they four had their faces and their wings.

The pilot of the small aircraft has his arms stretched out and his hands are on a flight control bar located under the wings. Keep in mind that Ezekiel can see all of this because he is looking up at an angle. Also, some of the text is not just additional information, it is how text

was written and given more expression, to something that was thought
to be very important. Scribes simply wrote the same thing twice in
the same sentence.

Ezekiel Chapter 1 vs. 9:
**Their wings were joined one to another; they turned not when they
went; they went everyone straight forward.**

Ezekiel could not understand how the aircraft, which he thought was
a living creature, could fly without moving its wings. He continues to
explain the wings of a bi-plane like structure. He has no concept that
the power to move the aircraft is in the engine, not in the wings.

Ezekiel Chapter 1 vs. 10:
**As for the likeness of their faces, they four had the face of a
Man, and the face of a lion, on the right side; and they four had
the face of an ox on the left side; they four also had the face of
an eagle.**

The symbolism used by Ezekiel in this text has confused people for
centuries. He describes four men who look alike because they are all
wearing the same flight suits and flight helmets. These are suits and
helmets similar to those used today. They are not wearing space suits
or space helmets. When reading this verse a mental scotoma develops
in the conscious mind. Our brain provides us with images from the text
we read. If the symbolic descriptions read, lion, ox and eagle, these
are the images produced in our conscious mind.

Now to break this particular scotoma, we have to look at things from
Ezekiel's perspective. He is filled with fear and watching things he
thoroughly does not understand. He is looking at a flight helmet with
a visor attached to it to keep the sand out of the pilot's eyes. Ezekiel
sees a human face behind the visor and to describe this face he uses
symbolism. The face has the solemn, fearsome look of deadly power.
The eyes of the face have a fierce intense look, like the bright sharp
look of an eagle. Looking at the same man he saw on the left side of
the face what looked like the nostril of an ox. This was the dust mask
the Man had to wear when flying inside the dust cloud. The dust mask
had two filters on the left side.

Ezekiel Chapter 1 vs. 11:
**Thus were their faces; and their wings were stretched upwards;
two wings of every one were joined one to another, and two covered
their bodies.**

Ezekiel is finished with the description of their faces, and the aircraft have landed. The small aircraft were sitting in an area, which would be blown about by the force of the wind created by large rotor blades, when the helicopters landed. The wings of the small aircraft could cause it to be blown over and damaged. The smaller rear wings were folded upwards, and the larger front, or main wing, was folded back along the sides of the aircraft. This is the same method used to store aircraft on aircraft carriers. This method of storage prevents damage to the wings.

Ezekiel Chapter 1 vs. 12:
And they went every one straight forward: whither the spirit was to go, they went; and they turned not when they went.

He is describing a team effort of the men as they set up a landing area. They were very intent on their business at hand and did not pay any attention to him or anything else.

Ezekiel Chapter 1 vs. 13:
As for the likeness of the living creatures, their appearance was like burning coals of fire, and like the appearance of lamps: it went up and down among the living creature; and the fire was bright, and out of the fire went forth lightning.

The landing site was set up using strobe lights that sent out brilliant flashes of light. Ezekiel mistook the brilliant flashes as that of lightning. The lights produced the effect of burning coals of fire. The up and down motions were simply the reflection of hand-held landing wands, or flashlights used to guide the helicopters while landing. This method is still used today. You put a light in each hand and guide the pilot.

Ezekiel Chapter 1 vs. 14:
And the living creatures ran and returned as the appearance of a flash of lightning.

This was all symbolic language, to show how fast they set up the landing area.

Ezekiel Chapter 1 vs. 15:
Now as I beheld the living creatures, behold one wheel upon the earth by the living creatures, with his four faces.

The secret to breaking the scotoma Ezekiel produced with this symbolic reference is to put yourself in his place. He was initially looking up, into the sky. What he is describing is the underneath view of an aircraft. Ezekiel's flying wheel within a wheel is the visual effect of rotor blades. If you view a helicopter in flight, the rotor blades produce the visual effect of outer and inner circles. Ezekiel says, as he is watching the group of four men, *behold*, this means he is astonished when he uses the word. Now one helicopter has landed. Because he can see the visual effect of the rotor blades, before the engine is turned off, he refers to the blade as one wheel. He is probably lying on the ground looking up.

Ezekiel Chapter 1 vs. 16:
The appearance of the wheels and their work was like unto the colour of a beryl: and they four had one likeness; and their appearance and their work was as it were a wheel in the middle of a wheel.

The term, "they four had one likeness," means three other aircraft had landed. The aircraft were aquamarine or greenish in color. Because the rotor blades continue to turn, he still remains puzzled regarding what he sees as wheels within wheels. He was looking at this aircraft head-on. It is possible they possessed an advanced system, which allowed the rotor blades to be tilted into the position of propellers, to facilitate movement on the ground. This system was advanced in the nineteen eighties and is still used by some aircraft today. The visual effect of seeing a wheel within a wheel would remain the same.

Ezekiel Chapter 1 vs. 17:
When they went, they went upon their four sides: and they turned not when they went.

This describes some type of movement, probably setting up for a preflight position. Ezekiel is using the terms their four sides to express that he is seeing solid objects, rather than something out of a dream or vision.

Ezekiel Chapter 1 vs. 18:
As for their rings, they were so high that they were dreadful; and their rings were full of eyes round about them four.

Here he is describing porthole type windows as what he believes to be eyes on the aircraft.

Ezekiel Chapter 1 vs. 19:
And when the living creatures went, the wheels went by them: and when the living creatures were lifted up from the earth, the wheels were lifted up.

Ezekiel still believes that the aircraft are living creatures. This verse was probably written out of sequence, but it describes a takeoff with the spinning rotor blades as wheels.

Ezekiel Chapter 1 vs. 20:
Whithersoever the spirit was to go, they went, thither was their spirit to go; and the wheels were lifted up over against them: for the spirit of the living creature was in the wheels.

I really enjoy this verse, because Ezekiel had figured out the wheels were part of the aircraft. He uses the term *spirit* because what he is trying to say, he still does not understand, but he is mentally working on a solution. The term spirit is Ezekiel's term for power. He was trying to say that the power of the living creature was in the wheels, meaning the rotor blades.

Ezekiel Chapter 1 vs. 21:
When those went, these went; and when those stood, these stood; and when those were lifted up from the earth, the wheels were lifted up over against them: for the spirit of the living creature was in the wheels.

Here he is trying to explain how he concluded the wheels were somehow connected to the movement of the main body of the helicopter.

Ezekiel Chapter 1 vs. 22-24:
And the likeness of the firmament upon the heads of the living creature was as the colour of the terrible crystal, stretched forth over their heads above. And under the firmament were their wings straight, the one towards the other: every one had two, which covered on this side, and every one had two, which covered on that side, their bodies. And when they went, I heard the noise of their wings, like the noise of great waters, as the voice of the Almighty, the voice of speech, as the noise of an host: when they stood, they let down their wings.

In these three verses, Ezekiel is describing a helicopter that has landed. The rotor blades have stopped turning. The likeness of the firmament is a flashing light coming from a crystal-like object, under which were the two rotor blades. The object is probably an upper strobe light which most aircraft have to prevent another aircraft from flying into them. The voice was the pilot talking to the four men who had set up the landing area. The speaker system was loud to overcome the noise created by the aircraft while landing.

Ezekiel Chapter 1 vs. 25:
And there was a voice from the firmament that was over their heads, when they stood, and had let down their wings.

This verse is the same as the last part of verse 24. The four men have received instructions from the pilot of the aircraft. They are preparing the small ultralight aircraft for flight by moving the wings from against the sides of the aircraft to their normal fixed position.

Ezekiel Chapter 1 vs. 26:
And above the firmament that was over their heads was the likeness of a throne, as the appearance of a sapphire stone: and upon the likeness of the throne was the likeness as the appearance of a Man above upon it.

This verse describes a pilot sitting in the flight seat, under a forward, tinted canopy windshield. The description, "as the appearance of a sapphire stone," was the dark blue color of the canopy. This is a tinted canopy to cut the glare of the desert sun.

Ezekiel Chapter 1 vs. 27:
And I saw the color of amber, as the appearance of fire round about within it, from the appearance of his loins even upward, and from the appearance of his loins even downward, I saw as it were the appearance of fire, and it had brightness round about.

This verse reveals Ezekiel could see most of the pilots exposed body within the canopy. He was also seeing the instrument lights, reflecting off the pilot.

Ezekiel Chapter 1 vs. 28:
As the appearance of the bow that is in the cloud in the day of rain, so was the appearance of the brightness round about. This was the appearance of the likeness of the glory of the Lord. And when I saw it, I fell upon my face, and I heard a voice of one that spake.

Again, we are told of the colors reflecting from the instrument panels and lights within and on the aircraft.

After the aircraft incident, Ezekiel reveals the personal character of the Lords of Sumer. The following provides insight of the lack of respect for anyone. Also recorded is what happened when native Man resisted their attempts to subjugate him.

Ezekiel Chapter 4

These remaining Lords put Ezekiel through a training phase, using a form of brainwashing psychology to make him believe he was worthy of becoming a prophet.

Ezekiel Chapter 4 vs. 9-12:
Take thou also unto thee wheat, and barley, and beans, and lentils, and millet, and fitches, and put them in one vessel and make thee bread thereof, according to the number of days that though shalt lie upon thy side, three hundred and ninety days shalt thou eat thereof. And thy meat which thou shalt eat shall be by weight, twenty shekels a day: from time to time shalt thou eat it. Thou shalt drink also water by measure, the sixth part of an hin: from time to time shalt thou drink. And thou shalt eat it as barley cakes, and thou shalt bake it with dung that cometh out of Man, in their sight.

This last verse does not require a lot of religious or historical interpretation. It shows a total lack of respect for the human condition.

Ezekiel Chapter 4 vs. 13-15:
And the Lord said, Even thus shall the children of Israel eat their defiled bread among the Gentiles, whither I will drive them. Then said I, Ah Lord God! Behold, my soul hath not been polluted: for from my youth up even till now have I not eaten of that which dieth of itself, or is torn in pieces; neither came there abominable flesh into my mouth. Then he said unto me, Lo, I have given thee cow's dung for man's dung, and thou shalt prepare thy bread therewith.

The Lords played a psychological game with Ezekiel. The more complicated the instructions, the more he believed the instructions contained religious significance. Being in fear of his life, he paid special attention to following the instructions. The use of religious fear diverted attention from those who gave the instructions.

Instructing someone to eat their excrement, while knowing that no one will do it, exhibits a very crude use of authority. Ezekiel did fall into the psychological trap that was prepared for him. He did not refuse to comply a second time. Instead of feeling anger at the suggestion of such subservience, he felt relief by performing lesser human degradation.

Ezekiel Chapter 9

In this chapter the errant Lords have arrived at the village temple to load food and other wealth left as offerings to the Gods. The Lords brought four helicopters because they had expected a large load of goods. The following verses indicate they did not find the amount they expected. The result of disobeying the Lords' instructions was death.

Ezekiel Chapter 9 vs. 1-2:
He cried also in mine ears with a loud voice, saying, Cause them that have charge over the city to draw near, even every Man with his destroying weapon in his hand. And behold, six men came from the way of the higher gate, which lieth toward the north, and every Man a slaughter weapon in his hand; and one Man among them was clothed with linen, with a writer's inkhorn by his side: and they went in, and stood beside the brasen altar.

Ezekiel Chapter 9 vs. 5-7:
And to the others he said in mine hearing, Go ye after him through the city, and smite: let not your eye spare, neither have ye pity: Slay utterly old and young, both maids, and little children, and women: but come not near any Man upon whom is the mark; and begin at my sanctuary. Then they began at the ancient men which were before the house. And he said unto them, Defile the house, and fill the courts with the slain: go ye forth. And they went forth, and slew in the city.

To clear up any religious significance regarding this brutality, there is none. The wholesale slaughter of people, including children, cannot be justified as a religious act. There were six men with weapons in their hands, and one supervisor that murdered because no tribute had been left in the local temple. "*Them that have charge over the city*" also translates as "*The Guardians of .....*" I find it interesting that their weapons are not identified as swords or axes but are only translated as "*deadly devices.*" The word *house* is a reference to a temple. The acts of murder were to affirm the Lords' dominance of the area. This dominance required tribute and subservience of the local population.

The phrase **"but come not near any Man upon whom is the mark"** shows us that although these Lords had no qualms about murdering children, they would not cause the death of a Masonic brother. It was a very warped sense of ego and honor. The "Mark" was the last letter of the ancient Hebrew alphabet, a "***Taw***," which resembles a modern day "**X**" with one upper arm hooked. This symbol is commonly known as a **"Hooked X"**. Masons could display this symbol as an X on the forehead or as a piece of jewelry. If circumstances permitted, they crossed their forearms in front of their body, right over left, and extended one hand. The "Mark" also protected their immediate families.

The Lords believed news of the slaughter would spread to other areas, and this would make extracting tribute, by extortion, even easier in the future. However, something went wrong with this plan. There is no historical evidence to suggest they were successful. Being few in number, it is quite possible they were eventually ambushed and killed by disgruntled villagers. It is also possible that a natural calamity claimed their lives. For whatever reason, this group vanished into history.

[Of all Organized Religions, I hold the Hebrew faith in highest esteem for their devotion to beginnings, reverence of The Supreme Architect of The Universe and of maintaining their bond through eons of attack. They remain strong and defiant in their religion and in the origins of their homeland and Nation. I certainly could not function having to follow their traditions, but I revel in their tenacity to survive as a people and kick ass when attacked.]

THE RISE OF A NEW ORGANIZED RELIGION

Pillars of Creation
Hubble - heic1501a

Galaxy;	Milky Way [Inner Spiral arm]
Constellation:	Serpens Cauda 7,000 LY away
Nebula:	M16: the Eagle Nebula

<u>YEARS CE</u>	<u>TL 8 Christianity</u>

1611 — King James Bible published

1534 — Church of England established

1533 — *Munich Talmud 1342 CE* only uncensored remaining—Pope burned Talmuds and censored future writings and teachings by Rabbis

1521 — Martin Luther excommunicated by Vatican

752 — Vatican becomes ruler of western empire and appoints emperors and kings

470 — Mitra reestablished as state religion

380 — Christianity becomes the state religion of the Roman Empire

321 — Pope Sylvester joins in worshipping Mitra Celebrations to become a recognized religion

080 — Linus, the son of King Caractucus of the Celtic empire becomes first Pope of Rome

067 — Paul [Saul] executed by Caesar Nero

058 — *Christianity* spreads to Rome - Paul arrested and sent to Rome to stand trial for Sedition

050 — *Church of Cephas* named by Judeo Christians to proclaim separation from Pauline Christianity

040 — Saul claims vision with Messiah - starts *Pauline Christian Church* with Mitra followers in Galilee

029 — Yeshua's disciples captured by Saul of Tarsus, tried by Sanhedrin and stoned

029 — Miriam visions Mitra ascending to heaven - starts her *Church of Mitra*
James starts *Judeo-Christian Church*

029 — Yeshua captured and tried by Sanhedrin, stoned and hung on a post

028 — Yeshu the Notzeri and Miriam worshipped as Mitra and Artemis lead a revolt against the Temple in a 10 month campaign

Mitra The Sun God Slaying the Great Bull

Spanish Inquisition

Chapter
7

CHRISTIANITY
THE RISE OF A NEW ORGANIZED RELIGION

ISAIAH 7:14 [NIV]: "Therefore the Lord himself will give you a sign: The virgin will be with child and will give birth to a son, and will call him Immanuel." [about 733 BCE]

In 733 BCE King Pekah of Israel [Samaria] was threatening to invade Jerusalem with the Syrians as allies. King Ahaz of Judah allied with the Assyrians and was holding against the attack. Ahaz was speaking with Yahweh and he was assured that the attack would fail. Apparently, Ahaz's advisors were skeptical and eventually Isaiah provided them with a prophesy to calm their nerves.

Isaiah's speech would be reinterpreted [recension by the Vatican] and the Christian "Virgin Baring a Messiah Myth to Save All of Mankind" began. The revised prophesy [NIV] is shown above. The actual interpretation of the Hebrew passages follows. [Compare Vs. 14] The rest of the speech is provided to give context to the conversation.

A Jewish [Hebrew] interpretation of the same passage [from on-line Jewish Bible, Book of Isaiah]

13 יג

"Listen, House of David," [Isaiah] retorted, "is it not enough for you to treat men as helpless that you also treat my God as helpless?

14 יד

Assuredly, my Lord will give you a sign of His own accord! Look, the young woman is with child and about to give birth to a son. Let her name him Immanuel.

15 טו

[By the time he learns to reject the bad and choose the good, people will be feeding on curds and honey.]

16 טז

For before the lad knows to reject the bad and choose the good, the ground whose two kings you dread shall be abandoned.

17 יז

The LORD will cause to come upon you and your people and your ancestral house such days as never have come since Ephraim turned away from Judah—that selfsame king of Assyria!

[Immanuel, in Hebrew, translates to "God is with us"]

These verses in Isaiah and countless other writings were changed by "Recension", which is, re-interpretation by "Devine Inspiration" to change the words "the young woman is with child" to "the virgin .... will give birth" and the meaning of the passages to something entirely different.

Amazing though, this blatant change to the meaning and context of the Hebrew Torah has been known about for centuries in the Protestant Religions. The Papal lie is still taught by "Evangelical" and other Protestant denominations because to acknowledge it would destroy the very fabric of their "religion".

There was never an Old Testament prophesy of a savior of mankind. A common Jewish prophesy was of the rise of a Jewish King, from the lineage of King David, who would lead a rebellion against the oppressors of the Jews, re-establish the Kingdom, rebuild the Temple and bring peace. The timing of this messiah's coming was never established, as the subject only came up when the Hebrews were captured by some invading civilization. Many Pharisees and Zealots claimed to be this "Messiah" during the Roman occupation of Jerusalem.

There was prophesy of a Savior of mankind, born of a virgin, in the religion of Mitraism; the State Religion of the Roman Empire. This was 250 years before the Yeshua epic story,

Why is the "virgin birth" myth still persisting after the Vatican admitted to the false interpretation of Old Testament scripture by

Papal "Recension"? Recension is the term applied to the revising of a text, which changes the context and meaning of the original, by the infallible papacy, to fit their church marketing plan. It means they were lying. The truth does not matter to "True Believers" because they have been indoctrinated since birth.

Why did it require the Vatican to admit to the recension rather than the vast Protestant movement admitting to it? The answer is because it literally destroys the foundation of the "Mother of God" movement. No virgin birth of God, no female virgin Goddess, and still followers will not look at the evidence of fraud in establishing the "Church".

It is called "The Greatest Story Ever Told", exactly; It is a story. Religion is the leading cash industry. It is greater than oil, industries or any of the marketplace money-makers. Religion has history, culture, tradition and a solid base in all societies. How did this occur?

Religion is not a belief in a Supreme Being or Entity. Religion is the group-think following of common core ideas and premises, which are based on ancient cultural influences rather than facts. This requires the followers of any religion presented to have a tremendous reserve of **"FAITH"**. Without faith there is no religion because the premises which are followed cannot be proven.

The Sumerian Enuma Elish was an historic "fable" about the Creator God and the establishment of Humankind. The Creator God was known by many names, but universally known as the Sun God and many religions were based on this fable. The Enuma Elish is also the most ancient "Holy Writ" found to date.

You will find the same basic structure and tenets of Religion and Gods practiced from the first Sumerians to the end of the Inca [Inki] Empire. In several variations, these beliefs include;

The Triune of Gods [Father, Virgin Mother and Son who saved Mankind].

The Principal God Council, usually 7 Gods [Elohim],

That "Man" was created from the blood of the Gods, by the Gods.

The Gods' Son taught "Man" all intelligence and "redeemed" Mankind by his sacrifice.

The Gods require Man to honor this sacrifice by shedding their genital blood.

"Moses'" Pentateuch was a plagiarized version of the Enuma Elish, combined with the history of Lord Yahweh's tribe and portraying Lord Yahweh as the Creator God.

The New Testament was developed over centuries using the plagiarized religion of Mitraism and the supposed letters between the Christian leaders and various groups of followers. The letters were apparently attempts to consolidate the precepts and foundations of a new religion within all of the followers. These revised letters are touted as "The words of God", how original!

Theos ek Petra [Greek]: "God from the Rock", is a staple beginning for Gods to be born in a rock cave [a grotto] of a virgin. To sound more religious, rock cave is replaced with "a Grotto". A grotto is a picturesque cave and was often created artificially as a religious shrine in gardens. Grottos were used to stable livestock and house herdsmen. In non-canonical writings Yeshua [Jesus] was born in **Notzeri** [Nazareth], not in a grotto in Bethlehem, which actually was a shrine to other Greek/Roman Gods.

According to legends all Gods of antiquity were conceived by "virgin birth". All Persian, Greek and Roman Gods held this remarkable beginning, as well as all Egyptian Pharaohs, Mayan and South American Gods.

From the time the Lords founded civilizations around the World; State religions were supported by the ruling class in whichever nation they flourished. Kings realized having their populations worshipping them as Gods, or as having been appointed by God, was necessary to maintain their rule.

Most Religions follow this proven success model of the Lords of Sumer. Whatever is necessary to establish a new following is done. Sort of like modern-day Politicians.

As with most cultures, which come to power, the Popes and Emperors destroyed all records which did not support the "Christian" teachings. This destruction is documented in Europe, Asia and The Americas. Other civilizations and religions did the same, destroying much of recorded history.

Nathan confronts King David for his adultery with Bathsheba, an affair that produced a mamzer. A Mamzer was an illegitimate child with a non-Hebrew.

[Bronze bas-relief on the door of La Madeleine, Paris]

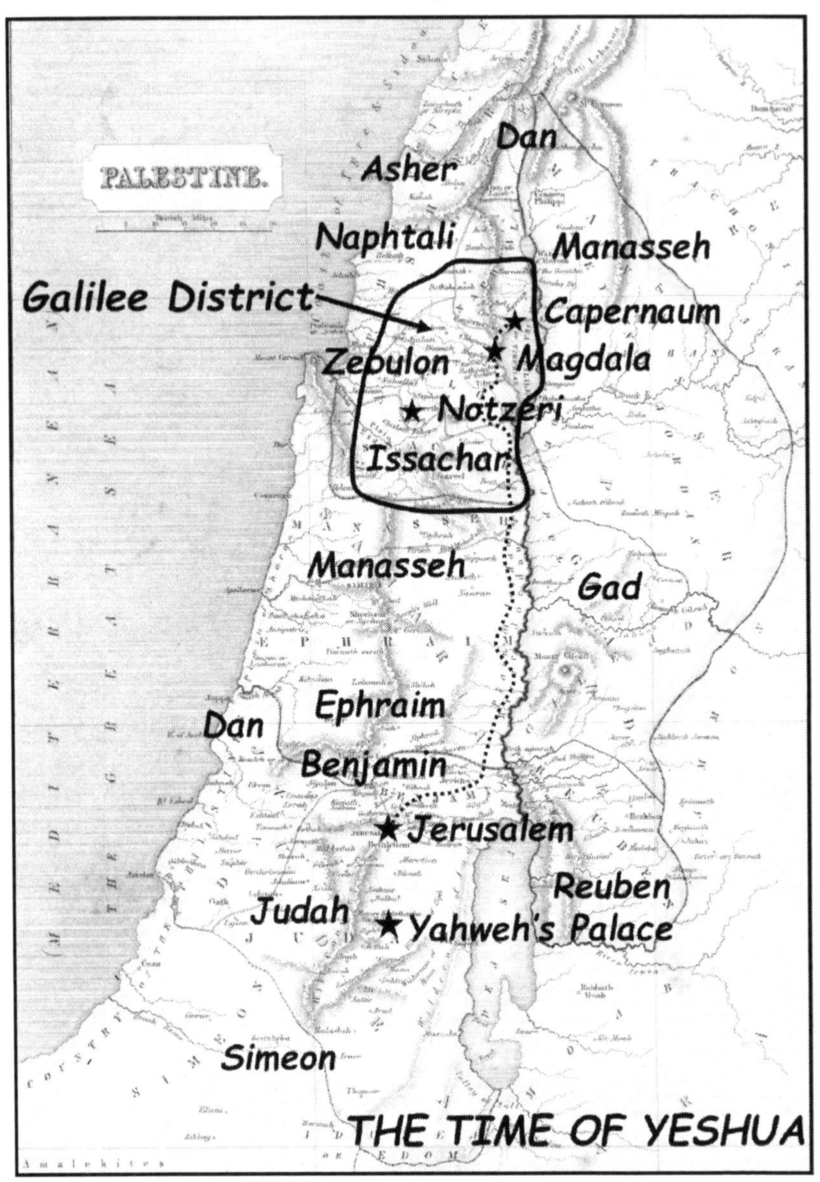

The general areas of the original lands of the 12 Tribes of Israel.
Galilee, the origin of many Revolutionary Leaders, Prophets and announced Messiahs

THE TIME OF YESHUA [JESUS]

This dialogue was developed using basic Holy Writ information, the Munich Talmud c. 1342 CE [the only remaining uncensored copy of the Babylon Talmud, completed c. 170 - 200 CE from the Jerusalem Temple records to 70 CE], also 1st and 2nd century writings and writings from Jewish rabbinical scholars c. 1900 CE.

Yeshua of Nazareth ["Yeshu Notzeri"] was educated by Pharisees, The Temple of On [Egypt], Zealots and the Sicarii. He campaigned for many revolutionary groups in the Holy Land and he was often referred to as "the Notzeri revolutionary" as this was his birthplace. The Zealots attracted followers using fiery rhetoric and producing "miracles". Their goals were the same, to overthrow the Romans and to occupy the Jerusalem Temple.

The name for the Sicarii sect of revolutionaries was derived from the sect members carrying and using a small concealable dagger, a sicarii. Their method was to approach a Roman soldier in crowded conditions and to stab him in a vulnerable spot, then disappear into the crowd.

The common languages of Hebrews at this time were Aramaic and Greek, although most understood many languages. Only the educated were proficient in Greek and Latin. The most devout Hebrews were proficient in the Hebrew language.

There was also a very powerful, long established, dominate Roman Empire State Religion:

If I were to profess to you that I worshipped **The Son of God, as part of the Trinity Godhead,** with the following attributes:

Son of God, Born of a virgin, in a grotto, on December 25th.
Placed in a manger and attended by shepherds.
Visited by Persian Magi.
Traveled widely to preach and performed miracles.
Promoted baptism for cleansing the soul and as a display of belief.
Had a following of twelve disciples, whom he taught.

Was addressed as "Teacher", "The way to Truth and Light, The Good Shepard and Messiah" Known as the Lion and the Lamb.
Observed the Sabbath and encouraged his followers too.
Knows all, sees all and cannot be deceived.
Held a Eucharist [Last Supper] with his disciples, "Eating the flesh, Drinking the blood"
Sacrificed Himself for all mankind and ascended to heaven.
His symbol is a cross.
His church is founded on "The Rock". Held midnight services.
This religion is based in Rome, on "Vatican Hill" and is organized with a Pope, Bishops and Priests.

Would you doubt that I would be a "Christian"?

These listed characteristics are from the worship of the Sun God Mitra. The Sumerian Sun God [circa 10,000 BCE] was known as Bel, later in Babylon as Marduk and in India and Persia as Mitra. This religion made it to the Roman Empire by 250 BCE as the Sun God Mitra. It was the primary [State] religion until the 5th Century CE.

Mitra was born in a Grotto [rock cave], fathered by "Ahura Mazda, Supreme God of the Universe" [The Sun], and the Virgin mother, Anahita [Immaculate], who was known as "The mother of God". Anahita was equal to, or portrayed as, Artemis, the Moon Goddess. Mitra was the "Voice of God to Mankind". These three primary Gods have been portrayed as the basis for religion, with different names, since pre-10,000 BCE.

In Roman times Mitra was portrayed as "The Invincible Sun God" riding in a chariot or as slaying the "Great Bull". Slaying the bull was relieving mankind of an evil God [one theory], or by eating the flesh and drinking the blood consecrates the Bull God and elevates Mitra to the sole Savior God of mankind [another theory]. This "Drink my blood, eat my flesh" ritual consecrated followers into Mitraism.

Mitraism ceremonies were held in underground labyrinths [mazes] or in structures to represent underground labyrinths. Mazes were used to initiate followers of religions, lodges and cults in Lord Yahweh's and Lord Bal's tribes. Mazes from antiquity are found in Asia, Europe, British Isles, Africa and The Americas. Initiates into the Mitra Lodge had to be male, of good character, citizens and uphold the values of the Empire [these are basic Masonic entry requirements]. There were seven to nine named levels of advancement with the final known as Pa-Pa, The Master Oracle of the Temple.

The worship of Mitra flourished into the 5th century, until the Emperors and the Catholic Church intensified the Inquisition. They destroyed all Mitra literature, killed the priests of Mitra, and destroyed or built churches over Mitra shrines and temples.

The Minoan civilization utilized labyrinth ceremonies with a woman priestess officiating over the Sun God ceremonies. She was known as the Labyrinth Priestess, symbolized with a double headed axe. The ax was actually a butterfly symbol on a staff.   Another prominent priestess was the "Snake Goddess", a tie to the Babylon Serpent.

Over 700 Mitra temples were built in Rome. The Romans extended Mitra worship throughout their Empire, building thousands of temples and requiring all Roman subjects to participate. In the 1960s a Mitra temple from Roman occupation era was located in London during construction. There are at least 35 remaining Temples of Mitra in Rome.

**Mitra Temple Room beneath the Basilica St. Clement,
Rome Italy**

The photograph is of the Mithraeum [Mitra Labyrinth Temple] beneath the Basilica of St Clement. The church is dedicated to Pope

Clement I, who was "*Bishop of Rome*" about 88 CE. I think this is wishful history as Mitraism was the State Religion at this time.

Vatican history revisionists claim the original "underground worship room" in year 88 was Christian, then c. 2nd century pagans built a Mitra Temple on the site. Christians again reclaimed the site in 385 and built a large meeting room, which was destroyed in an invasion. The current basilica was constructed in 1108. This is all amazing history, except that the lowest level, the oldest level, remains as a Mitra Labyrinth. In Medieval times the Vatican knew that about 1% of the population was literate and would believe anything the Church professed.

The Vatican hid these Mitra Temples in plain sight; they built their churches on the Mitra sites. This practice of building over religious sites continued worldwide with any religion they replaced.

Mitraism is noted to be a "Mystery Religion". It is a mystery because the Vatican destroyed all writings which could be found, for centuries.

Plutarch noted Roman soldiers of 70 BCE, led by Pompey, championed Mitra as their favorite God and put "His mark" [a cross, or X] on their foreheads and shields. This means the State sanctioned the religion and provided financial support and safety. The Mitra Temple [center of worship] was in Rome, actually what is now "Vatican Hill". The labyrinths beneath the Mitra Temple still exist beneath the Vatican. Did you make the connection of "his Mark" with "The Mark" in the Old Testament?

The Moon Goddess Artemis was worshipped as an equal to Mitra and was as popular. They were often portrayed as a couple. Mitra was portrayed in a chariot drawn by four white horses as the Invincible Sun God. The Goddess Artemis was portrayed as being in a stone tower, blessing her followers. Artemis statues were adorned with bees and bee larvae, and her temples contained numerous bee hives. Honey was stored in large vases in the temple storehouse.

Several extraordinary 2nd and 6th century documents of lost gospels, located in the British Museum, support the story of Miriam [Mary], a Hebrew, becoming pregnant by a Roman soldier, who was a Philistine. Also, that Yeshua knew who his father was and visited him often in Sidon. This Roman soldier, who worshipped Mitra, is mentioned by name [Pantera from Sidon] and eventually died in Germany. A monument to Pantera [Panther] is on display in a German museum. These documents are supported by historians and archeological finds.

Commentaries in the only uncensored Munich Talmud c. 1342 [a copy of the c. 170 Babylon Talmud] referring to the Jerusalem Temple Sanhedrin trials reinforce this history: Yeshu is referred to as "Ben Pandira". This means "Son of Pandira" who was "hung on the Eve of Passover".

Celsus, a 2nd century Greek historian who was anti-Christian, recounted the following story of Yeshua's mother:

> *Mary, a Hebrew, while engaged to Joseph of Nazareth, had a fling with the Roman soldier Pantera, a Philistine, and became pregnant. Joseph sued for divorce [as required by law] and it was granted.*

This claim is recorded in the Munich Talmud and was the subject of Rabbinical studies:

So "Joseph" got his divorce and Miriam married Stada instead of the soldier Pandira. And as the cliché so eloquently states; "the rest is history".

The Jewish laws of the time forbid intermarriage, and any child born of a union between Hebrew and Gentile was declared illegitimate, or a "Mamzer". The child, although raised Jewish, was forbidden to marry a Jew.

A Mamzer was treated as any other Hebrew except for the marriage issue. An educated Mamzer could prevail over an uneducated Temple Priest and could become a King.

Yeshua was forbidden to marry a Hebrew, and while traveling to visit his biological father in Sidon, he often stayed with Shimon Cephas in Capernaum, which is on the north shoreline of The Sea of Galilee. Capernaum means "village of Nahum" who was a "Minor Prophet" of the Hebrews. About 5 miles south of Capernaum Yeshua met a wealthy Philistine woman in Magdala. She was the **Priestess of Artemis** [Greek/Roman Moon Goddess] and was called *Miriam of The Tower*. *Magdala* translates as "*The Tower*", and results in the Holy Writ calling her "Mary Magdalene". Magdala had a large stone tower which served as the sanctuary for the Priestess of Artemis. The "Church" edited Miriam's history to that of a street whore, who followed Yeshua.

Yeshua was educated by Pharisees in Hebrew traditions and also by the Lodge in Egypt [the Priesthood of On], so was very well versed in the arts of "magic", healing and foretelling the future. Egypt's main God was Amun-Ra [Sun God] which was another name for Mitra. Yeshua was well schooled in Mitra and all Gods of the time. He paid homage to his father's religions, Mitra and Artemis.

Yeshua was a "craftsman" and hired out as a stonemason and carpenter. He was educated in Judaism by a sect of Pharisees who taught the existence of demons, magic and resurrection of the dead. The Pharisees were one of several anti-Roman zealot groups. The most active rebel groups came from the north of Jerusalem in the Galilee District.

South of the Galilee District Yeshua developed a following as a leader of anti-Roman occupation rebellions. He drew crowds of followers by performing healings and other "miracles". He also railed against the corrupt Temple Priests in Jerusalem. Yeshua proclaimed he was the Messiah for the Jewish people and would rule from the Jerusalem Temple after overthrowing the Temple Priests. His sole purpose in life was to become King of the Hebrews. He was vehemently opposed by the Sadducees Sect, which had a large influence on the Temple Priests.

Yeshua's family regarded him as "being out of his mind" and would not associate with him. He had many "step siblings", four brothers, Jacob, Jose, Simon, Judah, and as many sisters. As a mamzer he apparently did not bond well and "would not regard his mother in high esteem".

Yeshua's final campaign was launched from Shimon's home on the North shore of The Sea of Galilee, about 80 miles north of Jerusalem. Here he allied with several followers with the main one being **Shimon**, with the "nickname" of **Cephas** [Aramaic for rock] – called "*Simon Peter*" in Vatican writings.   These followers were fishermen of the Sea of Galilee and were considered one of the lowest classes of people [by the elite class of course]. They were hard working people with many different religious views with the anchor religion as Hebrew along with the regional Mitra religion.

His main meeting place was at the "House of Shimon" in Capernaum and he stayed there quite often. This was a few miles from where Miriam the Goddess of Artemis ruled in Magdala. Not far to go for a booty call.

This last campaign took place **"between the ripening of the corn about June of the year 28 and his death in March or April of the following year"**. Yeshua's main message was **"John the Baptist's message of the nearness of the kingdom of heaven and of the need of repentance in order to enter it."**

His group was based in the Capernaum/Magdala area and traveled to "adjacent heathen territories" to broadcast his message in preparation of overthrowing the Priests of The Jerusalem Temple.

His followers were radicals of the Zealots and Sicarii factions fighting against Rome. They were chronicled as being the lowest of the working classes, fishermen, who were literally the unwashed. People at Yeshua's meetings complained that his followers ate without even washing their hands. They had no hygiene principles and loved their wine. Obviously if they were Hebrews, they did not follow the strict hygiene laws of the Temple.

An interesting practice of antiquity was to marinate psychedelic mushrooms in wine and drink the brew to enhance religious experience and encourage visions. A 1st century document in **The Dead Sea Scrolls** revealed this concoction continued to be popular in Roman times and was used in Sun God and "Christian" rituals. Commentators of the time noted some attendees danced strangely and spoke in un-intelligible languages. This practice came to be called "speaking in tongues" while communicating with God.

A favorite wine of Yeshua was imported from Lebanon, a raisin wine which was very popular. The Apostle Petra [Shimon Cephas] wrote about his conversations with various animals while spending the night on a rooftop. He must have had some raisin 'shroom wine when he had these discussions, some might say, "drunk as a skunk."

Most of his converts lived around the Sea of Galilee, a region where the Mitra and Artemis religions flourished. They were undoubtedly followers of these established religions mixed with Hebrew teachings. Had they been devout Hebrews, they would have followed culinary laws and washed more often. This region was in the former Northern Kingdom of Israel [Samaria] which was resettled by Assyrian's after the exile of the Hebrews.

Yeshua's followers viewed him as the incarnation of Mitra. This was common for the time as these religions were very popular and sanctioned by the Roman Emperor. He welcomed this following and modeled his crusade using Mitra and all of his attributes and was viewed as the spokesman [Holy See] between God and Man

In the Galilee Yeshua was worshipped as the incarnation of Helios [Mitra], and Miriam of the Tower as Artemis. Miriam is referred to as "The wife of God" in Coptic Gospels [Coptic is Greek for Egyptian]. Mosaics depicting both, surrounded by portraits of twelve men, were discovered in the floor of a "church" in the Galilee.

Ancient writings never accounted for "Twelve Disciples" as an entourage for Yeshua. The most accounted for was the five disciples tried and stoned by the Jerusalem Sanhedrin.

The marriage of Yeshua and Miriam was celebrated by followers as the "Sacred Marriage" of Mitra and Artemis. The marriage was recreated in ceremonies called "The Bridal Chamber", and all followers were required to participate in this ceremony to enter the movement. The marriage is chronicled in 1st century writings as producing two children.

The Bridal Chamber ceremony is noted in the Gnostic Gospels and Holy Writs and is a staple ceremony in some modern religions.

The Vatican refuted the similarities of their new church with centuries of Mitraism and the same location of their temples in Rome by blaming it on "The Devil".   The Vatican said Satan had foreknowledge of Jesus and the Catholic Church and devised Mitraism to confuse true believers in God. The Vatican destroyed all known Mitra writings and public shrines declaring that the followers of this Pagan religion left no records.

Celsus, a 2nd century historian, was well read and mentioned many "gospels" which were never widely read and were eventually destroyed. 2nd century writers discussed the unexplainable reasons why people would worship a corpse. The Roman Gods were real to them, and answered their prayers, what else did you need?

The writings of Celsus were destroyed by Christians and Roman Emperors. His writings were preserved in quotes by his critics while refuting his statements. The Vatican library retained his writings and used them to rewrite gospels when he found errors in the Christian doctrines. Celsus was a gold mine for the Vatican in finding areas of contradictions in their Christian narrative. These teachings were refined and reformed into a more believable marketing plan. The Pope should have made him a Saint.

Talmudic records from the Jerusalem Temple indicate Yeshua was guilty of heresy against the Temple [claiming to be God and the new King of the Jews]. The Temple records state he was stoned by Jews and then hung up on a post for viewing. This would have fulfilled the punishment requirements of both State and Temple transgressions. The Roman Empire restricted the "Hanging" part after 200 CE.

[The following definitions may help you follow the ancient records]:

The **Written Torah** contains the Pentateuch [Five Books of Moses] and prophetic writings of Isaiah, Jeremiah, Psalms, Proverbs, etc., about 24 Holy Writ books.

The **Oral Torah** was not allowed to be written and it was required for it to be taught orally, a different section on specific week days. The written Torah could not be understood without the oral explanations providing traditions of Hebrew Law. The Oral Torah includes Midrash, an explanation of ethical and legal subjects. It also contains the Kabbalah, a tradition of mystical secrets of the metaphysical universe.

The **Talmud** explains all codes of Jewish law, and contains the **Mishna**, which is sixty-three tractates of Oral Law codified, and the **Gemara**, which holds rabbinical analysis of and commentary on the Mishna.

The **Oral Torah** was first published as "The Zohar" by R' Shimon bar Yochai [170 CE], and elucidated by the Arizal [1572 CE]. The decision to record the oral traditions was made after the fall of the Jerusalem Temple in 70 CE when many Hebrews fled to Babylon, Egypt and other areas for safety.

Pharisees were considered the most expert and accurate expositors of Jewish law. They believed in resurrection and of a coming Messiah, spirits and angels.

Sadducees were members of a sect of priests and aristocrats from the 1st century BCE to the 1st century CE that denied the resurrection of the dead and the coming of a Messiah, the existence of spirits, and the obligation of oral tradition, emphasizing acceptance of the written Law alone. Saul [Paul] chose this point of division to gain the protection of the **Pharisees** when attacked in Jerusalem.

Biblical names: Hebrew: Yehoshua Ha' Mashiach [Joshua the Anointed One] refers to OT Joshua.

From common Hebrew, Yeshua [Yeshu]; to Greek = Lesous; to Latin = Lesus; to English = Jesus of Nazareth; to Arabic = 'Isa

Names of Yeshua from the **Babylon Talmud** c. 170 CE [copied as the **Munich Talmud** c. 1342] from the **Jerusalem Sanhedrin** Trial of Yeshua c. year 28 CE:

> *Yeshu Notzeri, Yeshu ha [of]-Notzeri, Yeshu ben* [son of] *Pandira* [or Panthera], *Yeshu ben* [son of] *Stada*, from his mother's name, *Miriam Stada* [mother of Yeshua].

> *Yeshu the Notzeri* [Notzarine] had five disciples; *Mattee, Nakee, Nossree, Banee and Tadee.* A later follower was *Jacob of Kephar Sekhania.*

> *"Prominent Rabbis reviewing the 2nd and 14th Century "Written Talmud" determined the names Ben Pandira and Ben Stada, in reference to Yeshu Notzeri all referred to the same person. The references were included in the 2nd Century records to establish Yeshu's total family lineage with his father "Pantera", a Gentile, his mother Miriam, a Hebrew and his mother's later husband "Stada", a Hebrew. With this information they determined Yeshu was a Mamser [illegitimate Hebrew]."*

A composition of translations of the **Jerusalem Sanhedrin** trial of **Yeshu the Notzarie,** taken from the Munich manuscript states:

> *On the Eve of Shabbat they hung Yeshu the Notzeri. And the herald went out before him for 40 days proclaiming: "Yeshu the Notzeri will be taken out to be stoned for sorcery and misleading and enticing Israel [to idolatry]. Any who has words in his defence must come and declare about him." But none came to his defence so they hung him on the Eve of Shabbat.*

The Hebrew tradition of execution was stoning and hanging the body on a post for public viewing. One document adds after the public hanging **"and at sundown he was taken down and buried".**

A 1917 publication further elaborates on the Sanhedrin trial and execution: It is **"Yehoshua Nazir; Jesus the Nazarite; life of Christ"** by: Hanish, Otoman Zar-Adusht 1917

[see Appendix]

LIFE OF CHRIST 205
And proclamation was made every day for forty days, that whoever knew aught wherewith to defend Yeshu and prove Him not guilty, they should come forward and make it known: for Yeshu had been sentenced to be stoned because He had bewitched and led astray the people of the Jews.

But no one was found to speak in defense of Yeshu, except five persons, whose names were: Mattee, Nakee, Nossree, Banee and Tadee.

These were bold and said: "Why should we search for His good work; the wonderful things that He hath done are good evidences that He hath in Him a most godlike spirit."

The Sanhedrin perceived by the boldness of these men that they were disciples of Yeshu and gave orders that the matter be investigated. And when they discovered that it was indeed so, and that these men had been among the first to lead their fellow citizens astray after Yeshu, the Sanhedrim said unto them: "You will likewise be slain like your Master the sorcerer."

And they stoned all the five men to death on the same day.
I" "T" •!• T*

The Jewish sages did not wait for the Yom Tof, feast day, but this Yeshu was brot out on the day before the Eve of the Passover. That same day they led Him to the place where they used to stone all those who merited such death, and they stoned Yeshu.

Towards evening they wanted to hang Him on a tree but the tree would not bear His dead body, because before His death, Yeshu had, by the power of Shem, conjured all the trees that they should not receive His body. Then Rabbi Yehuda Ish Bari Totha ran and pulled out a large and thick root, like a tree, out of his own garden, and brought it, and they hanged Yeshu on it.*

And when the sun had set the body of Yeshu was taken down and buried outside the city. But the Jewish sages went away very much satisfied, and rejoiced at the wonders which God had done for them.

After reviewing Hebrew Traditions and Laws it is more likely that the stoning of Yeshua occurred on the day before the Eve of Passover celebration. The reference to "by the power of Shem" most likely refers to "Baal-Shem", which is a research job of its own, but interesting.

Yeshua's disciples; **Mattee, Nakee, Nossree, Banee** and **Tadee** were investigated and later all were stoned on the same day. There is no date given for this action but was most likely within a few months after Yeshua's death as the records indicate they were "**the first to lead their fellow citizens astray after Yeshu**". Another translation of the same incident lists the names as; **Matai, Nekai, Netzer, Buni,** and **Todah**.

These five disciples were also held in chains, the same as Yeshua, pending their execution. It is obvious that Shimon Cephas and his close allies were not with this group as Saul of Tarsus had not been able to capture them.

The Vatican claims these disciples were indeed the primary disciples of "the Gospels". How could this be is they were executed a short time after Yeshua?

This information begs one to consider the origins of the Vatican's Disciple Saints; Peter, Paul, Mark etc. These Vatican Saints names most likely rose from the ranks of the various Zealot revolutionaries. Saul and his followers spread the basis for these first "Saints" of *Pauline Christianity* and as writers of "*The Gospels*", which were created after 200 CE. These "Gospels" were continuously modified as tales of supernatural acts, by recension, for over a thousand years.

The Jewish-Messiah Sect [**The Church of Cephas**] led by Shimon as Peter; Yakov as James and Barnabas did not follow Paul [Saul] because they held to Pharisee Traditions. The addition of these "Disciples" was simply more Vatican Recension [God inspired lying]. The "**Jewish Didache**" listed the principles which these followers embraced: essentially those ideals of the Essenes and Qumran followers.

The Didache was a Hebrew document which was revised by "Paul" and the Vatican and became the primary building block for the "Gospels of The Twelve Apostles". It is portrayed by the Vatican as the founding sources to verify all writings of Pauline Christianity.

"Petra" [the Greek word for "rock"] is another connecting thread from Mitra worship to Christ worship as alluded to in "I will base my church on this rock" – the rock being the source of "God", which was the basis for the Temple of Mitra. I believe this quote attributed to Jesus was added to enhance the position of the Vatican, which was constructed on the Mitra Temple site on "Vatican Hill" across the Tiber River from Rome.

Most of the following references to Yeshua's disciples are according to the Vatican's **New Testament**.

Petra [rock] [Peter] was the nickname Yeshua gave to his disciple Shimon [Simon Cephas also called Peter]. He was known to give each disciple a nickname. Shimon believed his leader was the incarnation of the Jewish Messiah from God, not the incarnation of Mitra. These differences would create a schism between the Jerusalem followers and those who followed Paul and the incarnation of Mitra belief.

The custom of "Pauline Christians" holding midnight fertility rites and eating the flesh and drinking the blood of live animals was widely reported in the 1st and 2nd centuries. In the early formation of **Pauline Christianity,** the various churches followed their own local rites and were not acting of common accord. Paul's letters to these churches attempted to curtail these activities and bring common practice to all "churches". Paul called these letters the "Gospel from God".

EARLY CHURCHES EVOLUTION

Three "religions" evolved after the death of Yeshua

The name "Christ" and the derivative "Christian" developed from the Hebrew term "masiah" [messiah] translated to the Greek term 'khriein" [anoint] as "Khristos" [anointed] to Latin "Christus", to old English "Crist" to modern English "Christ".

The first religious group to emerge was the Hebrew Pharisee followers of Yeshua, who believed he was the Jewish Messiah, who was resurrected and would soon return and take all Jewish believers to "Paradise". This was the leading new religion until Saul entered the religious arena and consolidated the gentile and Hebrew Mitra worshippers.

After Yeshua's death, his brother Yakov [or Jacob], called James in the Testaments and Shimon [Peter] assumed control of the Hebrew rebel groups and formed the new Jewish religion. The Vatican claimed they also experienced Yeshua appearing and speaking directly to them. This new religion was Judaism with a returning Messiah twist. This following is properly labeled as **Judaeo-Messiahs**. Some historians relate the Essenes and Masada dwellers as followers.

The followers of Shimon and Yakov attended Synagogue, seated separate from orthodox worshipers, and strictly adhered to Jewish Law, with the exception that Yeshua was the promised Messiah and would soon return and escort them to paradise. They named their church **"The Church of Cephas"** so as not to be confused with Paul's church.

The Council of Jerusalem was convened in 50 CE [22 years after Yeshua was stoned] by Shimon and Yakov, due to conflicts with Paul and the Galilean followers. The council was to determine if Gentiles were required to observe the Torah, circumcision and dietary laws, to enter the movement.

The Gentile converts were observing the Mitra Eucharist by eating flesh cut from living animals and drinking their blood. They also held midnight orgies [Mitra and Artemis practices]. Paul agreed to a watered-down version of the Law of Moses for the Gentiles [no circumcision]. The Orthodox Hebrews conceded leadership of the Gentiles to Paul.

Although Paul agreed to these rules for the Gentiles, he later told his followers "to eat and do whatever they wanted". He proclaimed that even Jewish converts did not need to observe the Torah.

The separation of *"The Church of Cephas" and Paulinism* is supported by Hebrew researchers:

> **"The predominating point of view of the Synagogue was the political and social one; that of the Church, the eschatological one. May such as do not bear the seal of Abraham's covenant upon their flesh or do not fulfil the whole Law be admitted into the congregation of the saints waiting for the world of resurrection? This was the question at issue between the disciples of Jesus and those of Paul; the former adhering to the view of the Essenes, which was also that of Jesus; the latter taking an independent position that started not from the Jewish but from the non-Jewish standpoint. Paul fashioned a Christ of his own, a church of his own, and a system of belief of his own;"**

The **Church of Cephas** in Jerusalem wanted nothing to do with Paul's churches for they regarded him as an **"apostate from the Law"**, and indeed he was arrested and almost stoned when he arrived in Jerusalem in 58 CE. He only escaped death by surrendering to Roman soldiers and being imprisoned. Paul arrived in Rome, in chains, in 61 CE. This was Paul's first trip to Rome.

There are no historical records of Peter ever traveling to Rome. He had no reason to travel to Rome as he was active with his followers in Jerusalem. Many scholars mapped his travels and determined that he did not leave the Eastern Mediterranean. He is noted to not be fluent in Latin nor highly educated and also despised Paul and his new religion. "Peter" was aware of Paul's capture of the five disciples executed by the Sanhedrin.

There are records of heated exchanges between Paul, Peter and Barnabas about Paul's abandonment of Judaism. They were extremely upset that Paul would turn their Jewish Messiah into the incarnation of Mitra. This Jewish group severed ties to Pauline Christians and eventually died out.

The second religious group to emerge was the followers of Miriam of the Tower who worshipped Yeshua as Mitra incarnate, and Miriam as

"The wife of God". They believed the resurrected Mitra would return during their lifetime and escort all Mitra believers to "Paradise".

Miriam of the Tower [Mary Magdalene] founded her "**Church of Mitra**" by claiming Yeshua, the incarnation of Mitra, had risen from the dead and spoke to her. Miriam was known to have "spells", possibly epileptic seizures, and many visions. She was the first to declare Yeshua had risen from the dead and spoke to her.

Miriam already had a large following and in ancient meeting houses mosaics were placed in the floor to acknowledge the women who "supplied the meeting table". The women [wives of the Mitra disciples] were the power behind this religious movement because they financed the work and travels of the revolutionaries. These women had many followers north of Jerusalem, in Galilee, and started many "churches".

The floor of an ancient Galilean church contains a mosaic which proclaims Miriam of the Tower to be "The founder of the church". The Galilean believers of Yeshua as the Resurrected Messiah worshipped a mixture of Judaism, "Christian" and Roman Gods. These churches eventually disappeared when Pauline Christianity [Catholic] became the State religion.

The third religious group, and the one which would gain State approval and funding, were the followers of Paul who proclaimed Yeshua as the incarnation of Mitra the Messiah. Mitra was "The Voice of God" to all believers. About year 40 Paul claimed a personal blessing and conversation with a resurrected "Christ", which "converted" him to believe and to establish his Church. Paul proclaimed Yeshua would soon return as God and take all believers to "Paradise" during their lifetime. This church was and is **Pauline Christianity**.

Paul high-jacked the leadership and control of [a power, money and fame maker] the newborn religion of the resurrected incarnate of Mitra. He changed his Hebrew name to the Roman equivalent, Paul, to disguise his Jewish history. He used his education in philosophy to slowly remove women from any leadership roles in his new religion to redirect Mitra worshippers.

This branch of Yeshua followers would be slowly converted to a "**Pauline Christianity**." philosophy, occupying and rebuilding Mitra temples while replacing all vestiges of Mitraism. In 42 CE Paul sent an emissary to Alexandria to establish a following. This church evolved into "**Coptic Christians**". The Coptic believers had previous influence from **The Church of Cephas** followers who lived in Mecca. "Mitra" was replaced with "Messiah" and in Greek with "Christ" for addressing their God. It was an easy change for believers to get accustomed to. After a few decades it was standard mantra.

Some Yeshua followers were known as Gnostics [did not need anyone to intercede with God for them] and they were still trying to overthrow the Romans and reform the Temple. The northern Pauline Christians finally separated their church from Judaism near the end of the 1st century and into the early 2nd century.

SAUL OF TARSUS

Saul of Tarsus: Official of the Roman Empire as Inquisitor General for the Jerusalem Temple Priests and for the State to exterminate the Jewish Revolutionaries.   The Vatican recorded him as being an orthodox Hebrew and that he was educated as a Rabbi at the prestigious Jerusalem school of Gamaliel and was highly educated in the arts, languages, history and philosophy.

Hebrew scholars dispute these claims and found no records to substantiate these claims. One researcher stated "No records of Saul of Tarsus' early life could be found." From ancillary records it was apparent Saul was born of Hebrew parents but was neither active in Jewish orthodox lifestyles, nor educated as a Rabbi. His early life was devoted to following Roman Generals and their lifestyles. He is described as a "Hellenist".

> **<u>SAUL OF TARSUS [known as Paul, the Apostle of the Heathen]</u>: Rabbi Kaufmann Kohler (1843 - 1926)**
>
> **"The claim in Rom. xi. 1 and Phil. iii. 5 that he was of the tribe of Benjamin, suggested by the similarity of his name with that of the first Israelitish king, is, if the passages are genuine, a false one, no tribal lists or pedigrees of this kind having been in existence at that time (see Eusebius, "Hist. Eccl." i. 7, 5; Pes. 62b; M. Sachs, "Beiträge zur Sprach- und Alterthumsforschung," 1852, ii. 157). Nor is there any indication in Paul's writings or arguments that he had received the rabbinical training ascribed to him by Christian writers, ancient and modern; least of all could he have acted or written as he did had he been, as is alleged (Acts xxii. 3], the disciple of Gamaliel I., the mild Hillelite."** [a follower of more liberal interpretations of Jewish Law]

Saul's total history is sketchy at best. As a citizen and official of the Roman government, his mission was to find and destroy the Jewish anarchist groups. He is described in the Christian religion as a "Roman tax collector", but he pursued, captured and killed the Zealots.

Records of Saul's life suddenly appear after Yeshua was executed in Jerusalem. Saul was known to have had a "fiery temper" and was driven in his mission. Long before Saul became "Paul" he was in a fury to capture Shimon Cephas whom he considered the leader of **The Church of Cephas**. By whatever means he found out that Shimon was traveling from Capernaum to Damascus. He attacked a group of The Church of Cephas near the Jerusalem Temple and injured several of them. One outcome, if he was successful in capturing a revolutionary, would be information about the group.

He pursued Yakov [James, brother of Yeshua] and threw him down the steps of the Jerusalem temple during a battle. The fall broke Yakov's leg and he was carried away on a litter by his group, north to Capernaum.

I suspect Saul had a sizeable posse and was involved in the earlier capture of **Yeshu** and with this skirmish captured Yeshua's disciples **Mattee, Nakee, Nossree, Banee** and **Tadee**, who were executed. Saul was also implicated when a [another?] disciple Stephen [Nikud or Nakee] was stoned to death for crimes against the Temple. Shimon called Saul an enemy "acting in the interests of the High Priest".

The term "Christian" was coined about 44 CE, about 15 years after Yeshua was executed. Some revisionists claim early Christians were **Ebionites**, however this term referred to **The Church of Cephas**. Saul embraced his new Messiah as the incarnation of Mitra, a religion he had followed all of his life. He re-invented Mitra as the peace-loving God of all Mankind, cast in the mold of a meek, wandering worker of miracles [not associated with the Essenes] and established his "Christian" Church away from Jerusalem. He successfully removed women from all roles in his new church.

Paul's primary claim to his followers was that while pursuing *Judeo-Christian* anarchists, he had communed with Yeshua through visions and received his blessing as the church "Holy See" and actually ascended to "Heaven" for a tour. This "conversion" happened about 40 CE, while pursuing followers of Shimon Cephas, [the Vatican's "Peter"], during one of his seizures.

The reason Saul initially established his Church north of Jerusalem was to integrate the incarnation of Mitra [Yeshua] with the Mitra Temples located there. This would be acceptable to enough Mitra worshippers to gain a foothold. With his political connections he could gain favor and financial backing from the Roman government.

Historians made the following comments about Saul [Paul]:

"The actual founder of the Christian Church as opposed to Judaism; born before 10 C.E.; died after 63. The records containing the views and opinions of the opponents of Paul and Paulinism are no longer in existence."

"The conception of a new faith, half pagan and half Jewish, such as Paul preached, and susceptibility to its influences, were altogether foreign to the nature of Jewish life and thought."

"Still more is the partaking of the bread and the wine of the communion meal, the so-called "Lord's Supper," rendered the means of a mystic union with Christ, "a participation in his blood and body," exactly as was the Mithraic meal a real participation in the blood and body of Mithra."

As Saul gained state support, he managed to sway the Philistine churches to abandon any female leadership, using cultural arguments. Women were eventually driven from church leadership because it was not the custom for women to lead or instruct men, unless they were acting as an oracle or priestess.

Saul changed his name to "Paul" to disguise his Jewish heritage from the Roman leaders. He maintained correspondence with politicians, military leaders and followers throughout the Roman Empire. When traveling he would stay in comfort with the military officers he knew and receive safety and financial support. He continuously sent emissaries throughout the Mediterranean to establish followers.

Paul escaped assassination from numerous plots by the Sicarii sect led by James. Warned by his contacts, he would travel in disguise and bypass any towns that were hostile to him. Paul was arrested several times but was able to use his Roman citizen status to be released. It is recorded that he suffered the "Lash and the Rod" on several occasions for abuse of Jewish traditions. Apparently, James never "forgave" him for his attempted murder early on.

During this time the Government in Rome did not care about this new religion as long as it did not infringe on Roman life. Paul had no intentions of going to Rome; he was still consolidating his influence in the eastern Mediterranean.

Early Roman Empire Caesars

Augustus	27 BCE – 14 CE
Tiberius	14–37 CE
Caligula	37–41 CE
Claudius	41–54 CE
Nero	54–68 CE

Tiberius Caesar [14 CE to 37 CE], the Emperor of Rome could care less about these social matters, and was smothered to death at age 78, at one of his villas. The inbred families who controlled the Roman Empire were a constant source of plots, and murders of family members [mothers, sons, daughters etc.]. Becoming a Caesar was hazardous to their health, or to a lot of family members' health.

Caesar Caligula came to power and reigned from 37 CE to 41 CE. He was assassinated by poison and Caesar Claudius [41 CE to 54 CE] came to power. Caesar Claudius was assassinated in 54 CE.

The new religion was doing well until Caesar Nero came to power at age 16 [54 CE to 69 CE]. When Rome burned in 64 CE, he blamed the Christian sect as desecrators of the Mitra Temple and religion in Rome. He used the heretics as human torches to surround the Mitra Temple [Vatican Hill], and to light his private parties across the Tiber River.

Paul was attacked when he went to Jerusalem, in 58 CE, by an angry crowd from the Temple. Paul had desecrated the Temple by entering as an "unclean soul". The "Church" does not dwell on how many "Disciples" were in the crowd. He escaped death by surrendering to a Roman garrison. He was arrested and imprisoned for two years in Caesarea but the reason was not specified, possibly sedition and/or for the desecration of the Temple.

As a Roman citizen Paul demanded his right to plead his case before Caesar and was transported to Rome in 61 CE. This was the first time Paul had been to Rome.

Being a Roman citizen, Paul was allowed to leave prison and live in Rome even though he was a prisoner. Most likely he was "bailed out" by his political connections. Paul had several years in Rome to spread his brand of Christianity.   Caesar Nero finally imprisoned Paul and executed [beheaded] him in 67 CE.

The "Church" "recorded" Paul appointing Linus to be the Bishop of Rome [Pope] shortly before Paul's death. There are conflicting stories about the origin of Linus and his lineage as Pope. Vatican records indicate he was born to a Roman family and anointed by Paul.

Some historians insist Linus was a Celtic Prince, the son of King Caractucus of the Celtic empire. In 41 CE, Caractucus defeated another Celtic ruler who escaped to Rome.   The defeated king convinced Caesar Claudius to invade the British Isles, attack King Caractucus and help him regain his kingship.

Claudius defeated Caractucus and brought him and his family to Rome as trophies in 43 CE. History validates this part of the story, recording the speech by Caractucus to the Roman Senate. The Celtic King died in Rome in 50 CE. This is where the histories radically depart.

Prince Linus is said to have been a Celtic Christian, or introduced to it, by way of Christian influence coming to the Celtic region by a different path than "Paul".   The Christian influence was from James in Jerusalem, to the Middle East [Mecca area] and combining with influence from Alexandria Egypt. The Celtic church is said to have given women equal status in the religion.

Another story is that Linus was a convert to a Roman Christian sect lead by Jesus Justus, a converted Jew. It was this group of Christians who appointed Linus as Pope [The Bishop of Rome]. Their "church" was not located on Mt. Vaticanus as that was the site of the Temple of Mitra. Most likely these Christians met in secret at a local house. The Catholic Vatican would not come to be for about 300 years. Also, there was no physical contact with Paul, who arrived in Rome in 61 CE under arrest.

Vatican records say the Celtic Church was established sometime around 170 CE. The difficulty of resolving these stories is due to ancient records and writings being severely "scrubbed" by the Vatican. The Vatican also manufactured so much "church history" that not much is believable. An example of manufactured history is that "Peter" traveled to Rome and was crucified there.

Caesar Nero embarrassed the Roman nobility and Military by lowering himself to perform stage plays for the audience. Actors were viewed as the lowest form of humanity and it was a serious social breach for an Emperor to perform. More degrading behavior followed when Nero drove his own chariot in the races, a job for slaves, to portray himself as Mitra. This heresy angered the military who considered themselves as honorable soldiers of Mitra.

Nero's continued public excesses, such as performing homosexual acts for public viewing, while not tending to the business of Rome and its citizens, was his downfall. This was his last act of disgracing behavior, for when the military came to kill him in 68 CE, he committed suicide. After Nero's death Rome was in chaos for several years and Pope Linus continued to bring in converts to the new religion.

The "scriptures" were not invented at this time and when written several hundred years later were edited by Pauline Christians. Peter was written into the "Gospels" to establish the church lineage from Jerusalem. The gospels would evolve over the centuries to complete the story of the Messiah and the "Holy See" [Pope] as His Voice to mankind.

[Unless otherwise noted, all dates are CE in the balance of this section.]

TOMÁS DE TORQUEMADA

One of The Vatican's very own Medieval Sadistic Murderers. The legacy of this butcher, and many like him, of thousands of victims was rewarded with Sainthood. He also split the victims' seized property with the Vatican.

ESTABLISHING THE CATHOLIC CHURCH

Catholic *[Latin: catholicus]* means "Universal", or "All Encompassing". The title "Catholic" was first widely used in 107.

By 100 all of the original disciples had died. First and Second century writers recorded that many followers were disappointed, believing their Messiah should have returned as promised.

Mitraism was still the most dominant religion in the Roman Empire. Christians were tolerated, overlooked and often abused by society, but they were persistent holding to that promise of everlasting Paradise.

In 144 the Church split over the description of Jesus as God, Man or both. This divisive debate would continue to rage after the Council of Nicaea in 325. Gnostics and other heretics would continually cause unity problems. They were executed when found. The "Church" was still defining their dogma and "history". This would be a constant natural selection process [evolution] of beliefs and power.

In 195 the Pope excommunicated the Eastern Christians who observed Easter on the Jewish Passover, the 14th day of the Jewish calendar, instead of the proclaimed Easter Sunday. They are referred to these heretics as "Quartodecimans" and this debate would continue until the Nicaean Council established a firm Sabbath for the observance. Use of various vague terms to describe those who committed heresy would continue.

Emperor Decius, in 250, revived the killing and persecution of Christians in the Roman Empire. The acceptance of Christians would not be easy. They were persecuted, on and off, until Emperor Constantine's reign in the 4th century provided State protections and funding. Constantine allowed the Christians to function openly when they agreed to honor the established ceremonies of the Mitra and Artemis worshipers. This was after Christian soldiers allied with Constantine against his political enemies.

The "Vatican" derived its name from *Mons Vaticanus*, which translates as "The hill of prophetic cults'" or *Oracle*. This was the site of the

Mitra Temple and Labyrinths, which is across the Tiber River from the Seven Hills of Rome. The seven hills were the sites of many temples and official Roman buildings including the coliseum. The Oracle was the Mitra High Priest of the Temple. He was overseer of the Temple Priestess' who gave their life issuing predictions from the Oracle deep within Labyrinths. The Priestess' were "Virgins", women of great beauty with divine gifts.

After the Edict of Milan in 313, Constantine began building the first St. Peter's Basilica above the Mitra Temple and Labyrinths. The labyrinths became the Vatican Necropolis.

There was a myriad of religions located in this area. The Church removed or destroyed all traces of these declared Heretics which could be found.

The Church used as much symbolism from Mitraism as possible to afford an easier transition from Mitraism to Pauline Christianity. The High Adept of Mitra worship was known as the *Oracle* and *Pater Patrum*, or *Pa-Pa.* This title was used by the Church and became "Pope".

Mitra Oracles spoke for Greek and Roman Gods to communicate with followers, so the Christian Pope stepped in as the Chief Oracle for God's communications with all Mankind. The Mitra Temple [Labyrinth] Oracles were Virgin Priestesses who served until they became pregnant.

Around 480 the Vatican began using virgin women openly to serve as housemaids for the Priesthood. They were originally known as "Brides of Christ" and were able to serve until they became pregnant. They later became known as Nuns.

EMPEROR CONSTANTINE [306–337]
AND THE NICAEA COUNCILS

In the 4th century Emperor Constantine held Mitraism to be a valid state religion. Christian Pope Sylvester of Rome supported Constantine's victorious war against his brother-in-law, and political rival, Maxentius. Constantine was Emperor of the West Roman Empire and Maxentius was Emperor of the East Roman Empire. Maxentius invaded Italy but was later defeated at the Milvian Bridge, which connected Vatican Hill and Rome across the Tiber River. Maxentius was killed in the battle, drowned, and his head paraded on a lance.

Christian soldiers in this battle marked their shields with the first two Greek letters of the Latin word for Christian [Χριστιανός], Chi Rho, [XP] combined. The Roman soldiers marked their foreheads and shields with the mark of Mitra [X], which was the ancient "Hooked X". The Vatican later claimed it was the "Chi" and represented solidarity with Christians. Of course, The Roman Empire had been using the hooked X symbol for centuries before Christianity.

The Chi Rho combined symbol was also used in ancient times as a mark of approval in the margin of manuscripts, abbreviating the Greek word for good. This sign was mis-interpreted as a Christian approval of documents by some historians.

The combined Chi Rho letters [X + P] was the first universally recognized symbol for Christians.

The Milvian Bridge victory on October 28th, 312, and a few more victories, led to Constantine becoming Emperor of all of the Roman Empire. He was a superstitious man who paid homage to all of the Gods of the Empire. Although not impressed by the Christian God, he said it would not hurt to have another God, and in recognizing his new allies, it would bring religious peace to the Empire. This peaceful co-existence was a major goal of Emperor Constantine.

To achieve a lasting religious peace the **Edict of Milan** was issued to the Empire in February, 313. The edict was supported by Emperor Licinius of the Balkans and gave the Christians legal status within both Empires. This did not make Christianity the official State religion, it promoted toleration of a group with no social standing within the ranks of leading citizens.

In 321 Constantine made a deal with the Christians. They would no longer be persecuted if they joined in the celebration of Mitra on the winter solstice [known as "Venerable Day of The Sun"], the Spring Equinox and other celebrated days of the year. This was to show the Mitra and other religions' worshippers they could get along. Constantine would not tolerate religious uprisings or public disagreements. Pope Sylvester, the Bishop of Rome, the Holy See of Christianity, agreed to the deal. He became a close confidant of Constantine, promising his new God would protect the Emperor.

Emperor Constantine rewarded the Christians by building the Church of the Holy Sepulcher in Jerusalem during the 320's. The site is said to be the original sites of Solomon's Temple, The Jewish Second Temple and The Temple of Jupiter, the Roman Empire's highest God.

Jupiter was also known as "The Sky God" and "King of the Gods". This was the Roman name for the ancient Sumerian God Anu.

FIRST COUNCIL OF NICAEA – 325

Emperor Constantine called a meeting of all Bishops of several Christian factions who were causing considerable disruption in his Empire. Constantine wanted peace and tranquility among all of his subjects, and he decreed that conflicts would end, or else.

The site for the council was Nicaea and the time was May and June 325. The main topics were the Arien teachings which relegated "The Son" to a lower status than God. The son had a beginning and of course God did not. Also determined was which original letters, manuscripts and activities would be holy and who would be heretics.

The "holy" letters and manuscripts originated from the original four beliefs. The documents were from followers of the; **The Church of Cephas**, **Church of Mitra**, **Gnostics** and **Pauline and Arius Christians**. The revisions to bring conformity to the Church were controlled by the loyalists to Pope Sylvester, and his best ally, The Emperor. Sylvester did not attend the council but was personally represented and gave his support to Bishop Hosius from Spain.

The Council set the Spring Equinox as Pascha [Easter], celebrating the resurrection of Christ. The date was to be separated from the Jewish Passover, as some celebrated both as a single occurrence. The common name "Easter" came about in 1500s' England; it is something to look up.

Bishop Hosius of the Cordova Church was the close confidant of the Emperor in all Church matters, and an opponent of the Arien belief proponents. Constantine supported Hosius so that all of his proposals were passed, with opponents being summarily banished from the empire.

The 20 Canons of Nicaea set rules for clergy to disavow all Arien teachings or be exiled. For followers there were set procedures to gain entrance to heaven or be deemed heretics and suffer severe consequences.

An example of the dogma was the prohibition of self-castration and of kneeling during holy days. Standing was the normal posture for prayer at that time, and still is for Eastern Christians. Kneeling was considered appropriate for penitence prayer.

During the 325 Council the Catholic symbol of The Messiah crucified on a cross was adopted as the primary symbol of the Church. This was in addition to "The Virgin Mary" and many other 'Holy Symbols" for believers to pray to. The symbol of the crucifixion cross did not originate from the sight of a crucifixion, which was often done on a post. The Greek word which was translated, "stauros", means a post or stake. This word was translated by the Vatican as "cross" and in the "King James Version" sometimes as "tree".

Emperor Constantine was pleased with the results as the bishops assured him a place in Paradise. He lavishly rewarded the new Catholic Church with temples, funding and five Bibles for the Church at Constantinople. The Church had tremendous power in the Roman Empire, but Mitraism was still widespread and popular. It would rise to power several more times.

EDICT OF THESSALONICA – 380 CE

The **Edict of Thessalonica,** issued on 2/27/380, ordered the citizens and visitors of the Roman Empire to follow the Bishops of Rome, Constantinople and Alexandria in Nicene Christianity. This declaration made Catholic Orthodox Christianity the State Religion of the Roman Empire. "Catholic" meant universal, and "Orthodox" meant the true religion. The edict was issued by Emperors Gratian, Valentinian and Theodosius Augusti, at the direction of Pope Damasus.

This is "The Turning Point" in the power of the Church. There was considerable strife and outright war within the Christian factions in Constantinople. The followers of Arius, known as Arians, and other Christian sects had different interpretations as to whether "Jesus" was God or an anointed man. Constantine had been baptized by Arian Christian Bishops shortly before his death in 337. His predecessors supported various factions of Christians. The power struggles with Emperors came to an end when the Pope began appointing Emperors.

This important decree set the stage to kill or exile all "Heretics". The decree was clearly composed by Pope Damasus.

EMPERORS GRATIAN, VALENTINIAN AND THEODOSIUS AUGUSTI
EDICT TO THE PEOPLE OF CONSTANTINOPLE

It is our desire that all the various nations which are subject to our Clemency and Moderation, should continue to profess that religion which was delivered to the Romans by the divine Apostle Peter, as it has been preserved by faithful tradition, and which is now professed by the Pontiff Damasus and by Peter, Bishop of Alexandria, a man of apostolic holiness. According to the apostolic teaching and the doctrine of the Gospel, let us believe in the one deity of the Father, the Son and the Holy Spirit, in equal majesty and in a holy Trinity. We authorize the followers of this law to assume the title of Catholic Christians; but as for the others, since, in our judgment they are foolish madmen, we decree that they shall be branded with the ignominious name of heretics, and shall not presume to give to their conventicles the name of churches. They will suffer in the first place the chastisement of the divine condemnation and in the second the punishment of our authority which in accordance with the will of Heaven we shall decide to inflict.

GIVEN IN THESSALONICA ON THE THIRD DAY FROM THE CALENDS OF MARCH, DURING THE FIFTH CONSULATE OF GRATIAN AUGUSTUS AND FIRST OF THEODOSIUS AUGUSTUS

The Vatican's "Trinity" proposition of a "Triad of Gods" was mirrored from the Mitra religion, which proposed this established group of Gods from antiquity.

A noted philosopher of the Holy Writ stated, "Theology is the use of philosophy to try to understand God so it [*the premise*] is believable and understandable. What is not understandable is covered under *Faith*".

The Church now truly had ultimate power over the Empire. It would appoint Kings and Emperors, pass laws and award empires. They had finally established a Theocracy by Pope [Holy See of God]. All non-Nicene Christian groups and cults were banned, the members exiled, their writings burned and their property seized. Of course, the Vatican received the property.

Five years later, in 385, The Church flexed its power by executing their first Heretic. Priscillian was the Bishop of Avila [Spain] and was charged with sorcery for his unorthodox teachings of reading documents not approved by the Church. He was tried in a secular court and beheaded along with six others by the Emperor Maximus. Most of Priscillian's writings were destroyed, however his catalogue of Pauline gospels which he heavily edited and collated remained as gospel text. His considerable properties were confiscated and dispersed.

This caused a great political upheaval because the Pope said the Emperor did not have authority to intervene in Church matters. Heads did roll after this event; The Church was in power.

All non-conforming texts were searched for by The Bishops, Emperors and appointed emissaries of the early Catholic Church, and destroyed when found. The Apostle Barnabas, a follower of Peter and James [**The Church of Cephas**], claimed the Jewish God Yahweh was an imposter, an evil Angel who portrayed himself as God. Beginning in the 4th Century this Epistle and many others, which did not conform to the Church's new image of God, were banned and destroyed. The epistle of Barnabas surfaced again in Egypt in the 1940's.

Christians would continue to be overthrown, then regain power for several centuries. 5th century Emperor Julian renounced Christianity and established Mitraism in Constantinople as the State religion. Mitraism was popular from Scotland to India by the 3rd century and was difficult to overcome.

In the 400s Pope Augustine set many of today's ideas of Christianity. He promoted the idea that Jews were the cause of the world's evils and descendants of Cain [the devil]. He started the doctrine of a Hell-fire punishment for heretics. His denunciation of Jews set the stage for anti-Semitic actions which continue to present day.

Pope Stephen II [752 – 757] produced a document noted as the "Donation of Constantine", which titled all lands of the Western Empire [Italy and west to Briton] to Rome's Bishop Sylvester [314 to 335] and his successors. This afforded the Vatican tremendous power and wealth. The document was deemed a forgery by many, to their peril. There were claims of Pope Sylvester healing Constantine of Leprosy and other miracles performed. The authors of this fake document really produced it by *Divine Inspiration*.

In 1208 Pope Innocence III established the practice of *Inquisition* by attacking a group of Heretics known as Cathars. Cathars were a Christian sect in southwest France who followed different beliefs than the Vatican. They were Gnostics, vegetarians, did not believe in killing anything "made by God" and preached peace and tranquility. They would not participate in the Vatican Eucharist citing they would not eat a dead man's flesh nor drink his blood.

On 22 July 1209 the Pope's Crusaders began the "Cathar Massacre", eventually killing tens of thousands of Cathars, Catholics and any Jews who were in the neighborhood. The Pope had declared the "Jews bore the Mark of Cain", which made them Satan's disciples.

As I researched this era of the Church, I was surprised to find that any reference to Freemasons in the modern transcripts of Papal Buls was omitted. Freemason was replaced with Heretic. This is done in current history postings. The Period writings do not omit Freemasons because they were the Primary target even in the Cathar Massacres. My point is, do not rely on current documents alone if you research. Find the original documents and several sources before you decide what may be the truth.

The Knights Templars were Freemasons and were the Pope's Crusaders beginning in the 1st Crusade of 1095. The open killing of Cathars intensified until the Inquisitions of 1260 into the 1300s under Pope Clement V finally ended the religious movement. When the Knights Templars refused to kill the French citizens, who were Cathars, they were excommunicated and listed in an Inquisition Bul as heretics.

King Philippe IV and Pope Clement V were both heavily indebted to the Templars through borrowing to continue lavish living standards. They were also in debt from funding various "Crusades".

The Crusades have been well published and I will not spend a lot of time on this history. It is full of stories about how the Templars made their fortunes during the Crusades by establishing the first "banking system". For a fee, the Templars would hold money for travelers going to the "Holy Land" and provide them with an account which they could draw from once there. It was much more secure than traveling with your gold in a sack and the possibility of being robbed.

On October 13, [a Friday] 1307 King Philippe IV began arresting and killing Knights Templars because Pope Clement V had declared the Order to be Heretical and servants of Satan. All wealth and property of the Templars was seized by the King and the Vatican. Of course, the Templars were also protecting valued ancient knowledge and had removed considerable wealth, documents and artifacts prior to the date of the attack.

It may seem improbable that Masons would be Catholic. At least one Pope is known to have been a Mason. This "conflict" is due to one of the precepts of Masonic teaching, which is to be supportive of your government and the "State Religion". Revolts by Free Masons usually stem from abuses to human rights which become so great as to not be acceptable under any circumstances.

In 1533 Pope Clement VII ordered all Talmuds and other Jewish writings to be burned. All future rabbinical writings would be censored and teaching of censored writings would be punished by death. The "Munich Talmud" of 1342 was printed in 1520 and is the only remaining uncensored Talmud. The censorship was to destroy existing or future writings or teachings which dealt with the life or holiness of "The Messiah". This topic was the sole purview of the Church.

The Vatican would continue to spread its influence to distant empires by incorporating other religions' festivals and cultural practices into Christianity. This provided an easier path for converts to follow. This practice continues today.

Any religious following can produce tremendous power based upon the amount of influence the leaders of the religion are able to promote. Otherwise, why would millions of people follow a religion, which in the past, as recorded in history, enslaved, murdered, tortured and culturally denigrated them? Look at South American history about what the emissaries of Brother Pope did to the "Indios". And in return they love the Pope!

THE INQUISITIONS OF THE VATICAN

Papal BULS and Encyclicals with *Auto da Fe* directives, primarily targeting Freemasons, [Gnostics, infidels, Heretics, Jews, Lutherans and other nonbelievers] were issued for the destruction of these people. The accused were paraded before crowds by the Inquisitor General in an **Auto da Fe** [Act of Faith]. The accused were required to "confess their heresy by various means." These various means were the use of the most heinous of tortures. They then were "tried and condemned" and rendered to their slayers. The "lucky" ones were strangled, then burned.

The unlucky were burned while tied to a stake, others were "roasted" for the enjoyment of the crowds. Roasting was a long process, keeping the fires at the proper distance to exact prolonged pain.

After execution the property and wealth of the condemned were seized by the Inquisitor General with a cut of the profits awarded to the Vatican. If a dead and buried person were deemed a heretic their family would exhume the body [or bones] and burn the remains. Their property was deeded to the Church.

The following are a few examples of this "Murder by Devine Inspiration":

1481: Toledo, Spain:	2,000 Hebrews were roasted
1486:	27 Hebrews were burned
1481 – 1498:	Torquemada burned 8,800 men and women
1498 – 1506:	Friar Diego Deza burned 1,664 people
1507 – 1517:	Cisneros, a Franciscan, burned 2,536 people

From 1481 thru 1783: 34,656 Heretics were burned in Spain. 304,451 Heretics were killed by "heavy punishment". These numbers are documented for Spain, in other countries similar homicides occurred.

To illustrate the continuance of this Vatican practice, the following is proffered [I urge my readers to verify this]:

On 20 April 1884 Pope Leo XIII [1878–1903] issued a Papal Bul to American Catholics which reinstated all previous Buls of Auto da Fe against Freemasons. The Pope granted a 7 year "indulgence" for "any act committed" to all who would rise up against the Secular State the Freemasons had created. The goal was to place the Church in power and regain its Theocratic control. The timing for this Bul was to attack while the USA was weak due to the Civil War.

There was a reply to the Pope by Grand Master Albert Pike, Scottish Rite, Southern Jurisdiction, on behalf of American Freemasons. Freemasons are not governed worldwide. Each Nation has its own Charter and is governed locally by election.

The Papal Bul and Albert Pike's response is preserved in the book *THE POPE AND THE FREEMASONS*. Details are in the Appendix. It is true history which *Academia* does not want to discuss.

Freemasons may worship as they please without any question. The only requirement of "Faith" is a belief of God, as atheists are not permitted in the Lodge. Religion is not a question for discussion in Lodge business. Our Constitution is based with this principle in mind.

In 1633, twenty-two years after the King James Version of the Holy Writ was published, the Vatican Guys and Brother Pope held an inquisition for Heretics. They threatened Brother Galileo with disembowelment unless he recanted his writings supporting Copernicus' theory that the Earth, and other planets, revolved around the Sun in a vast Space. It was Holy Doctrine that the Earth was the center of the Universe, any other thoughts on this was heresy. It also screwed-up the taught system of Hell in the center of the Earth, and Heaven above the stars.

The Catholic Church accumulated its vast fortunes by following Yahweh's methods, have your followers pay for getting to Heaven. The uneducated and illiterate people had been taught from birth that displeasing the Church was disrespecting God. This was extremely hazardous to one's health. It was important to keep your Priest happy.

A payment was required for being born, for attending church [10% of your annual income], and for dying. The Church sold Relics, said to have been touched by Jesus or to have been in the same area as the Savior. The Priest would sell bits of cloth, wood, feathers from chickens etc. It was required that "good Christians" have relics in their homes to pray to. A follower could buy a dead relative out of

Purgatory and insure their passage to Paradise. There was no end to the sales of superstition, and the profits of the Church. Of course, there was the option of being a Heretic and the Church taking everything.

Centuries of indoctrination insured the Church would not run out of funding and they destroyed anyone who posed a threat to their income.

French Archaeologist Champollion in the early 1800s came against the Vatican for deciphering hieroglyphics which might contradict the Holy Writ, i.e., Noah's flood of 4029 BCE. He did find evidence of civilizations continuing unaffected during this time, but never published his findings. He was funded for his Egyptian archaeology by the King of France, with church approval, and was required not to publish anything which would cast doubt on the Holy Writ.

A new threat to The Vatican's world domination emerges in England.

THE MAKING OF A KING AND A NEW "HOLY WRIT"

In 1533 King Henry VIII, the King of England, defied Pope Clement VII and the Pope excommunicated him. Usually this meant the end of any King. In 1534 Henry VIII issued the *Act of Submission* of the clergy, barring Vatican interference in England.

Henry VIII formed his own **Church of England** and with the *Act of Supremacy* in 1536 he became the "Pope" of England. The Vatican grossly underestimated the unwashed masses on the Big Island.

The 1611 "King James Bible" was published by King James I, of England [1566-1625], to bolster his power against The Vatican and Brother Pope. He also proclaimed his position as the Head of the Church of England. He freely and openly persecuted the Puritans and Catholics to purge England of all heretics.

In 1567 Queen Elizabeth I of England forced Mary Queen of Scots to abdicate the Scottish Throne. With this abdication, Mary's son, 1-year old James, became King of Scotland as King James VI from 1567 to 1625 [dead at 58 years]. Scotland was ruled by Regents, appointed by Queen Elizabeth I, until young King James reached 16 years of age in 1583.

In 1587, four years after he was fully vested as King of Scotland, he did not intervene when Elizabeth I executed his mother, Mary Queen of Scots, because she would not renounce the Catholic religion. On the death of Elizabeth I, in 1603, he became James I, King of England, Scotland and Ireland.

At the age of 35 years, King James I was initiated into the Masonic Lodge of Scoon, located in Perth, Scotland, on April 15, 1601. He openly proclaimed the **Divine Right of Kings**, announcing to his subjects he was Head of State, Head of the Church of England, and appointed himself Grand Master of Masons of The York Rite [England].

The Divine Right of Kings is interpreted as "I would not be King if God did not make it so". Following this thought, the King is the Holy See of his country, as the Pope is to the Catholics. The King can do no wrong and to speak or act against the King is heresy, punishable by death.

King James I, was openly homosexual from his early days [introduced to this lifestyle by his regents] through the rest of his life, changing his favorites several times. As King he was also expected to produce heirs, thus his arranged marriages.

CONSOLIDATING POWER

England was in political and religious turmoil when Elizabeth died. Enemies of the State were active and King James I had to act to consolidate and maintain his power. King Henry VIII had produced the first complete Bible in English in 1539, so James I acted accordingly.

Use or possession of any bible other than the official version in England was considered heresy. William Tindale found out the hard way when he wrote and printed his version in 1535 and was, in great ceremony, burned at the stake by Henry VIII.

In 1604 King James I commissioned 54 translators known as "Divines" to review *approved* Greek and Latin translations, and at least six popular translations of the Bible [used in England] to arrive at an "Official Holy Writ" sanctioned by the State for use by all Protestants. These Divines were under the guidance and employ of Sir Francis Bacon, an extremely close friend and advisor of King James, and all were of Masonic affiliation. This group of translators insured that timeless secrets were disguised in veiled allegory throughout the Old and New Testaments.

Several Divines, including Francis Bacon were Knights Templars and were also known as "Ancients". Their knowledge included the codes, ciphers and secrets from time immemorial, preserved by the Ancients of King Solomon and of the Knights Templars. The draft manuscript of the Holy Writ was completed in 1609. To this day Francis Bacons' ciphers are reviewed and studied.

King James I was not an accomplished writer so he presented the draft to his close friend and confidant Sir Francis Bacon for final editing. The manuscript was edited and revised for near a full year and returned to the King in 1610 for publication. All secrets of the Lodge were well hidden by veiled allegory. Only those with proper training and the "Key" could bring those secrets to light. But that was in 1611.

Here is the unspoken secret of why the King James Version has survived virtually unchanged for 400 years. At the time of publication world class political and religious battles raged. Non-Catholic States [led by the Church of England] were pitted against the Vatican for rule of the World. Masonic and Catholic entities were blood enemies during this time. The Knights Templars were a mix of Masonic Lodge and ancient Vatican ties, a very complex group. With all of this political turmoil occurring, King James and his advisors needed to shore up their political and religious positions. Control of the population through religion was still necessary to maintain rule of the nation.

The King James Version of the Holy Writ established a consistent guide, or key, to Masonic veiled allegories, secrets and rituals. This guide was presented in the view of The York Rite [English Lodge]. These versions were prepared as best possible to offset Vatican destruction of old text mysteries.

Since that time, scholars using modern science have deciphered uncountable ancient manuscripts, Nag Hammadi scrolls and the Dead Sea Scrolls. Even with these advances, one must know the Key to unravel the veiled allegories in this 400-year-old masterpiece.

Sir Francis Bacon's expertise in prose and allegory was unequalled, and he is known to have written the Shakespearean works and used his friend's name on the titles. Shakespeare was in the close circle of friends of the King. It is documented that Shakespeare was "a dolt and somewhat of a dunce" in writing skills. His acting was mediocre and his financial dealings were even worse, but the ghost writing worked for both parties. Francis Bacon's position with the King and other royalty required his separation from the plays produced for the commoners, which were satirical of the Church and the Kings' rule.

The development of the King James Version of the Holy Writ is mentioned so that the next time you read from that Holy Writ you can imagine it as a Shakespearian play, and "know the truth of the matter".

Nothing has influenced history more than the power of Religion and "The Church". Nothing has subjugated people [Women, Races and Ethnic Groups] more than the influence of "The Church" professing the will of God. Have you ever considered the audacity of anyone who claims personal audience with "God" in order to give you guidance in your life?

MARTIN LUTHER VS THE VATICAN

In 1517 a Catholic monk made a pilgrimage to Rome to fulfill his duties to the Church. After a short stay he was so disgusted with the debauchery and selling of "Indulgences" to church leaders that he left Rome and decided to actively challenge these practices. An indulgence permitted any activity and could be purchased for the right price. Like buying a one-year permit to sexually abuse children, without Church intervention.

Martin Luther called the Doctrine of immortality of the soul one of the erroneous opinions of the "dunghill of decretals" in the Vatican. William Tyndale agreed with Luther, saying dead souls were not in Heaven, Hell or Purgatory. His followers were known as Protestants.

In 1517 Martin Luther penned the "95 Theses" to rebuke the Vatican's way of conducting "God's Business", which he described as "Rotten". Martin Luther did not want to leave the Catholic Church, he wanted to reform the blatant abuses of the Vatican. The Vatican would not agree to any reforms and demanded penitence from Luther. It was the Vatican who broke from Luther. This action set off the German Reformation and a break with Rome.

The Vatican was Supreme, the Oracle of God and would not be chastised. After Martin Luther called out the abuses of the Vatican, Pope Leo X demanded penitence from this ungrateful wretch. Refusing to acknowledge wrong-doing, Luther was excommunicated on January 3, 1521 by the Papal Bul *Decet Romanum Pontificem*. This was one of many papal blunders which cost the Vatican influence and cash.

Martin Luther translated the Latin Holy Writ into German and it was printed and widely distributed. He also published papers condemning Jews and freemasons. To this day freemasons are shunned by the Lutheran organized religion, which is mostly Vatican dogma without sending money to the Pope.

MOHAMMED AND FOUNDING ISLAM

Mohammed was raised with Christian teaching near Medina by a following which was banished after the Nicaea Council. He had issues with the Catholics about worshipping three Gods [The Trinity] and also sticks, feathers, rags and statues. He believed in One God, and also felt the Bedouins had been ignored by Christianity.

So, he had his own visions, discussions with God and wrote his own set of rules. He followed Christian Dogma and taught that women were property, and all Heretics should die. Mohammed promised greater rewards for believers who died in furthering the religion.

He must have been knowledgeable of the Lodge as the Islamic culture pursued the sciences, arts and mathematics. Islam produced great inventions and advances in science and architecture and allowed personal wealth. These ideas were finally discovered by Europeans such as Copernicus, Galileo and Da Vinci and ushered in The Reformation.

His religious structure was a Theocracy called a Caliphate, with high Priests officiating in Mosques. The religious teaching required learning to read Arabic. All teachings were in Arabic and the Arabs loved it. They told the Pope to "excommunicate this" and took the sword to the Christian Empire.

Mohammed was a camel driver on the caravan routes and finally met a wealthy widow in Mecca who became his wife. He had seven or eight wives and now had the means to pursue his vision of writing his book and uniting the Arab Nations under one language and one religion. His stories of flying great distances at night and going to Heaven and returning sound as if he encountered some remaining "Lords" and found the recipe for "Shroom wine".

There were several years of tribal conflicts in Arabia and Muhammed finally conquered Mecca. Islam slowly replaced the Tribal Gods which had been worshipped at Mecca. This movement eventually united the Arab tribes into a formidable nation and Theocracy. Islam mirrored the Christian practices of killing all heretics. Islam is a split religion due to disputes about the lineage of succession in the Caliphate when

Muhammed went to his "Great Reward" of being in heaven with more virgins than an old man could possible service.

This split in the cult resulted in each side declaring the other as heretics so they could openly murder each other. This is a religion which does not hide their true intentions. They also embraced the Vatican's propaganda that the Jewish People and Freemasons are the prodigy of the Devil and need to be exterminated.

THE CULT OF MORMONS
The Latter Day Saints

A 19th century historian declared: "The Latter Day Saints are the most successful of all American Communisms."

The Mormon's story is truly remarkable for 1800s' America. It is remarkable because so many joined the movement. With that statement in mind, I have to remind myself that today people will put their hand on a television set, "get healed" and send money to a total fraud! As I said before, ignorance can be overcome with education, but nothing will fix stupid.

The mindset of colonists in the 1700s and early 1800s was very similar to 1st Century Europeans. They believed in "Wizards, Spirits and Apparitions" as an everyday part of life. In 1649 Englishman John Sadler published the "Lost Tribes of Israel" declaring the "Lost Tribes" had traveled to America because it was awarded to them by God. Anyone proclaiming to have visions of, or visitations by, these "spiritual beings" would draw a crowd and many "Prophets" took advantage of the spreading religious hysteria of this "End of Times".

This epic of "Mormons" began with a network of grifters and conmen families in Vermont, the American Northeast, in the 1780's. They were known as the Wood Sect, or The New Israelites. They were treasure seekers [coin finders] and counterfeiters who used "divining" methods for their scams. Nathaniel Wood was impressed by Englishman John Sadler's 1649 publication. In the 1700s any claim which was published produced followers. Many New England traveling prophets and preachers found that preaching this story produced a following and more important, food and a cot.

In 1789 Nathaniel Wood, a preacher with the Congregational Church of Middletown Vermont, was excommunicated for preaching to his sect, who believed they were the descendants of ten lost tribes of Israel. He preached that America was given to the "New Israelite" followers, by God, along with a promise of salvation and that His believers would reconstitute the Nation of Israel and all heretics would be cast into Hell. His sect had several "Seers" and prophets who traveled the country with remarkable stories of visions and prophesies.

Wood's goal was to establish the New Israelite religion, complete with a Temple. An early follower of this sect was William Cowdery Jr. [1765 - 1847].   The Winchell and Cowdery families were essential in developing this new religion along with publications by English prophets. Several families intermarried and moved in the same areas, preaching to their followers and engaging in finding treasure with divining rods and seer stones. After "finding" coins on someone's property they would "work" for them looking for more treasure. This also meant a place to live and food to eat, provided by the "mark". A popular theme for these grifters was to claim contact with spirits, through seer stones, who would then lead them to the buried "treasure". Their communal funding was derived through "treasure seeking" scams, preaching their prophecies of the immediate coming of Biblical Revelations and selling printed tracts about the coming return of Jesus to occupy this new Holy Land.

The Joseph Smith Sr. family was part of this New Israelite sect by 1800 and they were using their divining rods to receive God's revelations as well as finding treasure. The common term for these conmen was "Rodsmen" after their use of wood divining rods. They operated in Vermont and upper New York, hiding out with different families when the authorities were hunting various members of the sect for swindles of the local citizens.

This area of New England was strongly Masonic, with Lodges in almost every community. The Lodges in this area were all York Rite, having their Charter granted by England.   The Southern Lodges were Scottish Rite, having their Charter granted by the French, affirming Scotland's Lodge which was separate from the York Rite. These Lodge boundaries would later form the "Mason-Dixon Line" between States during the Civil War.

The Masonic Lodges would spread the word whenever this sect would move into an area. Not all Rodsmen were known and a number of them were able to join the Masonic community. Even with warnings many people were convinced the Rodsmen could find treasure and were having communications with spirits. They believed this con right up to when they lost their life savings.

Joseph Smith Sr. and wife had a son born in 1805 and named him Joseph Smith Jr. The Smiths and the Cowderys were well known as seers and were often chased from villages throughout New England.

Over the next 20 years these families gained wealth, farms and printing businesses. Some would become Doctors and Pharmacists. It seems the Congregational church was attractive to a considerable number of the sect, and several of the men joined Masonic Lodges. The undertone of the "New Israelites" and the divining of treasure stayed with the intermarried families.

Some of the families in this sect were the Winchells, Woods, Bemis, Smiths, Cowderys, Rigdons and a multitude of others. They are prominent "Saints" of the Mormonism Cult. Members of this sect were continuously "warned out" of communities by the local authorities.

Family contacts included preachers in the Congregational and First Baptist Churches, publishers and physicians. They continued to spread the "New Israelite" doctrine and the preachers were asked to leave several ministries. Books and pamphlets were produced such as *View of the Hebrews* by Ethan Smith and printed with the assistance of the Cowderys in 1823.

1823 was the "Big Year" for Mormon history as Joseph Smith Jr. announced "A divine messenger" told him about hidden gold plates which bore the records of the "Lost Tribes" time in America. Smith originally related the vision, achieved with a divining rod and seer stone, was of a dead Native American warrior named Moroni. This was later changed to a "Divine Messenger" and finally to the Angel Moroni, or Gabriel.

This revelation occurred on the Fall Equinox to add the connection of ancient ghosts visiting these descendants of Israel. The Cowderys printed pamphlets of these visions and sold them from Vermont to Ohio. Many people of this era were near hysterical by printed reports of divine contacts because so many traveling preachers were predicting the "Second Coming" was about to happen.

One example of the hysteria was a prediction by a Baptist preacher named Miller who proclaimed that "Jesus Christ" would return in 1844 in an "Advent". When this advent did not come to be, it was explained as his error in computing the date from Old Testament prophesies. He and his followers founded the Seventh Day Adventist Church.

In 1825 William Morgan joined Batavia Masonic Lodge in upper New York, and received the Entered Apprentice Degree, but was denied further advancement when the brothers discovered his ties to the "Rodmen" [Mormons] and booted him from the Lodge. He then joined with the Mormon sect members to publish a book exposing the inner secrets of the Lodge.

Morgan "reportedly" received $500,000 for his manuscript. The Lodge published an announcement that Morgan was in the process of revealing Lodge Secrets in an upcoming book, violating his sworn oath taken in the Lodge. Morgan was arrested on charges of not paying his debts and of theft of property. He was jailed in Canadaigua, near Fort Niagara, on September 11, 1826 and friends came to post his bail.

What followed is murky but it is generally agreed that a group of zealous Masons arranged to pick him up from the jail on September 12, 1826 and applied the ancient punishment for a flagrant violation of his Masonic Word. He was never seen again. By the end of 1826 the printing business for the book burned.

His disappearance sparked public outcry with published articles from Mormon printers and a new anti-Mason political party was formed. This too disappeared in a few years. A major anti-masonic movement evolved and several masons were tried for Morgans disappearance and death. The local sheriff was convicted and served 28 months for the disappearance. Bill was just a memory after breaking his Masonic Oath.

Joseph Jr. continued to work as a diviner of treasure for various farmers but was evicted from the family farm. Times were hard for treasure diviners, usually getting only room and board for their time.

On September 21, 1827, Joseph Smith Jr. announced he had found the golden plates with the Book of Mormon text engraved on them. He had announced this would happen and apparently drew a large crowd of sect members and onlookers. Joseph Jr. claimed his seer stone [an artifact in Salt Lake] allowed him to see the spirits who led him to a stone vault on a hilltop, where he recovered the plates engraved with ancient Hebrew script.

In 1828 Jr. began "deciphering" the plates, which only he had seen, with the Harris family and "other followers". This effort became a "Charlie Fox", as we sometimes called things in the "War", and followers came and went.

By 1829 Jr. had new scribes and finished his "translation" of The Book of Mormon. His followers professed that although they never "physically" observed the golden plates, they had witnessed them by visions.   Maybe they discovered the recipe for Apostle Peter's "'Shroom wine" in the plates.

Everyone wanted in on the religious con and "Seers" began receiving revelations, finding more plates and writing their own stories. This went as far as Cowdery's followers founding a Church and usurping Jr.'s authority. Jr. said God told him he was the only one with the power of divining visions and "plates" and unless Jr. bestowed this gift, no one else could use it.

All of the "Witnesses" who found, saw and deciphered the "plates" claimed they received these revelations through the power bestowed by Joseph Jr. and the power of the seer stone and Rod. They journaled these sightings were in "their mind's eye", not a physical encounter. MY, MY.

Jr. bestowed the gift on Cowdery in ceremonies and gained help in finishing the book. The search for money to publish the book began after an attempt to sell the copyright in Canada failed. The Book of Mormon was finally printed in 1830 when a follower mortgaged his farm.

Joseph developed his "Endowment Ceremony" of giving the power of visions and conversing with ancient "Angels" to new followers along with a myriad of oaths and affirmations. All of these ceremonies and oaths were developed using Masonic Lodge rituals and legends as a template.   I repeat, as a template because the rituals are so bastardized it is only apparent they stem from Masonic due to certain phrases and actions.   Some of the goals of the indoctrination of initiates by these ceremonies follow:

The ceremonies are revealed by God.
They place an emphasis on the worthiness of initiates.
They include washings and anointing [the giving of special powers], a new name and sacred undergarments [with Masonic symbols imprinted].
They emphasize vows of non-disclosure or suffer punishment from God.
There are both "lesser" and "greater" rituals.

They feature presentation of the ritual through drama.

They contain an oath of chastity requiring strict purity and virtue of the participants.

They feature prominent use of the sun, moon and stars and other Masonic symbols as key Mormon symbols.

The purpose of the ritual is to assist mortals to attain to Godhood.

They employ titles and offices of prophets, priests, queens, princesses and kings to those in leadership.

They endow the initiate with supernatural powers.

In July 1838 Mormon President Rigdon declared a "War of Extermination" with Missouri Gentiles due to hostilities between Mormons and Missouri farmers.

The Governor issued Missouri Executive Order 44, known as the *Extermination Order*, on October 27, 1838. This was in response to the *Battle of Crooked River* between the Missouri State Militia and the Mormons. This period was known as the 1838 Mormon War when Mormons were expelled from the State of Missouri and they fled to Illinois.

The Illinois Governor was not a happy camper to have this group chased into his State. Joseph Smith Jr. traveled to Washington to appeal to President Martin Van Buren for compensation for his church members' lost property in Missouri. Van Buren, a good Mason, said "piss off".

Jr. called for his Democrat [Mormon] followers to join the Whig Party and planned on running for President. Jr. was really stirring the pot; Masons mounted an offense and Mormons were run out of several States in violent fashion.

Joseph Jr. founded Nauvoo Illinois as the base of operations for Mormons and was elected Mayor and Master of His Lodge by several thousand followers. Nauvoo had its own arsenal and militia and most all of the businesses were run by Mormons.

The Mormons prospered, Jr. married members' wives [8 or 9 recorded] and they all lived in Nauvoo Illinois. Then things went to hell in a handbasket. An outside group [anti-Mormon] founded a newspaper in Nauvoo and printed its only publication on June 7, 1844.

The article was an expose of Mormon practices, that they had opened a "Clandestine Masonic Lodge" [illegal in Masonry], and practiced polygamy with multiple marriages between married couples as well as very young girls. The article discussed a host of other items which included "glass looking". Glass Looking was another name for "coin finders" and cons with seer stones and walking sticks.

Jr. had a fit. As Mayor he had the City council declare the newspaper a public nuisance and seized it. The press was destroyed along with the building and furnishings. When neighboring towns raised arms to attack the Mormons, Jr. declared martial law and called out his militia.

The declaration of Martial Law resulted in the Governor of Illinois bringing charges of Treason and Conspiracy [a Capital Crime] against Joseph Jr. and many followers in Nauvoo. All arrested were able to post bail except for Jr. and his brother Hyrum.

On June 27, 1844 the "Man who would be President" and his brother were held in the Carthage City, Illinois jail pending the Capital Crime trial. It was not to be: The Lodge Brothers from near and far had heeded a call to arms and gave these renegade Masons what had been pledged in their oaths.

Joseph Jr.'s last words were an attempt to stop the execution. As he jumped from the second story Jail window he proclaimed "Oh Lord My God......" and he was shot several times, stopping an ancient plea before completion.

After Junior's and Hyrum's deaths Mormon seers popped up all over. Eventually Brigham Young went west with about 150 followers to The Great Salt Lake and declared "this is it". Tens of thousands of persecuted Mormons would follow, developing the State of Deseret, which stretched from Canada to Mexico with a port in San Diego. Brigham plotted for a secession of Deseret from the United States, allying with Mexico in the Mexican-American War [1846 – 1848]. He dispatched troops from San Diego to travel up the Colorado River to seize and hold the Las Vegas Springs against US troops. They failed to affect the outcome of the war. As a political cover Brigham provided a 500-man battalion to fight with the US.

The Mexican-American War ended on February 2, 1848 with the Treaty of Guadalupe Hidalgo. The treaty ceded Texas and large parts of the Southwest to the United States [previous Deseret territory]. Deseret was in peril and the Mormon leadership proposed an immediate statehood for the State of Deseret to Congress. Washington was leery of this "Theocratic State", since Freemasons had so openly declared a full separation of Church and State in the Founding Documents. Washington was, of course, densely Masonic, and anti-Mormon.

Deseret was reduced in size and scope and was designated "The Utah Territory".   President Millard Fillmore, in a compromise to end hostilities, appointed Brigham Young as Governor in the "Compromise of 1850".

The Mormons developed a stronger, better equipped military than the US government. There was a new movement within the church to declare independence from the US, ally with Mexico and take California in the move. California gold and the influx of eastern settlers changed the dynamics of the Nation and Utah. Tens of thousands of "Gold Rush" pioneers moved through Utah, the railroad was completed cross-country, and the Mormons had lost that great safety net of Isolation. With continued isolation the Church could have ruled its Theocracy and built a powerful State.

In the upcoming National elections of 1856 Deseret had two political faults which the Republican Party attacked, but only one fault for the Democratic Party. The top political issues of the day were Slavery and Polygamy, both embraced by Mormons under a political principle of "Popular Sovereignty". With support from the Democratic Party all slave states wrapped their slave status in this doctrine of States Rights, claiming the Constitution gave no powers to the Federal Government to override State domestic policies.

The Republicans brought in the Whig Party and ran candidate James Buchanan. The Party platform was for abolishing slavery and polygamy, openly challenging "States' Sovereignty". The Democrats were for slavery but realized they had to separate polygamy from the popular sovereignty doctrine to have a chance in the election. The Mormons were 100% Democrat and resisted this move by the party, claiming once again to be oppressed by the "East Coasters".

A primary Plank of the new Republican Party was to "Prohibit in the Territories those twin relics of barbarism: polygamy and slavery." They called out the Democrats as supporting both of these issues through "Popular Sovereignty".   Buchanan won about 60% of the Electoral votes. Popular Sovereignty politics would ignite The Civil War a few years later.

President Buchanan removed Brigham Young [LDS Church President] as the Utah governor and appointed Alfred Cummings, a non-Mormon. Tensions ran high and several parties of wagon train pioneers were attacked and killed by Mormon militia posing as local Native American tribes.

History will seldom mention the truth of the "Mountain Meadows Massacre" where 120 men, women and children [over 4 years old] were murdered, their property stolen and the young children adopted into Mormon families. What is not mentioned, except in Lodge records, is these settlers were Freemason families from Missouri and Arkansas.

As the Masons passed through Mormon settlements, arguments and fights erupted as the memories of the Masons eradicating Mormon families, from several States, were still fresh.

The Mormons' success worried Washington DC politicians.   With rumors of Deseret seceding from the Union, interference with federal officials in Utah and open rebellion beginning, President Buchanan sent the US military to secure the Utah Territory in 1857. This became a two-year guerilla war all over the West.

In the end, all Mormons received pardons, the appointed Governor Alfred Cumming took office and peace was restored in the Theo-Democracy. Brigham gave the appearance that his appointed federal judges were complying with the Republic, but all state matters were reviewed and resolved in the Temple before anything was presented in court.

To this day no Utah State business is formulated before a full review and concurrence by the Temple Administration is completed. It is a silent process, but anything you can do legally in Utah has been approved prior to the State Capitol getting a bill passed.

A 19th century historian declared: "The Latter Day Saints are the most successful of all American Communisms". And to their credit, they are one of the most successful groups in the world for financial and family stability.

The Mormons prospered through their tenets of strict observance of Church doctrine and absolute submission to the Leaders of the Church. They demand education, hard work, community action and reinvestment in their society for all members.

This is a formula for success in any enterprise, and if you are doing well and wield great wealth and political power, does it matter if your beginnings came from swindlers and con artists? The present-day Church fully acknowledges these beginnings as "God's Way of Restoring His Church" and "God's Guiding Hand Upon the Church", using these spiritually gifted individuals to reestablish Israel in a new "Promised Land".

"Blood Atonement" is a quietly held sacrament of the Church. Their belief is that Jesus shed his blood to cleanse sinners' souls, but some people's sins are so great that they can only be absolved by shedding their own blood when killed. This only applies to Latter Day Saints [New Israelites] and not to Gentiles who are viewed as heretics.

Were the beginnings of Christianity, Islam and Mormonism so much different? Both movements took advantage of gullible, uneducated masses by promising unbelievable returns for their devotion and participation in well promoted frauds. Unlike the Vatican, the Mormons delivered on their promise of great success.

The blood feud between Mormons and Freemasons continued for decades and finally, in the 1980's, the first Mormon [in Utah] was allowed membership in a Utah Masonic Lodge. The Mormon/Freemason feud was only eclipsed by the long running Vatican/Freemason feud. I believe that if the Vatican were to regain world power it would issue Buls with the Auto da Fe doctrine for Freemasons and other heretics.

THE CARINA NEBULA
**The Keyhole Nebula, which is part of the Carina
Nebula is +/- 8,000 light years from Earth**
heic1509a Westerlund [Hubble Project – see in color!]

2000 CE   <u>TL 3 - From the Beginning</u>

1,492 — Europe Discovers Americas

<u>YEARS BCE</u> — 0 BCE

1,020 — Hebrew Nation begins with King Saul

1,450 — Yahweh's Temple built on Mt. Gerizim in Samaria

1,533 — Ahmose I routs Hyksos in 1st "Exodus" sends Hyksos back to Canaan

1,628 — Thera explodes and Crete is decimated ending support for the Hyksos

1,900 — First Hyksos capital at Avaris—Minoan trade routes to the Americas

2,000 — Olmec—Maya— Moche — Nazca— Tiwanaku Civilizations in advanced stages

2,490
2,550 — 3 Giza pyramids built: Khufu [largest] Khafre [middle] Menkaure [smallest]

3,000 — Yahweh builds Minoan Villa in Samaria

4,400 — Scorpion Kings of Naqada [The Ka] rule Upper Egypt to 3,200 BCE
Minoan Palaces on Crete

6,500 — Parvaim palaces on Thera

7,000 — Indus Valley settlement
Sphinx Head Monument in place
Central and S. America Cultures advancing

8,000 — Egypt's Delta organized farming villages
Corn and Cotton grown in Americas

10,700 — Post Diluvian Sumer Begins

10,900 — Comet impact of Earth causes Pleistocene Extinction

20,000 — Lords establish civilizations in Americas
Tiwanaku Sun Temple in Bolivia

252 K — Alulim "Descends from Heaven" in Eridug

Book III

The Americas

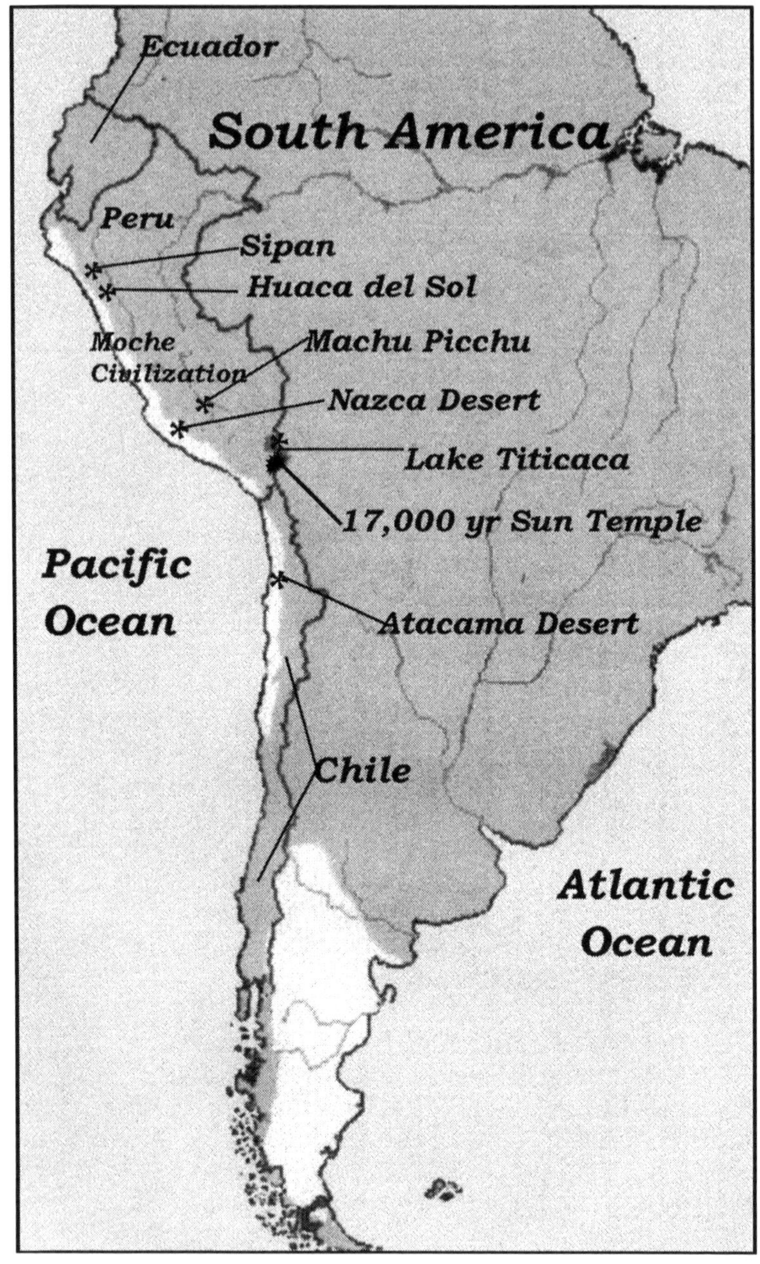

Ecuador
South America
Peru
Sipan
Huaca del Sol
Moche
Civilization
Machu Picchu
Nazca Desert
Lake Titicaca
17,000 yr Sun Temple
Pacific
Ocean
Atacama Desert
Chile
Atlantic
Ocean

El Abra Petroglyph - Columbia Cave Habitation Pre-Pleistocene Extinction during Last Ice Age - Site was Carbon-Dated to 12,500 BCE, 1,600 years before the Comet Impact.

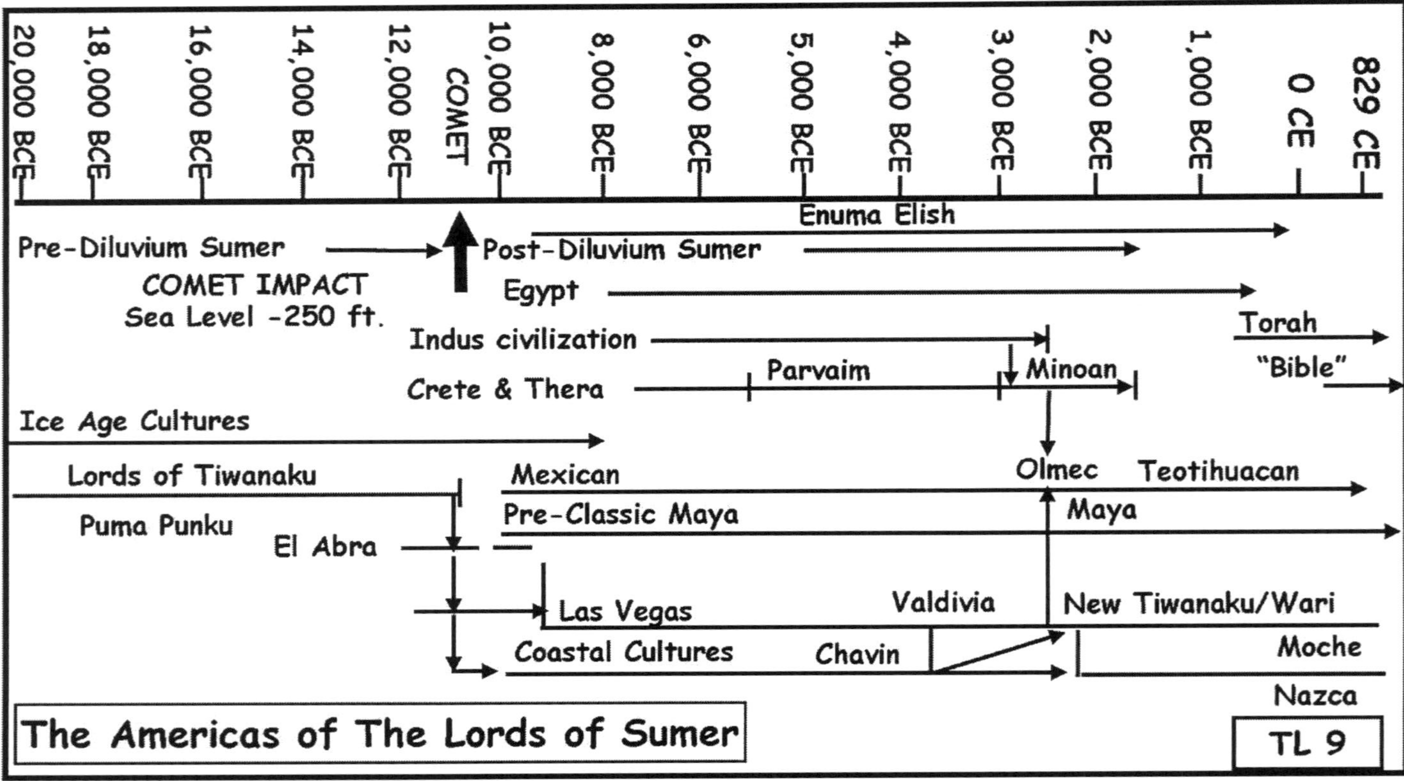
829 CE
0 CE
1,000 BCE
2,000 BCE
3,000 BCE
4,000 BCE
5,000 BCE
6,000 BCE
8,000 BCE
10,000 BCE
COMET
12,000 BCE
14,000 BCE
16,000 BCE
18,000 BCE
20,000 BCE
Enuma Elish
Pre-Diluvium Sumer
Post-Diluvium Sumer
COMET IMPACT
Sea Level -250 ft.
Egypt
Indus civilization
Crete & Thera
Parvaim
Minoan
Torah
"Bible"
Ice Age Cultures
Lords of Tiwanaku
Mexican
Olmec
Teotihuacan
Puma Punku
Pre-Classic Maya
Maya
El Abra
Las Vegas
Valdivia
New Tiwanaku/Wari
Coastal Cultures
Chavin
Moche
Nazca
The Americas of The Lords of Sumer
TL 9

Chapter

1

**The Gate of The Sun
Tiwanaku**

BEFORE THE COMET
THE LORDS FOOTPRINTS

The Lords established the Tiwanaku Civilization around 20,000 BCE in Bolivia, South America at Lake Titicaca. Tiwanaku and Puma Punku, 45 miles west of La Paz was the genesis of colonizing American advanced civilizations, developed to support the Lords' lifestyles and for the accumulation of valuable resources.

Tiwanaku and adjacent Puma Punku were constructed high in the Andes Mountains on the south shore of ancient Lake Titicaca in Bolivia. At 12,900 feet in elevation these magnificent structures housed an observatory, housing and administrative buildings, docks for vessels traveling the lake and underground religious worship centers. The grottos were used for Sun God worship ceremonies.

I believe that the "Lords" who originally established civilizations did so as a matter of colonizing the Earth. The accumulation of wealth was to either trade with other colonies or to export to their planet of origin. This is just basic reasoning given the fact these Lords were revered as "Mighty Ones" and Gods, and the accumulation of wealth would have no other reason than to influence some other colony. It is most likely Earth was strictly a combined colony effort by several different civilizations.

Prior to the Comet Disaster the Lords traveled and communicated from continent to continent, constructing palaces and great monuments while developing tribal followings.

These ancient ruins were dated to pre-15,000 BCE by one researcher. Another researcher dated site debris to 12,000 BCE. The site is called The Temple of the Sun. The construction reflects advanced building skills with close tolerance stone buildings, which appear to have been destroyed in a cataclysmic fashion and covered with a "massive mud flow." The Tiwanakuan Civilization was destroyed and survivors relocated to the Pacific coastline and other inland sites in the Amazon basin. This site was discovered by Spanish explorers when they first came to the Americas.

At the Tiwanaku ruins some of the stones, weighing hundreds of tons, appear to have been mechanically cut and are highly polished. The ruins contain a wharf and docking facilities implying that Lake Titicaca's shoreline reached the site and the lake was considerably larger and deeper.

A. Posnansky, in 1945, dated the **second** of three eras of enlarging the Sun Temple using the "variation of the ecliptic", that is, the variation of Earth's axis in alignment with the Sun to 17,000 years ago. He does state that if the scientific formula changes that this date could change. He further states:

> **"But it is an established fact that whatever calculation might be used to determine the age of The Temple of the Sun of Tiwanaku, on the basis of the variation of the obliquity of the ecliptic from times until today, would demonstrate that that American solar observatory is more ancient than any monument of man in the world of which we know up to this time."**

Other scientists have dated portions of the site to over 12,000 BCE. Of course, *Academia* would have none of it. In 1996 the Director of the Bolivian National Institute was forced to resign after validating A. Posnansky's findings. It was declared to be Inca era ruins and nothing else.

It is a site worth researching. I believe the evidence of destruction and "mud flow" covering the site indicates it also was destroyed in the comet/meteor strike. The adjacent site of Puma Punku, 45 miles west of La Paz, dated to over 12,000 BCE. This site is so advanced its construction cannot be duplicated with today's equipment and machinery.

Tiwanaku is a world-wide destination for travelers. The magnificent stone used to construct this site is machine cut and polished, with some pieces weighing more than 100 tons. Some estimates place weights near 400 tons, all cut, polished, precision bored and engraved.

The extraordinary thing about this site is that it was first discovered by Spanish explorer Pedro Cieza de Leon in 1549. It has been studied and pillaged since that time.

Academia will have no part of it, attributing the structures to Inca technology from years 500 to 600. A definitive statement by an archeologist, as to the scale and complexity of the site was; "We do not have existing equipment which can lift and move these stones, much less cut and polish the surfaces". In other words, existing equipment and technology cannot reproduce the construction at Tiwanaku.

Tiwanaku was destroyed in 10,900 BCE by the comet strike. Evidence of a massive mud wave, which covered the ruins is still evident. Most likely a meteor from the comet breakup hit the ancient lake area, causing widespread destruction. South America was heavily impacted by the Pleistocene Impact and Extinction.

To better understand the timing and precision of the construction of Tiwanaku I have included the following portion of an article by Arthur Posnansky:

Arthur Posnansky:

Mainstream science proposes the blocks were shaped by hand, with primitive tools that were available to the people living in the area in that era. Yet, engineers and architects who have had a chance to take a closer look at the ruins are positive that the builders of Puma Punku to achieve the results must have excelled in planning, logistics as well as have applied some sophisticated technology.

Even a brief examination of the stone work seems to suggest that some sort of precision, power tools must have been used to achieve the results. The stones are cut to a millimeter precision, with very accurate right angles. Sharp precision-corners and smooth drill-holes are carved in granite, which is one of the hardest materials on Earth. You need a diamond to be able to cut granite with that level of precision.

Massive granite and andesite stones carved with astonishing precision at Puma Punku.   Intricate drill-holes and precision-corners of the Puma Punku stones:

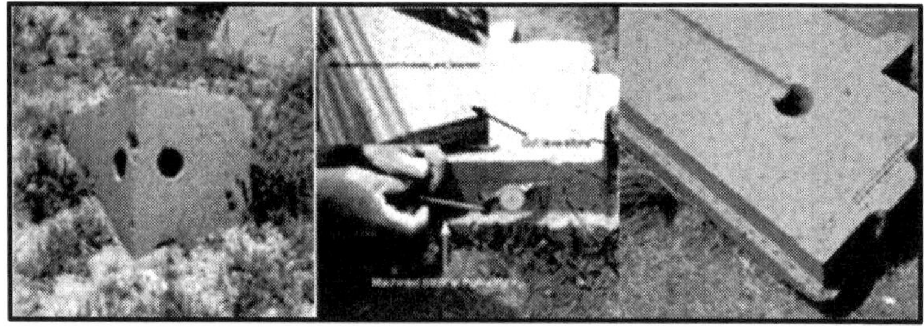

Posnansky reported about **machined drill holes for water systems and for stellar observations. Some of these holes were simultaneously precision drilled from each side of the stone, with "cross-hair" mounts inside for precision observations.**

Another interesting [and unanswered] question about Puma Punku is how the builders managed to transport the huge blocks of stone to the site and move them around the location. Mainstream science maintains that the blocks were quarried at a location 600 miles away and then rolled to Puma Punku on wooden logs.

> *However, the altitude at which the ruins are located*
> *excludes that possibility as no trees grow naturally this*
> *high. As mentioned before the biggest block of Puma Punku*
> *weighs in excess of one hundred tons. In order to*
> *understand the scale of such operation it is worthwhile to*
> *take a look how such challenge is tackled today.*

Academia maintains these are Inca era ruins, although there is no way we could duplicate this construction today. We do not have mobile cranes which can lift and move a 140-ton block of stone or move it 600 miles in the 12,900 feet elevations of the Andes.

If, and I stress "if" the indigenous people hauled these massive blocks using ropes of lama hide and logs, where are the ruins of the massive roads necessary to move them? They do not exist.

The Posnansky article concludes with:

<u>Arthur Posnansky:</u>
> *However, mainstream science maintains the Puma Punku*
> *megaliths were moved to location from a quarry 600 miles*
> *away by pulling/pushing the blocks on wooden rollers. Given*
> *that one of the construction blocks at Puma Punku weighs an*
> *estimated 440 tons [equal to nearly 600 full-size cars] and*
> *several other blocks lying about are between 100 and 150*
> *tons, this theory can hardly be accepted.*

Arthur Posnansky's [1873 – 1946] writings are difficult to find, but if you persist, they are fascinating reading with many surprises. Posnansky's team identified stone carvings of extinct Pleistocene animals. One of these carvings was of "Smilodon" a very large "Saber toothed cat".

Other findings were of pre-glacial stone structures on the islands of Lake Titicaca and progressions of labyrinth Sun Temples. There are many islands on this vast lake, some with Sun God Temples, Moon God Temples and temples to various other beings.

The work of Arthur Posnansky has been severely discredited and attacked by *Academia* as being totally insane. This site was built with its foundations sitting on *Pleistocene Alluvial* formations. I think I have presented sufficient evidence to discredit quite a bit of

Academia to show they are mentally locked into *Western Thinking* or bowing to religious pressure.

I included A. Posnansky's article because it was, and currently is, so vehemently attacked because it is such a threat to *Academia*. I equate it to the Vatican's influence to destroy all evidence which does not fit their marketing plan.

WE DO NOT HAVE THE TOOLS AND EQUIPMENT TODAY TO DUPLICATE THE PRECISION CUTTING AND POLISHING OF THE STONE BLOCKS AT TIWANAKU. WE DO NOT HAVE EQUIPMENT WHICH CAN TRANSPORT THE STONE BLOCKS AT TIWANAKU.

That statement is absolute, is not and cannot be explained away. Yet, archaeologists and scientific observers [*Academia*] continue to provide explanations of how these primitive civilizations moved stones weighing tens, and hundreds of tons using ramps, levers and ropes of Llama hide. Also, how they managed to carve and place the stones in such a close fit, that a piece of paper cannot be slipped between them. Attempting to explain the precision machining is also avoided.

Additional archaeological findings at these "Inca" ruins are andesite stone blocks which have been precision drilled with machine turned "bell and spigot" fittings incorporated in each block to build a pressure water delivery system. The archaeologist stated this was a mystery as the Inca had no such technology. MY – MY!

Some of the massive stones were secured with cast in place metal ties for stability during earthquakes. The identical system was used in the 11th century CE to keep the building stones of Angkor Wat Temple in Cambodia. Is this a "coincidence" of Stone Age brilliance which naturally evolved?

Academia insists all the above, of course, was accomplished by "*the perseverance of Neolithic Artisans*" without outside influences.

A similar ancient temple site with huge smooth stone columns and beams is located in the Beqaa Valley. The building stones weigh from 100 tons to 900tons and some researchers date these stone megaliths to 9,000 BCE.

The Comet Impact was immense, deadly and destructive. The survivors did what most survivors do; they relocated to places where food, water and shelter was available. These people, led by some of the original Lords, began new civilizations.

On the coastline of Ecuador, the ruins of the Las Vegas Civilization date from pre-9,000 BCE to 4,600 BCE. Near these ruins the Valdivia Civilization was found, dating to 4,500 BCE to beyond 1,500 BCE. Inland, in the Columbian Highlands the El Abra Civilization is validated to pre-comet impact and also surviving in the glaciers after impact.

There is evidence in the Amazon basin of massive planned farming communities, established in grid layouts. These were not accomplished by random jungle tribes.

The Earth was still in the Last Ice Age and tropical rain forests in Columbia did not generally begin to flourish until about 7,000 BCE.

In North America the Comet Impact ended the Clovis Civilization, which vanished with evidence of their sites found from the East Coast to the West Coast. The civilization was named from a spear point first identified near Clovis New Mexico.

Clovis flint tool making skills were distinct and extraordinary, using pressure flaking and a bi-facial striking technique. This flint tool making skill was mirrored in the Aurignacian and Solutrean civilizations located in Europe near the areas of Spain and France. Also, very interesting is that both civilizations [Europe and America] used a spear throwing device called an Atlatl. Central and South American civilizations suffered similar extinction fates, although there were more pockets of survivors.

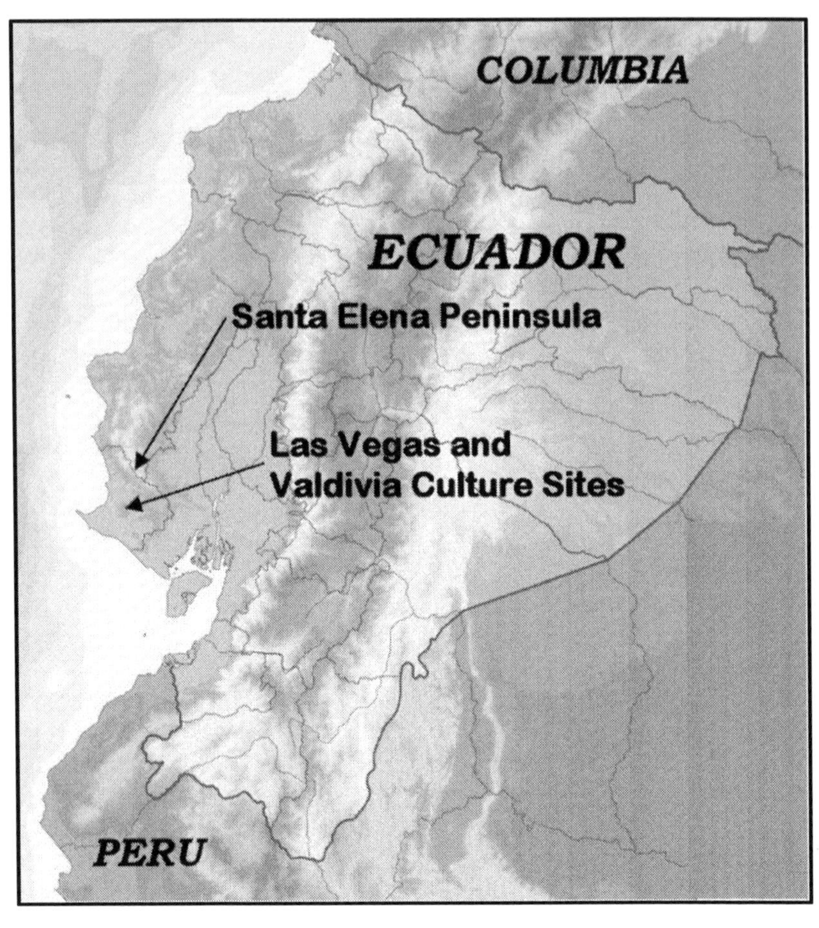

Las Vegas Culture
[9,000—4,600 BCE approximately]

Chapter
2

RISE OF CIVILIZATIONS
AFTER THE EXTINCTION COMET

Just as the Lords in Eurasia had fled the pending comet impact, so would have the Lords of South America. Those who left and those who remained would know the time required for a fleet to make the round trip to affect a rescue.

El Abra Culture
[12,500 BCE – 8,000 BCE]

El Abra is the site of a cave and rock shelter in the high plains [8,430 ft. elevation] north of Bogota Columbia. Occupation has been carbon dated to 12,500 BCE, 1,400 years before the comet impact and the Pleistocene Extinction. The Ice Age occupants of El Abra ate Mastodons, horses and camels while surviving in the pre and post-comet global winter.

This area was spared the total extinction of large fauna for about two thousand years after the comet strike. It was still glacier and savanna country without the tropical rain forest. Mastodons and other large animals were still viable in these highland areas

By 7,000 BCE the climate changed enough that the rain forest was returning and the last traces of horses and mastodons were vanishing.

Along the Pacific coastline numerous surviving cultures began their advancement to structured civilizations. These sites were located along the numerous river valleys from Ecuador to Chile. Most of the desert areas were vastly different until about 5,000 BCE. The river deltas were very productive agriculture and wildlife areas. The civilizations quickly utilized the ocean for fishing.

The trial and error method for creating various tools did exist worldwide and is documented as a true evolution of man's accomplishments. Over a great period of time, and without direct intervention, native Man did evolve the many tools necessary to create their civilizations.

However, hardened metal tools and equipment were necessary to create the intricate detailed stone carvings and the machine cut and polished stone slabs for the 17,000 BCE Tiwanaku Sun Temple at Lake Titicaca.

A very interesting segment of man's history is contained in this area. The coastal region of Peru and parts of northern Chile are barren deserts with almost no rainfall. It may rain once every fifty years or so. About forty river valleys, each separated by desert, cross the region. Although the soil is rich, it is barren desert due to the lack of water.

The cold waters of the Pacific Humboldt Current flow along this coastline producing one of the world's richest marine habitats. There is a great abundance of sea mammals, shellfish, and vast numbers of fish. This abundance of marine life provided an excellent source of food for tribal groups of hunter-gatherer and others. They became coastal dwellers, establishing settlements in the river valleys. By the year 6,000 BCE, villages were located away from the coastline and further upstream in the valleys. Here small-scale irrigation was used to water cultivated fields.

Several advanced civilizations emerged in the desert areas of Peru and Chile, supported by advanced agricultural projects. To bring irrigation to their crops a vast network of canals was constructed to carry the Andes Mountains runoff to their fields.

Prior to construction of the canals in the arid desert, indigenous tribes lived along river valleys near the coast. The people survived on their level of skills, fishing and tending small gardens. What they lacked to build the canals, was motivation, math, plans, tools and most of all, they could not read the plans if they had them. Plainly stated, based on population and civilization, there was no need for the inhabitants to move inland to an arid desert and build canals. There is an explanation for the canals, which will clearly explain why they were built. It is the same argument presented for the rise of the Sumerian Civilization.

The attitude of the intellectual community is that only a select few of the academic elite may propose answers to historical mysteries. This elite group produced the cute term *Neolithic Artisan* to explain a position of intellectual ignorance. This same group relies on the term *little green men from outer space* to discredit anyone who dares to intrude into their crystal palace of opinion.

Archaeologists provided the following information about the irrigation projects: *There is clear evidence that in a mass movement, a huge population of workers was brought to the region.* The group, described as pilgrims, created the foundation for the civilizations to come. What was not said was, to accomplish this feat; there was no time for trial and error. The population had to have food and water as they worked, but most of all they had to have hardened metal tools.

One of America's most renowned universities has published findings and conclusions describing the civilizations and agriculture of Peru and northern Chile as an *anomaly*. This area is a region with no rainfall and without any indigenous food crops. However, it became the center of great civilizations based on productive farming techniques.

There is extensive research regarding every level of evolution of the civilizations, with considerable effort expended to define specific time frames and settlement patterns. The research focused on the locations of major centers, the social structures within each area, agriculture, economy, and distinctive civilizations. It is apparent the Church has been involved, as much as possible, in defining the dates of the various civilizations' beginnings. Again, with enough research it is easy to find scientists not confined to "washing" their research with church blessings.

The terminology of reports contains some classic descriptive phrases, such as *manifestations-disseminations of iconographic elements,* or *along with concomitant changes in iconography.* The bulk of the text was saying, we know when and where it happened, but it was clear they did not know how and why it happened.

Clearly stated, the creation of civilizations based on agriculture in the middle of a coastal desert region is abnormal. It was a civilization that unless specifically created, should not have existed. Now that was not difficult to state and did not require the terms, *concomitant changes in iconography.*

To date there has not been an explanation, or any speculation, regarding the foundation of the desert coastal civilizations. The foundation for the abnormal civilizations was the building of long-range canals originating, in some areas, in the Andes Mountains. The canals zig-zagged down the mountain-sides bringing water to the desert regions. Year-round water for the civilization's crops was provided by hundreds of smaller feeder canals.

One project produced a major canal system that extended over 30 miles, connecting all of the small valleys with the same water source. From the primary canal, smaller secondary canals extended into arid areas, allowing for the extension of vast agricultural fields. The canals have been described as one of the most amazing engineering marvels of the world.

SOUTH AMERICAN CULTURE PERIODS

Preceramic*		
*[from the author, "Preceramic is not true", ceramics were found at the Las Vegas Sites and many others]		
Period VI	2500 BCE – 1500/1800 BCE	**Ecuador**: <u>Valdivia</u>; **Peru**: <u>Casma/Sechin culture</u>, <u>Norte Chico</u> [Caral], <u>Buena Vista</u>, <u>Casavilca</u>, <u>Culebras</u>, <u>Ventarrón</u>, <u>Viscachani</u>, <u>Huaca Prieta</u>; **Peru, Chile**: <u>Chinchorro</u>
Period V	4200 BCE – 2500 BCE	**Ecuador**: *<u>Valdivia</u>; **Peru**: <u>Casma/Sechin culture</u>, <u>Norte Chico</u> [Caral], <u>Honda</u>, <u>Lauricocha III</u>, <u>Viscachani</u>[disambiguation needed]; **Peru, Chile**: <u>Chinchorro</u>
Period IV	6000 BCE – 4200 BCE	**Peru**: <u>Ambo</u>, Canario, <u>Siches</u>, <u>Lauricocha II</u>, <u>Luz</u>, <u>Toquepala II</u>; **Peru, Chile**: <u>Chinchorro</u>
Period III	8000 BCE – 6000 BCE	**Ecuador**: *<u>Las Vegas</u>, 8000–4600 BCE; **Peru**: <u>Arenal</u>, <u>Chivateros II</u>, <u>Lauricocha I</u>, <u>Playa Chira</u>, <u>Puyenca</u>, <u>Toquepala I</u>; **Peru, Chile**: <u>Chinchorro</u>
Period II	9500 BCE – 8000 BCE	**Ecuador**: <u>El Inga</u>; **Peru**: <u>Chivateros I</u>, <u>Lauricocha I</u>
Period I	? BCE – 9500 BCE	**Colombia**: <u>El Abra</u>, [12,500–10,000 BCE]; **Peru**: <u>Oquendo</u>, Red Zone [central coast; **Argentina & Chile**: Patagonia

Note the date for El Abra habitation in the Ice Age, prior to the Pleistocene Extinction of 10,900 BCE, in 12,500 BCE. Even this early date is in question by researchers and could be thousands of years earlier. I believe the coastal cultures were in place during this era because of the Ice Age. The Ocean's coastal habitat would have provided a temperate climate for permanent habitation. This is a sensible conclusion as people are going to live where it is most comfortable and food, water and shelter can be found.

THE LAS VEGAS CIVILIZATION
[9,500 BCE to 4,600 BCE]

The Santa Elena Peninsula is on the southern coastline of Ecuador near the Las Vegas River. The ruins of one of the first South American civilizations to use planned agriculture are located at this site. The site is of the Las Vegas Civilization, dated to pre-9,000 BCE. This is 3,000 years before the Indus Valley Civilization but is concurrent with the beginnings of the Sumerian Civilizations. The El Inga Culture is labeled as a precursor to the Las Vegas, but I think it was the same widespread group.

The Las Vegas Civilization spread over an area of about 150 square miles. The sea level was down about 200 feet from present and this area provided excellent fishing for their sea-going boats. Farming was a major food source along with many game animals. Agriculture included the staple crops of corn, chili, beans, peanuts and squash.

Tropical root crops were introduced along with a plant which "is a mystery" to archeologists and botanists. It is the Calabash Gourd, which was previously found only in Asia and Africa. There are historians claiming the Gourd was brought to South America by ocean currents or people crossing the Bering Strait. Many researchers do not attempt to elaborate on this specific artifact found at Las Vegas sites. The remains of the Calabash [African] squash, which was carbon dated to 8,000 BCE, indicating that long range contact with The Lords of Sumer was established at that time. The Phoenicians would have brought this squash on their cross-ocean voyages.

Although not mentioned until the next civilization arrived, I believe the Las Vegans also cultivated cotton. Tools were found which are consistent with spinning and weaving cotton into thread and twine. This was woven into clothing, fishing line and other utility products. The same tools are found in later ruins for processing cotton.

Corn was also carbon dated to 6,100 BCE. I believe this civilization was the result of the surviving Lords and the Tiwanaku people remaining in contact with the Mediterranean group of Lords.

The site is at the northern end of the 2,000-mile-long desert which extends to the southern tip of Chile. It receives about 10 inches of rain per year, so these civilizations utilized canals to irrigate crops.

Upland sites receive much more rain annually and Human presence has been dated to about 9,000 BCE.

Burial sites were clustered close to religious and ceremonial centers. This civilization was well planned and organized on levels far above that of what scientists labeled it, as "A Holocene Hunter-Gatherer Society".

The scientists "speculate" this civilization had sea-going boats due to the remains of ocean fish species. That is an amazing deduction, Sherlock, since they had fishing lines and gear and left remains of deep-water species including whales.

Archeologists speculate that corn was first "hybridized" in Central America and brought to the Santa Elena Peninsula by couriers. I doubt this theory of couriers travelling on foot through the impassable Panamanian Peninsula. If corn was transported it was by sea-going ships sailing along the Pacific coast to Central America.

The civilization seems to have "vanished" about 4,600 BCE. The Scientists state "The fate of the Las Vegas people is not known" and claim there was no human habitation at this site for the following 1,000 years. That is an amazing speculation since the Valdivia Civilization is immediately established at this location at the end of the "Las Vegas" civilization. Someone does not read their counterpart's reports.

There is evidence various Civilizations thrived along the Pacific coastline, near river channels, dating to 9,500 BCE. These civilizations evolved, combined and relocated over the millennia. I truly believe that people lived along the coast for a much longer time, in the range of 100,000 years.

THE VALDIVIA CIVILIZATION
[4,500 BCE – 2,500 BCE]

Suddenly, about 4,500 BCE the advanced Valdivia Civilization emerged at the same location as the previous Las Vegas Civilization. Valdivia Pottery is dated to 4,000 BCE and it is labeled the oldest settled civilization recorded in the Americas. The Valdivia produced exquisite stone carvings, which is in contrast to the Las Vegas Civilization which existed for 5,000 years. This is another mis-step for *Academia*. I believe there was a change of leadership to guide the same people.

The Valdivia people continued with the same managed agriculture as their predecessors and added exquisite fired ceramics. These included figures of animals and humans, utilitarian pieces and some for other purposes. It is presumed to be the oldest pottery in the Americas, although less sophisticated pottery was found at lower levels of excavations. Most of *Academia* lists the Valdivia Civilization as "Pre-Ceramic". It is apparent there continues to be a massive immature culture in *Academia*.

The Valdivian Civilization continued along a long stretch of coastline and inland for a considerable distance. Their civilization has been classified as a "Tropical forest and Riverine Culture".

The Valdivians seem to have disappeared between 2,250 BCE and 1,800 BCE. Archaeologists state "There has been major re-evaluation of nearly every aspect of its culture". I suspect there is a very valid connection with the Olmec Civilization "suddenly appearing" in Central America as a "fully functioning Theocracy and advanced Civilization" within this timeframe of "disappearance" and "appearance".

Valdivia Owl Art

THE CHAVIN CIVILIZATION
[3,800 BCE – 500 BCE]

About 3,800 BCE, researchers concluded something very unusual began to happen in northern Peru. A great social reformation had begun with evidence of a mysterious higher authority. Although this higher authority has never been identified, it was able to mobilize and coordinate massive labor forces. This phenomenon is described as the sudden flowering of communities with ample work forces to engage in new construction projects.

The higher authority has been recognized as responsible for building a major temple complex at Chavin de Huantar, located in the northern highlands of Peru at an elevation over 10,000 feet.

The Chavin de Huantar temple complex was similar to those found in Central America, containing a very large flat-topped pyramid, sunken courtyards, various temples, public administrative buildings, and apartment complexes. Archaeologists state the higher authority appears to have been centered on a religious cult that worshipped a Sky, or Sun God. The Chavin Civilization extended to the coastal areas later ruled by the Moche and Nazca Civilizations. The site was abandoned by 500 BCE.

The Chavin Civilization relocated to the ancient destroyed Tiwanaku Sun Temple site at Lake Titicaca to oversee the final preparations to receive the rescue parties. The time for their arrival was quickly approaching.

THE NORTE CHICO CIVILIZATION
[3,000 BCE – 1,800 BCE]

Inland from the Central Peruvian coastline an advanced civilization flourished as early as 3,000 BCE and continued through 1,800 BCE. The principal site is called Caral and it was the center of a Theocracy which constructed "monumental architecture with sunken courts". They produced extensive advanced irrigation canals and multiple crop farming which included corn, peanuts and cotton. Cotton was widely used for clothing, fishing nets and lines. Unexplainable is the claim by

Academia that this civilization did not use pottery or possess cookware for its 1,200-year existence.

The Norte Chico Civilization built six stepped pyramids with platform tops about the same time Egyptians were building theirs.   Their Pyramid of the Sun has a large sunken circular courtyard in front of it.   *Academia* claims it is "One of the six sites where civilization originated independently and indigenously".   In plain terms, no outside influence occurred with these civilizations.   Really?   Maybe they influenced Teotihuacan!

To provide a time perspective, this equates to the same time period when King Menes was uniting Upper and Lower Egypt and when the Mastabas [stepped pyramids] with platform tops and the pyramids of Giza were built.

The Norte Chico people used vertebrae from Blue whales as footstools and chairs.   They enjoyed a vast amount of seafood and from other remains appear to have been adept at sailing.   The effort to chase down, harpoon and drag a whale to the beach is enormous. Historians give little credit to the seafaring abilities of these coastal civilizations.   And to think "they had no pottery or cookware", *Academia* does come up with some amazing conclusions.

A recent "Historical" program on this area titles the site "Caral" and the narrative distorts the site as "The first civilization in the Americas at 2,000 BCE, more ancient than the Olmec".   They also promoted the theory about no pottery or cookware.   They fail to mention the documented Norte Chico and many other civilizations. This is nothing more than *Academic* whoredom – for money.   Once anyone sells their word in knowing distortions of fact; it is worthless.

As you will soon read, Central America civilizations had developed open sea routes by this same time in history. I am certain these sea trade routes connected with South America.

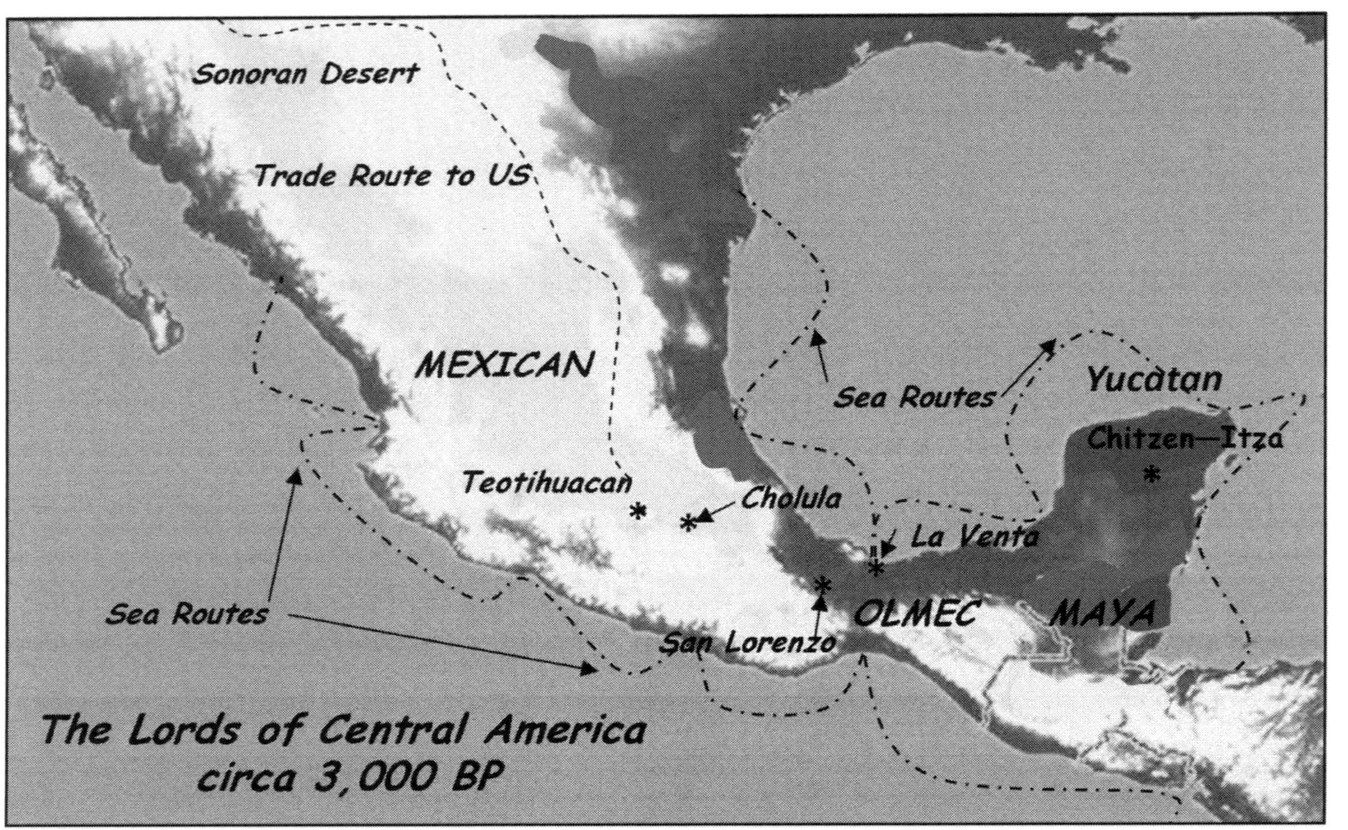
Sonoran Desert
Trade Route to US
MEXICAN
Sea Routes
Yucatan
Chitzen—Itza
Teotihuacan
Cholula
La Venta
Sea Routes
San Lorenzo
OLMEC
MAYA
The Lords of Central America
circa 3,000 BP

Chapter 3

Mayan Weaver
spinning cotton

CENTRAL AMERICA
OLMEC, MEXICAN AND MAYA

OLMEC STORY OF CREATION from Codex:

"So then there is just a little bit of dawn moving on the face of the Earth. There is no sun yet, but there is one who enlarges himself, 7 Macaw is his name. There is the first sky, Earth. Just hiding his face is the Sun, the Moon. This one [7 Macaw] says, "It is just the brightening of the people that drowned, like the spirit familiar people is their essence. I am great! I am placed over the human construction, the human form. I am its Sun, and I am its light, and I will also be its moon when it shall come to be! Great is my brightness! I am the walkway, and I am the crawlway for the people."

[From the Maya Codex <u>Popol Vuh</u>, <u>The Hero Sons destroy 7 Macaw and his Sons</u>, by Maya author Chilam Balam -- Translator undocumented, but appreciated.]

Lord Bal's final transition to Central America in 1,600 BCE elevated several great civilizations. These have drawn the attention of archaeologists since the early 1800's. Many of the archaeologists' early excavations were merely a search for treasure under the guise of archaeology. Beginning in the 1920's, a more serious effort emerged in the search for answers to the beginnings of the lost civilizations.

From the 1920's until the present, public interest in these civilizations has steadily grown. An aura of mystery produced by the ruins of Central and South America continues to gain in popularity. What could be more intriguing than to learn the secrets of civilizations buried by time and jungle growth?

The Americas were rich in natural resources with an abundant supply of human labor. All that was necessary for success was for the Lords to exploit the natural situation. Once again, the Lords were free from public scrutiny, social turmoil, and the possibility of encroachment by other civilizations. They again enjoyed the position of being received as Gods among ancient Man.

One of the most telling details, which led me to the conclusion of Lords Bal and Yahweh belonging to a Grand Council, was the evidence of fair skinned, red haired men in early Olmec and Mayan history [Lord Bal's descendants]. This was evidence of the multi-racial makeup of the Grand Council. Each member of the council projected their heritage in the various tribes of the areas they controlled. However, few members went as far as Lord Yahweh in promoting their individual lineages.

From beginning to end, the attitude of the Lords of the Grand Council toward Native Man was one of supremacy and indifference. This was the same attitude later explorers exhibited toward other races of people, that is, they considered other races as lower-class human chattel, to be bought, sold or killed without remorse. The "Grand Lodges" of the Middle East remained but were not established in the same manner in the Americas. In the Americas we will find lodges of sort, governed by different objectives, led by Priests and Shamen.

Compare the view of Gobekli Tepe with Southwest USA Kivas and you will see the same underground processes in play. This was the style of Lord Bal in developing clan leadership.

As was in the past 20,000 years, the view of good and evil depended on who held power and wielded the knife.

The Lords created an empire referred to as Meso-America. The history of this area is often misunderstood because of overlapping regional boundaries of the various civilizations. The second problem causing confusion is the time sequences of the civilizations.   It is possible to gain a clear picture of the era and the civilizations. The

Lords used a simple system of regions of control, with each region interconnected by culture and trade with its neighbor.

The Olmec Story of Creation by a Supreme God is a mirror of the creation stories of the Fertile Crescent. This story includes a Deluge with seven survivors, a tale similar to the Tower of Ba'Bel, and Sun worship. If you study it closely you will find enormous similarities.

The first civilization the Lords established in Central America was the Olmec. The Olmec territory was centrally located on the Pacific side of Central America. The Olmec passed into history after the establishment of Mayan northern and southern regions of control. The Mexican civilization centered near Teotihuacan and spread north and east to the Gulf coast.

The Mayan dominance of the area was because of the way it was established. The more than thirty tribes were set up as city-states, interdependent on trade. The Kings were the spokesman for God to his people, and kingship was patrilineal. That is, the power was passed from the king to his firstborn son. Is this beginning to sound familiar? And most familiar, all kings owed allegiance to the Gods of Teotihuacan.

The northern region of the Mayan empire began near present-day Mexico City and extended south to the Grijalva River, the heartland of the Olmec, just north of the Yucatan Peninsula. This region is a lowland strip along the Mexican-Caribbean coast, approximately 150 miles long and extending inland from seventy to one hundred miles. An exacting present-day location would place the area near Veracruz.

The southern region of control began in the area we currently define as the boundaries of the Maya civilization. The Maya civilization extended from the Yucatan Peninsula into the Central America states of Guatemala, Belize, Honduras, and El Salvador.

The Olmec civilization merged and co-existed with the two remaining civilizations of the Mexican in the North, and the Maya in the South. These civilizations were interdependent and existed in overlapping time frames. Each region had a special purpose to serve for the rescue of the Lords. The Mexican civilization controlled trade routes extending to New Mexico and southern Texas with another route into southern Arizona.

A group of Lords developed a third region of civilizations along the coast and inland in South America, centered in Peru. The development of this area coincides with the formation of both the north and south regions of Central America. The South American Pacific coastal area was used to provide rescue aircraft with the first recognizable features of the Lords existence. After the initial recognition, symbolic messages in the region would establish a flight path to Central America.

The grandeur of the rescue plan has confused scholars for over a century, and yet it was simple and effective. To add clarity to this era, a brief discussion of other popular civilizations, the Aztec, Inca and the US Southwest societies, is necessary. The popularity of these civilizations usually serves to cloud issues of the history we will examine. *These civilizations emerged after the Lords were rescued.* Their existence had nothing to do with the original development of the three regions. These civilizations are known as *Remnant Civilizations*, sometimes referred to as emerging cultures.

These civilizations most likely were established and led by Lords who chose to remain on Earth. Inevitably, when discussing the ancient history of Central America, references of these civilizations are interjected and confuse the events of earlier history. Native Man created history before the Lords arrived, and after the Lords who wished to leave were rescued. There were historical events that occurred simultaneous with that of the Lords' over which they had no control. For historical scholars, what will be presented is not an argument of history itself. What is presented is interpretation of selective events and regions, within that history.

Archaeologists' findings place the Lords' main intervention in South and Central America as early as 2,250 BCE. The advance group of Lords and craftsmen were involved when hybridized corn was introduced by 5,500 BCE in Central Mexico. One source stated that *Neolithic farmers* had successfully hybridized corn around 5,000 BCE, by converting the perennial wild corn to an annual corn plant, harvested twice a year. The story is the same as the one presented for hybridizing wheat in Sumer. Corn, not maize, was cultivated before 6,100 BCE in Peru.

Most of the Lords' early successes were due to enhancing crude agricultural systems and the introduction of new farming techniques. The Lords introduced new food crops and selectively improved native food plants to produce a more varied and greater crop yield. This allowed extensive labor forces to begin construction of temples and great cities.

As the civilizations progressed, the Lords developed factories and shops, which produced pottery and other items for trade. Long-range trade routes were established to connect North and South America to exchange merchandise with distant civilizations. A sect of astronomer priests ruled and controlled each area within the region.

This system of cultural achievement is an exact duplicate of that used to create the Sumerian and other ancient civilizations. Unfortunately, *Academia* has refused to acknowledge the achievements of the civilizations of the Americas in comparison with civilizations in "The Old World".

Another European statement regarding the scientific achievement of the Maya was "They had no concept of scientific analysis methodology because it [the methodology] had not been invented". This is classic "Western Thinking" where nothing exists before being invented or discovered by western *Academia*.

And one of the best: "The Maya were great record keepers but lacked the ability to project theoretical values." *Academia* choses to ignore the following achievements.

The Maya did understand the elliptical orbit plot of Venus occurring five times in a repeated eight-year cycle of 583.92 days per orbit. It is too bad they did not understand much about heavenly bodies, according to *Academia*. They did manage to develop several very precise calendars, predict Lunar and Solar eclipses into the 1990's CE, plot comets, track constellations and predict tidal changes. I guess this could all be accomplished without being trained by Europeans who had not yet discovered the Earth was round. The Americas' civilizations also developed metallurgy techniques for alloys and plating which surpasses some in use today.

A recent "amazing discovery" which the Western Press jumped on was a Mayan inscription "*deciphered*" to proclaim the "End of the World" in 2012 CE. This was raised to a fever pitch by the press and media hacks, all making money of course, and selling this prediction to the public. As I stated before, look at the original document before betting the family fortune on a fad.

The Mayan glyphs actually predict stability for the Ruling Gods in the future year of 2012. So much for the credibility of the Press and Media after creating global hysteria by publishing a pending catastrophe from unverified sources.

THE OLMEC CIVILIZATION

As a prelude to the Olmec Civilization I have paraphrased portions of an excellent article:

The Peoples and Civilizations of the Americas by Michael Adas:

The sudden appearance of the Olmec Civilization at Veracruz was as if a fully functional Culture arrived. Their advanced farming techniques, architecture, math, science, writing and established religion did not take generations to develop.

Their origin remains a mystery, but they are referred to as "The mother of Civilizations" in Middle America. Their sites range from the East Coast to the West Coast and spread throughout the highlands.

Their Culture is ruled by an Hereditary Theocracy, guiding a complex dominating religion which worships a Sun God Trinity with many lesser Gods.

The Olmec flourished during the same time Tut-Ak-Amon ruled Egypt [1340 - 1320 BCE] and many of their monuments reflect the African features of the Mediterranean Phoenicians.

I need to remark on this article that he went as far as he could without saying; "They arrived at Veracruz on trans-oceanic vessels sailed by Phoenicians."

I attempt to use dates substantiated by several Central and South American archeologists, which are more accurate than previous findings. You will find that many writers use the time-frames established 50 years ago for most of the civilizations in the Americas. *Academia* has not always respected the scientific views of Central and South American Scientists, believing they hold a lower level of education and achievement. It is Sad.

Archaeologists date the first advanced, organized civilization in Central America as the Olmec from 2,250 BCE to 1,250 BCE at the San Lorenzo site. The Olmec organized a conglomeration of about 16 similar tribal groups. The weather conditions of this low-lying coastal region are excessively warm with heavy rains. The hot, damp, swampy conditions caused the destruction of most of the archaeological evidence of the civilization.

Except for stone artifacts, many of the materials providing clues of the civilization have vanished. However, there remains enough evidence to piece together a general picture. Carved wooden human busts have been recovered in Veracruz sites. The wood artifacts were preserved in mud, and dated to over 3,500 BCE. Also recovered, among other artifacts, were *polished iron* concave mirrors [steel bowls], which focused the Sun's energy enough to start fires.

As with the dating of other ancient civilizations, I believe they incorrectly dated the Olmec beginnings by at least 1,000 years. The Olmec were in place, organized with administration and religion before they carved the large wooden human effigies.

Although the Olmec began their surge to prominence in the general time of 3,500 BCE, the foundation began far in advance of that date with the introduction of advanced farming with the local tribes in 5,500 BCE. This is when corn was widely harvested as a twice a year food staple along with year-round growing of beans and squash. Also, at this time cotton was grown and harvested for weaving clothing and bags. Cotton was also used for string, twine, fishing nets and ropes. Cotton production is not well published because it infers the people had to have the skills and tools to process and weave the material.

The first known site the Lords created was located on a river island approximately two miles square. Several existing rivers and streams form the island. The site is known as the Veracruz Site of San Lorenzo, inland about 35 miles from the Gulf Coast. The evidence establishing the site as one of the Lords is in the construction. There is clear evidence the entire site was planned and laid out before the beginning of any construction. In plain words, it was not a hunting site grown into a village, which continued to evolve into a structured city. The site was located near surfacing oil reserves, as many of the Sumerian sites were.

San Lorenzo was centered on a large stepped pyramid similar to Sumer's Ziggurats and Egypt's Mastabas. This pyramid was built on a general north-south meridian and sited for astrological observations. It was constructed of layered platforms of clay brick and rose to a height of one hundred feet. The structure provided for visual security of the area and signaled dominance by great powers over the land. As with all other great monuments built by the Lords, they proclaimed: *We are Gods, and we are here.*

The buildings of San Lorenzo have been labeled as religious centers by archaeologists. However, the Lords simply used the same methods of temple administration for their corporate endeavors. It is surprising that their methods have not been compared to the eastern civilizations. The comparison is so evident that the only reason it has not been promoted is because of the archaeologists' fear of being ridiculed.

The Valdivia Civilization from Southern Ecuador relocated and joined the Minoan Lords at San Lorenzo to establish a well formed and organized group of Lords and craftsmen. As the Lords completed the construction of the first temple administration centers, they employed a new technique to train or subjugate the native inhabitants. They used giant or medium sized statues portraying human figures in subservient positions.

The statues depict men standing or sitting in various positions. Many of the statues continue the subservient theme by depicting men in the position of half kneeling. The depiction of the body positions has previously been explained as an effort by native man to show the beauty of the human body. Evidently, because some archaeologists and historians find the statuary beautiful works of art, their interpretation is misguided. Using the intellectual level of the society as a guide, the correct explanation can be derived.

At the time of the creation of the statues, there were no common written glyphs or language for the indigenous tribes, although hieroglyphs were in use. Therefore, there were no common instructions for native Man to follow when they came before the Gods. If the statues had remained in the proper position from the time of their discovery, they would present a visual, symbolic message that would provide specific instructions to visitors entering a religious center. The message said, bow or kneel and assume a sitting position before the priest or God.

Stelae, large rectangular stone monoliths, [the same method used in Sumer and Egypt] were erected to depict visual messages to the populations in the areas controlled by the Lords. Many of the stelae were carved with scenes of a human figure rising from the mouth of a jaguar holding a child in its arms. The jaguar was recognized as powerful, fearless, silent death. The Lords used this image to depict their power over the land.

The figure with the child was a visual representation of the Lords' creation of civilization. Smaller versions of the stone monoliths were placed throughout the travel routes in the Olmec region. Eventually each stela was covered with hieroglyphics presenting various messages to the general population marking routes and territorial boundaries.

Numerous colossal, carved stone heads were discovered in the area, varying in size, but all are extremely large. One was measured at eight and a half feet in height with a base circumference of twenty-two feet, and an estimated weight of twenty tons. A leather helmet covers the upper part of the skull. Each helmet is adorned with different identifying glyphs. The facial features appear to be those of large young men of African ancestry.

From the time of their discovery to present day, historians have been reluctant to make specific statements regarding the possible identification of the men depicted in the stone carvings. This is rather strange because there is sufficient information available to make a plausible statement regarding the identification. If you examine American civilizations during this time and compare the headgear, and the facial features, they clearly indicate the race was not Native Americans. They were Phoenicians who ruled North Africa and the oceans of the area. This should lead to the conclusion the race is, just as depicted, African.

Phoenicians, organized by the Lords of Thera and Crete, were the only group of seafaring people capable of Trans-Atlantic voyages. Phoenician carvings clearly show their African heritage and their oarsmen wearing the same helmets depicted on the Central American carvings. The oarsmen wore the helmets to protect the top of their heads. The ends of the massive oars of the Phoenician ships could injure them. As they pulled the oars, their arms were extended, head bent forward, and from this position the oars were pulled toward the body. This rowing position caused the oars to be pulled directly to the forehead. These helmets also protected the Phoenicians in battle.

The Phoenicians were a diverse, multi-cultural society, made up with people from Africa to the middle East, including Egyptians.

OLMEC HEAD SCULPTURE AT LA VENTA

The Lords used the features of Phoenician sailors as boundary markers due to human nature and behavior.   When the native population first saw large muscular black men, they were filled with terror. The oarsmen appeared to the smaller native people as Gods or as their worst nightmare. Having observed this reaction to the Phoenicians, the Lords took advantage of their fears.

The Lords created the stone heads for the specific purpose of controlling the local population. One of the stone heads, found near a huge earthen mound, contained a speaking tube that ran from behind the ear down through the head, and emerged between the lips. This is a feature used in ancient Sumerian and Egyptian civilizations, which allowed the voice of a priest to appear to be coming from an idol.

The numerous stone stelae provide evidence the Lords promoted the belief that they were the incarnations of the jaguar spirit in human form. The stelae were carved depicting the Lords evolving from the jaguar form, beginning with mating with a woman, and producing a human figure with jaguar features. Some stelae present the Lords with jaguar skin. The entire scenario promoted the belief the Lords were the product of a powerful spirit. In the religious centers, statues portrayed the human figure in animal forms, particularly the jaguar.

The Lords were worshipped as Gods who controlled the forces of nature, and as the living incarnations of the great Sun God. From this position of authority, the Lords were able to control vast pools of laborers. Anthropologists have estimated the population of the Olmec region at approximately 350,000 people. This was sufficient to provide all the labor necessary to expand the Lords' regional control.

From the creation of the first site of Veracruz at San Lorenzo, the Lords established a series of smaller ceremonial centers. Workers living in groups of small villages maintained the grounds of each site. The population of the villages is estimated at approximately one thousand. The ceremonial centers were governed by an elite council of priests and maintained by specialized craftsmen who lived in elaborate residences next to each center.

This model of management is an exact duplicate of that used at the Palace of Knossos on Crete. A short distance from the ceremonial center was a second group of villages with larger populations. These villages provided labor for specific area projects, without the maintenance of the entire region suffering neglect.

As the Olmec civilization progressed, the foundation for the civilizations of the northern and southern regions was being established. Beginning in the Olmec region, long-range land and sea trade routes were improved. As the populations became dependent on regional trade, the Lords spread their influence into the areas. Over time the outer regions were incorporated into the empire. The overall area was a confederation of city-states with interdependent trade

The San Lorenzo site was not built to last through extended periods of time. Unlike the stone cities of Mexico and the Maya temple centers, San Lorenzo was built of sun-dried mud bricks identical to temples in Sumer. This type of construction would be destroyed by the elements, and around 900 BCE, the site was abandoned. The great stone monuments were disfigured, toppled into trenches and buried. The purpose was to destroy the visual messages of the monuments. Throughout the entire area, stelae depicting the human-jaguar spirit were also toppled and buried.

When the Lords abandoned San Lorenzo, they moved to a more elaborate site. This site is known as La Venta, and is located East of San Lorenzo, about 6 miles inland near a coastal estuary in the western Tabasco region. As was San Lorenzo, La Venta was built above oil reserves. The Lords appear to need a continuous supply of petroleum products. The tar from seeps was widely used by the local populations as mortar for brick and tile construction. This seemingly unique application is another clue the Lords were involved. This same unique construction practice, using tar, was used in Sumer.

The Olmec Casajal text [scribed on Serpentine] was found near the Olmec La Venta Site and dated to before 900 BCE. The writing is undeciphered [as with the writings of Teotihuacan, Sumer and Minoan] and is proof the American civilizations had written communications. There is no logical reason to believe this was not normal practice long before this time, and that it continued to be used in various formats in Central and South America through the end of the Inki Empire.

Academia would have you believe written communications was a select activity for isolated cultures, developed independently of other influences. This premise is absurd; it is another reflection of "Western Thinking".

The abandonment of San Lorenzo caused considerable speculation among historians and archaeologists. The general opinion is the abandonment of San Lorenz was the product of an insurrection, or an unknown religious philosophy. Based on the evidence at the site, there was no warfare or insurrection. There was only evidence that a powerful administration had moved from one location to another.

The La Venta site was more elaborate, decorative, and comfortable. It was built on high ground for security. This move was well planned and was first developed as a farming community in 2,250 BCE.

The stone statues and reliefs of San Lorenzo were buried to ensure the power they projected would never be used by native priests for future insurrection. The Lords must have considered that generations later a local leader could use the statuary against them. Secondary to this, once the figures were buried there would be no evidence of where the Lords religious practice originated. Future native leaders were totally dependent on receiving their authority from the newest ceremonial center of La Venta. By 2,000 BCE the Maya began to represent the Lords from this new center of power, administratively and with new religious power.

La Venta was built of clay bricks with apartment complexes to house the Lords and elite visitors, administration and ceremonial buildings, and a large pyramid. The pyramid was constructed of clay fill and mud bricks. The entire complex was ornate luxury complete with mosaic pavements.

Most Mayan, Olmec and Mexican pyramids were oriented a few degrees off of north. The degree of orientation from north depended on the particular location of the pyramid, and the date of the construction. These particular orientations provided alignment with the Seven Sisters, or Pleiades Star System, in the Taurus constellation as it set in the western horizon.

Also constantly charted was the movement of the three central stars of the Orion constellation. Each pyramid observatory charted the exact distance, location and speed of these star systems, which served as a celestial clock.

Some distinct interior features of the Mayan pyramids were built using the exact construction methods of the Egyptian pyramids. The pyramids were basic rubble filled, stone veneered structures with ornate stone carvings. In the main interior burial room of some of the pyramids a vaulted ceiling was constructed using two huge wall slabs, tilted inward, with a horizontal ceiling slab resting on top of the walls. This creates an A Frame type interior room, which when photographed, you will not be able to identify whether it is Maya, or Egyptian.

On both continents these vaulted rooms were decorated with paintings depicting travel to the afterlife. As with the Pyramid of Ra [Sun] in Egypt, the Temple of the Sun pyramid in Teotihuacan was constructed with a celestial observation gallery. Both galleries were underneath the pyramids. The Temple of the Sun gallery was oriented to the western horizon position of the Pleiades star system. This type of architecture was typical construction throughout the region, from Mexico to the southern areas of the Maya.

Data from modern archaeological excavations indicate a progressive spread of ceremonial centers throughout the region. The Tres Zapotes Site, north of La Venta, has indications of construction as early as 1,400 BCE, and continuing through 600 BCE.

The areas of Oaxaca, Chiapas, Guatemala, and El Salvador all contain administrative religious centers. From the central ceremonial centers, the Olmec were responsible for the creation of a regional trading system unifying all areas of Mesoamerica, from the Gulf of Mexico to the Pacific Ocean. The sea routes provided access to the South American coastal civilizations. Each region contained distinct trading complexes. The extensive trading, supplemented with the religious authority of the Lords, produced their ultimate goal of corporate control of the entire area.

Hardened metal tools were a necessity in producing a considerable amount of this stone construction. The Lords maintained the utmost secrecy in any ore deposits and smelting processes. They did not want a repeat of native Man obtaining this knowledge for unsupervised use, as occurred in Sumer. This is evident in that iron artifacts were found only in ceremonial centers. Brass was produced in the Americas using a copper and nickel alloy, which is a more durable alloy than copper and tin.

The "brass alloy" statement means: The American metallurgists had to know what they were looking for to locate nickel ore and also how to smelt it. Guatemala has a myriad of locations containing nickel ore deposits.   The most concentrated ores are in placer deposits containing Nickel-Iron-Sulfides with adhering serpentine. Commonly found deposits are Nickle-Cobalt alloys in the sulfides. The ore is usually 60-75% Nickle-Cobalt and 25-35% Iron. I do not intend to bore you with the technology of smelting these metals. I do not believe it was done with "rocks and a campfire" by "Neolithic Artisans" and that they would discard the other metals.   The Lords had previously alloyed iron and cobalt in Egypt, leaving exquisite knife blades in tombs.

The Lords, from Sumer to the Americas, had technological uses for these various metals and elements. Artifacts recovered which show evidence of advanced Cobalt-Iron and high Nickel-Iron alloys did not happen by accident.

In the 1990's I worked with high-nickel alloy metals designated as "Inconel". Working with this material required advanced technology, plasma cutting tools and knowledge of the properties of the metal. I mention this because the technology to work with this metal had only recently been developed for industrial applications. Producing these nickel and cobalt metals in 2,500 BCE required no less advanced and sophisticated methods. Man has not developed the "Knowledge of the Universe" beginning in Medieval Europe and advancing to today's level.

The Olmec civilization was the key to all civilization advances in Central America. I believe they were descendants of the Tiwanaku Civilization, through the Las Vegas civilization, of South America. Their Leaders would have maintained contact with Lord Bal in the Mediterranean area. I believe this is the group from the Las Vegas civilization which "disappeared" when they relocated to the San Lorenzo site.

With the advancement of the Olmec civilization, the Lords introduced common hieroglyphic writing, the calendar, measuring time, posting stelae for instructions, and a form of the alphabet. These features are the clearest indicators of a civilized world. Other indicators of the complexity of this civilization were metallurgy, astronomy and advanced mathematics. However, not until the rise of the Maya did astronomy become the most significant focal point of the priests.

After 600 BCE the intensity of trading and building slowly declined. The area entered a passive phase as a distinct region within an empire. After several hundred years, the civilization could be observed as an outlying supportive area, slowly engulfed by another phase of civilized growth. The Olmec civilization did not disappear; it was just replaced as the center of power. Olmec influence is found in the buildings and artifacts of Teotihuacan into its height of building.

The *La Mojarra* stelae, found near the San Lorenzo site contains the earliest hieroglyphs *deciphered* for Central America. Deciphering the text required experts of four ancient languages, which included the Olmec language. The text of these stelae was meant to be read by several distinct groups, all living and traveling in the same area. The date of these stelae is about CE 100, and they were found in the center of Maya control. The point is, the Olmec were still around, just not in power.

Olmec Lord with hand basket riding with God Kukulkan [The Feathered Serpent] in his flying craft.
[reference hand-baskets at Gobekli Tepe and in Assyrian carvings]

Some commentators from Academia insist the "God's" headgear is a ceremonial human jaw-bone. I believe the explanation of the headgear is very obvious, just as the explanation of his hand and feet on the flight controls.

The "hand basket" feature I have noted from Gobekli Tepe carvings, Sumerian Gods and Olmec Gods is a "royal stamp" from the ruling gods. In ancient times a "pass" was required from the "King" for unlimited travel.

THE MAYAN CIVILIZATION

Archaeologists agree that the Mayan "Archaic" period begins in 8,000 BCE and advances in 1,600 BCE. Most of *Academia* would have you believe they were only around after 400 BCE. All of the historical dates are approximate, as dating greatly depends on who is offering the information.

The Maya began their rise as the religious and warrior culture about 1,600 BCE when Lord Bal moved from Crete to the Americas. They became the leaders of the efforts of the Lords to rule Central America. Their first cities of prominence were Nakbe in Guatemala, El Mirador and the crown jewel of the period, Tikal.

MAYA CHRONOLOGY

Archaic	8000–2000 BCE
Preclassic	2000 BCE – 0 CE
Classic	0 CE – 830 CE
Terminal Classic	830 CE – 900 CE
Final Destruction	1519 CE -

The Mayan Civilization was thriving when Cortez found them on the Yucatan Peninsula in 1519 CE, and the Maya still exist today. Their Theocratic Rule is the only thing that "Disappeared" in about 830 CE.

On the Pacific coast the cities of Takalic Abaj and Chocola were the centers of Maya power and influence. The Pacific Ocean trade routes were governed from this area, extending south to Ecuador and Peru and north to the Sea of Cortez.

Teotihuacan would become the "Home of the Gods", with the Maya governing the vast Central American tribal systems. Their power was absolute, with no tolerance for independent actions from the ruling Kings of each area.

Local priests retained absolute power in each tribe or political group within the Lords' empire. Most priests had the power of life or death over local inhabitants. They settled disputes and dispensed justice within their region of control. The element of supreme religious authority, which was passed from the Olmec civilization, was in the form of an emblem representing a serpent, a snake. In some areas it was seen as a flaming snake or as a feathered serpent. This was the identical symbol for Lord Bal's power in Babylon.

Regardless of how it was presented, the emblem of the snake reflected the supreme power of the Lords over the land. As was the custom in Egypt, anyone wearing a snake headdress emblem was recognized as supreme royalty. There is clear evidence recorded on the Maya stelae of supreme visitors from the northern region of Mexico wearing the snake emblem.

Although the region of Mexico was developing parallel to that of the Maya, the Maya became the more popular civilization. The supremacy of the religious snake emblem can also be found in the construction of a specific ceremonial center in the Maya region. This construction validates other evidence, such as the stone stelae, which depicts royal visitors wearing the snake emblem. Think of the Maya as the "anointed" of God, like the Priests of Israel.

The Mayan center at Palenque is an amazing site. The Mayan name is B'aakal and its first *ajaw* [king] was named K'uk Balam. When I first read this name, I thought of the Sumerian Gods of Bal and Balaam. Am I stretching connections? It appears almost too good to be true. His name is also interpreted as Quetzal Jaguar.

Palenque had a pressurized water system fed by a closed aqueduct into the complex. Archaeologists cannot determine why this existed. It could be the Maya wanted a water system, I don't think that was difficult to figure out.

A main feature of Palenque is the tomb of *ajaw* K'inich Janaab Pakal the Great. He was buried in a stone sarcophagus with a seven-ton stone lid. The relief carvings have created many alien theories for decades. The burial chamber is located in the pyramid, Temple of Inscriptions. The chamber is a vaulted [A-frame] room which was elaborately painted. This is an exact duplication of Egyptian pyramid burials.

The carved lid seems to portray Pakal sitting in a woven hammock type chair, at the controls of a mechanical device.

Archeology Photograph - Pakal Sarcophagus Lid 1 by Gary Keesler
[Photo altered by author to remove color saturation for detail]

Top: Pakal's Vaulted Tomb and 7-ton carved stone
Sarcophagus lid in Palenque. Bottom: The carved stone
Sarcophagus. Photos by Gary Keesler

The Maya ceremonial center of Chichen Itza is located on the eastern portion of the Yucatan Peninsula. It contains the pyramid El Castillo with the Temple of Kukulkan on its flat top. This pyramid was constructed with engineering genius. El Castillo sits on top of an underground lake formed by a limestone cave system. When a roof of this cave system collapses it forms a huge freshwater lake, called a cenote. The pyramid was sited where the center of four cenotes intersected. This put El Castillo in the center representing the four quadrants of the Mayan universe. The cenotes were the source of fresh water as there are no streams or rivers near Chichen Itza.

Kukulkan is the Feathered Serpent God [Plumed Serpent]. This ceremonial temple is built on the top of a stepped pyramid. There is a large stairway leading from the ground level to the upper building. At the bottom of the stairway, the head of a great serpent is carved into the stone.

This type of temple pyramid is typical of Maya construction. However, the building is oriented to a specific position to the rising of the Sun, and twice a year the orientation produces an awesome display. The steps of the structure were engineered to catch the Sun's rays, causing the shadows of the steps to form the body of a great snake crawling up or down the stairway.

During the spring equinox, the Sun's rays cause the shadow of the great snake to crawl up the stairway and disappear into the ceremonial temple. The reverse of this event occurs at the autumnal equinox, as the rays of the Sun again form the body of the snake at the top of the temple steps. From that position it now slithers down the steps and disappears at or near the carved snakehead. It is truly an awesome display that evokes spiritual and superstitious grandeur.

The Palace and temples at Chichen Itza were built to display the power of the empire. It demonstrated the religious power of the king and knowledge of the Gods. It is apparent the location could not provide viewing for the entire Maya population. However, priests, chiefs, and sub-leaders of the various Maya districts could view the symbolic snake. This awesome display twice a year reinforced the authority of the Lords, and stories twice related to the commoners would certainly have grown in content.

The Maya occupied a region that encompassed most of Guatemala, part of Honduras, El Salvador, and in Mexico all the Yucatan, Campeche, Quintana Roo, almost all of Tabasco, and eastern Chiapas. This is an area of approximately 600 miles from north to south and 350 miles east to west. Most likely it was the area the Lords could travel in a day's time to check the status of their immediate empire.

Just as the Sumerian civilization grew wheat as a staple food crop, the Maya grew corn. Like wheat, the evolution of corn shows signs of managed growth. Without cultivation, the corn of 8,000 BCE was about the size of a small adult human finger. With management and cross-pollination of several species, it was close to what we recognize as corn of today.

A new breed of university investigators provided the information regarding the agricultural foundation of the Maya. Along with archaeologists, researchers now use a group known as mappers and settlement-pattern research teams. These teams provided extensive insight into the physical effort required to create and maintain the districts within the Maya region.

These investigative efforts provided evidence that labor forces extensively modified and improved existing features within the region. The labor forces created buffer zones, strips of untended land, which separated rival Maya districts. On each side of the buffer zone, the land was kept well cleared of unnecessary trees and vegetation. Many of the districts show evidence of managed forest areas by the planting of selected trees. This management practice produced selected wood products and provided for hunting areas for individual tribes. The focus of keeping the areas well cleared of intrusive vegetation was to facilitate farming.

Each Maya region operated in a similar fashion and was managed from large, ornate ceremonial centers. The local population usually did not visit the centers except for religious festivals or ceremonies. Each center was built in a similar architectural design of spacious open courts flanked by pyramids and multi-roomed buildings.

The centers contained large stone palaces complete with private courtyards. Areas directly adjacent to the ceremonial centers were restricted to a group of special craftsmen and selected priests. Homes for the craftsmen and priests were constructed of ornate stone and plaster with thatched roofs and encircled the center. Each house contained a water tank, which provided running water to facilitate modern plumbing and sewer systems.

Continuing outward were residences for servants, with buildings used for administrative purposes where the priests held court and dispensed various forms of justice. The outlying area was a large open market place used when people gathered from the surrounding countryside to market local merchandise.

Ceremonial centers varied in size depending on the region and population. A very popular center, known as Tikal, covered an area of approximately one square mile. The center was almost a city with palace buildings. Mayan palaces were built on a grand, but different architectural design than those located on the island of Crete. The buildings were meant to blend with the culture and what is more important, to blend with the concept of Maya religion.

The function of the Mayan and Knossos palaces was exactly the same, which was to provide the Lords with an opulent lifestyle. Like the palaces on Crete, residential areas had fresco paintings decorating the walls in brilliant colors. Interiors of Maya temple complex buildings were also painted in the same manner.

In Sumer the Lodges of Lords Yahweh and Bal were created so each God would be worshipped as the Supreme God. The Lodges also provided the necessary labor and skills to carry out construction projects. Yahweh did not make it across the pond to continue his fraternity, but Bal reconfigured his "Lodges" as clans with Priests, Priestess' and Shamen.

The frescoes of the Palace of Knossos depicted the Lords ego and conceit by leading the power of Egypt on a leash with butterflies surrounding the male figure. *The Butterfly was the Minoan symbol for resurrection and eternal life.*

Maya paintings and art reveal the same exhibitions of human conceit revealing a startling secret:

> **The visual expression for resurrection and eternal life in Maya art is the butterfly. One of the Maya Gods is the Butterfly God, the symbol of resurrection and immortality.**

The mathematical probability of two distinct ancient civilizations, on different continents and an ocean apart, combined with the differences in culture, accidentally using the same symbolic reference for resurrection and eternal life is near impossible. The use of such a reference had to be deliberate and initiated by the same influence.

Neither historians nor archaeologists have ever pursued the revelation of this particular reference to the afterlife. This failure of the intellectual communities is due to preconceived, prevailing attitudes and limited historical vision regarding the Earth's civilizations as a whole. *What we have here is a failure to communicate.* The elitists continue to debase the level of sophistication of the civilizations of Mesoamerica, and others, using simple terms such as *Old World*, and *New World*.

Had the paintings been regarded as history instead of marvelous works of art, more attention would have been paid to the subjects of the paintings. In the Minoan and Mayan paintings, the message depictions of the butterflies would have been discovered long ago.

The terminology used to describe paintings found in the Minoan and Maya civilizations detracts from investigative motivation. In the Minoan civilization the term *fresco* alludes to a separate cultural setting. The culturally correct intellectual uses this term to describe a wall painting. In the Maya civilization, often viewed as less sophisticated, the paintings are referred to as murals. The term *mural* alludes to simplistic paintings of little or no historical value. And yet, both have the same value. They present the earliest form of a technology to view details of past civilizations.

To clear any misunderstandings, a fresco is a painting applied to a wall while the plaster is fresh, requiring the plasterer and painter to work in concert. A mural is a painting applied to cured plaster. The Minoan and Maya civilizations both produced frescos and murals.

The Maya economy was based on agriculture and trade. A large number of people were farmers and craftsmen, and to achieve agricultural success they carefully controlled the landscape. Swamps were drained, and in other areas, dams and canals were built to stabilize the land for cultivation. Their primary food crops were corn, beans, peanuts and squash. Each region supplemented dietary needs with large garden plots of many other vegetables and a variety of chilies and peppers. Cotton was widely cultivated to provide for textiles and fishing needs.

Where the land trade routes crossed particularly dangerous rivers, the Maya constructed magnificent suspension bridges. These bridges were supported with stone masonry abutments and center piers to carry the loads from classic rope-cable and plank suspension construction. One site located near Yaxchilan was a three-suspension bridge, with two stone center towers, spanning over 600 feet. This technology and engineering proficiency predate the suspension bridges of the United States by at least 2,500 years.   Is this the "*Perseverance of Neolithic Artisans,*" or the result of introduced intelligence?

The Mayan roads were constructed with care about drainage, alignment and had engineered sub-base material with surfacing which would not deteriorate with traffic and weather.

The Lords maintained control of the entire Maya region and population through the formation of city-states. The Maya region is believed to have supported a population of twelve to sixteen million people. If the civilization was considered on the basis of one unified political force, under the rule of one king or priest it would have presented a formidable force in the area. At any time, it could have expanded its territory either north or south without much contest.

There is no evidence of extended territorial aggression among the city-states, and each cultural phase was designed to strengthen the region internally. The Lords controlled the area by fragmenting the authority and power within the civilization. They dominated the fragmented power by the authority of being perceived as living Gods, and yet, if necessary, they could command the power of the entire region into one force.

There were no standing armies within the region. Each village had a defined leadership that instantly called together a disciplined force of citizens, acting on the same system as a National Guard or reserve army force. The Priests responded to the needs of the ceremonial center within its area and could quickly marshal the forces of the numerous villages within its area of control. Although the ceremonial centers were designed and built of stone, there were no massive stone fortifications.

The lack of fortifications is unique in the history of native Man and mirrors the history of Sumer. This indicates there was no fear of outright invasion from within or without the region. The fragmented districts engaged in ceremonial warfare. This type of warfare in itself was neither extensive nor used for territorial aggression.   The restricted warfare, usually in the form of small raiding parties, and at times as an individual effort, was used to release tensions and hostility. The primary purpose of these limited raids was to provide prisoners for ritual sacrifice during festivals and religious ceremonies.

At present, archaeologists have found one instance of an invasion of a ceremonial center during the reign of the Maya. A large force from an adjacent district invaded a ceremonial center and executed a king along with his entire royal family and supporting lower priests.

If Mayan Kings became full of themselves and defied the power of Teotihuacan, they were summarily removed without negotiation. In 378 CE the King of Tikal, Chak Tok, got frisky and Teotihuacan detailed a warrior named Si'yaj K'ak [Born of Fire] to remedy the issue. Chak got a one-way ride to paradise with his head on a stick. A new King and dynasty was installed and Tikal continued to be a regional power.

The Lords governed the larger ceremonial centers and entrusted ruling priests to the smaller centers. The raid on Tikal indicates a local ruler overstepped his bounds of authority, or he became insubordinate to the authority over him. The Lords' response was quick and deadly, destroying the entire lineage of the ruler.

A more prominent and popular method of providing sacrificial prisoners was to have teams from different districts compete in a form of soccer. These games were held at the larger ceremonial centers. Points were scored by kicking a rubber ball through a stone hoop attached to the wall of a stone courtyard. The sport was very competitive as the losing team was ritually killed shortly after each game.

Two other popular social features of the Maya bound the civilization together. The first was the amazing use of advanced mathematics and the physics of astronomy. The second, and apparently very popular, was ritual sacrifice. Both of these areas of interest have withheld two prominent secrets. Astronomy and mathematics are generally viewed by a greater segment of our population as existing between a mental plane of interesting and that of boredom. The Maya's use of these sciences usually produces explanations such as, amazing, astounding, or having been far ahead of their time in the exploration of astronomy. The use of these phrases indicates *Academia* has no interest in breaking the bubble of thought identified as "Western Thinking". It would be disastrous to the academics' egos to admit these ancient civilizations were capable of creating and utilizing advanced scientific knowledge.

Researchers determined the Maya charted the Pleiades star System of the Taurus constellation. The Maya charted several hundred stars in this system. However, today you can only see six of these stars without the aid of a high-powered telescope.

Depending on who conducts the research regarding this unusual Maya talent, we receive different answers. First there is the answer of mystical spiritual. In this answer the researcher states the Maya priests possessed clairvoyant powers. This answer hardly lies within the realm of physical reality. A second answer promotes the theory that Maya priests had acute sight that enabled them to view all the stars within the constellation. And further, because this feat cannot be duplicated today, human sight must have degenerated through the years. For those researchers who disagree with both solutions to the apparent mystery, we are returned to a very safe answer of amazing and astounding.

There is a plausible answer to the practices of Maya astronomy. First, the term *priest* is usually viewed as an entity of one person having vast knowledge of everything pertaining to a civilization. This view is very incorrect. All the civilizations of Man, including those not influenced by the Lords, had a defined hierarchy within the societies of priests. Each priesthood was trained to different levels or planes of knowledge. In the Maya priesthood, this same system was used. As an example, there were specific groups of priests who dealt with the science of astronomy for planting and farming. These priests passed information to the lower groups, who then determined when to start the planting of fields and hold various festivals.

The answer to the question, of how the highest group of astronomer priests charted several hundred stars, which cannot be seen by the human eye, is simple. If you need a telescope to duplicate the event, that is the answer. They used a high-powered telescope, provided to them by their living Gods. The clue that provides information on a telescope is in the convex steel mirrors found in some temples. The same technology is required to produce telescopic lenses and parabolic reflectors used to start fires.

In conjunction with the information gained from astronomy, the Maya needed a method to process the information as usable and meaningful information. Using the astrological information, the Maya determined the time and distance between Earth and other celestial systems.

The Maya used stone tablets; each called a codex, carved with symbolic math symbols, to perform complex calculations. The stone tablets are sophisticated functioning calculators. Across the face of the tablets are symbols, each with numeric values. The combinations of the symbolic values were used much the same as buttons on our calculator. Depending on how they used the symbols, vertical, horizontal, or diagonal, the symbols provided solutions to mathematical problems. The Maya calendars, which were round, interfaced with each other in the same manner as sets of gears.

With these devices the Maya calculated the intervals of the return of the planet Venus with an error rate of one day in six thousand years, or less than 15 seconds per year. The examples of the planet Venus and the Pleiades star system are used to show the specific knowledge the Maya priests had regarding the systems within the universe. However, these are just examples and should not be viewed as the total content of their knowledge of the universe.

At present, like the information regarding the great pyramids of Egypt, there have been many books and scientific papers written detailing the extent of Mayan astrological observations. And yet, within this vast area of research, there is an avenue of thought that was never explored. The pervasive attitude regarding the Maya's knowledge of the universe is based on the premise that great civilizations proceed through a series of evolutionary learning phases.

These evolutionary phases allow the civilization to slowly gather and collect their vast knowledge of the universe. However, what has actually occurred, since the earliest civilization in Mesopotamia, namely Sumer, is the continual use of the same system. The Sumerians mathematically mapped the circumference of the Earth and charted constellation stars in seconds of an arc. Researchers regard this feat as very interesting. It is interesting because ancient Man was able to devise a system to measure time and space. The information should have been explored on a higher plane of thought. If we combine the information regarding the Sumerians with that of the Maya, we find that what is being measured in seconds, is time. These astrological measurements are relative to the time and space of the universe, in relation to the time and space of Earth.

Maya Astronomer charting planets and stars. He is looking through an instrument which extends his vision. An arrow points from the end of the instrument indicating distant vision. Could this simply be a telescope? It definitely is!
Image is from The Dresden Codex

The image from the Dresden Codex is the only surviving image by the Maya of an astronomer using a telescope. This image has not been just recently discovered, it has been known about for centuries. Academics did not have the courage to go against their peers and the Vatican to tell the world of the level of scientific abilities of these "sub-humans"; as the Vatican had labeled them long ago. The Vatican missed this very revealing documentation when they destroyed all writings they could find in the 1500's.

Quotes from *Academia* demonstrate their mindset for ancient American cultures as being extremely low achievers in scientific endeavors: Thompsons' speculations are still given weight by scholars of today. A solid example of "Western Christian Thinking"

Thompson, J. Eric S. [1950]. Maya Hieroglyphic Writing, an Introduction. p. 236

> **"The people of Mesoamerica didn't know about the Copernican nature of the solar system — they had no theoretical understanding of the orbital nature of the heavenly bodies."**
> [Certainly, Brother Pope did not understand when Copernicus explained it, but the Maya had long known of our planetary system.]

The Mayan computations of synodic returns of the planet Venus have been challenged by scientists as being in error. Researchers determined the Maya used a set of mathematical calculations to offset a discrepancy caused by rounding off extended numbers. The offset of the discrepancy reduced the error to one day in six thousand years.

A researcher of the Mayan computations in the Dresden Codex stated;

> **"A 'mathematical subtlety', which scholars have long known about but considered a numerological oddity, serves as a correction for Venus' irregular cycle, which lasts 583.92 days, just like our own Gregorian calendar incorporates leap years."**

If the researchers had realized the Sumerians and the Maya used the same mathematical system, the avenue they should have explored was what caused the error of the Venus computation? Or was it an error at all? It is believed that the Maya rounded off extended mathematical computations because of limited calculation values provided by the Codex. The term *limited* infers the stone tables could not project extended decimal places. The common attitude is that the tablets may have been able to produce numbers into the thousands or millions, but were unable to calculate beyond certain fractions, or decimal points. Therefore, it is believed the Maya rounded off the numbers.

However, the Maya compensated for what appears to be a mathematical error, they created exact stone calendars. Two separate codices have been found that were used as calendars for the returns of the planet Venus. They are the Dresden and Grolier Codices. The Grolier codex is considered to be a perpetual calendar. It is the only perpetual calendar ever produced by ancient Man. The Maya produced many variations of the codex, and in each the mathematical functions have been described as incredible. Simply stated, the Maya produced stone tablets, which functioned as computers, able to program and retrieve mathematical data.

As there is no argument the Maya were brilliant mathematicians, what if there was no mathematical error? It occurred to me that what had not been considered was a secret of Maya astronomy. The secret being the Maya, or more properly the Lords, had expressed their knowledge of an expanding universe.

Our contemporary scientists label this view as the *Big Bang Theory*, which in essence says; the universe is in a slow continual expansion. This knowledge, combined with the amount of time that has passed since the creation of the codex systems, would account for what has been perceived as a mathematical error.

The Maya recognized the increasing distances between stars and when they determined the values of time and distance, at that specific time, they were correct. As the universe continues to expand in each thousandth of a second, the results of the equations also change. This constant expansion is physically depicted in some of the Nazca Desert Lines. One series of lines target the positions of the constellation Orion. Over several hundred years, at least four different lines were constructed to line up with Orion as it set on the horizon.

The expanding universe theory would also explain why the Lords continued to promote astrological observations across the eons of time. This would explain why they were required to have astronomer priests in each civilization as a continuing means to determine the exact date of their rescue. The great distance from their origin, compounded by an expanding universe, would require serious mathematical computations. These computations were necessary to determine exact distance, time and the speed of rescue craft. Is this the end of the unexplored avenue of thought about Maya excellence in math? Not yet.

The Maya produced exceptional scripted books. Three, which survived *the cleansing* of the early Vatican, are the **Books of Chilam Balam**. They are titled "Secrets of the Soothsayer," "Popol Vuh," and "The Annals of the Caqchikel." These three particular books were dictated to, or copied by, a scribe about 550 BCE. The Popol Vuh is extremely interesting reading. It is the Maya story of creation.

**Caracol – Chitzen Itza: Ruins of Mayan observatory
with interior spiral staircase and observation windows**

A considerable number of Maya books deal with mathematics, astronomy, and seasonal necessities. The Maya math system was based on 20 repetitions. As our present system is a base 10, their primary system was a base 20. The Maya possessed a unique mastery of advanced mathematics.

This secret math ingredient is the value Zero [0]. The 0 may not appear significant, but without it there are virtually no advanced math capabilities. Simple algebra, Physics, Quantum Mechanics and on and on could not happen without the 0 concept.

One system of numbers is represented with face and other glyphs which are "keys" to Lords and their personal "God" number. Numbers 0 through 19 are represented on first level. 20 is represented by a dot on the second vertical level.

The vertical system advances from 1s to 20s to 400s [20^2] to 8,000s [20^3] and continues in powers of 20. After the first level maximum number of 19 [3 bars/4 dots] is reached the math extends vertically in powers of 20. To inscribe 20 a dot is used in the second level [20^1; **1x20 = 20**]]; to add3,600 inscribe a bar/4 dots [9] in the third level

[20²; × 9 = 3,600]. The total of this three-tier number is: **19 + 20 + 3,600 = 3,639**.

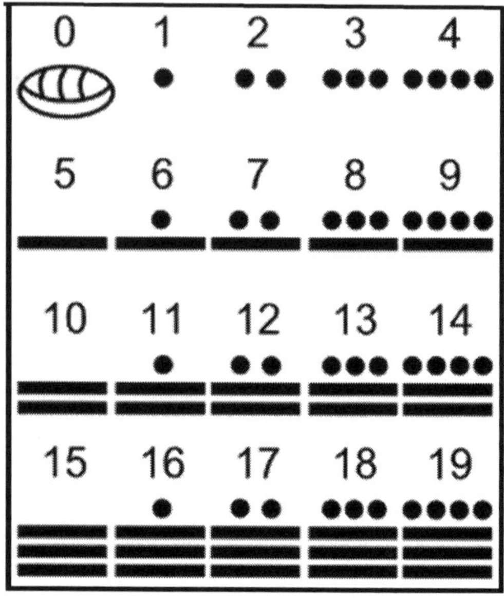

These are First level number representations:
As the levels progress vertically these values are multiplied
by 20²; 20³ and so on.

The Olmec base 20 math system, which the Maya and other cultures used is a vertical system beginning at the bottom. On the 1st level the dot is 1 and the bar is 5. On the 2nd level the dot is 20 and the bar is 100 and continues by 20², 20³ and so on. Zero is represented by a shell glyph. There are also complex systems included with base 18 and base 13. Other complex variations have yet to be fully understood.

The complex system means the glyphs and numbers work both ways when identifying Gods. This is a multiple meaning writing system which can be converted into numbers, or "Keys" for hidden messages. The same type of system was used in the ancient Hebrew alphabet.

Academia claims the Maya were the first civilization to possess the 0 concept. Also implied is that the Sumerians did not have this math concept. How then did the concepts of astronomy, physics and even simple algebra occur with the Sumerians?

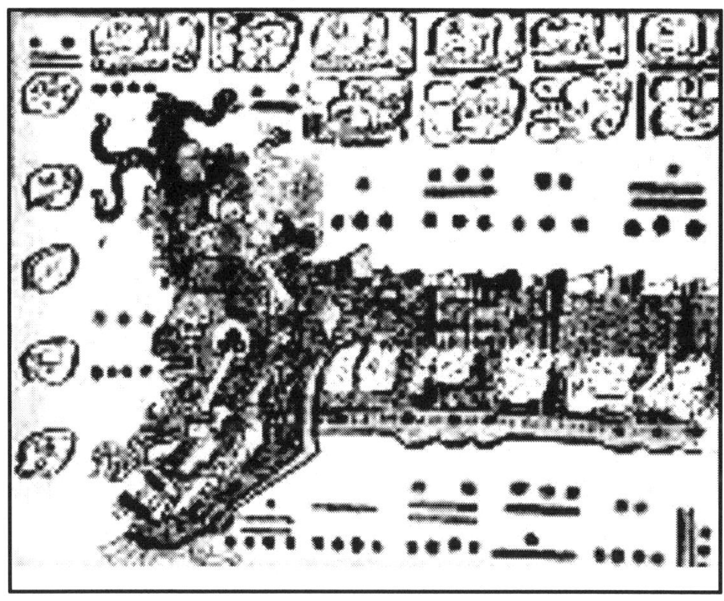

The image [difficult to read] is of a Codex scene with the Mayan number system included. In the lower left, the two dots over four dots represents the number 44 [20 x 2 =40 + 1 x 4 = 44]. Three dots and 1 bar over 1 dot and one bar represents the number 166 [20 x 8 = 160 + 1 x 6 = 166].

The following excerpt is from an article on the Indus Civilization's high level of math and engineering development, and use of the decimal system for calculations:

"Harappan engineers followed the decimal division of measurement for all practical purposes, including the measurement of mass as revealed by their hexahedron weights.
These chert weights were in a ratio of 5:2:1 with weights of 0.05, 0.1, 0.2, 0.5, 1, 2, 5, 10, 20, 50, 100, 200, and 500 units, with each unit weighing...."

The use of the decimal system is explanatory in itself that the [0] zero concept was not only necessary but was widely used in ancient Sumer. Aside from the decimal system, counting and recording numbers using a base 10 system requires the use of the zero placeholder. This is another claim by *Academia*, which is worth 0 [zero]. These are the same academics who can describe an entire civilization, including their religion and sexual orientations, from a single lithic artifact or symbol on a rock.

The Maya were the most advanced theoretical mathematicians on this Earth. They were able to accomplish these advanced calculations using inscribed stone tablets, a codex.

The Maya had several calendars running concurrently. They used a Long Count, 360-day annual calendar, based on eighteen, 20-day units. These were recorded on stone stelae. A round, 365-day calendar and a round 260-day ritual calendar were also used. The round calendars [365 day and 260 day] coincided every 18,980 days, or every fifty-two 365-day years and was celebrated as a major occurrence. The long count days were recorded in descending units of time. The long count of the stelae was counting backwards or counting down. The first unit, the Baktun, recorded units of 144,000 days, or 400, 360-day years. The Baktun, 400 years, represented a revered religious cycle. The next unit, the Katun, recorded units of 7,200 days, or 20 years. The next, the Tun, utilized a base 18 placeholder, the Uinal [18] x the Winal [20] which equals 360 days. The last units were the Winal for 20 days and the Kin for one day. The computations involved base 20 in descending exponential powers and one inserted Uinal [18] multiplier.

The Maya produced calendars which coordinated Earth and Venus solar revolutions. Their variations of days, months, and years are too extensive to even briefly explain. The Mesoamerican culture [all of these interrelated civilizations] was extremely advanced in astronomy and mathematics.

Maya religious writings claim the Earth has been destroyed twice. Their third and current era began in 3114 BCE and they projected time forward to October 4772 CE. The long count calendar stelae, recording this time span, account for 7,886 years, which is one **Piktun** of time. Researchers describe the starting point of August 13, 3114 BCE as a *mythical starting point.* The word mythical defined as, imaginary or fictitious. The word mythical was used to describe something for which no one could find an answer.

Archaeologists clearly state the stelae were used to record *prominent events,* past and future, for the Maya civilization. Most stelae were specifically dedicated to commemorate the history and hierarchical life of the Maya. Archaeologists and historians use the stelae to pinpoint the history, political events and the passage of time of the region. The stelae offered valid historical data, and yet with the Long Count stelae, the term *mythical* is interjected. Which is it going to be, valid historical data or mythical historical data? The determining factor is, of course, the author of the research.

The continuing argument is; why did the Maya go to so much trouble to specifically record explicit historical data and mathematical computations? It is very improbable they would resort to creating a mythical starting point in time for the purpose of counting backwards.

Like all of their other works, there was a specific reason for the Mayan Long Count stelae. The reason was probably not understood by the Maya priests themselves, but the Lords understood. The starting point of the Long Count stela was far from being mythical. For the Lords, it marked the last time their Brother Lords returned with rescue craft.

The Long Count stela began with the year 3114 BCE, and, there is no recorded Maya history for this date because the *Advanced* Mayan civilization did not exist [precursor civilizations did exist]. The Maya Long Count Stela is the most important item of all historical and archaeological traces of the Lords. The Stelae are time-fixed to our current calendar, and to ancient history.

Although the Long Count Stela is correlated with our current calendar, there are several different correlations of the dates proposed. These correlations vary by **260 years or more**. A majority of archaeologists use a correlation that produces a long count beginning date of 3,114 BCE, which is the Goodman - Martinez - Thompson correlation date. The Spinden correlation sets the date at 3,373 BCE. This dissertation on date correlations serves only to point out that no system is perfect. We should not discount historic events because the "dates" appear to be off by a few hundred years.

A very popular media aspect of Maya history is human sacrifice. Most all programs, television, movies, and books dwell on the subject. This completely valid scenario is also clouded investigative archaeologists over the years. There is evidence the continuous sacrifices held an intriguing secret. The historical aspect of human sacrifices is not unusual. Many cults and religions have engaged in such practices.

In Maya culture human sacrifice was used to celebrate religious events, sporting events, festivals, and victorious capture of an enemy in mock battle, losers being sacrificed. Usually these ceremonies were planned in advance and drew huge crowds to watch the mass sacrifice of human life. Many were volunteers, to be presented as gifts to the

Gods. In Maya culture, those sacrificed would immediately join the Sun God in his daily journey across the heavens, living forever as Gods.

Ceremonial sacrifices of prisoners were conducted in much the same manner. All the victims had their hearts cut or torn out as a specific offering to the Gods. Logic tells us, if the Lords were in control of the Maya civilizations, they were also in control of the extraordinary number of people being sacrificed. An unusual medical practice for this time was the Maya and South American priests routinely practiced successful brain surgery. Archaeologists have recovered human skulls with clear evidence of these operations.

The skulls contain areas of healed bone, usually as square cuts or neat circular bores, slightly behind and above the level of the ear. These healed areas in the skulls clearly indicate the patients survived the surgeries. Brain surgery was taught to the Maya priests by the Lords, as were the Egyptian Priests. It is very possible the brain surgeries were connected with some research aspect of the extended life spans of the Lords.

The explanations provided for these surgeries have been *attempts to explain something for which no one really has an answer.* Their statements are that the operations were probably used to relieve headaches or to release *bad spirits.* These backward tribes certainly could not have been practicing advanced medical science.

The idea of living for thousands of years is quite unbelievable. Several authors have approached the subject based on the Sumerian Kings List, or the writings of Genesis as a foundation for evidence of extended life. For the existence of the Lords, even this aspect fell short of a viable, realistic explanation.

The Maya civilization offered the most recent available database to solve this mystery. They were trying to duplicate the effects of a medical process. In this case, they already had knowledge of the results, which was extended life spans. The evidence suggests they either did not understand how to recreate the process or they were searching for a medical alternative, the substitute for a substance they no longer possessed.

There were tens of thousands of victims of the same type of head wound. The wound was a blow to the upper temple area of the head. The resulting hole extends from the temple area to just over the ear. Archaeologists have long noted that the same type of wound in so many victims is very unusual.

The only explanation has been the wounds were the result of extended warfare among the Maya tribes. That explanation is not valid because extensive warfare did not begin until very late in Maya history, after the Lords had vanished and an extended drought began. Like the Sumerian civilization, this type of warfare did not arise until after the Lords had relinquished control and civil authority broke down.

The missing skull fragment revealed the Pituitary gland. It is very small and is located under the brain between the cerebrum and the cerebellum, just forward of the ear canal. The gland contains an Anterior lobe, Posterior lobe, and a stalk that is attached to the brain.

The Pituitary gland is the master endocrine gland controlling several other glands, which secrete a number of hormones and peptides [proteins]. The gland controls the growth of the human body, including the replacement of cells. An overactive Pituitary produces spectacular changes in the production and reproduction of human cells. An enzyme is also produced which acts to accelerate chemical reactions within the human body. Some reaction rates have been estimated to be one billion times faster than the normal rate of living cell production.

The result of this is speculation that the Lords were attempting to create an anabolic-androgenic steroid derivative from the chemicals contained in, or produced by, the Pituitary Gland. In plain words, they were searching for a chemical substance that would stop the aging process.

The skull wounds were an essential part of the experiment. The Lords crushed the skulls in a specific manner as step one in the experimental process to harvest the enzymes produced by the gland. Next, the operations on the brain of living persons were experiments in which these chemicals were introduced to the Pituitary gland to control the aging process. There is strong evidence, in the form of royal burials of Lords in the Maya regions and in Peru, that they were not totally successful.

Scientists have discovered a primary Pituitary gland enzyme named Telomerase, which allows for cell reproduction without mutations or aberrant growth. One application of these enzymes is an attempt to combat cancer.

A very recent medical research group reported their study on life spans of humans. The possible life span can be projected with some certainty by the length of the Telomerase protein chain in one's cell structure. This can be measured at an early age and a longer chain of Telomerase indicates a longer possible life span. Cellular Telomerase chains reduce in length throughout a person's life after reaching maturity. An interesting find!

We have entered an era of scientific manipulation of DNA structures, supposedly with the ability to remove detrimental protein chains and implant beneficial protein chains. Could be that in the next 100 years we could harvest new "Gods", a really great step in the evolution of "Man".

Pyramid of the Sun and Plaza Ziggurats

TEOTIHUACAN
BIRTHPLACE OF THE GODS

The city of Teotihuacan emerged in an area known as the Valley of Mexico. Some historians and archaeologists refer to the civilization that occupied the Valley of Mexico and Teotihuacan as the Teotihuacanian Civilization. I believe the correct and proper term is the Mexican Civilization.

Teotihuacan is the birthplace of the modern Mexican civilization, with roots to all of the past civilizations that ruled there. Teotihuacan translates as "Birthplace of the Gods". This name is important as historians would have you believe the rulers of this great metropolis came to be after it was a city. It is not logical to give a name which indicates original habitation to Gods who arrived after the city was established.

The Maya name for this city was Puh, as recorded with hieroglyphs. It meant "Place of reeds". The area was a collection of lakes and swamps at an elevation of 7,500 feet. The entire area was laid out in grid fashion, for construction of the farms and the city.

Channels were dug along grid lines with the rich muck filling raised farming plots. The result was a great agriculture area which could be travelled by canoes. With the raised bed feature the crops were spared killing frosts and freeze periods. This same grid process was used in Bolivia at much higher altitudes, and in Eridu, built in the marshlands of the Euphrates River.

The city expanded around the pyramids, temples and marketplaces along The Avenue of The Dead. The city was made up of about 30 ethnic communities for all different tribal systems. These contained workshops for artists and metalworkers, and apartment complexes with up to 80 family sized apartments. Housing areas for the elite classes were separate from the industrial and tribal areas. At its peak the city had about 250,000 residents and spread over 12 square miles.

Near the Citadel are grand temple-like apartment complexes for an elite group of individuals. Outward from the royal apartment complexes is the "urban area" and covers approximately eight square miles. This area housed high ranking public officials, the city administrators and the more important shops and small factories. Spreading outward from the urban area for approximately twelve miles were thousands of apartment complexes and numerous workshops. These housing and factory complexes reflected the tribal and cultural status of the individuals who lived there.

The ethnic neighborhoods contained hundreds of shops that produced figurines, pottery, jewelry, and numerous other items for trade. The shops producing obsidian knives, blades, ax heads, arrow and spearheads served millions of customers. Each tribe constructed their homes in the traditional manner of their homeland. From this construction archaeologists have determined the origin of the workers in each neighborhood. The city continued to spread outward from the urban area.

Beginning about twenty miles from the city center, a residential settlement area stretched for an additional sixty miles. The greater the distance from the city, the smaller the settlements became and the agricultural fields became larger.

What has been described is a web with its center at Teotihuacan. Beyond the eighty-mile radius are *corridors of settlements*. The corridors extend out of the Basin of Mexico along established trade routes. One corridor ran southeast, past the Pyramid of Cholula, to the Gulf Coast. Other corridors ran south to the Maya region and southwest to the Pacific Ocean. The corridors provided an aerial view of the outer strands of the giant web.

The Lords used the city as the focal point of religious and political power. The Olmec civilization evolved on the premise of religious authority and that concept was passed on to the Mexican and the Maya civilizations. The city kings of all tribes held the same position as the Prophets of Sumer; they relayed God's instructions to the citizens.

This element of the Lords' complete power over all regions has generally been overlooked. It provides the most important and significant evidence that these regions were under the control of one political force. It was a vast Theocracy exceeding the Theocracies of the Fertile Crescent.

The statement that entire regions, including South America, Mexico and the land of the Maya, were under the control of one Theocracy is in direct contradiction to established historic norms. Present day historians insist that each region was independent with distinct languages, although interdependent regarding trade.

The fact of having many distinct languages in a given area is somehow presented as an impediment to cultural exchanges. Maybe these tribes were multi-lingual; they most likely were, as with other ancient cultures speaking multiple languages. Another *Academia* "Western Thinking" idea shot down.

In the North, all trade routes led to the city of Teotihuacan, the center of all commerce and power. The influence of Teotihuacan reached far to the North. The Cerrillos area of New Mexico, south of Santa Fe, produced Turquoise from its mines for trade with Teotihuacan. The items of wealth were dependent on supply and demand. At times, colorful bird feathers were more precious than gold. The feathers were used to enhance the splendor of costumes used in ceremonial rituals. The common people prized colorful feathers for decoration when attending festivals and ceremonies. Along with feathers, salt, pottery and jade were prized trade items for obsidian, used for making knives, tools, and weapons.

Another trading outpost was in southern Arizona near Phoenix. The Hohokam Civilization thrived with massive irrigated agricultural areas and trade goods. Crops and trade goods were transported in semi-finished and raw form to the craftsmen in Teotihuacan who fashioned finished items.

Land and sea trade routes were established to move goods throughout the entire region and into neighboring areas. A Gulf of Mexico sea route extended from the northern Mexican coast south around the Yucatan peninsula, and on to Panama and Columbia. The northern Gulf route connected with the early Cahokia Culture in the Mississippi floodway. A Pacific Ocean route served the West Coast of Mexico and extended to South America. The sea routes were connected to inland routes which completed the trade networks for North, Central and South America.

In Teotihuacan a pyramid, named The Pyramid of The Plumed Serpent, stands near the Pyramid of The Sun and the Pyramid of the Moon. These pyramids provide an important tie with Egyptian civilization. The center of power at the Giza Plateau and its counterpart at Teotihuacan had three massive Pyramids. At each location the largest was "The Pyramid of The Sun," the second in size was "The Pyramid of The Moon," and the third was dedicated to the local "Living God."

Archaeologists state that Teotihuacan emerged in 100 BCE and the Pyramid of the Sun was completed by 100 CE. They also state "*The early history of Teotihuacan is quite mysterious, and the origin of its founders is uncertain."*

That would be very remarkable construction for the world's third largest city, pyramid and civilization. There was monumental building during those dates, but it was in addition to the existing framework. There is evidence The Pyramid of The Sun was enlarged over a smaller pyramid, as yet dated to its origin. Building larger pyramids over smaller pyramids was common practice in Egypt and in The Americas.

This is a bit out of sequence, but very compelling. The Pyramid of the Sun at Teotihuacan is the third largest remaining pyramid. The Pyramid of the Sun at Giza is the second largest remaining pyramid. The largest remaining pyramid is about 80 miles southeast of Teotihuacan, located at Cholula.

The Pyramid of Cholula is the largest remaining pyramid and monument known to be built in the world. It was built as a palace for the God Itzama. Construction began about 500 BCE and continued until Teotihuacan collapsed about 850 CE. The entire structure was covered with earth and abandoned. Today the pyramid complex appears to be a wooded hill with a Catholic Church on top of it. The Vatican always hijacked places sacred to local populations and constructed their churches on these sites.

The structure is about 1,500 feet square and 220 feet high, with a total volume of material of 5.9 million cubic yards. Although higher, at 455 feet, the pyramid at Giza contains about 3.3 million cubic yards of material. This pyramid and temple have been looted by "archaeologists" over the centuries, as others were, and damaged by highway construction.

I find it amazing that the largest ancient pyramid receives so little attention compared to other ancient sites. Of course, the "Church" has the site well controlled. The original native language name for the site translates as "Place of refuge for the Gods".

The Aztec relayed a fantastic history for The Great Pyramid of Cholula to Catholic Priests. The Aztec believed one of their seven mythical giant founders, named Xelhua, built the pyramid.

The Great Pyramid of Cholula Legend:

The legend continues; 4,800 years after the world was created the land was home to giants. A great flood enveloped the world and killed all of the giants except for seven who sought refuge on a sacred mountain in paradise. After the disaster Xelhua, also called "The Architect", built the pyramid as a refuge for the seven giants.

The pyramid was being built so high it was reaching the heavens and the Gods became enraged that anyone would dare try to reach them. They showered the construction with fire, killing all of the workers and destroying the pyramid. It was then dedicated to Quetzalcoatl.

There is much more to the legend but several things piqued my interest. They are: The Parallels of this legend to The Flood, destruction of The Tower of Ba'Bel, The Seven Gods of Old [worshipped by the Hebrews, Babylon and the Priests of On], the Great Architect of The Universe, and the reference to 12 cycles of the Maya Baktun, the 400-year cycle, equaling 4,800 years. If you go back in time about 800 years from the time this legend was told you would be at the time of the Rescue of The Lords. It would also be the end of a Baktun and the imagined travel time for rescue craft. Just a few things for your personal mind games.

An Artist's rendering of The Great Cholula Pyramid and Palace from details of early explorations and modern seismic and ground penetrating radar. "The Refuge of The Gods" is the name given in legends.

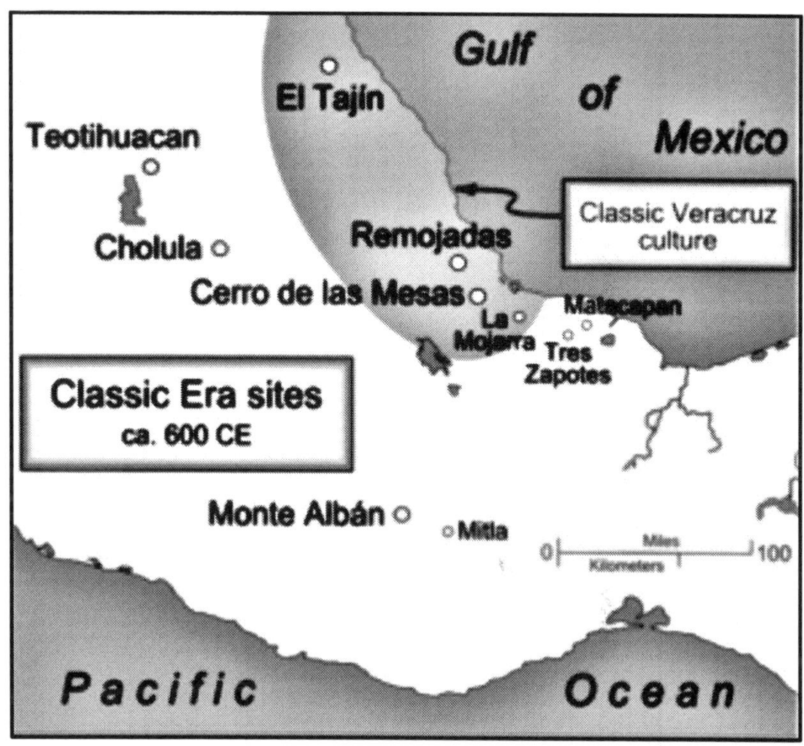
Gulf of Mexico
El Tajín
Teotihuacan
Cholula
Remojadas
Classic Veracruz culture
Cerro de las Mesas
La Mojarra
Matacapan
Tres Zapotes
Classic Era sites
ca. 600 CE
Monte Albán
Mitla
Miles
Kilometers
0
100
Pacific Ocean

El Tajin Pyramid in northern Veracruz
['Tajin" is derived from "Twelve old men who were Lords" from Teotihuacan]

RELIGIONS OF THE AMERICAS

Lord Bal would not repeat the mistake of creating a society which possessed complete knowledge of the principle arts and sciences. The Lords would, however, use previous methods of initiating and mentally preparing new followers to obey their Gods without question. This time the priests only possessed sufficient knowledge and powers to facilitate the culmination of the rescue of the Lords.

The Lords did establish a knowledgeable society of Shamen and priests inculcated with the knowledge of the universe, mathematics and medicine. This would be on the level of Shaman who occupied Lord Bal's site of Gobekli Tepe. With few exceptions their knowledge of metals would be limited to the noble metals to increase the Lords' treasure houses.

In the Americas a trinity of Gods was worshipped from Teotihuacan. Itzama [many other names] was the Creator, or Sun God, and the Virgin Blood Moon Goddess Awilix [sometimes called the Great Snake Goddess, or the Spider Goddess], with their offspring as the third and Savior God called Kukulkan. He was best known as the "Feathered Serpent", the night flying destroyer God. He was also known as Jacawitz, the Mountain God and later Quetzalcoatl by the much later Aztec civilization. This basic assemblage of triune Gods will be found throughout the Americas, with the addition of many lesser, or personal Gods.

One of the Teotihuacan **Tajin** [derived from "Twelve old men who were Lords"] names translate as "Hummingbird" and this branch of Gods is honored with hummingbird symbols in the Nazca Desert. The Pyramid **El Tajin** is an extremely unique structure located on the Gulf Coast north of San Lorenzo.

El Tajin Pyramid [Pyramid of the Niches] construction was completed in the 700s CE with six stepped platforms, sixty-five feet high and eighty-five feet square, with placed [poured] **concrete** roofs. Construction of El Tajin began about 500 CE with several stepped pyramids and ball courts.

The Pyramid of the Niches was constructed with 365 niches (possibly one for each day of the calendar year). Each niche measured about 24 inches square. The complex contains many ball courts and was the site of human sacrifice.

The El Tajin complex was a major religious and trade hub for Teotihuacan with corn, vanilla, cocoa and tobacco as the primary trade items.

The El Tajin Complex was destroyed and burned about 1100 CE, coinciding with the same destruction of the Toltec capital city of Tollan when the last Lord died.

The reference to the Maya using concrete in 600 CE is not widely proclaimed, the same as their advanced metallurgy. The Greeks produced a cementitious material about 600 BCE, but the Romans successfully used concrete for structures in 200 BCE. This knowledge somehow made it to Central America by 500 CE. I suspect the use of cementitious materials, such as volcanic ash, occurred much earlier in the use of plaster.

The *Great [Snake or Spider] Goddess of Teotihuacan* was the lead deity of the city. The vast grotto beneath the Pyramid of the Sun was first thought to be a natural cave. Recent investigations show it was excavated. The Great Goddess held underground religious ceremonies for initiates and followers, identical to the ceremonies of the Minoan "Butterfly Goddess" and later Roman Empire Mitra Ceremonies.

The Lords were fallible Gods and left distinct evidence of their existence.   The example of the butterfly tying two civilizations together was a conscious act of the Lords' ego. I believe this next example was a subconscious act, of depraved authority. Lord Yahweh required his people, the Israelites, to shed genital blood of newborn males as a sacrament to God. This was required of any male joining the Hebrews.   This was performed on the male population by circumcision of the penis foreskin.

In the Americas, the Lords required the Maya High Priests to perform ritual genital bloodletting by cutting the penis foreskin and collecting the blood for a burnt offering to the Gods. This was also performed on young boys of about 4 years old. What are the odds of two distinct civilizations, on different continents, performing this similar religious blood ritual?

The liquid metal Mercury appears to have a unique place in Mayan religious ceremonies. Mercury was found in chambers beneath several pyramids.   There is evidence in Teotihuacan that mercury was produced by heating red cinnabar ore. Natural occurring mercury is found in several areas of Central America.

An interesting observation about pyramids and mercury comes from the Qin Dynasty in China about 250 BCE. A flat-topped pyramid of earth covers his burial chamber. The chamber includes apartments for officials and a flowing river of mercury simulating the Yalu River. His wives were killed and placed in his tomb, along with a myriad of needed items for comfort in the afterlife. The tomb ceiling was painted with a celestial scheme of stars. These burial customs are very similar around the world during this time.

Constant contact was kept between the Central American and the South American Lords and the influence is openly exhibited by all of the societies in religion and architecture. While the trade flourished in the North, providing great wealth, South American civilizations had a very different purpose. Their mission was to construct visible markers to attract the returning rescue craft.

heic1007a Mystic Mountain - Carina Nebula
Hubble photo

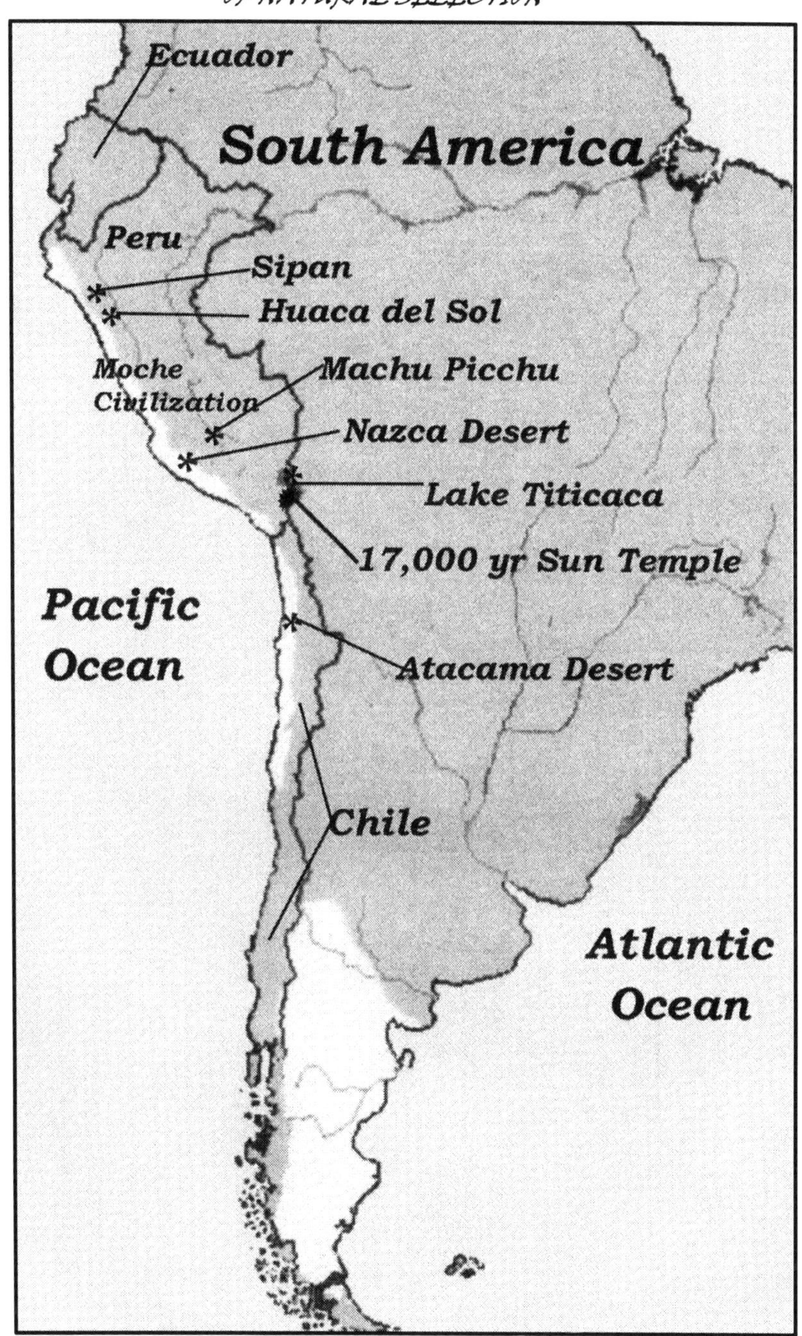
Ecuador
South America
Peru
Sipan
Huaca del Sol
Moche
Civilization
Machu Picchu
Nazca Desert
Lake Titicaca
17,000 yr Sun Temple
Pacific
Ocean
Atacama Desert
Chile
Atlantic
Ocean

This is the only six-winged Nazca Hummingbird I have found in all of my research [Nat. Geographic - May 1975] I have been unable to find this again online. It is the only geoglyph to show an ultralight aircraft within the geoglyph. This is a special glyph for one of the Tajin "Hummingbird" Lords from Teotihuacan.

Chapter

4

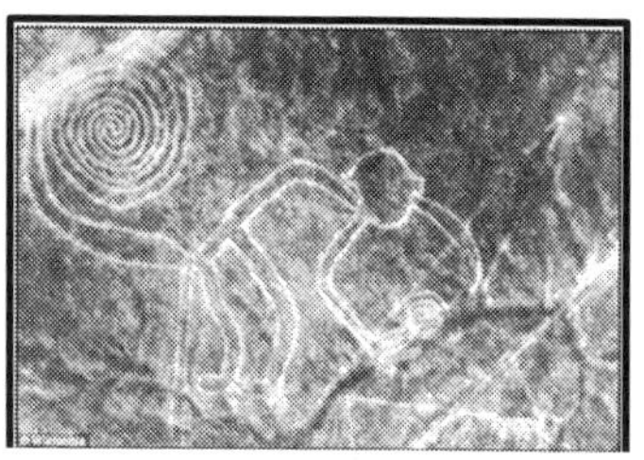

RESCUE OF THE LORDS
Tiwanakuan and Wari [Huari]

The lords developed and expanded two major religious centers to control the South American development. The Tiwanaku Empire located in present-day Bolivia, on the shoreline of Lake Titicaca, was the most powerful and controlled the southern areas, mainly the Nazca Civilization and construction of the Nazca symbols.

Tiwanaku is the site of the 17,000 BCE Sun temple. It is referred to as the center of a pre-Inca civilization. Academia refuses to acknowledge the previous civilization at this site, claiming it all began about 1,500 BCE and collapsed around 1150 CE.

By 2,500 BCE Tiwanaku and adjacent Puma Punku were re-occupied by Lords and craftsmen from The Chavin Civilization. The Sun Temple was rehabilitated and it became the center of power for the Gods.

The Tiwanakuans developed about 50 square miles of raised bed agriculture, gridded with canals, identical to those of Teotihuacan. By 1,000 BCE This site supported over 1,500,000 people with trade routes extending to the Peruvian coastline. They also wielded the religious power of South America as ambassadors of the Feathered [War] Serpent. They refurbished the ancient Sun Temple site and added new structures.

Their religious activities centered on subterranean grotto ceremonies with a "Moon Goddess" in charge. The balance of the Gods mirrored those of Teotihuacan.

In 500 CE priests of the Sun Temple sent a large group north of Tiwanaku to establish the Wari [Huari] Empire. The purpose of this empire was to control the Moche Civilization of the northern regions of Peru and Ecuador. The several Moche regions functioned the same as the individual districts of the Maya. The Wari were based in Huari Peru and built a Palace complex, temples and apartments for visiting Lords at Cerro Baul.

Cerro Baul is a mesa towering almost 2,000 feet above the valley. This was the home to a Mountain God and the destination for pilgrims bringing offerings to the God.

The Nazca Civilization to the south was controlled from Tiwanaku. The separation of the Moche and Nazca Civilizations was to insure they did not deviate from their assigned tasks. With direct oversight from the Lords the rescue plan was staying on schedule. The reconstituted Tiwanaku and satellite Wari Empires oversaw the Moche and Nazca Civilizations to about 800 CE.

The leadership of The Lords preferred to live in high altitudes, with remote Palaces whenever possible. It seems to have been in their nature to avoid the masses when they could and they appear to have been more acclimated to living in higher altitudes.

Everything the Lords constructed was to ensure their rescue. They built observatories to track time and stars and specifically designed their construction to create images the returning rescue groups would recognize. The Lords knew their rescuers would soon fly in to find them, and any signs of the Lords' existence had to be seen from the air. It was necessary for the construction to be massive and recognizable.

To attract the attention of rescue craft, an isolated area geared for new construction was necessary. South and Central America offered the solution to all their problems. In comparison to other landmasses, it is relatively small. The distance from the Atlantic to the Pacific Ocean offered the best possible landmass for overall visual recognition of surface construction.

THE MOCHE CIVILIZATION
[0 – 800 CE]

From about 0 – 800 CE this coastal region of Peru and Chile was home to two distinct cultures. They were the Moche of the northern coast and the Nazca of the southern coast. The Moche of Peru consisted of five Moche "bands" beginning in the north with The Moche of Piura [inland], the Northern Moche, the Moche of Lambayeque, the Moche of Jequetepeque and the Southern Moche. In the same region, but inland, were the Recuay of the northern highlands, and the Huarpa of the south-central highlands.

Precursor civilizations were established at these sites by 2,500 BCE. The various coastal cultures interacted over the millennia, from 8,000 BCE, as they advanced in size and political power.

Along the coastal areas of the Moche there were smaller religious/administrative centers in each of the larger valleys. The following information should begin to sound very familiar. Archaeologists and historians have noted that tremendous wealth and power was concentrated in the hand of a few individuals. The mysterious authority figures lived a life of royal opulence. They were attended by a large group of priests who ranked as a sect of nobility. Each valley had one or more royal residential complexes, or palaces.

The living standards of the ruling Moche authority have been compared to the Kings of Europe. This is degrading to the Moche because the Kings of Europe lived in deplorable conditions of no hygiene and rampant disease outbreaks. As with the Maya, the status of Moche royalty was recognized by their religious insignia. These High Priests had the power of life or death over the general population. The Moche cultivated over one hundred thousand acres of food crops, which was very excessive for their needs. The excess food supply allowed massive labor forces to complete construction projects in other regions.

Although there were at least four distinct cultures controlled by the Lords, all of the cultural phases were basically the same. The Moche civilization should provide enough information to substantiate the existence of the influence of the Lords.

Only in recent years have the Moche become of interest because of the early intense popularity of the Maya region. The Moche civilization occupied an area of the Peruvian coastal region approximately two hundred and fifty miles long. The locations were along the valleys from Lambayeque to Nepena. Their settlements extended inland, usually no more than fifty miles.   In this area, the Lords built religious administrative centers complete with royal courts and pyramids.

The construction techniques used to build the centers are basically the same as used in Mexico and Central America. The primary difference of the architecture being, the construction was not built to last. The primary building material was sun baked mud bricks, which when compared to stone, deteriorate at a much faster rate. The erosion of the mud bricks held off the popularity of the area. Had the Lords used stone, the popularity of the area would have been the same as that of the Maya.

This is one secret the region has kept through the years; the structures were meant to deteriorate. The evidence for this can be found in the region itself. There was an abundant supply of labor sufficient to bring stone into the area. Also, there would be no jungle growth to cover these buildings and pyramids. They would simply appear as normal desert mounds centuries later.

A Moche site located in the Lambayeque Valley, known today as Pampa Grande, contained an urban center with a population of approximately ten thousand.   The religious center was complete with several pyramids. A second Moche site, Huaca Del Sol, is located in the Moche River Valley. The area is located about 350 miles north of the present-day city of Lima. The nearest town to the site is Trujillo.

The pyramids in Mexico and Peru are directly related to those of the Giza plateau. The design of the pyramids would have been easily identified. The secret of the pyramids is the design would be familiar to the returning rescuers. It was a structure they had seen before. The design provided conclusive evidence the Lords had survived in the area. The pyramid structure was not built to provide a message for future generations of native Man. It was produced as a tool for rescue. The pyramids of Central and South America were used as directional flight path markers and as stellar observatories. The directional markers would lead the rescue craft to the final location.

Another feature of many Moche Temple sites was the construction of very large "Temple Mounds", which were surface finished with giant figures of various animals and mystical god figures. These features were completed using colorful paints, tiles and other bright materials.

Again, these gigantic features were not discovered by ground surveys; they only came into recognizable features when viewed from the sky.

The Lords always implemented backup plans for being located. One certain plan was the construction of a pyramid with a base six times larger than the Great Pyramid of Egypt. The pyramid is known as El Tigre. It is located in northern Guatemala at the Maya site, El Mirador. Today El Tigre Pyramid appears as a forested hill from an aerial view.

Huaca Del Sol contains a pyramid almost as large as the Great Pyramid of Giza. The massive structure covers an area of twelve and a half acres with a height of 135 feet. The pyramid contains more than 140 million mud bricks and is estimated to contain about four million tons of material. The name Huaca Del Sol means Pyramid of the Sun. Across a nearby plain is another pyramid, somewhat smaller, named the Pyramid of the Moon. The third and smallest is the tomb of an exalted ruler.

All of the pyramids located in Egypt were built on a precise north-south alignment. Some of the pyramids of Mexico, Central America and South America were sited to a precise north-south alignment. However, most were sited a few degrees off of north to provide specific orientations for star systems, and to mark the vertical passing of the Sun. There are other pyramids in this region as the Moche built a string of at least eighteen pyramids along the coastal area, and probably more.

The purpose of using this site as an example is to illustrate the massive construction and the use of labor forces for this site alone. The Moche are not known for the use of advanced mathematics or the study of astronomy. This leads us to the question of, what was the purpose of such a massive structure? The answer to the question lies in what was not present. There were no massive fortifications and no standing army. It appears there were no worries of being invaded from other regions or from the sea.

This leaves two distinct possibilities for the massive structures. First, the Lords used these structures to illustrate dominance over the land. The common people of the region viewed such construction as a clear visual picture of the power of the Gods who ruled them. Second, the structure was built for the same reason as all other massive construction. It was meant to be seen from the air, as aerial markers for the rescue craft.

Moche history provides many intriguing mysteries. One of these mysteries occurred along the coast of the Casma Valley, at about the middle of Peru. The site is Sechen Alto, a pyramid with a base larger than the Pyramid of the Sun, along with ceremonial centers. The site appeared as a giant mud hill, with evidence of continuous occupation and construction dated to 3,500 BCE.

Sechen Alto was originally constructed as a ziggurat with a base of about 1000 feet by 820 feet. Over 60 million stones were cut to construct the base of this "pyramid," and then an unusual finish was added to this base. The top of Sechen Alto was completed with hand formed adobe cones. Finger marks are captured in the dried adobe. The local inhabitants were later summarily sacrificially butchered after losing a brief battle to invaders.

Archaeologists are in a quandary as how to explain the mixed construction of the pyramid and the massacre of the local inhabitants. The academic storyline is the local people built a pyramid, starting with stone. They ran out of stone and finished the structure with adobe cones. An invading army, led by religious priests, entered their area and captured the local people after a brief war. The conquering army and priests sacrificed the losers to a Sun God, or "Weather" God.

This is what I believe to be the true story of Sechen Alto. It fits all previous history, and the evidence of this explanation has been excavated at the site. The quarried stone "base" [a ziggurat] of Sechen Alto was constructed by 1,000 BCE. The top was constructed about 200 CE. Sometime after the completion of the "Pyramid", an army led by Priests from Teotihuacan arrived at the site and slaughtered the inhabitants of Sechen Alto.

Sechen Alto was huge, the oblong stone structure, some 1000 feet by 820 feet, with sloped sides and flat-topped, stood as the largest ziggurat in South America. It was an integral part of the visual display, meant to be viewed by returning aircraft. The Lords of Teotihuacan had commissioned this construction, as with all other major centers. At some point after completion of the ziggurat the Priests and workers departed, leaving behind a contingent to maintain the area. After several generations of isolation from the Lords, the local priests encouraged the people to "complete" the pyramid. This would bring certain favor from the Gods.

When Teotihuacan learned of the desecration of the ziggurat, they sent an army to remedy the problem of independent thought and construction. The local priests and their families were sacrificed. Their flesh was flayed and stripped from their bodies, and the intact skeletal remains were made to dance on puppet strings for the remaining population.

With all remaining inhabitants watching, the priests from Teotihuacan drank their blood and ate their flesh, sending an unmistakable message to anyone who might think of desecrating another site.

The proof that the conquering priests were from Teotihuacan was what was found at the ceremonial center. Frescoes depict combinations of Jaguar and Feathered Serpent Gods on the entrances to the center. Mummified corpses had jaguar tattoos, and the stelae are of unmistakable Maya influence.

MOCHE RELIGION

The Moche religious ceremonies were led by a High Priestess, attended by several priestesses. Once again, the religion is of a trinity of Gods. The trinity is composed of the Creator God or Mountain God, *Al Paec*, The Moon Goddess *Si* [a virgin], and their Son, The Sun God. There are several lesser Gods in the ceremonies.

Archaeologists go to great lengths to distance the Moche from Teotihuacan influence, insisting on independent growth of the civilization. The jewelry mirrors Maya glyphs, the Gods are portrayed with snake ornaments, and one God is of a half man/half jaguar. This God is referred to as a spotted cat. The Decapitator God is said to have feline features rather than jaguar features. There is no doubt the Moche were led by Lords from Central America.

The God Al Paec is always depicted with a jaguar headdress and snake earrings. The Moon Goddess officiates over the human sacrifices where the elite drink their blood and eat their flesh. A giant Spider God flays, dismembers and mutilates his victims. This God is the ultimate in power and fear, eating the flesh and drinking the blood of victims.

Sex was openly displayed in art and ceramics, and prisoners were subjected to about anything you can imagine in the way of intercourse.

These religious and open orgy lifestyles, with human sacrifice are the same as practiced in Babylon under the leadership of the Lords. All aspects of this culture combined with a Sun God, Virgin Moon Goddess and Son of the two as a War God is not a coincidence or "independent growth" of cultures.

The Moche civilization had a distinct class system. Priests and warriors were highest and were obeyed immediately. Next were the Royalty and their families, followed by artists and then the laborers.

An unusual pictograph in the Nazca desert is a giant spider. The pattern is out of character with the other pictographs, and there have been few attempts to decipher and understand its symbolic meaning. The significance of the spider came from Moche burials of political and religious authorities. These burials indicate the Lords were beginning to age and die.

An ancient royal Moche tomb was discovered near Sipan, Peru. The Sipan occupation was prominent from 100 BCE to 700 CE. Archaeologists named the buried Lord the Old Lord of Sipan. The status of Old Lord is established by the immense wealth of gold found in the tomb.

Old Lord was buried with a gorgeous necklace of ten golden spiders. Each spider is sitting on a golden web and on the back of each spider is the likeness of a human face; each face is of a different person. The spider played a part in Moche religion as the great devourer, so the necklace is a sign of the High Lord of the Moche. It held a special meaning for the person who wore the necklace, showing the faces of his counterparts as wrinkled, glum looking, old men. These representations of old men are undoubtedly referring to the Tajin of Teotihuacan ["12 old men who are Lords"] who all were referred to by a "Hummingbird" reference. This is speculation; I believe this reference was due to the aircraft they used for travel.

A Lord took the faces of ten other dead friends with him to the grave on the necklace. The aging process must have affected each Lord differently. It appears some were dying well ahead of others. The symbolism recorded in the necklace is quite interesting. The spiders and the webs are symbolic of builders and this was the symbol for "The Great Goddess of Teotihuacan. The faces on the backs of the spiders are symbolic messages that the men, to whom the faces belonged, were objects of Teotihuacan religions and were Lords.

The Old Lord of Sipan was The Spider of Sipan, and his sign was permanently etched in the desert. Some Sipan legends relate stories of a tall white God who was kind to his followers and performed healing miracles in the villages around Sipan.

I have always thought the giant desert symbols were "call signs" for different Lords, possibly another "key" type of message. I think my speculation is allowed given all the speculation from *Academia*.

THE NAZCA CIVILIZATION
[100 BCE - 800 CE]

The Nazca Civilization evolved from the Paracas civilization [800 BCE -200 CE] after new leadership arrived.

As the Moche constructed in the North, the Nazca constructed in the South. One of the great mysteries of modern Man is the Ancient Nazca Lines. With the construction of the irrigation systems, the agriculture and cities provided for the needs of massive labor forces. Bringing water to the Nazca cities was as much of a problem as the Moche encountered in the northern deserts.

One of the water projects in the Nazca area is also an engineering marvel. This system began by tunneling into the mountains until an aquifer was located. They next tunneled an underground aqueduct system with access points to retrieve the water. These aqueducts are known as *puquios* and remain in use for current residents. The underground system is ingenious in that it limits water loss due to desert evaporation.

An original puquios access site in use today shows continued maintenance. Some researchers are trying to find meaning or purpose for the spiral design. They are confounded by this structure but have financial grants to eventually solve the mystery. I don't think I need to insult you by telling you the reason for the spiral design. *Academia* remains amazing!

The water systems in this area are now being compared to the identical system developed in the Sumerian civilization. Underground aqueducts are still in use in the Middle East. Yet, except for time and location, the Peruvian system is a duplication of Sumerian history. The next interesting factor regarding this great civilization built on agriculture is the source of the food crops.

A well-maintained Nazca puquios with spiral access to the aqueduct

Archaeologists have specifically stated there were no indigenous food crops in this desert area. Yet, advanced civilizations existed to the north, along the coast, which grew a great variety of crops. The Valdivia and other civilizations used advanced agriculture and building methods. I finally found a very short statement that simply said the issue was *hotly debated* about the existence of corn and other varied crops.

Most reports will state the native people of Peru cultivated maize. Maize is the accepted word used by persons of a higher intellectual plane. Remember the famous words, "*read my lips*", the Civilizations of Peru did not cultivate maize, they cultivated corn.

Maize is a form grain, still grown today. Early corn cobs were about the size of a small adult finger. The Peruvians of the coastal desert grew corn, because there was no maize. The reason the source of the food crops is hotly debated is that the corn could not have evolved from maize in this entire area. Maize does not grow in the higher elevations of Peru, and there were no indigenous crops in the desert. Academics use the terminology of maize to infer a biological evolution to modern corn. It did not happen.

The mystery of the Nazca Lines begins in an arid desert region inland from the southern coast of Peru. The area lies primarily between the towns of Nazca and Palpa. Both towns are south and inland from the Peruvian coastal town of Paracas. Between the towns of Nazca and Palpa are thousands of square miles of arid plateaus and desert. The ancient Nazca people created numerous giant geoglyphs that can only be fully recognized from the air.

Many of the figures etched into the desert surface appear to be geometrical quadrangles, triangles, and trapezoids. Other figures are of a whale, spiders, monkeys and hummingbirds. On a hillside overlooking the pictographs is the giant figure of a man. One arm of the figure points skyward, while the other arm points downward to the Earth. Covering most of this desert is a series of straight lines that run for miles without known purpose or meaning. It is possible the lines mark rising stars.

Millions of tons of stone and desert rubble had to be moved to create the landscape pictographs. The massive labor force that was involved had to be fed and watered. There has been widespread controversy regarding what motivated the Nazca people to spend so many years creating this aerial mural. And the most interesting aspect being, *it was a creation they could never see completely* from the ground. One researcher stated the geoglyphs were constructed so their Gods could see them. This was correct. There are legends the "Mountain God" flew at night, surveying his realm.

There have been many proposed answers to the Nazca lines and art. The most interesting speculation was some of the markings might have been used as airfields for spacecraft. Also, that such aircraft had used the area during the Neolithic Period. The reason for this speculation is that the geometrical lines of quadrangles, triangles, and trapezoids are overlain creating what appears as two or more perfect airports. The airports are complete with takeoff and landing runways. They are images only and were never used for aircraft landings, or takeoffs.

Maria Reiche [1903-1998], a German mathematician, spent half a century charting the Nazca lines and attempting to solve the mystery of their meaning. She was very successful in the detailed charting, but unsuccessful in solving the mystery. One popular article regarding her research stated that she scorns the suggestions that the Nazca lines may have been airfields for outer space visitors. She further stated that once you remove the stones, the ground is too soft to support any type of aircraft. Her last comment was, "I'm afraid the spacemen would have gotten stuck." And, she was absolutely correct. What was not correct was the prevailing attitude.

The published statement, *"I'm afraid the spacemen would have gotten stuck,"* ended all speculation that could have led to a more productive investigation. The conversation was meant to be counter-productive. The use of the word spacemen immediately shifted the conversation into the realm of science fiction. Once that occurs, all further meaningful speculation is useless. Her attitude was, the Nazca lines could not have been used to alert intelligent humans from across the universe. That attitude was incorrect.

The amateur archaeologist's original profession was that of a mathematician. Her work in archaeology consisted of charting the lines and geoglyphs in the Nazca desert in an attempt to mathematically solve the mystery. Although she spent more than fifty years in the area, she never developed a plausible explanation for the Nazca lines and symbols. Her conclusion, which was drawn from her attitude – as evidenced by the fact that her conclusion was a non-explanation, was accepted in some pseudo intellectual circles as an authority.

Her situation in Peru is more interesting. She was born in 1903 in Dresden, Germany. At the age of eighteen she enrolled in Hamburg University and excelled in mathematics. In 1932 she immigrated to Peru and obtained a job as a teacher. She also held a secondary job of translating scientific papers in the capital city of Lima. At the end of World War II, in 1945, she suddenly quit her jobs and moved to the region of Nazca.

Not only did she chart the Nazca desert, she also traveled the coastal area of Peru. In these travels, she measured and mapped many other unusual symbols that were meant to be viewed from the air. And yet, all her reported work was conducted from Nazca northward. *I found it strange she never studied the coastline to the south of Nazca.* If she did conduct such a study, I was unable to find any published reference to it.

Some facts of this period in the 1930's are; the leaders of Germany, the Nazis, held a passion for archaeology and the occult. Millions of dollars were spent sending Nazi teams all over the world attempting to discover ancient secrets. At the end of World War II, the United States hired every German intellectual to be found. This could be the answer to why she came to South America, and why many of her reports remain unpublished but in the control of the US government.

The coastal desert of Peru continues southward into northern Chile. Six hundred miles to the south of the Nazca desert is the Atacama Desert of Chile. The nearest town is Tarapaca, and the Lluta Valley. Here lies another secret to the Nazca lines and symbols. *This area contains the worlds' largest Man-made figure, and it can only be seen from the air.* The figure of the man has a series of strange symbols above his head, which have been incorrectly called a crown. The crown effect is created by a series of straight lines of various lengths that overlay each other.

The area where the giant man is located, like Nazca, has numerous large strange symbols. The symbols appear to be letters of an unknown language. Early archaeologists thought the symbols were similar to ancient Chinese or Asian languages. The message the letter symbols portray continues to remain a mystery. It is strange that the Nazca archaeologist never expressed, or published, any knowledge of the area. The giant Man figure and the strange letters can only be seen from the air. Therefore, you would expect she would have shown an intense interest in the figure.

I suspect the Nazca and Atacama deserts' symbols were never meant to be publicly tied together. Although we may never be able to decipher the exact message of the Atacama symbols, we can determine parts of their meaning by examining how they were presented. The symbols can only be seen from the air, so they are a message for persons in an aircraft. That message could only have two possibilities. The first purpose was to establish that the Lords created the message and that they were still alive. Next, the symbols would contain information regarding time and a directional flight path to locate the persons who created the message. The flight path would lead rescue pilots to the second message located in the Nazca desert.

As the rescue craft flew in from the south, they would first fly across the giant man and letter symbols. The distance from the Atacama Desert to the Nazca symbols is approximately six hundred miles. This information was provided by the symbols on the desert floor. The Nazca region symbols would provide information for a continued flight to the location of the Lords. It was also six hundred miles from Nazca to the location of the first large Moche pyramid. The three specific locations, each placed six hundred miles apart provide the evidence for a deliberate south to north flight path.

The purpose of the entire Nazca region, the geoglyphs and lines etched on the desert floor, was to attract attention from the air. This factor alone should clearly indicate that aircraft were expected to fly over the area. It will become evident that the Lords possessed and used light aircraft, particularly in their work in South America. These aircraft would be the same as was used in the Mediterranean Areas.

The next mystery of the Nazca plateau appears to be sets of straight lines continuing for miles, crossing valleys and traversing hills. The numerous lines appear to be set on the majority of the azimuths of our present-day compass. The visual effect of the lines extending outward creates a gigantic circle at the base of the lines. However, not all the azimuths of a compass are indicated. There are several lines very close to each other, then a blank space, continued by another group of lines, followed by a space and the cycle repeats itself. The completed pattern is similar to a sunburst effect. This could be a form of communication.

The next geoglyph is easily defined. This is the picture of the giant man located on a hillside overlooking the other geoglyphs. One hand and arm of the man points to the sky, while the other hand and arm points to the ground. This is a symbolic message that is easily read as, I am Man who came from the universe and I am here.

The various geoglyphs contained messages when combined. The hummingbird clearly represents flight and the whale represents the coastal region of an ocean. If you use the information to create a message, the message will say *fly along the coastline of the ocean.*

There is a Nazca geoglyph called "The Tree of Life", which I urge you to research and view. The image and title have already implanted a "scotoma" [blind spot to thinking] in your mind. When I first viewed this glyph, I turned the view several times and came up with another possible image of this glyph.

The usual view presented shows a large branched tree with roots. If you look at the roots, these appear to be feathers [same as the hummingbirds], but could also be flames. The "branches" are easily viewed as smoke. Removing these two parts of the glyph reveals a sleek aircraft. I could be hallucinating on **'shroom wine** of course. Indulge yourself, take a look.

This "Tree of Life" was a symbol of immortality used by the Sumerians, Hebrews, Christians and American Civilizations. The Nazca symbol

which has an aircraft imbedded as the trunk is a distinct image for
the returning Lords' Rescue Team.

Nazca Desert Giant Man

When the pilots followed these instructions and flew along the
coastline approximately 130 miles north of Nazca, they would see a
giant candelabra carved into the hillside in an area known as Pisco Bay.
The Candelabra is approximately 595 feet in length. The design shows
three distinct arms, which is a physically real version of a candelabra
holding three candles. This message clearly states "We are from
Sumer", where this symbol was widely known. The hillside where the
Candelabra is carved drops off to a rocky cliff at the water's edge,

providing no beach for a boat landing. This location clearly indicates the Candelabra was meant to be seen from the air.

The Candelabra is one of the greatest symbols of ancient religion and of the Ancient Masonic Lodge. From the time of antiquity until present day, it depicts a special symbolic message and meaning to all Masonic Lodges. For those nonmembers the information regarding the candelabra may appear exaggerated. However, for members of the Lodge, this information should provide clear, specific evidence of the connection to the Ancient Masonic Lodge.

Giant Desert Candelabra Geoglyph

Several of the glyphs gave the rescuers messages that important Lords were to be found. The six-winged hummingbird represented one of Teotihuacan's highest Gods, the spider represented the Great Goddess and the monkey confirmed who was still around. The six-winged hummingbird was the only glyph with six wings containing an aircraft image. All of the other hummingbird glyphs were three winged and plain. The spider was a particular call sign key, which local priests had revered and copied in costume. The monkey's tail reveals a circular maze, identical to mazes throughout the world.

The maze, or labyrinth, was recognized throughout the world. In the Minoan Civilization it was refined into the "Seven Circuit Labyrinth". It was used as a ceremonial passage in Sun God worship initiations and in Lodge teachings. The maze was another message which could not be mistaken. A quote from a 33° Mason is a great insight to the use of the maze in ceremony: "Masonic circumambulation, like walking a labyrinth or maze, is an allegory for introspection, self-awareness, and the journey of life." This is the eternal message imbedded in Lodge teachings spanning time from Minoan to Hopi ceremonies.

Continuing along the coastline rescuers entered the region of the Moche. A series of pyramids, eighteen or more, all of which are situated on a careful north south alignment, would point north towards Central America.

The spider is usually found at the center of the web, or at least somewhere within the web. In this case the figure of the spider indicated the Lords could be found in the center of a web of civilization.

As the rescue pilots continued north into Central America, they would view an unusual sight. From the air, the pattern of ground construction in the Maya regions led the pilots north to Mexico.

Beginning in southern Mexico the pilots would see the visual effect of a giant spider web. The construction that created the center of the web was the Mexican city of Teotihuacan. Here at the very center of the city was the great ceremonial center. This was where the Lords would gather for their rescue.

On the completion of the Nazca project, the Lords relinquished control to native Man. It is probable the Nazca priests continued creating pictographs and lines in the desert. The practice would continue as long as the priests believed it produced or reinforced religious powers. It is apparent Old Lord and others stayed to be served by their extended families and subjects.

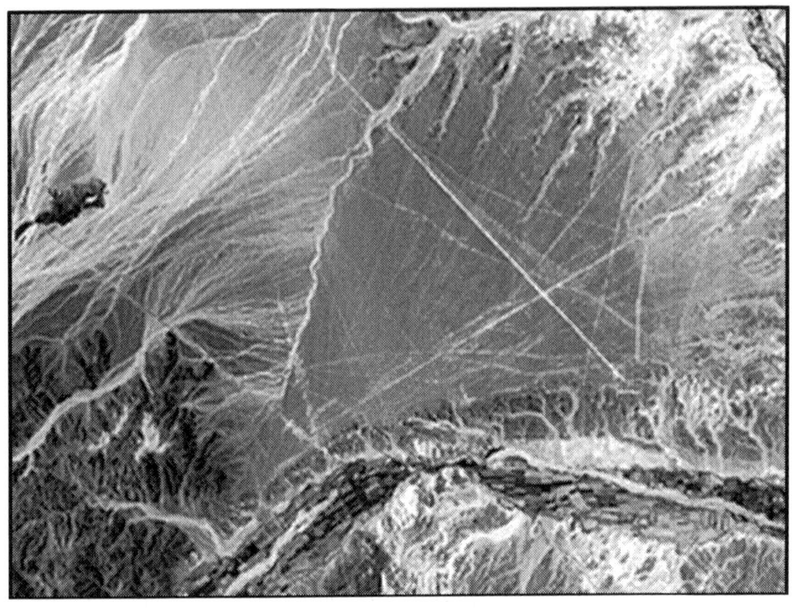

A satellite view of some of the Nazca lines. These straight lines span great distances. This view dispels the argument that the lines were constructed using strings for guidance.

RESCUE MISSION RETURNS

A major social event began in the regions of Mexico and Central America about 600 CE as the Nazca projects neared completion. Following the completion of the projects in Peru, the Lords relinquished power and control to local priests. Like the history of the Sumerian civilization, the Lords slowly removed themselves from public view.

In the Maya region the lords removed themselves from public view much earlier. However, they continued to rule through a well-established lineage of kings and priests. The major event of 600 CE was also the beginning of a final construction phase. In the Maya region, new temple structures were built over many of the existing temples. The new structures raised the height of existing temples well above the tree line.

In Mexico, particularly in the southern region, existing ceremonial centers with pyramid temple structures were abandoned and covered with soil. The interiors of the religious centers were burned out. Following the burning, the entire complex, including the pyramids, was covered with millions of tons of soil, allowing the jungle to reclaim the areas.

A layer of soil approximately twenty feet in depth covered some structures. From the air, the covered temples took on the appearance of small hills. This practice was duplicated in specific areas within the Maya region. For over a century historians and archaeologists have been puzzled by the mystery this event created. Early investigations by archaeologists determine there was insufficient time for the dirt to have naturally formed over the ceremonial centers. All subsequent efforts to unravel the mystery failed. In the end, historians simply stated the event had occurred, but there was no plausible explanation for it.

The secret of the event came in two parts. First, around 600, from the Lords' calculations, their rescue was drawing near. The Lords entered this final construction phase and began to relinquish authority and control to local priests. That control was based solely on the life and death authority of the Lords. If problems or difficulty arose, direct intervention by the Lords prevailed. It was a very sound system that facilitated a smooth operation.

As the ceremonial centers were closed, burned out and covered with soil, the Lords of these areas departed to live at the ceremonial center in the Mexican city of Teotihuacan. The local population and interconnecting trade routes remained in service. After the completion of all the projects in the Maya region, the remaining Lords also left for Teotihuacan.

The trade and religious cooperation of the tribes continued to function smoothly for a number of years. Then, like the Sumerian cities, the loss of a central authority began to take its toll. The authority, power, greed, and natural mistakes of human behavior lay in the hands of local kings and priests. Civil authority had broken down.

The second part of the event is the end result of the new construction phase. Investigating archaeologists could not deduce that the covered temples represented a complete transfer of authority and power, but this intensive labor effort should have caused some independent thought. The most intriguing secret was what was physically accomplished by covering the temple complexes. The Lords were cleaning up the outer regions of what a pilot would see from the air. They covered structures that interfered with the visual effects of the strands of a web. Today we see the dense jungle or forest in the area. This is the result of centuries of neglect allowing nature to reclaim the land. However, at the time of the Lords' rescue, the land was well maintained.

The rescue pilots recognized the outer strands of a web of civilization as they entered the southern Mexican region. Concerning the importance of the aerial view, the Lords had a secret that applied to both the Maya and Mexican regions. Historians have noted the unusual fact that such an advanced civilization, which existed in both the Mexican and Maya regions, had never produced the wheel. At the same time, archaeologists have discovered numerous toys with wheels. What should have been said was that the wheel was produced but never used. But without any further speculation or investigation, the subject of the wheel fell to the wayside as unimportant. The reason the wheel was never allowed to be used was that it would have created a situation the Lords could not control.

In the Middle East the wheel led to chariots giving armies great power. This led to independent nations and continuing wars. This could not happen again as it would disrupt the plan for rescue.

The use of horses and wheeled wagons would have scarred the landscape and caused uncontrolled travel. This is another reason the Lords did not introduce the horse to the Americas. If native Man had been allowed to use the wheel and the horse, the result would have been exactly like Sumer and Egypt. The irregular road building or cross-country travel would interfere with the final ground construction pattern. The use of horses and wheels could also lead to civil insurrection. To avoid any aerial confusion regarding the specific strands of the web, the Lords prevented these introductions.

The location of the Lords' rescue was the city of Teotihuacan, which holds the greatest secret of the Maya region. The Mayan Temple of Copan is very important as it is near the center of the landmass of Central America. Copan would provide a pilot flying into the region from the south the first view of major construction. The first thing the pilot would see is the replica of a giant spacecraft. The replica totally reinforced previous information that set the rescue pilots on their flight path.

As the pilots flew over Copan, they entered the area where pyramids and temples could be seen above the tree line. The structures provided aerial markers guiding the aircraft to the beginnings of the giant web. The strands of the visual web led the pilots to their final destination of Mexico and the city of Teotihuacan.

The aerial image of Copan was completed about 600 CE. This coincides with the time of the last great building phase in the Maya region. Another secret of Copan is that it was never built or used as a city. The term *city* has simply been applied to describe the construction found in the area. Archaeologists have noted the city was not built to serve a mass population. It was built as a retreat to serve a sect of royal nobility. About three thousand service people were necessary to maintain the complex and surrounding area. The lack of a supporting population, public buildings, evidence of trade and agriculture indicates the complex was used as a resort, a safe, quiet, or secluded place.

The history of Copan is preserved in the carved reliefs of the High Priests who ruled the site. Archaeologists of today refer to these Priests as "Kings" because the term alludes to local empires, as Priests allude to a controlling religious authority. The reliefs of the sixteen consecutive nobles are carved into a huge square altar, each with their name in Mayan glyphs, and their combined reign spanned a Baktun, the 400-year Mayan Holy cycle.

Some of the rulers, or High Priests, are named after the Jaguar, some after the Plumed Serpent, but the title of the very first ruler, the founder of Copan, was a mystery until his name was finally discovered. His name was simply "Lord."

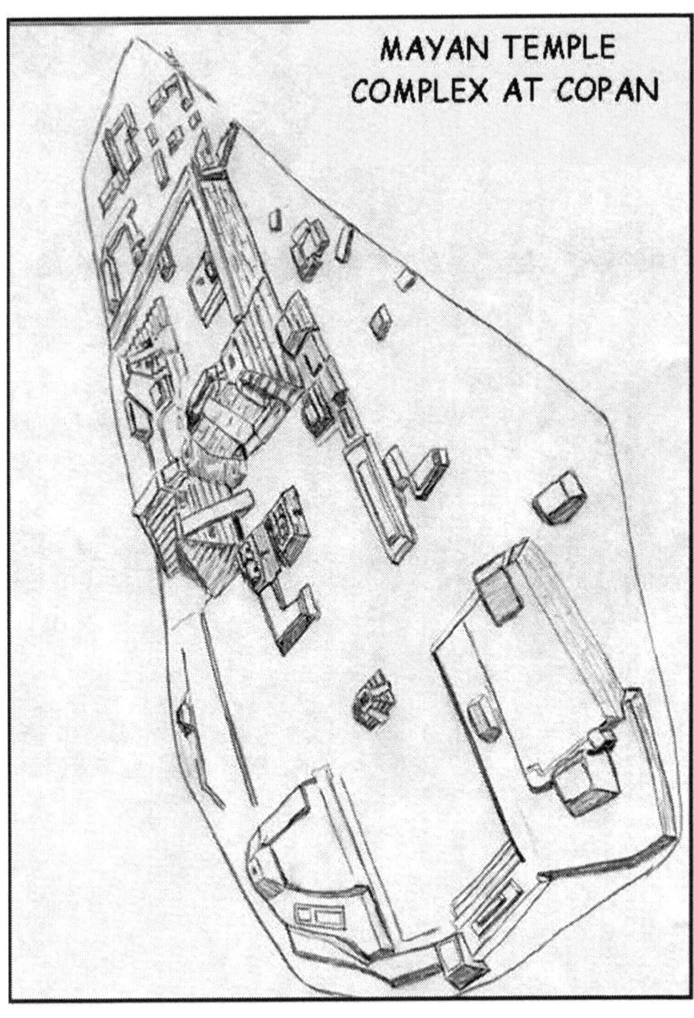

Copan was constructed as a replica of how the Lords recalled their main spacecraft appeared when viewed from the top side.

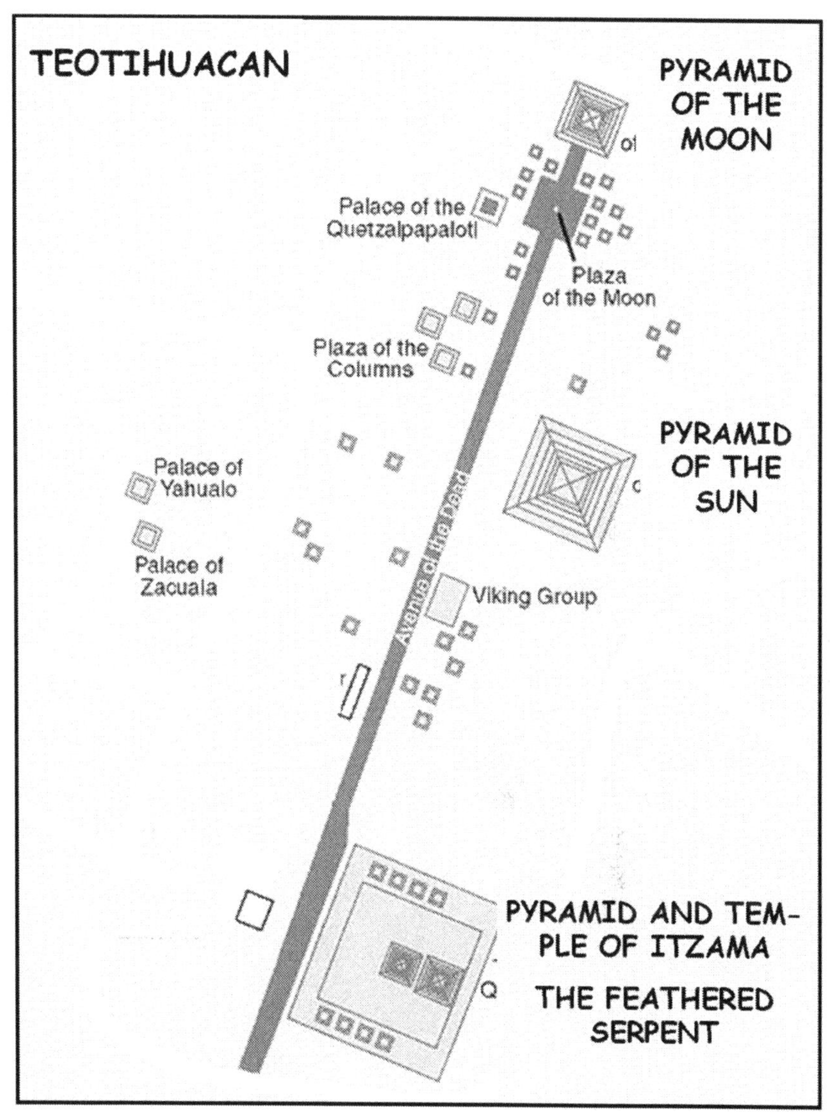

The city of Teotihuacan never attained the popularity achieved by the Maya region, yet its architecture is more elegant and magnificent. The disparity of popularity appears to be in the lack of mystery that usually surrounds ruins found in a jungle. Yet Teotihuacan holds the answers to more mysteries than all the Maya ruins. Teotihuacan was looted since it was abandoned in the 800's, and more so in the past four centuries.

Teotihuacan is located in the Basin of Mexico and is situated about twenty-five miles northeast of present-day Mexico City. There is evidence the foundations for a planned civilization began about 2,250 BCE, one being the building of the Purron Dam. The dam provides clear evidence that an irrigation system was built to facilitate an agricultural foundation for the civilization emerging in the region.

Teotihuacan was a great metropolis by 100 BCE. Historians and other experts agree the city was planned prior to its development, but exactly who conceived and developed the city is still in dispute. The general consensus is the plan originated from a mysterious group of priest-architects. All experts agree that the city was developed with a precise urban grid plan. The grid encompassed a rectangular area of about eight square miles. This city plan was followed for several centuries accommodating populations well over 250,000.

Teotihuacan holds many mysterious secrets and provides a great number of clues and evidence about the reign of The Lords of Sumer. The greatest mystery is there are no definitive records identifying the administrators of the city. There are no records to indicate what language was used in Teotihuacan. There are no records to indicate the volume of commerce, or the accumulation of wealth. One prominent archaeologist stated only a few remnants of the original language were found, glyphs similar to those found in Egypt. The glyphs contained faces, animal heads and figures, and odd geometric figures. Some of these mysterious writings stand alone, encircled with an oblong border. The archaeologist would not use the word **cartouche** because he feared peer ridicule if he dared make a connection of Teotihuacan with Egypt. These cartouches and glyphs of the original "Gods" have not been deciphered.

No Mayan glyph writings have been found in the central area of Teotihuacan. The number system used by the Maya and over 20 major clans [tribes] from all over Mexico and Central America was absent. The base 20 bar and dot math system used on calendars, and administratively to record census and product inventories, was found only on a few pieces of stucco covered sea shells. The religious shrines with accompanying paintings and carvings are the only informative messages left in Teotihuacan.

The religious and ceremonial centers were at the core of the city. Within this area were three main avenues with numerous connecting side streets. At the north end of the central core is a massive pyramid known as the Pyramid of the Moon, dominating the large Plaza of The Moon. All of Teotihuacan's pyramids are built of volcanic rubble with stone veneer, using a series of rising platforms. From the base of the structures, each layer became smaller, and the top of the upper layer was a wide level square area.

Beginning at the Plaza of The Moon, the main avenue, the Way of The Stars, was oriented about 12 $\frac{1}{2}$ degrees west of south, through the center of Teotihuacan. This avenue is known by two other names, The Way of the Dead, or the Avenue of the Dead.

View from the Pyramid of the Moon Goddess along the Way of the Stars, with the Pyramid of the Sun in the background

South, about one-half mile on the Avenue of The Stars, there is a second and much larger pyramid, the Pyramid of the Sun. The Pyramid of the Sun was built in the same manner as the Pyramid of the Moon, and geometrically speaking, it is only slightly smaller than the Great Pyramid of the Giza plateau in Egypt. The top of the Pyramid of the Sun is a large horizontal platform, which once contained a large temple. The Great Pyramid of Giza [The Pyramid of the Sun] was bejeweled with gold, and the Pyramid of the Sun at Teotihuacan was bejeweled with mica, a shining crown.

The primary burial under the center of the pyramid was looted, but it was evident that a supreme ruler of Teotihuacan was interred.

Continuing south on the avenue, about three-fourths of a mile, is a much smaller pyramid, The Pyramid of the Plumed Serpent. The very top of this pyramid is also completed as a horizontal platform.

The Pyramid of The Plumed Serpent is located in the compound known as the Citadel, or Ciudadela, which contained a grand royal palace. This palace was the ceremonial home of **God Kukulkan**. East Avenue begins on the Citadel's east side. Directly across from the Citadel compound, on the west side of the Way of The Stars, is The Great Compound.

The Citadel compound is a huge quadrangle, with a perimeter of approximately one mile, and contains almost forty acres. The entire area of the Citadel is enclosed in a rampart; an embankment topped with a parapet. The rampart was built as a raised platform that caused the interior ground level to appear sunken. Facing the avenue, the rampart was 30 feet in height and 132 feet in width. The other three sides of the rampart were constructed in the same manner, 30 feet in height and the width changes to 262 feet.

The Great Compound was created by two enormous U-shaped platforms that face each other and are approximately twenty feet high. Both platforms have front recessed areas that form three sides of a rectangle. Looking down on both platforms, the recessed areas form a vast central plaza. On the right side of the plaza, an entrance opens to the Way of The Stars. A second entrance on the left side of the plaza leads to West Avenue. The outside perimeter of both raised platforms forms the visual effect of a giant rectangle, approximately half the size of the Citadel. On top of both platforms are the remains of several buildings. From an archaeological view, the use of the buildings has yet to be determined. There is no evidence of either residential or administrative use.

The Pyramid of The Plumed Serpent compound is regarded as a royal palace and shrine. It contained a temple flanked to the north and south by grand royal apartment complexes. Early Spanish explorers were awed by the grandeur of the temple and pyramid carvings. Archaeologists discovered mass ritual burials around and in the engineered foundation sections of the pyramid. The mass burials were on the perimeter of the pyramid, arranged as guards, and in the interior as attendants and worshippers to **Lord Kukulkan** who ruled from there.

This pyramid and temple are known by several names. The Pyramid of the Plumed Serpent and the Temple of Kukulkan are the most common. It is apparent this pyramid was the spiritual and cultural center of power for all of Teotihuacan. Surviving stelae reveal Kukulcan was worshipped as the God who created the Maya and as the God who introduced corn and all the arts and sciences to Mexico and Central America. He was revered in Mayan civilization as the God of all civilization and of the forces of good and light.

Recently, after a flooding rain, researchers discovered a vertical shaft [30 to 40 feet deep] in the Great compound which connected to a tunnel. The tunnel extended to the center of the Pyramid, revealing a grotto with numerous religious icons and a "considerable amount of mercury".

Raised platforms are a unique feature of Teotihuacan architecture. These platforms provide the answer to the greatest secret of Teotihuacan. This type of architecture is found throughout the twenty-mile center of the city. Previous publications have used the word *hallmark* as the only explanation for the unusual platform construction. What should have been said was; at the time of the creation of the great city, it was the only city on Earth with such architecture. The platforms provided the final clues to the rescue of the Lords. As in ancient Sumer, the staircases to the top of the pyramids and platforms were known as "Stairways to the Gods."

Over one hundred raised platform temples were scattered throughout the twenty-mile interior web of Teotihuacan. These single ornate buildings were completed with a massive flat top. There is no evidence the buildings had any practical use. The platforms were relatively small when compared to any other functioning temple, about twenty feet in height with a flat roof. The roofs were 131 feet wide and varied in length. The secret of the numerous platforms is that they provided raised landing pads, well above street level, for a host of aircraft.

Beginning at the wide Plaza of The Moon, at the base of the Pyramid of the Moon, and continuing south on the Way of the Stars, each side of the avenue was filled with these structures. The Moon plaza had four platforms on each side, with two others, one on each side of the stairway that led to the top of the pyramid. The Pyramid of the Moon had a large flat top, providing for the landing of one extremely large aircraft and ten smaller aircraft. Continuing south, each side of the avenue contained numerous platforms facing the avenue.

The base of the Pyramid of the Sun was built on a raised platform that extended out from the structure on three sides. The front area contained a large stairway, and the border was approximately twenty feet in height and one hundred thirty feet in width.

The Temple of Kukulkan, although smaller than the Pyramid of the Moon, had a large flat platform top that was sufficient to provide landing for an extremely large aircraft. The two large compounds of the Citadel had fifteen raised platforms spaced around the enclosure. Across the Way of The Stars was the Great Compound with the giant raised platforms that formed the square plaza.

The following is speculation based on the number of platforms in the city. At the time of the Lords' rescue, numerous aircraft landed on the platforms along the Way of the Stars. Two extremely large aircraft landed on the two large platforms in the Great Compound. Based on the close proximity of both compounds, the Lords gathered in the Citadel and walked across the avenue into the Great Compound plaza square. It was from this area they were rescued.

The other hundred raised platforms scattered throughout the city served a different purpose. Archaeologists and historians explain the event in the following manner: *Sometime around 750 CE a great holocaust descended upon the city.* The inner core of the city was systematically and deliberately burned. Most of the city temples and public buildings were totally destroyed. The buildings and the surrounding charred areas provide evidence of sudden extensive and intense heat.

The fiery destruction of the city has been described as sudden and catastrophic. The catastrophic end of the city at about 800 CE establishes the time of the Lords' rescue. After the Lords were aboard the rescue craft, the other platforms scattered throughout the city were used as specific points to destroy the urban core. The destruction was completed either by support aircraft of the initial rescue, or by a vast number of other aircraft that had settled on the platforms. After the fiery holocaust, the city was a ghost town. The civilization never recovered and the city was nearly abandoned.

After escaping from the city, thousands of people were free from the yoke of the Lords' authority. The effect of the aircraft destroying the urban center must have caused the people to believe the spirits from hell had arrived. Once they were free from the area, the inflicted fear guaranteed they would never return.

The same pattern of destruction was used in the Peruvian regions, except on a smaller scale. In these areas, the Lords burned the temple complexes as they abandoned the regions.

ON THE ORIGIN OF GOD BY MEANS
OF NATURAL SELECTION

MAYAN STELAE DATES AND HISTORY

Now that the date of the Lords' rescue has been established, here is the key to events, past, present, and future. As previously mentioned, the Long Count Stela is dated to our current calendar by several different correlations. These correlations vary by 260 years or more. A majority of archaeologists use a correlation, which produces a long count beginning date of 3,114 BCE [others set the date at 3,373 BCE], and an ending date of 4,773 CE, or 7,887 years. A point to think about, in reference to the date correlations, is that with minor adjustments, or averages of the various correlations, one can come up with a very important Mayan number. That number is 8,000 years, which is 20 cycles [the Katun] of the religious Baktun cycle of 400 years. This will produce a more mentally manageable beginning Long Count date of 3,200 BCE, and an ending date of 4800 CE.

If, for conjecture, we use the Maya religious cycle of 8,000 years, then half of that cycle is 4,000 years. I believe that number, 4,000 years, is the time required to complete a trip from Earth to their origin, and return. Here is the argument for this theory.

If we start with the future Maya stelae date of 4800 CE and subtract 4,000 years, we have the date 800 CE. This was the approximate date of the Lords' rescue. Going back another 4,000 years gives us the date, 3,200 BCE, the beginning of the Maya stelae count, and the last previous date of possible rescue. This last possible rescue date correlates with the development of Egypt before Crete and Thera were destroyed in 1,628 BCE. The failure to be rescued would explain the expansion of Egypt and the Americas' civilizations. Continuing with this line of thought, if we back up another 4,000 years from the stelae's earliest date, we arrive at 7,200 BCE. This date began the Lords' previous countdown to rescue. The Lords organized their tribes in the Fertile Crescent and continued developing the area. By 6000 BCE temples and ziggurats [raised brick watch towers] appeared in the land between the Tigris and Euphrates rivers. The Lords needed support to survive the next 4,000 +/- year cycle, the time needed for round trip travel to and from their origin.

Around 3200 BCE, their rescue from Earth failed to occur. I suspect that spacecraft did arrive and bring communications and supplies, but for whatever reason could not effect a rescue of all personnel or did not leave. The Lords made plans for surviving through another travel cycle. Realizing the Sumerian civilization would overrun their control;

the Lords began their secretive settlement of Crete and started the abandonment of Sumer. The Lords brought Egypt's First Dynasty to power in 3200 BCE, and put a firm plan in motion to relocate to Central America.

Going back to the Comet Strike of 12,900 years ago, which has been verified and correlated to our present calendar, this is about the date Gobekli Tepe was backfilled. With the Lords rescue at about 800 CE this accounts for 12,100 years. If three travel cycles fit into this time it would equal about 4,000 +/- years for a travel cycle. This time can be extended some depending how long before the comet impact that the original party of Lords left Earth. This does seem to verify a maximum travel cycle time of about 4,000 years for the Lords to travel to their homeland and return. I believe the Baktun travel cycle [400 years] to be more likely the travel time.

If you wish to play mind games, estimate the maximum speed of travel, and the distance to the nearest star [solar] system. Good luck with that. A "Light Year" of travel is about 5.88 Trillion miles.

Academia says nothing can travel faster than the speed of light. Could they be correct? No possible "Warp Speed" of multiples of light speed? I remember in my childhood when Chuck Yeager was going to achieve Mach 1+ [speed of sound] over the Mojave Desert and become the first human to travel faster than the speed of sound. I think it was 1947 and many radio news stories quoted scientists as projecting that a man's body would liquefy due to the harmonics encountered when matching the speed of sound. Yeager was going to die! *Academia* was wrong.

The published position of Scientists about light-speed travel:

"As an object approaches the speed of light, its mass rises precipitously. If an object tries to travel 186,000 miles per second, its mass becomes infinite, and so does the energy required to move it. For this reason, no normal object can travel as fast or faster than the speed of light."

Could *Academia* be wrong about this, as they were with traveling at the speed of sound? They are saying that the spacecraft and people would become a "Singularity" at the speed of light, a mini "Black Hole".

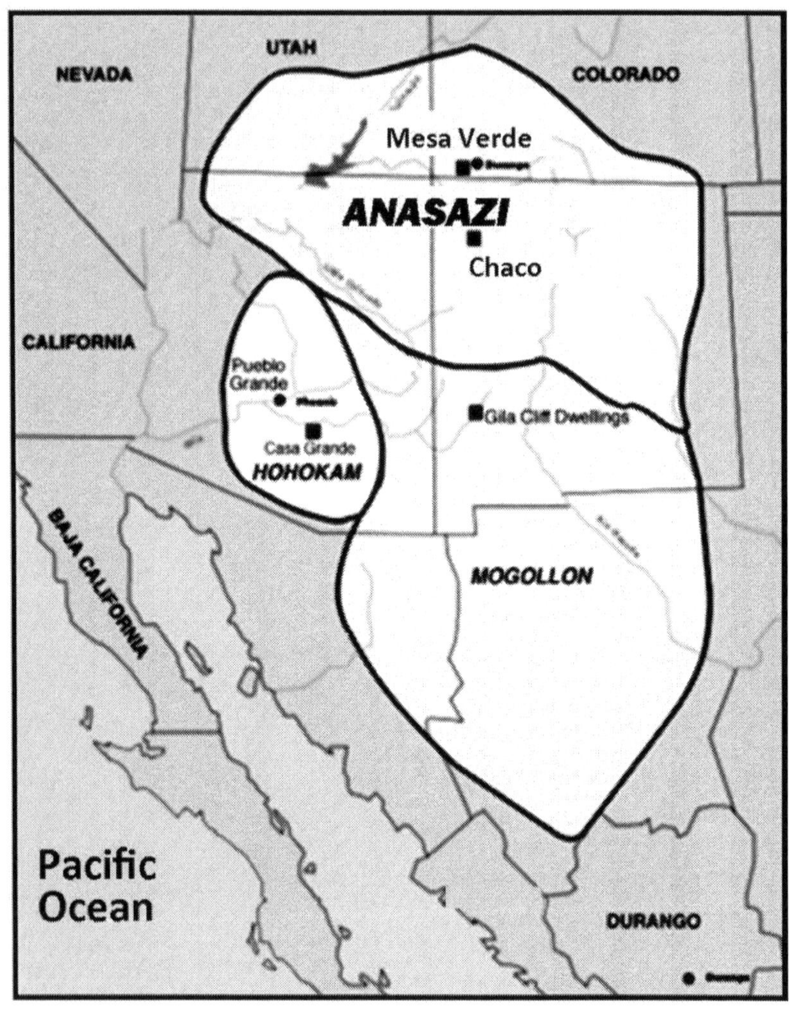

"Four Corners" Region of Southwest USA
Named for the common corner of the four states
Home to the "Ancient Ones", The Anasazi –
Descendants of Teotihuacan.

Chapter
5

**Long House Ruin
Largest at Mesa Verde**

REMNANT CIVILIZATIONS
The Last Teotihuacan Lord Dies

MEXICO BASIN AND YUCATAN

When the Lords were rescued from Teotihuacan, and destroyed the city, chaos ensued. With the absence of a central controlling religion and absolute authority figures, the leadership of these civilizations of Mexico, Central America, and Peru simply fell apart.

Beginning around 800 CE, after the destruction of Teotihuacan, these civilizations began a steady decline and some were absorbed into other tribal communities within a hundred or so years.

What later emerged were *Remnant Civilizations*, which retained some of the cultural and religious mythology passed from one generation to another. The Maya civilization's decline was an exact duplication of the fall of the Sumerian civilization. The various kings began regional warfare for territorial power.

With no governing authority, and the living Gods gone, local rulers vied for control. Tens of thousands of prisoners were sacrificed in an effort to bring back the Gods. Another natural disaster caused widespread famine in Central and South America; it was a major drought which lasted at least 100 years.

As the drought continued, the water levels in the cenotes of Central America continued to drop. These water holes were the only source of drinking water for many temples and religious centers. Human sacrifices were offered to the Gods for the return of rain with no effect. Temples and cities were abandoned with the inhabitants traveling to distant sites to find food, water and shelter.

As these civilizations disbanded and moved to more livable areas, new societies began. Archaeological evidence and Native American legends indicate there were two small groups of Lords that elected to remain. One group remained in the Mexican region, while the other stayed in Peru. Following the rescue, there is no evidence that either group attempted to communicate with the other. Apparently, as the remaining Lords began to age, they decided to live the remainder of their years as Gods among their own extended families.

THE TOLTEC AND THE AZTEC
[900 – 1150 CE]   [1325 – 1521 CE]

Little is known of the remaining Lords in the Basin of Mexico. After the destruction of Teotihuacan, the structured civilization of the city completely disintegrated. The Maya continued in the Yucatan and Guatemala highlands as the major power until the arrival of the Spanish. The remaining Lords and their followers maintained the legends and religious practices of their ancestors.

In the Basin of Mexico, the foundation of a remnant civilization, known as the Toltec, emerged around 900. The civilization did not achieve the popularity of the Maya. It appeared to be a combination of architecture and religion from both of the civilizations of Teotihuacan and the Maya. The history of the Toltec almost duplicates that of Teotihuacan. The difference of the civilizations was the Toltec were an aggressive and warlike society. When compared to Teotihuacan, the Toltec were a crude and unrefined copy of the Teotihuacan society.

The name of one Lord emerges in the Toltec and the later Aztec empire. This Lord is the traditional founder of the Toltec civilization, and his name was Topilzin Quetzalcoatl [Mayan Kukulkan]. Other than he was a living God among men, there is no other information regarding his existence with the Toltec.

The Toltec established trade with the existing Hohokam and Anasazi civilizations to the north and north-west of their capital. The Toltec may have been source of the "renegade" priests who took over the Chaco Canyon site for about 100 years before the collapse of the Anasazi in 1150. Archaeologists found evidence of cannibalistic ceremonies during this occupation. The end of the Anasazi correlates with the demise of the Toltec.

The major accomplishment of the Toltec was their capital city of Tollan. The city was built about thirty-five miles north of modern Mexico City, known today as the city of Tula. The Toltec came to a sudden end around 1150. I believe this is when Quetzalcoatl died. Civil war ensued to fill the power vacuum and after 1200 the Toltec capital city lay in ruins.

The last great civilization to emerge in this region was the Aztec in about 1325. Their empire extended north into the United States along the old trade routes of the Anasazi. The Aztec believed they were the descendants of the Toltec. After the fall of the Toltec empire, a large group, led by a former Tollan Priest, moved out of the Basin of Mexico to an area northwest of the Mexican region. It is speculated they joined the Hohokam in the Salt River Valley. Sometime around 1300 they migrated back to the Basin of Mexico. Once settled in the area, they began to build their empire and their history is quite interesting.

The first ruler of the Aztec empire claimed to be a direct descendant of Quetzalcoatl. His statement of being a descendant clearly indicates their last Lord was dead. As the lineage of rulers and history continued, the name Quetzalcoatl was used in a legendary religious context. The end of the Aztec Empire will be discussed in detail in Chapter 6 – Discovery.

In the Yucatan area the Maya city of Chichen Itza declined as localized warfare increased. A brief Mayan resurgence occurred, centered at the city of Mayapan and along the Gulf coast. Mayapan was abandoned about 60 years before the Spanish arrived in 1511.

Cahokia Mound Builders
Mississippian Culture [600 CE – 1200 CE]

The Cahokia mound-builder culture was directly and intricately tied to the Toltec Culture.   The Mound Builders Culture began in the late 600's and attained its height about 1100 CE.   The Mississippi drainage system was occupied by this culture. The civilization was as advanced as the Toltec and declined at the same time as the Toltec when the last ruling Lord died. The Cahokia followed the same established religious, building and social organization practices as those in Central America.

The Cahokia Mounds were layered pyramids using local materials as stone was not available.   The pyramids were constructed using raised platform exteriors and contained burials for the hierarchy along with extensive human sacrifice to provide company for the dear departed.   Astrological observations were extremely important in the planned layouts of their cities and various structures.

Cahokia Religion was centered on The Sun God, The Moon God and Mother Earth God. I mention this culture as it is directly related and is a thread for your own research.

Cahokia Falcon Dancer

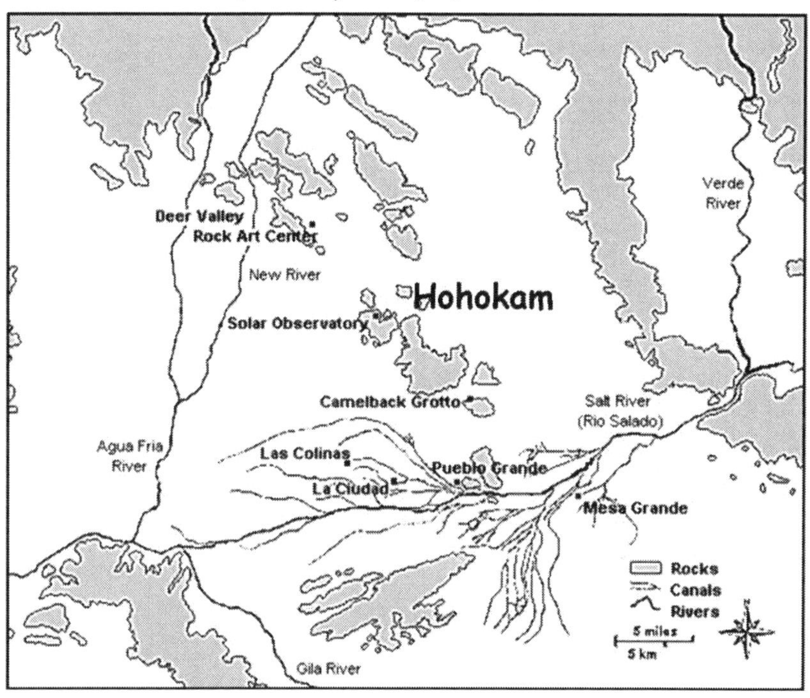

The map above is based on work done by **Omar Turney** in 1929. According to him, the system encompassed *"the largest single body of land irrigated in prehistoric times in North or South America, and perhaps in the world"*. The system utilized at least 1000 miles (1600 km) of canals and irrigated over 100,000 acres (40,470 hectares) of land. The area shown measures about 50 miles (80 km) West to East, by 40 miles (64km) North to South, and encompasses approximately 2000 square miles (5200 km). It was built c. 500 - 1,500 CE By the 'Hohokum' people. (4) Arizona has a tradition of ancient canal building that dates back almost 3,000 years, although the earliest ones found are on a smaller scale, archaeologists have uncovered a complex canal system that dates between 1,200 and 800 B.C. Known as Las Capas ("the layers" in Spanish), it was the earliest large-scale system of its kind in the Southwest, and was built by people belonging to what archaeologists call the San Pedro Phase Culture. "It is the best exposure of an early canal system of just about any pre-Columbian time period in North America to date," said project director **James Vint**.

The Hohokam [1,200 BCE -1,500 CE]
The Anasazi   [30 CE - 1,150 CE]
Mesa Verde and Chaco Canyon cultures

After the rescue a group of Lords remained in the Mexico region. There is evidence these Lords were involved in the formation of two civilizations and the resulting cities. Although difficult to define, the time from 800 forward indicates the remaining group split into different parties.

In the Mexican region, history between 800 and 900 is almost a blank. However, something very unusual was occurring well north of the Mexican region.

In the United States, there is a region commonly called the Four Corners area. Here the states of Utah, Colorado, Arizona, and New Mexico come together on The Colorado Plateau. Neolithic tribes categorized in the Basket Maker eras populated the area. Southwest of this is the Sonoran Desert with Phoenix at the northern edge.

The Lords who chose to remain rather than be rescued planned their stay well in advance of 800. They established cultural followings in several areas of civilization. In southern Arizona, centered in the present-day Tucson-Phoenix area, an advanced agrarian society developed. Known as the Hohokam [1,200 BCE - 1,500 CE], they constructed Sun temples. They were noted for extensive irrigation systems, pyramidal mounds, sunken ball-courts with rubber balls and other structures similar to those of central Mexico.

Hohokam translates somewhat as "those who left". Here, along the Salt River and the Gila River, the Hohokam began their civilization about 1,200 BCE. The area was populated by pit dweller groups and nomadic tribes. Sun dried adobe bricks were the major building component with clay plaster dressing the walls. Their greatest accomplishment of all was the extensive 1,000 miles of irrigation systems.

Today, large canals and other water conveyance systems follow the exact layout of the Hohokam canals, delivering agricultural and municipal water. The Hohokam canals were so accurately engineered the water flow had a perfect *silting velocity*. A good silting velocity for water flowing in a canal allows enough silt to be carried along and slowly fall out to seal the canal against leakage, without plugging the waterway. Canals were excavated through rock to an exact grade.

One canal diversion at the Salt River immediately enters a large excavated basin before continuing. The large basin causes the velocity of the water to slow considerably. The lower velocity allows sediment to settle out, keeping the canal from plugging. The sediment can then be flushed back into the river. In desert regions high runoff carries tons of sediment, which if not managed will destroy irrigation systems. This Hohokam construction exhibited an extremely high engineering ability. Silting basins are widely used in modern desert runoff systems.

Shortly after 500 CE a major trade route extended from Teotihuacan to the Hohokam, and on to the Anasazi region. The Hohokam introduced the bow and arrow, pottery, corn, squash, chilies and beans to the Chaco Canyon and Mesa Verde areas. Priests introduced religious ceremonies centered on the Sun, Moon and local Gods. This provided for a common culture and purpose.

Anasazi is the Navajo word given to the builders of Chaco and Mesa Verde and is translated as *Ancient Ones*. The Anasazi emerged as a civilization in this area about 30 CE. They were led by Priests from the Hohokam Civilization, who organized the various hunter-gatherer and pit dweller groups into a construction and agriculture-oriented society.

To build a shelter a pit dweller dug out a shallow pit in the ground, placed rock slabs on edge around the pit edge and covered the pit with a primitive roof of limbs, branches, and shrubs. These "Pit Sites" could have up to 20 dwellings per group. Other small groups walled the entrance to rock caves to create a home. The Anasazi's evolution into a civilization was slow and natural until the year 500 CE. By this time, they had progressed to living in single story houses and growing the staple crops of corn, beans and squash, with a myriad of other food crops.

Archaeologists have determined around the year 750 CE major urban complexes emerged in Chaco Canyon and on Mesa Verde. The Chaco complex is located southeast of Farmington and Aztec, New Mexico in a semi-arid desert canyon area. A major Chaco outlier site is near Aztec New Mexico. Mesa Verde is about 90 miles north of the Chaco Complex near Cortez Colorado.

*Mesa Verde - Cliff Palace Ruins with
Circular Kivas for religious ceremonies
One of many sites*

*Chaco Canyon - Pueblo Bonito
One of Eleven Sites
Circular Kivas for ceremonies - note damage from canyon
wall collapse [modern]*

Chaco Canyon
Spiral Maze with Solstice Sun Dagger
The maze is still used in Hopi and other Pueblo Tribes initiation ceremonies

In 700 CE multi-storied building began in the Chaco complex. Archaeologists agree that some of the larger structures and complexes were built using one specific plan and were constructed over decades in sections as the population required additions. The lower apartments were often filled with trash and debris, with the new apartments constructed over them.

The additions are clearly evidenced at Pueblo Bonito in the distinct masonry styles. The master plan was used for over one hundred years. The average Anasazi had a life span of forty years, which infers a continuous authority, other than the builders.

After the rescue of the Lords and the destruction of Teotihuacan an improved, advanced building phase began in the Anasazi region. A group of Lords who declined to be rescued followed the established trade routes north. On arriving in the Anasazi region, they once again began the foundation for another empire. All of the evidence in the Pueblo Bonito area supports this assumption.

The urban complex at Chaco Canyon contains a building from which the entire complex derives its name. Pueblo Bonito is a massive multistoried structure that contains several hundred rooms and is unique to the entire Anasazi territory. This architecture was completely unique to the region. The architecture provides evidence of an outside influence on the Anasazi civilization. In and near the canyon there are eleven other structures that produced an additional two thousand rooms.

Chetro Ketl Great Kiva of Chaco Canyon
The major buildings of Chetro Ketl were Palaces for Royalty

The entire complex contains many other structures, including large gathering areas for public meetings, and kivas for ceremonial or religious events. There are also sunken ball courts. Throughout the Anasazi cultural area, the circular spiral maze, the symbol for the spiritual journey to the center of the Universe, is found.

Five major ancient roads begin at the complex and continue for several hundred miles. Regardless of the terrain, the roads were engineered to remain straight. To reinforce the magnitude of this construction, the routes are roads, not trails. The roads are designed to a defined width, and some were thirty feet wide. Such a width indicates the roads were built to facilitate heavy traffic to and from Chaco Canyon.

Each roadbed was constructed to produce a firm foundation of bedrock or in some areas, hardpan. The roads were constructed by hand and are unique considering this culture never produced a shovel, pick, or the other tools required for this construction.

In close proximity to the primary complex are seventy other communities constructed on the same pattern, using the same architecture. The only difference from the primary complex is that the communities were built on a smaller scale. It appears the structures in this region were built as a foundation for a great city and civilization to come.

The civilization development pattern is exactly the same as used by the Lords in other regions. Many trade items found within the region provide clear evidence of a trade route from Mexico through southern Arizona and the Hohokam. Some items, such as copper products and colorful Macaw feathers, came from the Mexican regions.

The construction of the Pueblo Bonito complex was completed shortly before 1100 but by the year 1200 the entire area had been abandoned. The Southwest was in the grip of another extended drought.

The Hohokam and the Anasazi, which includes the Chaco cultures, simply disappeared. There is definite evidence to support the theory that extended drought ended their ability to obtain water for agriculture and basic living needs. When this happens, the people lose their faith in the leaders and Shaman to provide for basic living standards. When you are starving you usually find somewhere else to live. Many small tribes moved to remote canyons which still had streams and shelter.

The reason for the sudden abandonment of the Anasazi areas was that the central authority had vanished. The Lord, or Lords, had finally died.   A recent archaeological find at the Chaco site is very interesting. It appears that around 900 to 1100 a renegade group, originating in Mexico, took charge of the Chaco site and conducted ritual cannibalistic ceremonies similar to the Mayan ceremonies.

The Anasazi civilization, as well as many other similar North American civilizations, has always been viewed as a rather romantic mystery. The mystery being the people suddenly vanished. The most popular explanation for the disappearance of this entire civilization has been; extended drought forced the population to leave the region. Another popular explanation is that the civilization frequently moved to different regions. However, anyone, including many archaeologists who view the civilization with serious intent knows there is something wrong with these simplistic tales.

To establish drought patterns, a specialized team located the oldest trees and removed core samples. The core samples provided rings for each year of growth and the width of each ring indicates the amount of rainfall in the local area. These wood ring patterns are the foundation for the theory that extended drought caused the Anasazi to abandon their region.

The point most historians fail to note is the area the Anasazi lived in was already semi-arid. The people simply lived on a basis of more or less water. It did not have to rain in the specific region for the people to survive, as most areas were already going through seasonal droughts.

The people were resourceful and constructed water catchment basins at Chaco Canyon. These basins were on the canyon rims and in the side canyon areas to store water for future use and prevent uncontrolled seasonal run-off. As the drought periods lengthened, the regular seasonal flow through the canyons became more uncontrollable and devastating since it now came less often and was more destructive when it did arrive. The argument that the people relied on corn crops to survive is very lame. The plains Tribes of North America never grew corn and had a thriving civilization. And as for food, if there was an extended drought the animals would congregate at a water source, the bottom of the canyon. If anything positive came from a drought in this region, it would have been to make hunting easier.

In the early foundation of the Anasazi civilization there were frequent moves to expand and find better sites. They learned that due to drought, the ideal locations for habitation were canyon areas, which contained a river or numerous streams. At the height of this cultural phase, ideal locations were found and massive building began. The Anasazi lived in these dwellings for hundreds of years. During these extended occupations weather patterns produced many droughts, yet the civilization did not move. The perception that one drought forced the entire civilization to abandon the region is misleading.

Mesa Verde begins with the northern edge of the mesa at 8,000 feet elevation. This slopes to the south and into numerous canyons. Magnificent cliff dwellings are spread throughout these canyons, with storage sites positioned in precarious locations. On the mesa above the canyons the Anasazi constructed dwellings, farm plots and raised turkeys. There are tower structures and granaries throughout the mesa and continue far to the North and West into Utah.

The Mesa Verde Anasazi extensively raised semi-domesticated turkeys and used the feathers for clothing and bedding. They constructed outlier settlements and perfected dry-land farming of beans, corn and other crops far north of the cliff dwellings they are famous for. The ruins of their civilization are so widespread the stone blocks from the ruins were used for building materials into the 20th century. Their ruins extend into Utah, Arizona and of course, New Mexico.

The earliest photographs of the excavation of Mesa Verde cliff dwellings and other Anasazi sites show ancient baskets filled with corncobs. This indicates the corn was present when the people left. The comments from 1920's and 1930's were that this indicated the inhabitants had left in great haste, as the stored supplies were not taken as the people left. This contradicts the current argument that the Anasazi had been finally driven out of their settlements by drought as they certainly would not have excess food to leave behind.

The question of what happened to the Anasazi population, we will never know with complete certainty. The popular view is that these societies were at the height of their civilization when they collapsed.

I suspect they were only beginning to complete the foundation of a civilization to come. In the establishment of the foundation, great labor forces were needed. The population in and around Chaco Canyon, the area of Pueblo Bonito, was not sufficient to have completed the system of roads, much less the buildings in the area. Some of the abandoned Anasazi sites are the results of the Lords moving entire groups to form the labor gangs. If we compare the history of Peru, this is the exact method used to construct the first canals.

Where there is evidence the Anasazi population left in great haste, they most likely did. When the ruling authority, or living Gods, leave a civilization in haste it is not unusual for panic to overtake the population. They flee for a multitude of reasons. Following the breakdown of civil authority, chaos follows and the system falls apart. The civilizations are left to follow any leader available. These people became the Pueblo civilizations of today, the Hopi, Zuni, Acoma and others. The Navajo tribes were established in this region by the 1500s CE, originally identified as Navajo Apache, their heritage is Athapaskan, descendants of the North-West Canadian Tribes.

I read a recent article on the Chaco complex. It seems that *Academia* once again is changing history. Any tie of Chaco to the Anasazi Civilization has been omitted. Chaco is now described as a Pre-Pueblo Culture, and even the ancient road system to Mesa Verde, and Mesa Verde, has been omitted from the article and accompanying maps. I believe this is due to political correctness and pressure from the Pueblo Tribes. It portrays an entirely different view of these ancient cultures.

It is similar to the Vatican removing ties to the Mitra religion. What a shame to distort history for political purposes.

FOR NOTES

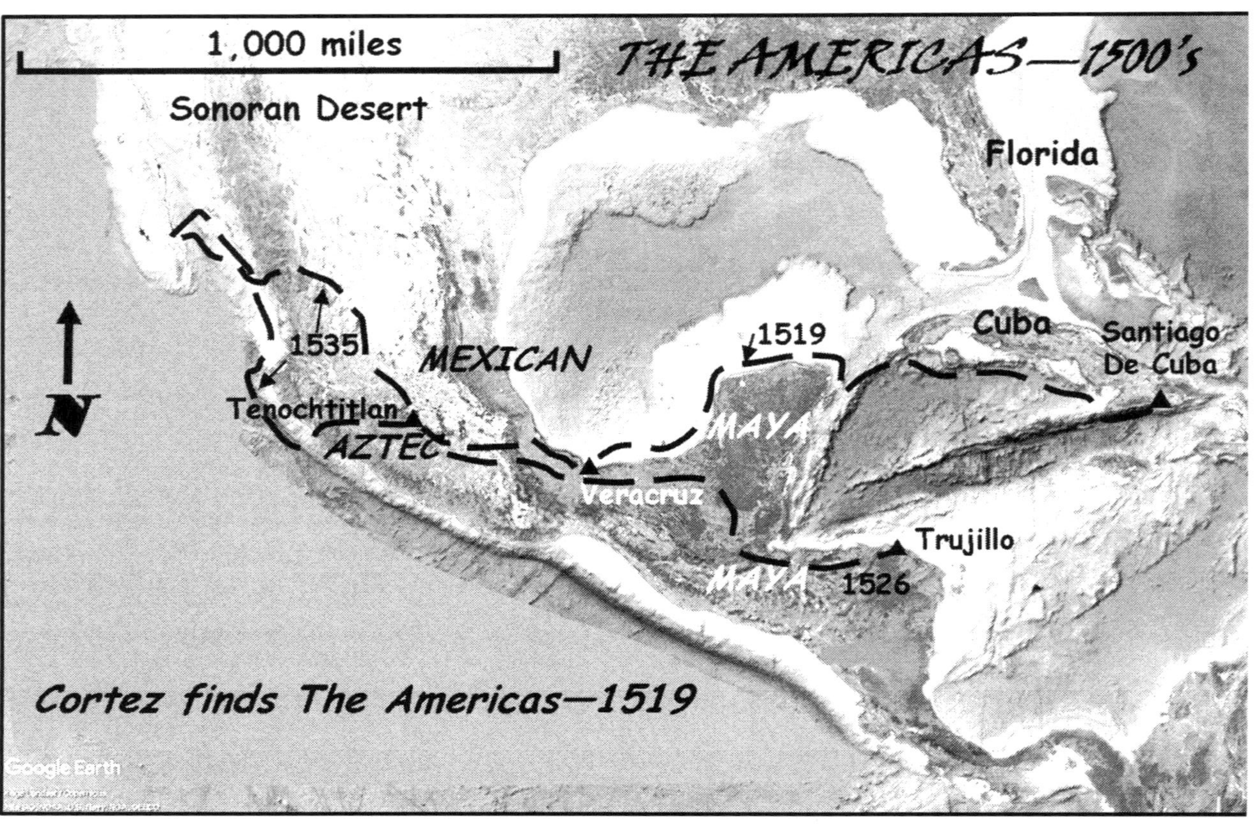

1,000 miles
THE AMERICAS—1500's
Sonoran Desert
Florida
1535
MEXICAN
1519
Cuba
Santiago De Cuba
N
Tenochtitlan
AZTEC
MAYA
Veracruz
Trujillo
MAYA
1526
Cortez finds The Americas—1519
Google Earth
Twenty-Seven Years after Columbus Landed

Chapter 6

DISCOVERY
The New world is found and pillaged

Lord Quetzalcoatl

The people of the Aztec were led into the land by Lord Quetzalcoatl. The Lord had ruled all the people before us. The Lord left the Aztec to return to his own people. After many years, the Lord returned and found that his followers, who had remained in the land, had married native women. His followers had raised families and had created many towns. The Lord wished for his followers to return to their native land, but they refused to go. After some time the Lord departed, but we have always known he would return to rightfully claim us as his vassals."

[Aztec King Montezuma, 1519 CE, addressing Hernan Cortez, believing he was Lord Quetzalcoatl returning, delivered this speech.] [from: A legend of the Aztec, Descendants of Teotihuacan.]

This speech provided the last faint trace of the Lords' existence on Earth. This event occurred approximately 700 years after the rescue of the Lords. Was this a promise made by a Lord who chose to remain on Earth? Or have we overestimated the round-trip travel time for the Lords to return? It does raise a lot of speculation. Was it the calculated 4,000-year cycle? Or, was it the religious cycle of the Maya, The Baktun, a 400-year cycle?

The End of the Aztec Empire

In 1492 Christopher Columbus, an Italian explorer with ties to the Vatican's outlawed Templars [Freemasons], persuaded the Royalty of Spain to finance his adventure to show the Earth was a globe. If true, the trip to the orient would be shorter and result in fortunes made from the spice trade. Spices were as valuable as gold in some markets. Chris was successful, using carefully guarded Templar maps and charts. These charts were called "Rudders" by ships pilots and were jealously guarded.

His and others' success resulted in transmitting deadly viruses and bacterial plagues to the new lands.   Tens of millions of original Americans, named after Amerigo Vespucci [Americus Vespucius, in Latin], died from influenza, smallpox, measles and many other bacterial plagues, which caused minor discomfort to Europeans. A later Spanish explorer of North America would write "There were no humans found during weeks of travel through lands bounding with game."

After Columbus' discovery of the "West Indies", a thriving market in the form of "licenses" to sail the new route was in place. The Italian "House of Medici" controlled a vast trading empire and the Vatican during this time. They virtually controlled who would be the Pope. They had an office in Spain which controlled the sale of licenses for ships sailing to the "West Indies".   Everyone assumed the land discovery was coastal islands of India. Medici had signed a monopoly deal with Columbus to control their trade empire by limiting who sailed this new trade route.

A young Italian employee of Medici was sent to Spain to spy on their Cadiz Spain operations because of rumors of corruption in the sale of licenses. His name was Americus Vespucius and he was successful in finding the crooks.

Americus became wealthy through various business dealings and put together 12 ships and crews for the Spanish Crown.   Americus' business supplied all ships with supplies for their voyages. The Vatican forced the cancellation of the monopoly on licenses when they realized they had lost control of this valuable resource.

In about 1500 Americus sailed under the flag of Portugal on the voyages which mapped the extent of the South American Atlantic coastline. Through his writings and influence it was agreed that the new lands were not the Indies but a new continent. In honor of his work the New World was named The Americas on maps by 1507.

After Columbus made his historic journey the Church granted slavery rights to Spain and Portugal for "All soulless masses living in the New Lands". The Blessed Conquerors slaughtered or enslaved millions of the "soulless masses" under the guise of *Devine Inspiration*.

In 1493, Brother Pope divided the world into two equal parts, Pole to Pole, awarding half to Portugal and half to Spain. The Conquistadors were not obliged to defer any actions to the Vatican for activities in any place not "governed by a "Christian Monarch". That is, a Monarch appointed by the Vatican.

The Papal Bul *Inter Caetera*, awarded colonial rights by the *Patronato Decree*, in which State authorities made all clerical appointments and these Priests would report to the Governors rather than to the Vatican.

This decree created the famous "Spanish Main" which included North and South America, except for a portion of eastern Brazil and Argentina.

Rising criticism of the slaughter and slavery in the Americas caused the Vatican to review the matter. The Pope heard the arguments that "the Indios were not truly human so could not be baptized". Also, and very important, he had no control of the Conquistadors and was not receiving his share of the profits. Pope Paul III issued the Papal Bulls Veritas Ipsa and Sublimis Deus in 1537, rescinding his previous Buls, and confirmed that although the Indios were not fully human they were human enough to receive baptism. This move put the Vatican back in charge of the "New World".

The decree was a shrewd political move. He mandated the Indios were "mere children" compared to real humans and should be wards of the Church under the care of church priests. The real meaning of "Mere Children" was that they had not fully evolved. This put them in the category of cattle and the Pope was claiming the herd. This provided for the construction of thousands of missions in the Americas and put the Vatican back in charge. If a Governor did not agree with the Church he was threatened with excommunication. This of course would be the end of his career and his head, so the Church always won.

This did not stop the missionaries, who searched for gold and gems, from tying Indios to turnstiles for crushing ore, blinding them with hot pokers and working them until death. There was an endless supply of unbaptized labor. The slaves were used in the gold and silver mines or for any other labor necessary.

Hernan Cortes [1485-1547 CE], the Spanish Expedition leader, after resupplying in Cuba, landed on the Yucatan Peninsula in 1519 CE with 600 soldiers and priests. He found an advanced civilization rich with gold and with teaming marketplaces. Cortez and his army were greeted with gold, food and women. The infection of both groups began. He sailed north along the coast, and eventually travelled overland, led by Aztec guides, to the Aztec Capitol Tenochtitlan. On the way his priests would preach to the locals, in Spanish, and when they did not convert to Christianity they were killed.

On November 8, 1519 Cortez challenged the local Aztec guards and entered Tenochtitlan to meet with the Aztec King Montezuma. King Montezuma believed Cortes to be the returning God Quetzalcoatl [Kukulkan in Maya era, The Feathered Serpent God of Teotihuacan], and received him with great honors.

According to ancient Mayan prophecy, Quetzalcoatl would return in the year 1519 CE, land on the eastern shore of Mexico, and greet his people with blessings. According to Aztec legend the God Quetzalcoatl was red haired, blue eyed and light skinned [this was Lord Bal's description]. At the Aztec reception for Cortes, Montezuma related the previous religious legend of the creation of the Aztec civilization.

After being welcomed and given a reception fitting a God, Cortez captured Montezuma and held him ransom for a room filled with gold. Eventually Montezuma was killed and war ensued. Cortez did not defeat the Aztec by force; his hidden weapon was smallpox and other diseases.

After six months Cortez was driven out of the city in July 1520, with severe losses. Men and seized gold overloaded the main bridge out of the city, which collapsed, with heavy losses to Cortez. Cortez waited and regrouped while 80% of the Aztec died from Smallpox, measles and other European diseases. A year later he attacked the city again and captured it on August 13, 1521.

Hundreds of thousands of Native Americans perished and Cortez was rich beyond belief. The Aztec capital was destroyed and Cortez built Mexico City on the ruins of the old Gods.

In 1549 Catholic priests, notably the Bishop of the Yucatan, destroyed everything he could find relating to Maya history. One of the Bishop's priests, who possessed a very high degree of intelligence, was able to decipher Mayan script. He dutifully gathered and read all the available script of the area, then destroyed every document that infringed on the teachings or authority of the Catholic Church. The remainder of the documents was sent to the Vatican archives, never to be seen again. These actions had a serious impact on the historical perspective of the area.

The destruction of the Mayan Codices by the early church was for the same reasons the early church destroyed Mitra documents and any writings not conforming to Vatican teachings.   As with all men, the priests were fallible in their efforts to destroy all of the historical records of the Maya, as they did with the beginnings of the western Holy Writs. The Vatican used the same tactics in the Americas as they did in Europe to eradicate previous religious followings. They killed all non-converted people and built their temples on the sites of previous temples.

Conquistador De Soto meets the Inki of Peru
Depicted as 1530's

Desoto and Cortez meet the Inki – 1532

South America
THE INKI
[1,438 - 1,533 CE]

The reconstituted Tiwanaku and satellite Wari Empires oversaw the Moche and Nazca Civilizations up to about 800 CE. The Moche later became the Chimor Empire [900 – 1100] centered at Chan Chan, located along Peru's coastal desert. These various civilizations continued to combine under new Inki leadership and build new temples and palaces over the centuries.

Chan Chan translates as "Sun, Sun" and is doubled as a method of increasing the stature of a name. In this case the Sun God was worshipped. Similar double name usage is found in several Sumerian languages. This society also worshipped a Moon Goddess and the warrior God [Son of the Sun and Moon Goddess].

The great city of Chan Chan emerged in the Moche Valley of Peru around the year 900 CE. The life source of this civilization was based on a fifty-mile extension of the existing canal system. The canal brought water across a desert area to facilitate an agricultural foundation for the city. The methods used to create the city were the same as all the other endeavors of the Lords.

At the time of Quetzalcoatl's death in the Toltec's Capital city of Tollan, the Tiwanaku and Wari Empires joined forces at the city of Cuzco. This was about 1100 CE. They then relocated the wealth and royalty from Chan Chan to Cuzco, a distance of about 600 miles. I do not believe in very many coincidences in history. I mention this because I assumed these remaining Lords did not communicate with each other. I believe this was a wrong assumption due to the immediate reorganization in South America. The last Lord, or Lords, knew their time was over and planned for their descendants' future.

This was the beginnings of the Inki Empire [Inca]. The empire was expanded by offering neighboring civilizations the benefits of the Empire if they would adhere to the Inki leadership and their religious followings of Inti, The Sun God. If the neighbor declined, they were invaded and after replacing their leaders they became part of the Inki

Empire. Although part of the empire, they were not "Inki". The Inki could be viewed as the Priests of the Empire.

Inki meant "Lord" and the population of the Inki was 15,000 to 25,000 people. They governed from 10 to 37 Million inhabitants of the Inca Empire, which ran most of the length of South America. The various tribes operated as city-states, borrowing and exporting labor for massive projects throughout the Empire. The Inca Empire encompassed thousands of miles of the western portion of South America, from Ecuador, through Peru, and south through Chile. Their cities and highways continue to be a marvel of engineering feats.

Cuzco functioned much the same for South America as Tiahuanaco functioned for Central America. Cuzco was the last vestige of the Lords in the Americas. The legend of the founder of the Kingdom of Cuzco was Manco Capac, the leader of all of the Gods on Earth. Then the Sapa Inca [Highest ranking Lord] of Cuzco, whose name was Pachacuti-Cusi Yupanqui brought in neighboring empires under the authority of Cuzco. This Lord's name translates as "Earth Shaker". Earth Shaker conquered those empires that refused the offer to join Cuzco. Earth Shaker was the War God son of Inti [Sun God] and Mama Killa [Moon Goddess].

From the Inca capital city of Cuzco, the remaining Lords built their last empire. When the last Lord died, the central authority was passed on to local priests. The history of the Inca Empire is relatively short in comparison to other regional civilizations.

Cusco was an absolute marvel of a planned city with a grid layout, water and drainage systems along with housing complexes connected by paved roads for quick exits and entry. The stone buildings of the Inki were clad with gold inside and out. Nothing in Europe compared with the excellence and grandeur of Cusco.

I believe the last of the lineage of the original Lords died around 1438. This is when the recorded lineage of the Inki began; when Pachacuti created the Tawantinsuyu. Tawantinsuyu was name of the Inki Empire centered at Cuzco with four districts, which were governed by "Strong Lords", most likely direct descendants of the original Lords.

From near the Inca site of Machu Picchu to Tiwanaku, the stone walls were reinforced with cast-in-place metal ties. The ties were formed by molten metal poured into carved recesses in two adjacent stones. This provided additional stability in an earthquake prone area. More Neolithic Artisanship? I doubt it!

Pachacuti-Cusi Yupanqui built Machu Pichu as a royal palace and center for religious ceremonies. The religion and Gods followed the same grouping and beliefs which were introduced in Sumer and followed by the Minoans, Egyptians, Romans, and in Teotihuacan. They just used different names based on local language.

Machu Pichu also served as the corporate headquarters for managing trade goods throughout the Empire. Machu Pichu was the site for the Inki Emperor God who controlled trade and religion. Cuzco served as the administrative warehousing and distribution center for the entire Inki Empire. This is identical to the structure the Lords created on Thera and Crete.

The Inki tracked goods using knotted twine bundles. These served the same purpose as clay tablets in the Mediterranean. The Lords always kept meticulous records of people and trade. Academia insists the knotted twine bundles are the only "language evidence" of the Inki.

Inki Religious Dogma
[Similar to Mitra and Christian dogma]

The Creator God was Viracocha:
Viracocha, or Pachamac, created all living things, plant and animal. Man was a descendant of God.

Pachamama was the wife of Viracocha and Goddess of Earth

Inti was the Sun God, with his worship based in Cuzco.

Mama Killa, the wife of Inti, was the Moon Goddess.

Manco Capac was the Son and God who descended to Earth to teach and save the Inca.

There were many other Gods for solutions to all of life's situations, from a bad hair day to no rain.

The Inca practiced mass human sacrifice, infant sacrifice and believed in an afterlife. If their corpse was burned, they could not go to heaven and would be eternally bound to wander the Earth. Heaven was a place of serenity and flowered fields with no worries.

There is much more about the Inki Empire but as with other Empires, they came to an end by circumstances unanticipated. This one fell to foreign diseases and religious zealots guided by God and Gold.

Conquistador Francisco Pizarro discovered Inca territory in 1526 along the Ecuadoran and Peruvian coastlines and found a very rich Empire. He returned to Spain and reported the wonders and treasures of this very wealthy country. In July 1529 the Queen of Spain gave Francisco the charter to conquer Peru and appointed him as Governor of all conquered lands.

He returned to Peru in 1532 accompanied by Hernando de Soto, but during his six-year absence about 94% of the Inca population had died from Smallpox, Typhus, influenza, measles and diphtheria. These epidemics raged from Columbia to Chile. It is presumed the efficient Inka road system prompted the spread of death throughout the empire.

The end of the Inca came with a meeting of the Spanish, and the Inca ruler God known as Atahualpa, "The Inki", to his followers. The meeting was to convert the heathens to Christianity and to accept the rule of King Charles I of Spain. At this meeting a Spanish priest reportedly handed a copy of the Holy Writ to The Inca and explained it was "The word of God". The Inca held the book to his ear, and hearing nothing, threw the book away. This was cause enough to declare the Incas as heretics or sub-human and kill or capture every one the Spanish could find. Many who escaped eventually died of the new diseases the Spanish brought to America.

In 1572 the last Inca Lord, The Inki, was captured and executed. The Vatican continued its methods of destroying all writings and monuments to past empires and religions and building their churches on the destroyed sites.

The Inki lasted from their beginning [1438] to the death of the last Inki [1572] a total of 134 years. As a functioning civilization they lasted about 94 years before disease wiped them out.

The entire demise of the Civilizations and Empires of the Americas took place between 1492 and 1572, a very short period of 80 years; to conquer, kill and subjugate an entire hemisphere. It does demonstrate the power of biological warfare combined with religious power.

The descendants of the survivors of the original Americans were indoctrinated with Vatican objectives for the World. I doubt this history I have presented has ever been objectively presented in educating young people. I find it ironic that most of these descendants worship the organized religion which destroyed them. A final note, it is believed by researchers that the Inca had no written language. These same researchers believe another entire civilization had no way to cook food.

I find these conclusions difficult to believe. It is unimaginable to think the rulers of 37 million people relayed edicts of their entire history and religious mythology verbally to the entire sub-continent of South America. I find it more believable that the Vatican was more proficient in destroying all Inki language documentation and glyphs in South America than they were in Central America with the Maya and in the Middle East and Europe with the Mitra followers.

I think that once the Vatican priests deciphered the religious mythology of the Inki, they realized the similarities to their religion would be devastating. As usual the Vatican acted to remove any threat to their religious mythology. This was one of the reasons the Inki and their leaders were all hunted and executed as heretics, to exterminate any possible avenue of compiling true Inki history.

What is known today about these ancient civilizations comes from the journals of early explorers and from modern archaeologists. I believe a new class of archaeologists has emerged, one which will be guided by valid findings and scientific analysis. The time has come to end the suppression of truths due to political and religious bias. I applaud their efforts and at the same time condemn the prostitution of history by tin-hat "researchers".

The Inki is Executed as a Heretic
"The Inki" was the last Leader of all Inca - 1572

Book IV

Final Secrets

FOR NOTES

Chapter 1

**Mystic Mountain
heic1007a Carina**

EINSTEIN AND THE MAYA COMPUTATIONS

Modern Theories and Discoveries from The Maya

During the 1800s a lack of mobility and technology limited access to jungle areas. Archaeologists did not have easy access, nor did they possess technological support of modern equipment. Since that time, like the history of Sumer and Egypt, there has been constant exploration of all regions of Central and South America. Each expedition has revealed new secrets of the ancient civilizations.

Although considerable information has accumulated, authors continue to present information based on their own special interests. Some slant the information to impress an inner circle of intellectuals. If ecology or religion was popular, then the rise and demise of the civilization was based on that premise. Their research papers all presented bits of valid information, but the presentations only served to cloud reality. From the 1940's to present day, archaeologists and historians have presented an attitude that is pervasive today. The prevailing attitude is the Mayan civilization was like no other civilization on Earth.

The intellectual presentations continue to state the motivation of the Maya was religion, created by a sect of priests who were unusually gifted astronomers. The Maya are generally regarded as a people without a written history or language. That is absurd and is not true. The "sudden disappearance" of this civilization is simply regarded as the passing of a unique civilization, which rarely had to deal with serious problems. It is ludicrous for a group of learned intellectuals to put forth such a view. And yes, the Maya had a written history. Most of the written history was destroyed by Brother Pope and his minions. The same policy was used to obliterate the history of Mitra worshippers in the Roman Empire. The Maya did not "disappear", they continued to live, as well as possible under European attack, in their ancestral homelands.

If you exchanged Mayan, for Sumerian, Indus, or Egyptian, you would have a description of all the civilizations. No one wanted a close comparison of the cultures because history had already been set in an acceptable format. Today, although attitudes are shaped by university tenure, they have managed to evolve.

An important fact about the history of The Americas is that a very advanced culture and civilization [Tiwanaku Civilization] was established about 20,000 years ago. This is on par with the civilizations established in Euro-Asia, Africa and possibly others. Academia would have you believe Man encountered The Americas by way of the glacial land bridges and ate the large animals lost in the Pleistocene Extinction of 12,900 years ago.

Today when historians and archaeologists compare the civilizations of Sumer, Indus, or Egypt to Central America, we are presented with statements of, *strikingly similar*. As a new class of the archaeological community continues their excavations, more evidence of *strikingly similar* comes into view. Younger archaeologists are less hesitant to speculate on the connotations of their finds, and attitudes are changing.

Have you ever wondered how, in many instances in past years, some brilliant young minds have been able to conceive even more brilliant theories regarding universal time and space? The deciphering of Maya codex tablets in 19th Century Germany inspired and triggered the brilliant minds of researchers in several Universities. The deciphered data of several codices revealed the theories of time and space travel.

In 1832 a European genius studied the Dresden Codex and deciphered the Maya's math system. In 1880 a German mathematician,

Förstemann, working at the Dresden library, decoded the Maya's astrological tables and calendars.

After considerable investigation it was discovered that the codices are mathematical in nature. The codices were then analyzed by the most brilliant mathematicians available to unlock the complete use and secrets of the stone time calculators.

In the early 1900's, the group of scientific geniuses was relatively small. The sharing, or exchange of information, was limited to people following the same interests. Within this rather limited group there is a very human practice of finding out how much your friends know, and on which projects are they working. The object of the intellectual game is to publish your findings or theories ahead of your peer group.

The most prominent group of mathematicians was that of Albert Einstein [General Theory of Relativity], Erwin Schrodinger [Theory of Wave Mechanics], Werner Heisenberg [Quantum Mechanics], and Max Born [Atomic Physicist – Quantum Mechanics/Physics]. During the early 1900s this group was working on various projects regarding theoretical physics. The group, some acting as individuals, produced theoretical papers on complex numbers. Also produced were papers on physics known as, the theory of relativity, wave mechanics, matrix mechanics, and finally the concept of the link between classical physics and quantum mechanics.

Very coincidentally, in the same time of the emergence of the Maya codex systems, Einstein began to diverge from the mainstream thoughts of the group. The following information comes from a bibliography of Einstein. The information is Einstein's response to the group's production of the matrix mechanics theory.

Albert Einstein [1879-1955] greatly influenced many areas of science; however, he diverged from the mainstream theoretical concepts of the group. He published the **General Theory of Relativity** [Die Grundlage der Allgemeinen Relativitätstheorie'] in 1916. The theory is based on the geometry of universal space-time, and the elements that would influence the measurement of how we view time. Einstein believed the use of his theory of relativity was necessary to attain a correct measurement of time-space if a moving body approached the speed of light. Einstein produced a **Special Theory of Relativity** as part of his overall Theory.

A small portion of his General Theory predicts the time-space relationship of a body at rest, near a concentration of mass [star or planet], is different than the time-space relationship of a body traveling at extremely high velocity in open space. Simplified, this proposes that a vehicle traveling at or near the speed of light, in open space, will occupy very little physical area, and time on board the vehicle will differ from the relative time on Earth.

My additional thought to this theory is: If we can accept this premise of time and volume condensing travel, then it would follow that this effect would geometrically increase if velocities greater than, or multiples of, the speed of light were attained. The effect would continue until the travel vehicle came within the proximity of a planet or star. However, although I am not a scientist, I cannot get my mind to agree that time is not time. To me time is a fixed past event. Einstein's theories certainly provided great leaps in the study of complex math and physics, I do think in years to come these theories will be revised to include hyper-light-speed travel as a possibility.

The General Theory of Relativity predicts how to correctly measure time and space, rather at rest [motionless] or at multiples of light speed. The codex does exactly that. Could Einstein have started with the correct answers to space travel and worked backwards, attempting to explain how the codex achieved the correct result?

I also find it strange, that in the 1920's when Man was still using double winged *aeroplanes* and trying to determine how to advance the technology to improve them; suddenly we are provided a theory of mathematically measuring time-space and traveling across the universe in relatively short periods of time. Or more correctly said, how to measure the distances and travel time variations within the universe. Of course, it could have all been coincidence.

Archaeologists continue their excavations in Central and South America at several hundred sites. The system used to explain the lost civilizations remains the same as it did fifty years ago. Emphasis is placed on finding royal tombs of ancient rulers, and the treasure of precious stones, gold, and other artistic artifacts. The deeper the archaeologist excavates, the less the historian sees. We are presented with glittering jewelry instead of promoting the motivation, intelligence, and discipline it took to build the civilization.

From an historical perspective, the system slowly advances. In Central America progress can be measured in attitudes of *strikingly similar*, to finally the statement of; *It becomes very apparent there was interdependency between the cultures and civilizations.* A small group of scholars has finally managed to use some internal fortitude to make the following statement.

"The accumulated evidence is so impressive and overwhelming that Phoenicians reached the shores of both Central and South America, it is hard to understand why it continues to be disregarded."

An interesting article by a researcher for a prominent American university regarding Mayan civilization made a reference to the introduction of foreign stimuli, which led to the Classic Maya Period. And, that such foreign stimulus continued at an increasing rate well into the Preclassic Period. The author should have defined the term, *foreign stimuli.* I wondered if by using a form of intellectual drivel, he was trying to make a statement of introduced intelligence. The author went as far as he could in making the statement. However, so there is no confusion regarding the statement, it is possible the author was referring to the influence by the Lords from the city of Teotihuacan in Mexico. If this was the case, he was correct.

There is physically real, hard evidence of foreign stimuli in the Mayan region of civilization. Mayan stone relief pictures clearly depict men wearing the attire of the Semitic culture. The stone reliefs also show braided or curled beards and hairstyles of ancient Sumer. Painted murals show these curled beards as red and brown in color.

Comparing the stone reliefs, paintings, stone masonry, mathematics, engineering feats, astronomy, and other strikingly similar features of Central and South America with the Sumerian and Egyptian civilizations provides unmistakable answers.

For Notes

Chapter

2

1950's SR-71
Blackbird

THE ROSWELL, NEW MEXICO INCIDENT

The following is presented as entertaining history to simply provoke you to wonder what is truth or fiction in our recent past. This rendition of history is decades old.

This is a dissertation of "The Roswell Incident", which led to the secret advanced development sites for aircraft, weapons and computer science. "The Skunk Works", "Area 51" and "Area 52" information was compiled from existing records and a few undisclosed sources privy to Projects Blue Star, Moon Dust, Blue Fly, Badger and several others best not disclosed. Most of this was originally presented 30 years ago and is history only, but it may be entertaining and thought provoking for you. Consider this as another "Old War Story".

An historic event will hold the public's interest only if that event produced an unsolved mystery. One unsolved mystery has held public attention for over eight decades. This event produced the possibility that Earth received visitors from across the Universe. It is known as the **Roswell Incident**. For those who are unfamiliar with the Roswell story, the following is the general scenario of the mystery. This was originally written about 30 years ago. Many revelations since have sharpened the focus of this incident.

On July 4, 1947, shortly after the end of World War II, a rancher reported to the sheriff of Roswell, New Mexico that a UFO had crashed near his ranch. The local sheriff responded by notifying the

Base Commander of an Air Force installation also located near the town. Subsequently, the Base Commander made a public statement that a spacecraft had been recovered. The following day, the Commander changed his story and reported that a damaged weather balloon, not a spacecraft, had been recovered. Although there continued to be conflicting accounts regarding what had been recovered, the Air Force remained steadfast that a weather balloon, not a spacecraft, had been recovered.

As the Roswell Incident is explained it is very important to understand there were two parallel situations. The US Government devised a solution dealing with both. First, there was intense public interest in the event, and second, the Government was protecting the secret of Roswell from foreign military intelligence. The time was one year after World War II, and hostilities were escalating with the USSR.

Based on the spacecraft recovery story, one Hollywood film was produced. This movie was followed by what appears to be an investigative television program that was indeed interesting and provided valuable insight into the event. In the program, an eyewitness reported four alien bodies were found, and also stated a fifth alien appeared to be alive and well. The program included parts of what appear to be a film taken of an autopsy performed on a dead alien humanoid creature.

The film was presented as explicit proof that indeed a spacecraft, complete with aliens, had been recovered. Following the film clips of the autopsy there was an interview with some person of reported scientific prominence, focusing on the authenticity of the film clip. The conclusion being, if the film was authentic, the recovery of the spacecraft could be totally verified.

The program also presented information that the owner of the film refused to release it to be examined. There was a continuing effort to obtain the film from the reluctant owner. The media depiction of the Roswell scenario was very cute. The word *cute* is defined as "deceptively straightforward" and the Roswell scenario was a "cute" psychological trap.

To understand what developed with the "Roswell Story" you must enter the world of reality. One of those realities is, of course, that the film is a hoax. The film was made so it could be found to be a hoax. Once the film had been scientifically determined to be a hoax, the whole Roswell scenario would lose public credibility.

It is necessary to reveal the secrets of the Roswell Incident because what has been publicly released is historically deceptive. The hoax created by the film, of the dead aliens, caused people to exchange their mental image of historical reality for that of science fiction. This episode was manipulated using multiple frauds. Following the multiple frauds was selective disinformation fed to the Press by our CIA. The CIA and other "intelligence agencies" continue to use this effective strategy.

The combination of these deceptions can create any psychological atmosphere desired. As an example, in the 1950's it was very common for people to voice a belief in the possibility of "Alien" visitors from across the universe. The foundation for this belief was based on the Roswell Incident. However, today such views are usually met with public ridicule. Public officials shun even discussing the possibility of humans living in a distant galaxy.

This prevailing attitude is the result of selective disinformation, and the process is very simple. At selected times a television program concerning the possibilities of life existing outside our own solar system is presented. Before the taping of the program, the producers make sure that all guests appear to be mentally dysfunctional in one form or another. They always have one or two that relate stories of being abducted by aliens.

A prime example of selective disinformation occurred on July 4, 1996 at Roswell. As a humorous event, the local people of Roswell sponsored a UFO landing celebration, in conjunction with the celebration of Independence Day. The parade and celebration were covered by national media reporters. After a short introduction that related the origin of the celebration, the cameras focused on the local parade. The parade was filled with people dressed in comical spacesuit costumes. One spacesuit was bright pink, with the occupant wearing what appeared to be a space helmet with extended antennae.

Following the view of the parade, the news commentator conducted several interviews with the people of the celebration. The results of the conversations were as expected. All the people interviewed appeared to be somewhat discreditable and inebriated. The program implied that anyone who was interested in the Roswell event was a crank, drunk, or merrymaker, and a lot of tourist dollars crash-landed in Roswell. The result was a program, which knowing or unknowing, promoted selective disinformation.

As for the actual 1947 event of Roswell, a different and more effective method was used to discredit the witnesses. Each person provided a view of their own individual involvement, or that of gained knowledge. These credible witnesses provided enough information to substantiate that something unusual had happened in the area. There were too many witnesses, or people who had access to information, to totally discredit them all.

The solution to the problem was to create a multiple fraud situation. First, the Air Force officer used the only credible information available to begin the fraud. He stated that a damaged weather balloon had fallen in the region. This was the first level of the fraud. The second level involved military personnel at the crash site. They were probably instructed to add false information that was somewhat believable. The false information was that the spacecraft contained occupants. The third level was to create a film showing humanoid creatures being autopsied. The overall intent of the fraud was to totally protect what had been found near Roswell. The plan was, if necessary, a last-ditch effort to expose the film to the public as a fraud. The psychological impact of exposing the film as a hoax would result in the total collapse of interest in the subject.

The result of this process guaranteed the secret of Roswell would remain hidden from public view. However, someone underestimated the depth of public attention for this specific event. Instead of the public becoming interested in one specific location, the age of Unidentified Flying Object sightings came into being. In the following years, thousands of UFO sightings were reported. This popular phase of American culture filled a very necessary void needed to divert attention from the Roswell event. The UFO phenomenon blended reality with science fiction.

The result of this popular phenomenon was exactly what the government needed to maintain independent control of unusual events. By appearing to be responsive to public concern, the government-initiated Project Blue Book. The project was geared to investigate every reported UFO sighting and publish the results. Project Blue Book existed for many years and served to quell public concern. The results were rarely compared to the Roswell event. Year after year, each investigated sighting proved to be something other than a UFO.

After some time, the general public forgot about the events of Roswell. During those years it was unnecessary to publicly reveal the hoax of the Roswell film. Instead, public interest was focused on the Blue Book reports. When public concern mounted regarding the validity of the ongoing investigations, the government graciously explained every detail of each investigation. The reason for such an open response to public concern was the investigators were employees of the Federal Government. Being paid employees, what would you suspect the investigators findings would be?

In researching this historical period, I could not find any evidence of a civilian review board regarding Project Blue Book. I do recall a television series produced based on Project Blue Book, which apparently kept the general population happy. Many people viewed the entire scenario as another government tap dance provided to a gullible public. Personally, I am not a UFO enthusiast, but for a public to allow the government to assign a military group to investigate UFO phenomena is unbelievable. That is like sending a weasel to the hen house to count the chickens. However, there were no UFO's found by the intensive efforts of the government investigation. At least none were found that fit the description used by the writers of science fiction. In any event, the secret of Roswell was safe.

The Roswell event can now be explained, devoid of fraud and disinformation. On the morning of July 4, 1947, a rancher reported an unusual object had crashed on an area of his ranch. An Air Force sergeant reported he was given orders to bring a semi-truck and flatbed trailer rig to the crash site where a spacecraft was loaded onto the rig. The spacecraft was then driven to an aircraft hangar located at the nearby Air Force base.

There have been conflicting information releases regarding the size of the spacecraft. There were reports it was twenty-five to thirty-five feet in length, and that it was fitted to seat four or five small occupants. If this information is correct, the spacecraft was small enough to fit on the flatbed trailer. The relatively small size can be substantiated, as there was no mention of the use of heavy cranes to lift the object. Apparently whatever equipment was on hand at the Air Force base was used to load the spacecraft. Typically, the equipment would have been tow trucks, forklifts and small truck-mounted two-ton cranes known as "bomb loaders." Someone was very confident, before ordering the truck and trailer that the spacecraft would fit on the flatbed trailer.

The Government next began a disinformation campaign using the psychology of the 1940's and telling half-truths. The spacecraft was relatively small and had been seen by many possible future witnesses. Therefore, it was very possible the existence of the spacecraft would become known at some future date. Because the spacecraft was small, the fabricated crew members would also have to be physically small. So, a small crew was created for a small spacecraft. The reported physically small crewmembers also fit the psychological profile of what people thought visitors from across the universe should look like.

In the 1940's and 1950's, there was a popular conception that advanced technology would reduce physical labor. The idea was, if an entire civilization did not have to engage in physical labor over a given time, their bodies would shrink. And, at the same time their brains would expand to an enormous size. The result would be small people with oversized heads. The general idea was, the larger the head the more intelligent the person would be. This perspective of thinking was the mind-set of most of our population when the Roswell film was made.

The occupants of the supposed spacecraft coincidentally met the mental image of what the general public believed strange visitors should look like, *Little Green Men from Outer Space.* If the same event occurred today, the Roswell filmmakers would produce a crew such as seen on a popular science fiction program.

Only one major American movie company had the resources, and top security clearances, to produce an elaborate, almost technically correct movie. For the film to be made on relative short notice would have been expensive. If we combine the cost of the film and the event it was related to, the source of the funding would have to be the US Government. The filmmaker most likely was Howard Robard Hughes, owner of RKO Radio Motion Picture Studios. Mr. Hughes was a great American and performed many untold services for his country, and the CIA.

Fabricating this hoax in 1947 was both easy and necessary for National Security. We possessed something extremely important and needed to maintain absolute secrecy. World War II had ended only two years earlier, and the greatest perceived threat to the United States was Russia. The Russians had one of the finest intelligence services in the world. The hoax film could surely convince the general public that the Americans were in possession of a spacecraft and its dead crew.

Under the examination of Russian intelligence experts, the film would be discovered to a fraud. And that is exactly what happened. In one manner or another, the CIA allowed the KGB to obtain a copy of the film. After an examination, the Russians concluded the dead crewmembers were fakes and wrote the incident off as a crude attempt to fool them. This response was exactly what American Military Intelligence wanted. The Russians never suspected the crew was faked and the spacecraft was real.

This leads us to the spacecraft itself. The size of the spacecraft indicates it was too small to support life for any long duration. The idea that this small spacecraft came from a mother ship is not very realistic. There were too many telescopes and observatories on the Earth for a large spacecraft to orbit unobserved. An explanation of later American history will bear out the following conclusion. The Air Force had recovered a space probe. The term *space probe* is defined as an unmanned spacecraft.

Although the space probe was a great deal more sophisticated, its purpose mirrors that of space technology today. The United States has been launching known space probes for years. I would suspect, based on the events of the last 50 years and the advances in technology, that the spacecraft was mapping solar systems. This spacecraft was most likely programmed to home in on radio signals, which provided the directional course to Earth. Another way of explaining this is, it is very doubtful the spacecraft was purposely sent to Earth. Of course, that is just an opinion.

There was a huge burst of radio wave energy launched into space about two years before the space probe landed near Roswell. This high-energy wave was sufficient to cause the probe's sensors to lock onto the origin. The radio wave burst occurred at Trinity Site on July 16, 1945. The world's first Atomic Bomb was detonated in the pre-dawn hours, sending a blast of light and burst of high-energy radio waves, of all frequencies, into space.

This phenomenon had not occurred in the modern history of Man. Trinity Site is located about 100 miles west of the Roswell Landing Site.

The unmanned probe did not burn up as it entered the Earth's atmosphere and did not destroy itself due to extreme impact. Therefore, it had to have internal guidance systems that would place the spacecraft in the proper attitude to obtain an Earth orbit. After the spacecraft achieved orbit, it again had to slow itself for a landing. The reason the spacecraft was not destroyed through an impact, was that it landed.

The landing was in rough desert terrain, and a crash would have spread debris across a wide area. There would not have been any reason for a flatbed trailer to be dispatched to the site to recover debris. The flatbed trailer indicates the spacecraft was in one piece. The debris reported to be at the landing site was most likely the foil-like material from the deployed drogue, or landing parachute.

It was 1947, and the United States had a spacecraft, but did not possess the technology to understand its secrets. At some point, it was determined the spacecraft had purposely homed in on radio signals. Have we slipped off into the world of science fiction? It could be argued that past and current space programs do not prove another civilization could do the same thing. Or it could be said we are the only persons alive with the ability to send out unmanned space vehicles and land them on distant planets. Or, more simply stated, the Earth's space programs are indeed real, but anything else is science fiction. Instead of creating a debate on the issue, we need to carefully examine history subsequent to 1947. The following information is available at most local libraries. This information has previously been presented but is used now to reiterate subsequent information.

In the mid 1960's, I believe about 1967, Congress began "publicly" funding radio dish signal stations. The initial funding was ten million dollars a year for six years. This same program has continued to be funded for almost forty years. The public had been told the radio dish sites are used to attempt to receive radio signals from possible civilizations, somewhere in the universe. And this information is very true. But, what has not been said is, that purpose is secondary.

The primary purpose is sending signals, not receiving signals. I am sure that initially it was possible to obtain sixty million dollars based on the mathematical probability that civilizations exist somewhere in the universe.

But what would it take to have such a program continue for the next fifty years? Would you suspect that somewhere along the way you would have to produce evidence? Or would you simply give the same presentation each time you appeared before Congress? At some point you would have to provide viable evidence to receive continued funding. I suspect the funding was initiated, and continued, based on the theory the Roswell spacecraft had homed in on radio signals. The secret to the extended funding is that a second unmanned spacecraft made a hard landing in the state of Ohio.

The available information is from these two fragmented stories with parallel history, and begs for a conclusion. In the mid 1970's a second unmanned spacecraft was recovered. The event was thought to be very unusual, but the event occurred twenty-five years after the Roswell spacecraft landing. The public never tied the two events together because; both events were submerged in the realm of science fiction.

In the second recovery, an unmanned spacecraft made a hard landing near a small town in Ohio. Several witnesses viewed the spacecraft, which appeared to be similar to that of a nose cone of a large missile or rocket. One man who had a close look at the spacecraft said it was inscribed with strange symbols. He said the symbols looked like those used in ancient Egypt. He explained the Egyptian description was as close as he could come to describing what he had seen. Very shortly after the spacecraft landed, a military unit closed off the entire area.

As in Roswell, a semi-truck and flatbed trailer was used to load the vehicle. The spacecraft was then covered with a large tarp. The truck and trailer departed the town under military escort. The entire scenario has been labeled the *Hangar 18 of Ohio Event*. For anyone interested the specific details are available.

Combining all of the information available regarding the two separate events of Roswell, New Mexico, and of Ohio leaves considerable speculation, conjecture, suspicion of, and a myriad of conflicting information. There is no hard evidence the two unmanned spacecraft actually exist. Given the secrecy of governmental agencies, you will probably never have specific evidence of either spacecraft.

Reviewing these stories from a different perspective will establish that the government has an ongoing program using radio signals to contact, lead, or lure unmanned space vehicles. The evidence of such a program would be in locating specific receivers and sending stations. These facilities would blend in with many other projects involving radio astronomy. Several facilities are in operation for these specific purposes.

An example of a project that sends and receives deep space radio signals is the Arecibo Observatory located in Puerto Rico. The Arecibo Observatory was the worlds' largest radio telescope when constructed. The receiver dish is one thousand feet wide. The observatory is used to search for radio signals from other civilizations somewhere in the universe. The Chinese have since constructed a

500-meter Aperture Spherical Telescope which has unbelievable capabilities of monitoring very deep space.

If you were going to build a station to send or receive homing or directional signals, you would locate the station near your best region for success. If the first spacecraft homed in near Roswell, that is the region where I would build a station to broadcast for another vehicle. Researching information for receiver and sender stations that would meet all the requirements, the first area of interest was possible locations similar to Roswell. I found what I was looking for and I must say, it was very easy to locate. The nearest town is Socorro, New Mexico, which is about 154 miles west of Roswell, and only 30 miles west of Trinity Site.

The Socorro station contained a very large array [VLA] of twenty-seven mobile, directional radio dishes. The radio dishes are termed parabolic antennas, which transmit to a central computer. The dishes are built on a special railroad laid out in the form of a Y. Each arm of the railroad is thirteen miles long. The dishes can be moved and grouped along any point of the railway. This system provides for 351 possible combinations of interconnected antennae. The receiving resolution as well as the transmitting capabilities exceeded that of any optical telescope on Earth, at that time.

In July 1947, after successfully confusing the public and subduing the Russian military intelligence interests, the American government had a spacecraft safely in their possession. But they also had a problem; they did not have the capability to effectively understand the technology of the spacecraft. There is no doubt the public of our present day will never be told the truth regarding Roswell. Therefore, we must turn to history itself for evidence the Roswell spacecraft did indeed, exist.

The spacecraft recovered from Roswell was transported by secure railroad to a site near Oakridge, Tennessee. What our government had in their possession caused the birth of an extremely remote, super-secret site. The site was located north of Las Vegas, Nevada and we know it today as "Site 51." The spacecraft was removed from Oakridge and transported by rail to Las Vegas, and on to Site 51 by truck. To maintain absolute secrecy of the site, the Nevada Test Site for nuclear testing was established and provided a vast perimeter around Site 51. An older brother of mine worked on building the roads to these sites. They were designed to appear as unimproved desert roads but were able to support vast loads of material to "51".

In the twenty years following Roswell, dramatic changes occurred in the technologies of flight. Another way of saying this is, everything regarding advanced technology changed. New avenues of thought suddenly emerged. I believe the technology onboard the Roswell spacecraft created new avenues of thinking and present-day technology simply evolved as a natural result.

In early 1948 our government established "The Skunk Works" in Southern California and "Area 51" located near Groom Lake, Nevada, both for secret aeronautical developments. The Skunk Works was the analysis and design center, and Area 51 was the center for research, development and field trails. Hailed as a monumental success, the highly classified project "Tacit Blue" resulted in, to name a few, microchips, new metallurgy, composite materials, advanced radar systems, stealth technology, and the impulse propulsion power units. Both sites continued their remarkable work until recently.

Area 51 has resumed life as a secure research and development location. Also, Area 52 in Utah has been in use since the 1940's.

Before the end of World War II, the Germans and English had produced the jet engine. After the war many countries were continuing to improve the jet engine and made considerable progress. Larger and more powerful engines were successfully designed in a relatively short time; however, the flight engineers were faced with difficult problems. One problem was the heavy metals used to produce the frames of the aircraft greatly reduced the full capability of the new engines. The aircraft were simply too heavy for the jet engines to reach maximum speed. Another problem was the jet turbine metal alloys could not withstand the heat produced by full power without quickly burning out. This is where the US advanced; reproducing the internal engine alloys from the recovered spacecraft.

Quite suddenly American flight technology made astounding progress. In less than three years after the Roswell event, in early 1950, the United States had a fully operational spy plane known as the U-2 aircraft. The aircraft was constructed with new forms of lightweight metals. These new materials were combinations of titanium and aluminum/cobalt base metals combined with carbon elements. These newly developed metals for the aircraft skin, and jet engines, allowed flight at maximum speeds and altitude.

The metal skin of the U-2 aircraft was so unique that it expanded and contracted back to natural form when subjected to various temperature changes.   The total weight of the U-2 aircraft was 17,000 pounds. Considering the aircraft's function, size, and design, it was considered to be very lightweight. Early on, the aircraft had a cruising altitude above 80,000 feet and the camera capability of taking two thousand highly detailed photographs over a nine-hour period.

As history has indicated, it is very conceivable the Roswell spacecraft provided the means to develop the new forms of metals. It is also very possible, or probable, the spacecraft provided the information necessary to catapult American technology into the Space Age. A spacecraft from across the universe would be able to provide technology relating to metals, microcomputer chips, camera lenses, possibly plastics and a new form of aerodynamics known as lifting bodies. During the next 30 years these technologies made dramatic advances.

One production of the Roswell event provided a witness who drew a picture of the spacecraft. In this hand drawn sketch, the witness described what appeared to him as a cluster of cells located on the underside of the spacecraft, similar to the cells in a beehive. For a spacecraft that was charting solar systems, the cells would have been long-range camera lens. The sketch also provides a crude view of the upper front of the spacecraft. If you compare the sketch to the same front portion of the SR71 Blackbird spy plane, you will find the comparison very interesting.   The SR71 appears to have the same design features.

For those who are unfamiliar with the SR71 Blackbird, it was the second spy plane developed in 1950's. The Russians shot down the slower U-2 with new missiles. The SR-71 aircraft can still [today] fly at altitudes in excess of 90,000 feet and speeds of over 2,200 miles per hour [Mach 3.5] [government admitted data]. We know it can perform well beyond those admitted limits. As one pilot explained in debriefing after a flight over Russia in the Late 1970's, "The Soviet S75 SAM [surface to air missile] locked on at 60K [60,000 feet altitude] and I went to the wall [full throttles] and outran it." I can assure you that the second stage of a Russian S75 SAM punched up well beyond 2,200 miles per hour. The secret of the SR71 is that the area forward of the canopy and along the body is very similar to the unmanned lifting-body spacecraft from across the universe.

1950s "Skunk Works" SR-71 Blackbird over Area 51 - built by Lockheed-Martin: Unclassified as existing in the early 1960s. Ceiling of 90,000 feet @ Mach 3.5

The advances of the SR71 program were accomplished about eight decades ago. We now have spacecraft, which are ground launched, that can achieve orbit and return to a controlled landing for continued use. These spacecraft are both manned and unmanned and can be armed and can exceed Mach 7.

The "Skunkworks" has produced several evolutions beyond the SR 71. A developed SR-72 [unmanned capable with Mach 6+ capability] has been introduced, so it has been flying for at least 40 years. Our super aircraft [Spacecraft] must be kept secret as the world powers have an easy way to reverse engineer our developments. Rest assured the USA has capabilities which are difficult to imagine.

A note about Howard Hughes always assisting the CIA. When a Soviet nuclear submarine [K-129] sank with all hands in the Pacific Ocean in 1968, the Agency depended on Mr. Hughes to pursue the recovery under "**Project Azorian**". K-129 sank approximately 1,560 nautical miles [2,890 km] northwest of Hawaii. Hughes built the Glomar Explorer and used the "**Mohole Project**" as cover for his operation. Project Azorian was one of the most expensive and secretive intelligence operations of the Cold War and cost about $800 million, or +$4 billion in todays' dollars.

The Mohole Project was an effort by scientists to drill into the upper portion, or lithosphere, of the Earth's mantle and provided excellent cover for the Hughes operation.

In 1972 and in 1973 two unmanned American spacecraft left Earth to begin their journeys across the universe. The first spacecraft was the Pioneer 10, launched on March 2, 1972, the second was Pioneer 11 launched on April 5, 1973 after Pioneer 10 had successfully traveled through the Asteroid Belt. Each spacecraft carried a metal plate bearing a message in the form of symbols that would convey the existence of the human race to any intelligent life forms that may intercept it. The spacecraft, powered by plutonium generators, returned high resolution photos of Jupiter and other Planets.

Pioneer 10 traveled over 8 billion miles and finally lost power on January 23, 2003. It was the first American spacecraft to fly to Jupiter, Saturn and on to the interior of the Milky Way Galaxy. Pioneer 11's transmissions ended September 30, 1995. These spacecraft carried less computer capability than a pocket calculator has today. The average smartphone has 1,000s of times more computing capability than Pioneer 10 had.

Lockheed Martin SR-72 Venture Star Version – A true Orbit – Re-entry capable Stand-alone Vehicle above Area 51.   Enclosed in the fuselage are docking ports for the ISS and arms for deploying satellites.   These spacecraft are fitted with deep penetrating ground radar and cameras with extraordinary resolution.   Some versions are capable of attaining Mach 8, remaining unmanned in extremely high orbit for instant recall.   Only your imagination can come close to what this vehicle is capable of.

More space probes were launched in 1977 named Voyager 1 and 2, which have also left our solar system. Voyager 1 reached Interstellar space in 2012. These probes also carried digital recordings from Earth. The accomplishments of the *little green men of Earth* provide the necessary evidence that it is very possible the *little green men* across the universe could also launch unmanned space vehicles.

In the last and current century several payloads of unmanned spacecraft made soft landings on the planet Mars. The payloads were vehicles which photographed terrain, sampled the soil and atmosphere and transmitted reports back to Earth.

We, as individuals, on a daily basis still lie, covet, stretch the truth, and shade circumstances to improve our personal position in life. Governments will always lie, take our money, and perpetuate multiple frauds on its people to extend its power and control. These basic instincts are the exact same personal instincts that **The Lords of Sumer** brought with them when they discovered Earth. And last, if logic does not fit the lifelong or official explanation of an event, it does not mean the event did not occur. It means you must find the real explanation of what happened, and why, or if the event actually occurred.

SETI and METI

The SETI Institute constructed a VLA in Northern California. It contained 350 programmable parabolic dishes capable of scanning thousands of star systems simultaneously. The Institute was formed because of two major issues. First is the Freedom of Information Act [FOI], and second is the famous "WOW" transmission.

The FOI Act requires disclosure of information produced or obtained through publicly funded projects. These disclosures, such as the WOW transmission, could not be permitted to continue. Although funding is public, monies are laundered through various Government and corporate accounts to hide the funding sources.

The "WOW" transmission was labeled such because that is the note the PHD wrote next to the printout of the binary transmission received. The analysis of the transmission revealed it was not of any known language or database. It was determined to "most likely" be a portion of transmission between two spacecraft, "several" light years from Earth.

During a follow-up meeting of high level SETI, METI and Government Scientists the discussion pointedly centered on whether we, The Earth, should be attempting to contact some unknown advanced intelligence. It could be hazardous to our health if we succeed. Think about the introduction of European diseases to the Americas and how quickly 90% of the inhabitants died.

With what you have just learned, do you think it is science fiction to believe we Humans of Earth are the only Humans in Space? If it is science fiction, why are we spending Billions of dollars every year to fund the various projects, which you will probably not know about in your lifetime?

Currently Arecibo can send and receive frequencies from 1 to 10 GHz, with 2,400 MHz of transmitting power. There are two foundations for the operation of Arecibo: first is the Search for Extra Terrestrial Intelligence, SETI, and second is the Messaging to Extra Terrestrial Intelligence, METI.

The following are observations I made while fact checking Arecibo data;
Cornell University_managed the site for about 50 years operating under the control of the National Astronomy and Ionosphere Center [NAIC]. NASA and other federal funding exceeded $10 Million per year.   About 2001 changes were made beginning with funding by forming a myriad of political and private conglomerates, and Cornell University was fired from its managing position in 2011.

Arecibo is now operated by the **University of Central Florida**, **Yang Enterprises** and **UMET**, under a cooperative agreement with the National Science Foundation [NSF]. It is funded by the US Congress and numerous federal, public and private groups. The principals of management are:

UMET: The **Metropolitan University of Puerto Rico [UMET]**, a private non-profit.

Yang Enterprises - founded as an engineering consulting firm in 1986 by Dr. Tyng-Lin [Tim] Yang. In 1993, Mrs. Li-Woan [Lee] Yang assumed management.   **Yang Enterprises** is listed as a high-technology disadvantaged/minority/woman-owned business.   This business is disadvantaged near a Billion dollars annually.

Yang Enterprises holds contracts for Development and Maintenance of IT systems at UMET, Arecibo and myriads of US Airbases and Government facilities.

Amazing are the connections of people involved with the Arecibo site. A past Director of the CIA holds patents for the antennae and his relatives and business partners are doing well. Many USA, Puerto Rico and Mexico politicians, including Hillary Clinton and TeleMundo head the various funding organizations, and control the commercial applications of the site. Their families profit from appointments and board positions. Puerto Rico politicians funded millions for SETI but would not provide their people with decent electrical power systems and many basic needs. The entire situation will not pass a "Smell Test" for the level of corruption and graft perpetrated under cover of scientific endeavors. It is as corrupt as the Vatican's selling of licenses to plunder the Americas.

Arecibo produces fantastic scientific findings using very qualified scientists. What I am railing about are the low-life operators using Arecibo as a mechanism for fraud and riches. The installation also plays an important role for National and World security.

This railing and dissertation of "old war stories" is just that, for entertainment. It is meant to make you aware of the advances in technology after WWII and to remind you that you do not know about everything your government is doing or developing. You definitely do not want to know what is "under the covers" of your favorite institutions. Or, maybe you do.

Opinions From The Author

I hope this has been entertaining and informative for you. It has been a passion of mine since childhood to find the most truth I possibly could which pertains to the history of Man, and of Man's Religions and Civilizations. In the last three decades computer advances have afforded fantastic resources for the research of ancient documents and archaeological finds. Scientific advances in the last decade have brought to light some amazing contradictions to the way we have been indoctrinated with Western Thinking.

I "discovered" ancient documents online which caused me to "Go down the rabbit hole" of research and the information is so critical because it exposes Pauline Christianity and Vatican censorship of the original Hebrew writings. I had to revise this work, delaying publication. One of the main documents I found is the "Munich Talmud", which is the only uncensored copy of the "Babylon Talmud". [see references in Appendix]

I use the term of "Going down the rabbit hole" not as a bad thing to do but as a necessary anal pursuit of a singular subject to verify information as much as possible. So, the information and definitions are the result of such an undertaking.

I have found the ancient Torah and Talmud [Rabbinical discussions of the Torah] writings about the founding of Christianity to be more historically correct than the censored writings of the Vatican. This does not change my research and views about the *origins* of the Torah.

One of the greatest scientific discoveries of the last 1,000 years is of the Comet Impact of 12,900 years ago, which caused the Pleistocene Extinction. *Academia* will not consider the work of these 30+ scientists, engineers and geologists because *"we know ancient man ate the animals to cause the extinction"*. How myopic, how disgraceful to mis-lead the world with the same "Earth is Flat" dialogue.

I am neither a Physicist nor Scientist, but I do have an opinion on an Academic mass following. It is the "Big Bang Theory" of the Universe. The Theory says all matter in the universe was compressed to a "Singularity". This is the term *Academia* uses to describe a mass in the Universe which has compressed to an indeterminate small volume and huge unmeasurable mass, i.e. a black hole. I love to read Professor

Hawking's work and theories. But these are only theories caught up in a social acceptance network as *Academia* often does. It is not socially acceptable to doubt a world lauded Physicist, or Brother Pope.

The "Big Bang" theory was developed on the premise that if a system is expanding with time passing, then one can reverse the coefficients of expansion and arrive at a time when expansion began and also reveal the distances to the beginnings of the Universe. The Big Bang theory assumes all matter [and energy] in the entire Universe was compressed in a "Black Hole" to a "Singularity" and then exploded, creating our present Universe.

The true test of this theory is: If a black hole was compressed to a "Singularity", where did the black hole come from? Black Holes are the result of a star imploding and the remaining mass attracting all matter and energy surrounding it. By rational process, there had to be a Universe prior to "The Big Bang" occurring.

Give this "Theory" some rational consideration; proponents believe [?] one can peer back in time, using telescopes, and find "The Edge [beginning] of our Universe". Their expected result is because they propose the deeper our instruments penetrate space, the older the source of light. This is in fact true, but their premise is that eventually we will discover "the beginning of light emissions", which in turn will define distance to the edge, or beginning of the Universe. These are dual dependent theories, each depending on the other to prove both.

There is no edge of our Universe; that is why the term "infinity" is used. Infinity defines "no beginning or ending". The human mind attempts to attach limiters to anything in order to measure the magnitude of our understanding of that item of interest. If one rationally considers the theory, it is ludicrous to apply the minuscule phenomena of a black hole exploding to the creation of the entire Universe.

If you give this theory some rational thought it should sound like a miracle from Genesis in the Holy Writ. It has no basis other than; observations of stellar bodies indicate an expansion of the area and distances between these bodies is occurring. This has no relationship to their theory of a pinpoint singularity explosion.

The theory infers that the Universe is a "bubble" of material and energy, in what? If nothing is beyond the bubble, what is nothing? When reviewed rationally it is simply a mind game to impress other

Academics. There are extremely valuable discoveries yet to be made exploring the Universe and we do have tremendous photos and scientific data gathered from deep space studies and probes.

I think it is more important to research how Man colonized Earth and what has caused our world civilizations and religions to develop as they have, than to debate the "origins" of the Universe.

How about this thought on their theory; it is something which will never be proven or dis-proven in many lifetimes. It cannot even be equated to medieval scientists proving to Brother Pope that the Earth revolved around the Sun and that the Earth is round.   You can be certain that this Big Bang Theory will result in uncountable Millions of dollars bankrolling various studies which hopefully will make everyone's life better.

The distances to stellar observations can be 7,000 light years and much more. Recent deep space photographs have captured "Black Holes" freely existing in the Universe. The black holes were without surrounding stars or gasses being devoured by massive gravitational forces.   This discovery will radically change the physics of the Universe and *Academia* will go nuts over this.

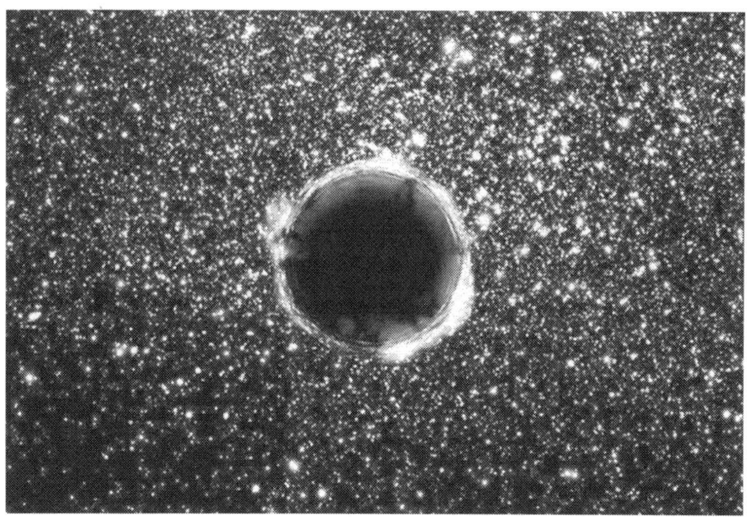

**Free existing Black Hole [Artist's rendition from
NASA photos]**

Understand that for scientists to produce the above image rendition required a vast amount of observations of light spectrums, magnetic patterns, stellar shadow variations, various radio and energy waves and much more. It also required a collaborative effort of imaginations to depict **an image which does not exist in reality**. The image is based on a rendition of data, not a visual observation.

Widespread Human acceptance of the *theory* that unseen "spiritual" entities can enter our minds and communicate Devine messages, or create demonic actions is the result of a massive collaborative effort of imaginations. This collaborative effort has been ongoing for thousands of years, and is the result of teaching, rather than independent thought processes. As with the imaginary rendition of a "Black Hole", the imaginary renditions of "Mind altering Gods" requires a tremendous amount of mindless acceptance of superstitions. Each of us creates enough mental images and superstitions to complicate our own sphere of existence. We have that ability as Humans to delve into the imaginary realm.

As we Earth Humans may soon colonize Mars, these same academic experts will not even entertain that Man could have discovered Earth, and as I have presented, it is more likely to have happened than not. Mars may have had life at some time, but as for now there is no atmosphere, no food and no internal engine driving planetary processes.

<u>But it is there, Man is here, so Man will go there because it is our nature to do so</u>. I provided this categorical syllogism on purpose to illustrate how Theologians and Politicians "Prove" their arguments. The underlined statement provides two known facts to arrive at a suspect conclusion.

Academia's statement decrying the Sumerian Kings List as a "Fable", stating "There is no evidence of habitation in the Fertile Crescent to support the Sumerian Kings List as authentic", it is obvious it was blindly proffered. Is it *Academia's* position the Fertile Crescent was only occupied by wandering groups of "Hunter-Gatherers" while the balance of the continent supported widespread cultures, civilizations and established settlements? The premise of *Academia* that "since there is no physical evidence of cities in Ante Diluvian Sumer, there were no cities. Therefore, the Sumerian Kings list is false history." This is another blatant categorical syllogism to arrive at a corrupted conclusion.

Observe a satellite view of the total area of the Tigris and Euphrates Rivers and you will see a vast flood plain from the northern mountains to the coast. Any remaining ancient ruins located in this area are buried under meters of alluvial material. Destruction of any remnants of civilization was the result of many flooding incidents and was not unique to this area of the world.

Reviewing geology and the impact on Earth's geomorphology [surface features] due to worldwide flooding for centuries after the comet impact, it is not a mystery as to why many ancient cities are gone. This ancient disaster is most likely the basis for the "deluge" references in ancient myths and manuscripts. As I previously noted; one of these "Kings" of Sumer recorded that he had read inscribed stones from "before the flood".

My goal is to find what is verified knowledge versus what is taught by *Academia* for us to "believe". I intended for this work to be an enlightening exposure of *Academia's* politically motivated myopic grip on censored history and of the groups who promote their intimate association with "God" as a means of gaining absolute power over humanity, over nations and the world. Organized Religion is, and always has been about power, control and wealth.

Current debates about the "origins of the Universe and life" are limited to the spiritual aspect of "In The Beginning" there was nothing and God created everything, or to the scientific explanation of the "Big Bang" with the Universe being created from the detonation of a "Singularity" which created everything. Some religious arguments say the "Creation" was for the Earth only, that the rest of the universe already existed.

To analyze these theories in reality, consider the spiritual theory of creation. If there was nothing except God, has God existed forever? If so where did this entity reside if there was "nothing"? In the scientific venue of creation from a Singularity, that is a Black Hole which contained all matter of the universe, how did this black Hole come to exist? If this is the answer to creation, the black hole had to attract all of this mass from – what? A previous universe?

I believe the answer is the simplest; The systems of the universe, time and space, have no beginnings or ending, which we can possibly wrap our minds around. So why worry about it! Live your life, get some 'Shroom Wine" and go fishing.

History is what it is, and religion is the same. If believing in a "Vicar of God" to address all of mankind, or believing prayers to feathers, sticks or a "Virgin on An Abalone Shell" trip your trigger, good for you. If you believe God has descended and bestowed the power of the Universe on an individual who has visions and dream conversations with The Almighty, good for you. Just keep sending these "Prophets" your money, buy a prayer hoodus and keep "God" happy. But above all, never doubt that God personally guided the many "Prophets" who penned the Holy Writs of the World.

If your social connections in Organized Religion greatly influence your life, if this is the all controlling influence for you, then stay with it. Be Happy! If, on considering what you have discovered, you are enlightened then make changes and have a worry-free life while continuing to expose the myths of history.

Many people stay with their organized religion after knowing the true beginnings of that particular religion. Good! Live your own life because I am not attempting to recruit anyone away from, or to, a particular religion. I personally might enjoy some good Christian 'shroom wine and time with a Mitra Oracle Sporting Lady.

I am neither an Atheist, nor a follower of any organized religion. Beyond this information it is no-one's business what my beliefs are because this book sums up what my views of life are.

To enjoy my dry humor, I will often openly wear a Star of David if I expect to be around a group of "religious people" to gage their reactions. It is absolutely the best entertainment available. Most will be near apologetic that they were not born into the faith, while thinking how to get the hell away from me without appearing rude. Try it, you will be amazed, or let a Baptist think you are about to join the Latter Day Saints.

If I were to follow a religion, it most likely would be one which affords me the greatest opportunity for social equality within the organization. Children do not need to be taught right from wrong by clergy or soothsayers. Parents can teach their children social skills and proper demeanor without ancient fears and prejudices. Ancient Sumerian Kings put forth edicts of acceptable behavior for citizens of their nations. These principles have not changed in millennia and if followed, one can lead a very honorable, prosperous life.

Being a member of an organized group of like-minded people is a necessity for an orderly civilization. The group can represent many factions of society; religion, political, crafts and so on. I do not decry joining any group, my point is you should know the truth of the origins of the particular group.

If you enjoy your Organized Religion, by all means stay with it. If you do not like it, and need an organization for fulfillment then search around. You will find a group you like.

Thank You for reading my lifelong work, I hope it provided some level of knowledge and entertainment for you.

"Anyone who sells their Word by knowingly distorting facts has rendered their Word worthless."

"Knowing the truth, those without the courage to resist tyranny will follow myth and rumor into bondage and ruin."

Mac A Caves   2018

FOR NOTES

450 *CAVES*

FOR NOTES

APPENDIX

INTRODUCTION TO THE AUTHOR

Readers seldom know the true mindset of the author so as to gage the validity or purpose of their work. I provide the following micro view of my early life to give you this view into my obviously non-politically-correct mental processes and sometimes dry humor.

I have been interested in the mysteries of religion since my early childhood. As a child living from Southern Arkansas in share-cropper housing to West Coast Migrant Camps we were barefooted, unwashed, dirt-floor, tarpaper shack migrants. We worked for poor share-croppers. In Arkansas in the 1940s we were called "white niggers" and accepted our place in the social hierarchy.

In 1940s southern Arkansas we lived in a small log cabin with a dirt floor and our water was available by a hand pump located outside. I vividly remember the fall season when the hogs were rounded up from the swamp by horseback riders and sent to market. Two or three hogs were butchered in the yard, yielding items for the smokehouse, lard for the coming year and various other things. One item always made was lye soap.

My job [as a four-year-old] was to recycle the bucket of water poured into the top of a wood ash-barrel, with a spigot at the bottom. The liquid would take on a green hue with each cycle and was complete when the liquid was a bright green. This was the lye which was placed in a large cast iron vat over a wood fire. Hog fat and lye were boiled together and when later cooled formed a two-inch-thick curd on top. This was cut into bars and was our soap. I remember standing in a wash tub and being soaped with the lye soap, watching the barn fleas jump off my skin.

These are not unpleasant memories; they are just a child's view of the world. This was our normal life without any thought of life changing. Traveling Tent Preachers told us God would care for the low-class humans, it was written and it was so. Work hard, don't look up, Jesus loves little children.

Tent preachers awed us with stories of God and Paradise where you would not go hungry or be worked from dark to dark and you would live forever in a wondrous cloud. That is, if God liked you. If you ever thought of nasty things, much-less do them, then God would burn your ass in Hell.

We would go to the back door of "The Big House" and ask the "House Niggers" for anything we needed. Field hands and low-class workers, of any color, were addressed as niggers.

The 1940's were a turbulent time for America, World Wars, rampant racism, many people trying to recover from the Depression and the Dust Bowl. I remember walking the few miles to "The Corners" which consisted of a board walk country store with a tall glass, hand pumped gas pump in front. I was approaching the Corner with my brothers and Dad when I noticed two Black Men hanging from the floodlights of a billboard. This was mid-morning and no-one seemed to notice the sight. I tugged on my dad's pant-leg and pointed and he said "not your business son – just look straight ahead". This was the mind-set of the times; do not get involved unless something actually directly affects you. Later in life my older brothers told me these men had apparently "disrespected" the matriarch of this area because they did not get off of the boardwalk when she passed them.

I do not use pejorative language lightly. I use it because it was the social and religious "*truth*" in the 1940s [and in many venues today]. My use of this language also gets your attention and lets you know I have first-hand knowledge of society's prejudices. I lived these circumstances rather than just reading about them. It would be a lie to pretend that the use of these terms to describe social status and skin color prejudices were not widely used and taught in churches and in schools. The Civil War ended slavery in America; it did not end religious fables and unrepentant prejudice.

In today's USA politics terms of "White Privilege" and "White Guilt" are tossed around to intimidate and disparage a population strictly because of the politics of Socialism. The same politicians teach some Americans they were born victims of injustice and must "rise up" to defeat this injustice. When taught these destructive tenets of life as a child it is extremely difficult to realize they are false. Once realized, any American can achieve their life dreams. Politicians need victims of any social issue to maintain power over the masses, just as Preachers need "sinners" to flex their social influence.

A renowned writer and social historian recently gave the clearest explanation of why this is happening. First, some accept the "Guilt" language and "PC Rules" in fear of being labeled "Racist". Second, and most important, "minorities" now have total "Freedom", but some do not know how to live with personal freedom without creating a "victim drama" based on widespread class-distinction standards of decades and centuries ago. Part of the difficulty of freedom is resolving one's life challenges without Government assistance. Real racists could care less about being labeled as Leftist Fascists [True Nazi's].

Racial or social prejudice is not a moral stance of disliking someone. Prejudice is true hate directed at anyone who seems different because of appearance, religion or social status. The really sad thing is that most people do not know why they are in the mindset to believe they are superior to other humans. The answer is because they were taught to be. I was indoctrinated with this hate, by illiterate parents and preachers, as a child but changed my mindset in adult life to a dislike of an individual's actions rather than their "status". [This personal "Light" came on after about 3 months in a combat zone.]

Religious leaders and politicians are most responsible for spreading and maintaining the prejudices of our nation and world. Even those who are the objects of these social and religious views have been taught to accept that they are somehow the eternal victims and must live with this perception. The teachings by religious leaders of; "Jesus loves you" and "God has put this burden on your life to challenge your Faith" are mental perceptions to keep groups of people in a fairy-tale state of mind that they deserve to be an underclass.

If you were not born into riches and proper social status, you are a victim, but if you "Get Jesus" you can love being a victim. If you are not born a victim, Christianity teaches you are still a worthless, undeserving wretch at birth; until you "Get Jesus" in your life and can love being in an upper social class.

Unfortunately, for Americans with dark and light skin, preachers and politicians have convinced them they cannot achieve success without the assistance and intervention of the ruling class. Like the Vatican over the millennia, with each generation being taught rules to live by, these Americans have perpetuated their mindset of needing assistance to think.

Have you ever thought how conversations would proceed if in America people were not described as hyphenated Americans? Hyphenating anyone's heritage is just another method of dividing a nation into class warfare. Heritage is important as it provides a positive basis for anyone's history. It should not become a social weapon.

If you can reach a mindset of your own importance, a "me first" attitude that one must educate themselves, realize that if anyone has a problem with some aspect of your being that it is not your problem, it is their problem. Any individual's personal problems only become your problems if you allow it to happen. In other words, "screw them" as you do not need the drama. Set your own goals and find a way to achieve them. And last, why argue with a fool? You will never change their mind-set; so, are they important enough to spend your life trying?

RESEARCH AND DATA SOURCES

The following individuals, organizations and Universities provided valuable information and are deserving of recognition:

[I do not rely on on-line information other than to find research clues, which I need to further verify. In my opinion on-line sites are most often heavily censored on any subject which contains political or religious content.]

DISCOVERY OF 12,900 YEARS AGO COMET IMPACT

Dr. Richard Firestone and Dr. William Topping of Lawrence Berkley National Laboratory, and Geologist Allen West, along with over 20 scientists who published their findings in 2005.

NASA Scientists and other researchers – Hubble and other photographic missions, deep space probes.

ANCIENT EGYPTIAN MYTHS AND LEGENDS

Author: LEWIS SPENCE [1874-1955]
Originally published in 1915
DOVER EDITION 1990 ISBN 0-486-26525-0

The Codex Nuttal, Edited by Zelia Nuttal, introduction by Arthur G. Miller,
Copyright © 1973 by Dover Publications, Inc.

THE DEAD SEA SCRIPTURES, Author Professor Theodor H. Gaster, Copyright 1956, 64, 76 - ISBN 0-385-08859-0

The following is a book well worth your time, true history of the Vatican vs. Freemasonry:

THE POPE AND THE FREEMASONS

The Letter "Humanum Genus" of the Pope, LeoXIII, [1878-1903]

Against Free-Masonry and the Spirit of the Age
BY POPE LEO XIII - 1884
Westphalia Press – 1527 New Hampshire Ave., NW
Washington, DC 20036

ISBN-13: 978-1935907244; ISBN-10: 1935907247

westphaliapress.org

THE DEAD SEA SCROLLS DECEPTION
Authors Michael Baigent and Richard Leigh

A fascinating book about the Dead Sea Scrolls was published by Summit Books, Simon & Schuster Building, New York Copyright 1991. The book, **THE DEAD SEA SCROLLS DECEPTION**, ISBN: 0-671-73454-7, authors Michael Baigent and Richard Leigh, provide a unique account of the difficulties some Dead Sea Scrolls scholars faced when they did not follow the proscribed agenda for releasing interpretations of these text.

Although this book is focused on the Christian era of The Holy Writ, it is a testament to the very problems I have voiced about Western Theology mindsets and accurate translations of ancient text. I highly recommend this book to anyone who seeks the truth about ancient history.   A fascinating read! The cover comment reads: "**Why a handful of Religious scholars conspired to suppress the Revolutionary contents of the Dead Sea Scrolls.**"

Mac Caves comment - 2010

A very interesting 100-year-old publication:

"life of Christ"
by: Hanish, Otoman Zar-Adusht
"Yeshua Nazir; Jesus the Nazarite"
Yeshua Stoned at the Temple

Publication date 1917
Publisher Los Angeles, Cal., Mazdaznan Press
Collection New York public library; Americana
Digitizing sponsor MSN
Contributor New York Public Library
Language Hebrew; English

Interpretations from the Original Uncensored "Munich Talmud" a copy of the "Babylon Talmud" section on Jesus of Nazareth's Trial in Sanhedrin 43a
Dr. David Instone-Brewer

Senior Research Fellow in Rabbinics and the New Testament, A Baptist minister
Tyndale House, Cambridge.

SAUL OF TARSUS (known as Paul, the Apostle of the Heathen):
By: Kaufmann Kohler [Rabbi Kaufmann Kohler (1843 - 1926)
JewishEncyclopedia.com

Scripture quotations and some Masonic information are taken from:

THE HOLY BIBLE
THE GREAT LIGHT IN MASONRY
According to The Authorized or King James Version
TEMPLE ILLUSTRATED EDITION
Copyright © - 1924, A. J. Holman, Nashville, Tennessee

Additional Scripture [and translation notes] taken from:

THE HOLY BIBLE
NEW INTERNATIONAL VERSION,
Copyright © 1973, 1978, 1984, International Bible Society. Used by permission of Zondervan Bible Publishers [Notes paraphrased].

1917 HEBREW BIBLE - On-line edition used for direct scripture verses.

The Munich Talmud c. 1342 CE: A copy of The Babylon Talmud c. 170 CE.

MITRAISM RESEARCH [MITRA]
D.M. Murdock's research, and her many noted sources, into ancient religions have provided significant connections for my work. A great source of information for anyone who wants more detail.
www.truthbeknown.com/Mitra.htm

Many other researchers have provided substance for this work, too many to list, but again I must caution against premature acceptance of anything published, as there are more published tin-hat writers than you would believe!

I must remind readers of the vast amount of literature from ancients and modern researchers. I have extracted portions of these documents for this writing. You can immerse yourself in your own journey as you follow the threads of these writers. I attempt to give as much credit as possible.

Ancient text suggested reading:

Most of the following tablets were recovered from the Library of <u>Ashurbanipal</u> (668-627 BCE, located in Nineveh.

Elba Tablets – Sumerian, Third Millennium BCE
        Political and cultural texts of Northern Syria

Sumerian Kings List – Third Millennium BCE
        Sumerian Kings beginning 254,000 years ago

Enuma Elish – Akkadian, Second Millennium BCE
        El and son Marduk – Creation God

Gilgamesh Epic – Akkadian, Second Millennium BCE
        Survivor of The Deluge [Great Flood] basis for "Noah"

Athra-Hasis Epic – Akkadian, Second Millennium BCE
        Creation and early history, The Deluge

Sargon Legend – Akkadian, First Millennium BCE
        Sargon The Great, King of Akkad, rescued as an infant from a
        reed basket floating in a river.

Mayan Codices – Archaic Central America
        Creation and Mayan Kings, political and daily life

<u>**Some of the few surviving Codices are located in Dresden Germany**</u>

Ancient-origins.net: Great articles

Bahrain University
Faculty of Arts
Department of Antiquities
Manama, Bahrain

National Geographic Society
Washington, D.C. - For excellent publication of articles and data from
hundreds of dedicated researchers.

New Mexico State University
Las Cruces, New Mexico

Smithsonian Institution
Washington, D.C.

University of Cairo
Faculty of Arts, Egyptology Institute
Ancient Languages Section, Orman Garden

National Park Service
Mesa Verde National Park
Mancos, Colorado

National Park Service
Chaco Culture National Historic Park
Nageezi, New Mexico

Northern Arizona University
Flagstaff, Arizona

El Jeffe de Tecnico Operations
El Centro 17
Santiago, Chile, SA

Consular a Peruvian
Attache de Culturo
Lima, Peru, SA

Consular a Bolivia
Attache de Scientifico
La Paz, Bolivia, SA

NASA Technical and Photographic sections

University of Minnesota
Department of Anthropology
Ancient Mesoamerican Civilizations

University of Amsterdam
Faculty of Science
Astronomical Institute, Mssr. Michiel B. @
 www.astro.uva.nl/~michielb/maya/astro.html
[Maya Mathematics]

LATE QUATERNARY PALEOENVIRONMENTS OF THE SAHARA REGION

E.M. van Zinderen Bakker, Sr
Institute for Environmental Sciences, University of the O.F.S.
Bloemfontein, South Africa.
Maley
(ORSTOM), Laboratoire de Palynologie (CNRS, E.R. No. 25),
Université des Sciences e t Techniques du Languedoc, Montpellier
34060,
France.
This is an exceptional study with great detail and clarity. [MAC]

12,900 years ago Comet impact findings and debate by *Academia*

Report Titled:

Evidence for an extraterrestrial impact 12,900 years ago that contributed to the megafauna extinctions and the Younger Dryas cooling.

Team Members:

R. B. Firestone a,b, A. Westc,   J.
P. Kennettd, L. Beckere, T. E. Bunchf,   Z.
S. Revayg, P. H. Schultzh, T. Belgyag,   D.
J. Kennetti, J. M. Erlandsoni,   O.   J.
Dickensonj, A. C. Goodyeark, R. S. Harrish, G.   A.
Howardl, J. B. Kloostermanm, P. Lechlern,   P.   A.
Mayewskio, J. Montgomeryj, R. Poredap,   T.
Darrahp, S. S. Que Heeq, A. R. Smitha,   A. Stichr,
W. Toppings, J. H. Wittkef, and   W. S. Wolbachr
[26 Primary members of Team]

The 12,900 years ago Comet impact discovery by Dr. Firestone and team was a history clarifying scientific report; his summary report and reply to skeptics in Academia who claim no impact occurred, follows:

Dr. Firestone et al – Pleistocene Extinction brief summary:

"*A carbon-rich black layer, dating to ≈12.9 ka, has been previously identified at ≈50 Clovis-age sites across North America and appears contemporaneous with the abrupt onset of Younger Dryas (YD) cooling. The in-situ bones of extinct Pleistocene megafauna, along with Clovis tool assemblages, occur below this black layer but not within or above it. Causes for the extinctions, YD cooling, and termination of Clovis culture have long been controversial. In this paper, we provide evidence for an extraterrestrial (ET) impact event at ≅12.9 ka, which we hypothesize caused abrupt environmental changes that contributed to YD cooling, major ecological reorganization, broad-scale extinctions, and rapid human behavioral shifts at the end of the Clovis Period.*

Clovis-age sites in North American are overlain by a thin, discrete layer with varying peak abundances of (i) magnetic grains with iridium, (ii) magnetic microspherules, (iii) charcoal, (iv) soot, (v) carbon spherules, (vi) glass-like carbon containing nanodiamonds, and (vii) fullerenes with ET helium, all of which are evidence for an ET impact and associated biomass burning at ≈12.9 ka. This layer also extends throughout at least 15 Carolina Bays, which are unique, elliptical depressions, oriented to the northwest across the Atlantic Coastal Plain.

We propose that one or more large, low-density ET objects exploded over northern North America, partially destabilizing the Laurentide Ice Sheet and triggering YD cooling. The shock wave, thermal pulse, and event-related environmental effects (e.g., extensive biomass burning and food limitations) contributed to end-Pleistocene megafaunal extinctions and adaptive shifts among Paleo-Americans in North America."

Dr. Firestone's rebuke of several academics' attack on his work:

"Surovell et al failed to confirm the YD Impact data because their sampling methods were fatally flawed. We discovered that the impact layer was very narrow, often millimeters thick, and used painstaking microstratigraphy to find it. Although the impact layer initially was deposited just before the formation of the black mat, the magnetic and organic fractions containing the most compelling information often moved about due to turbation of the sediment following deposition.

Surovell et al did no microstratigraphy and analyzed substantially wider sediment layers that included mostly normal sediment. Thus their results greatly diluted the impact layer contribution to their samples. Also, Surovell et al chose to recognize only magnetic microspherules that are round and shiny. It is well known that meteoritic dust is generally not perfectly round, often pitted and dull, and generally weathered. Despite all of these failures the distributions of magnetic grains and microspherules shown by Surovell et al at all of their sites do show increases at the time of the YD impact which are consistent with our own results after correction for the sampling dilution effects. Surovell et al's conclusions are clearly influenced by their own bias and not by a fair analysis of their own data."

Recent studies and reports which have validated Dr. Firestones' Report:

The Younger Dryas climate change: was it caused by an extraterrestrial impact?
(Utrecht Studies in Earth Sciences 054) NARCIS (Netherlands) van Hoesel, A. 2014-01-01

The reluctance of *Academia* to embrace these historic findings and discoveries is all too familiar. The work of Dr. Firestone and his team has destroyed many fairy tale papers about ancient activities and events, which were concocted without verified evidence or plausible connections to reality.

Last, thanks to a great many [thousands] of on-line ancient history articles which provided leads and clues for further research into ancient names and places. Remember, you do not have to agree with these writers of sci-fi and conspiracy theories to discover important names and places to begin your research.

I send a huge thank you to family and friends who provided feedback and encouragement for this work, especially to my life-long best friend, lover, confidant, advisor and keeper of our home, my wife.

ON THE ORIGIN OF GOD
BY MEANS OF NATURAL SELECTION

Mac Caves
ISBN-10: 0-9676191-1-4
[Chuparrosa Press]
Published 2019

ISBN-13: 978-0967619118
[Caves Land and Cattle Company]
Published 2019 - Amazon Kindle Direct Publishing

IF NOT AVAILABLE AT YOUR LOCAL BOOKSTORE GO TO: www.thesecretofthegods.com for orders from Caves Land and Cattle Company [Chuparrosa Press] or link to amazon.com.

Orders from the website will be available with author's signature and a note to specified individual at no additional cost.

Limited quantities of *THE SECRET OF THE GODS* by Mac A. Caves [published 12-1999] are available from the web site and also from Amazon.

A readers' comments format will be provided on the website.

ISBN-13: 978-0967619118 [Kindle Direct Publishing]
(Caves Land and Cattle Company)

ISBN-10: 0-967619114 [Chuparrosa Press]
Mac Caves

For Notes

For Notes

Made in the USA
Lexington, KY
29 November 2019

57820351R00269